JAPAN

The Ultimate Cookbook

13-Digit ISBN: 978-1-40034-508-3
10-Digit ISBN: 1-40034-508-1

This book may be ordered by mail from the publisher. Please include $5.99 for postage and handling.
Please support your local bookseller first!

Books published by Cider Mill Press Book Publishers are available at special discounts for bulk purchases in the United States by corporations, institutions, and other organizations. For more information, please contact the publisher.

Cider Mill Press Book Publishers
"Where good books are ready for press"
501 Nelson Place
Nashville, Tennessee 37214

cidermillpress.com

Typography: Adobe Garamond, Brandon Grotesque, Lastra, Sackers English Script
Image Credits: Photo on Page 29 used under official license from Shutterstock.
All other photos courtesy of Bea Omura.

Printed in Malaysia

24 25 26 27 28 COS 5 4 3 2 1

First Edition

JAPAN

The Ultimate Cookbook

YUTO OMURA

CIDER MILL PRESS

BOOK
PUBLISHERS

CONTENTS

Introduction   9

Ingredients, Techniques & Tools   13

Ichiju Sansai: The Japanese Concept of a Meal   31

Homemade Ingredients   37

Gohan (Rice)   79

Shirumono (Soup)   113

Aemono (Salads & Sides)   147

Nimono (Simmered Dishes)   181

Fish   219

Meat   239

Agemono   271

Tsukemono (Pickles)   307

Donburi (Rice Bowls)   335

Ramen   371

Udon & Soba   413

Nabemono (Hot Pots)   463

Sushi & Sashimi   483

Yoshoku   527

Chuka   561

Izakaya   593

Yataimeshi (Street Food)   627

Desserts   645

Appendix   677

Index   687

INTRODUCTION

From ancient times to the present, Japanese cuisine has evolved alongside societal, cultural, and religious lines. The unique geography of Japan—an archipelago stretching from north to south—plays a crucial role in shaping its diverse food culture.

Japan's varied landscape encompasses ocean, mountains, rivers, and plains. The country spans from the tropical climate of Okinawa in the south to the frigid winters of Hokkaido in the north, with most regions experiencing distinct spring, summer, fall, and winter seasons. This geographical diversity has given rise to a rich tapestry of regional cuisines, each of which makes the most of local ingredients and flavors.

The stark differences in food culture between the north, south, east, and west of Japan are indisputable proof of the country's diverse culinary landscape, though all Japanese cuisine is defined by its emphasis on seasonal ingredients, reflecting the culture's deep connection to the cyclical character of the natural world.

In modern times, Japanese food culture has continued to evolve, maintaining traditional elements while incorporating influences from China and the West. Ramen, now globally recognized as a Japanese staple, originated in China before developing its own unique identity in Japan. Similarly, tonkatsu (breaded pork cutlet) and tempura drew inspiration from French and Portuguese cuisine, respectively. This fusion of influences showcases the simultaneously traditional and multicultural nature of Japanese food.

Fermented foods represent another distinctive element of Japanese cuisine. While fermented foods exist in many cultures, few countries boast such a wide variety or incorpo-rate them so extensively in daily meals. Miso paste, soy sauce, katsuobushi (dried bonito flakes), and natto (fermented soybeans) are staples in Japanese households. The prevalence of fermented foods in Japan can be attributed to the country's high humidity, which creates ideal conditions for fermentation. Our ancestors, either by accident or design, ingeniously harnessed local bacteria and microorganisms to produce nutrient-rich, preservable foods, and that legacy continues today.

An intriguing aspect of Japanese culinary history is the long-standing prohibition on meat consumption. From 675 to 1872, a period spanning nearly 1,200 years, eating meat was officially illegal in Japan. During this time, the general population adhered to what we would now call a pescatarian diet, though some individuals did consume meat in secret. This extended period of meat abstinence had a profound impact on Japanese cuisine. Culinary experts honed their skills in creating flavorful, satisfying dishes without relying on meat. This resulted in a rich tradition of vegetable, fish, and seafood-based cooking that continues to influence Japanese cuisine today.

When the ban on meat consumption was finally lifted in 1872, Japanese cooks began to experiment with combining their traditional techniques and flavors with new ingredients. This fusion led to the creation of unique dishes that would not have existed otherwise. For example, combining meat with a broth made from dried bonito flakes and kelp—a staple of traditional Japanese cooking—gave birth to entirely new flavor profiles, which are found in many modern Japanese dishes.

This cookbook presents 300 authentic Japanese recipes across 19 categories, designed to be as accessible as possible for home cooks outside of Japan.

The recipes are organized into categories based on ingredients, settings, occasions, and cooking methods, providing a comprehensive look at Japanese cuisine. For example, the Homemade Ingredients chapter guides you through creating essential Japanese components from scratch, perfect for those without access to specialty stores. In the Chuka and Yoshoku chapters, you'll discover how Japan has adapted Chinese and Western cuisines, respectively, creating unique fusion dishes that are now integral to Japanese food culture.

With 300 recipes, you might, at some point, feel overwhelmed by all of the unfamiliar ingredients. Please don't let this deter you. The essence of Japanese cooking is its ability to adapt to local conditions and ingredients. While some key seasonings are irreplaceable, I encourage you to experiment with your local ingredients whenever possible. This spirit of adaptation and respect for local resources is at the heart of Japanese cuisine and is what makes it truly authentic.

As you explore this book, start with recipes that appeal to you or seem manageable. The goal is to enjoy the process and gradually expand your repertoire of Japanese dishes.

If you have any questions or need clarification as you cook your way through these recipes, please don't hesitate to reach out. Visit my website, sudachirecipes.com, for additional resources and support.

Remember, the joy of cooking lies in both the process and the result. Embrace the spirit of Japanese cuisine, adapt it to your local context, and, most importantly, have fun cooking and eating with your loved ones.

As you embark on your journey through Japanese cooking, it's essential to master two fundamental elements: dashi and rice. These form the backbone of many authentic Japanese dishes.

Dashi is the secret to unlocking the essence of Japanese cuisine. A well-made dashi can dramatically improve the taste of any dish. Learn to prepare a rich, umami-packed dashi and you will significantly enhance the depth and complexity of your Japanese cooking. This cookbook will guide you through various methods of making dashi, from traditional techniques to convenient modern approaches.

Many Japanese dishes, whether main courses or side dishes, are designed to complement freshly cooked rice. Fluffy, warm rice is not just a staple; it's an integral part of the meal that enhances the overall dining experience. Rice is also the star ingredient in sushi, making it crucial to master the art of cooking it perfectly.

In this cookbook, you'll find detailed instructions on how to prepare rice to achieve the ideal texture and flavor, whether you're using a traditional rice cooker or cooking on the stovetop.

Once you've mastered these two fundamental elements—dashi and rice—you'll have the keys to unlock a wide array of Japanese dishes. This solid foundation will enable you to create and enjoy many of the recipes in this cookbook with confidence and authenticity.

An important aspect of cooking, especially when exploring a new cuisine, is understanding your own taste preferences. Japanese food, with its unique flavor profile, may seem either too subtle or too intense depending on your background and the flavors you're accustomed to. As you work through these recipes, don't hesitate

to adjust the seasonings to suit your palate. This is especially important when you're first starting out with Japanese cooking.

One of the most fundamental principles in Japanese cooking and dining is the celebration of seasonality. This concept, known as "shun" in Japanese, extends far beyond the selection of ingredients—it influences every aspect of the meal. In Japanese cuisine, the best ingredients are those at the peak of their season. Nothing can compare to the flavor, texture, and nutritional value of seasonal produce at its apex. And, of course, this principle aligns perfectly with the idea of using local substitutions we discussed earlier. By choosing ingredients that are in season in your area, you're not only ensuring the best flavor, but also staying true to the authentic spirit of Japanese cooking.

INGREDIENTS, TECHNIQUES & TOOLS

In Japan, there is a time-honored concept known as "Sa-Shi-Su-Se-So" that has been passed down through generations. This term is shorthand for the five most commonly used seasonings in Japanese cuisine, and it also represents the order in which they are typically added to dishes.

- Sa: Satou (sugar)
- Shi: Shio (salt)
- Su: Su (vinegar)
- Se: Shouyu (soy sauce)
- So: Miso (fermented soybean paste)

It is believed that adding seasonings in this sequence, especially when preparing simmered dishes (nimono), helps the ingredients absorb the flavors more effectively. However, this order is not always strictly necessary, so don't feel obligated to follow it precisely every time you cook.

SUGAR

In Japanese cuisine, sugar plays a multifaceted role that goes beyond simply adding sweetness. It enhances the luster of dishes, while also contributing to a deeper, richer flavor profile. Sugar is typically the first seasoning added in the "Sa-Shi-Su-Se-So" sequence due to its large molecular size, which makes it more difficult for the sweetness to penetrate the ingredients. Additionally, sugar can help to soften and tenderize the food. Most Japanese households use johakuto, which is the equivalent to caster (superfine) sugar and can be substituted for granulated sugar at a 1:1 ratio. It is also common to use kibisato, a light brown cane sugar that is useful for both cooking and baking, and can be substituted for another light brown sugar. Where sugar is listed in this book, caster or cane sugar can be used according to preference, unless otherwise stated. Depending on the dish and the desired flavor profile, I sometimes reach for dark brown sugar (kurozato or muscovado) or coarse light brown sugar (zarame or turbinado) to achieve a more robust and complex taste.

SALT

I recommend using natural sea salt or kosher salt instead of refined table salt. The former not only provide a more nuanced flavor but also contain minerals that are often stripped from refined salt. In Japanese cuisine, salt serves multiple purposes: enhancing flavor, firming up ingredients, drawing out excess moisture, and bringing out the natural umami flavor of ingredients.

VINEGAR

In Japanese cooking, when a recipe calls for vinegar, it typically means rice vinegar or grain vinegar. These types of vinegar have a milder, slightly sweet flavor that complements Japanese dishes well. Rice vinegar, in particular, is a staple in Japanese kitchens and is used in everything from sushi rice to pickles. If you can't find rice or grain vinegar, white vinegar can serve as a substitute in a pinch.

SOY SAUCE

Soy sauce is a cornerstone of Japanese cuisine, used for many purposes. For the best flavor, add it towards the end of cooking, as prolonged heat can diminish its aroma and even grant the dish a burnt taste. Japanese soy sauce comes in two main varieties: dark (koikuchi) and light (usukuchi). Dark soy sauce, primarily used in the Kanto region (which includes Tokyo), has a rich umami flavor that adds considerable depth to dishes. Light soy sauce, favored in the Kansai region (including Osaka and Kyoto), is perfect for dishes where you want to highlight the natural color and taste of the ingredients. In this cookbook, when we simply say "soy sauce," we're referring to dark soy sauce. Interestingly, despite its name, light soy sauce actually has a higher salt content and tastes saltier than dark soy sauce. While there are other varieties like tamari and white soy sauce, they're less common in everyday Japanese cooking.

MISO

Miso is one of Japan's most important fermented seasonings. It comes in several varieties, primarily differentiated by the main ingredient used in fermentation: rice miso, barley miso, and pure soybean miso. The type of miso commonly used varies by region in Japan. Miso can also be classified by color: red miso has a strong, salty flavor; yellow miso is medium in strength; and white miso is mild and slightly sweet. For those new to Japanese cooking, yellow miso is the most versatile and easiest to use, though don't worry if you can't find yellow miso—you can create a similar flavor by mixing equal parts white and red miso. It's also important to note that when Japanese recipes call for "miso," they always mean miso paste. Powdered miso, while available, is rarely used in everyday cooking. A crucial tip for using miso, especially in miso soup: never boil it. Boiling destroys miso's delicate flavors and beneficial enzymes. Instead, add miso at the very end of cooking, after you've removed the pot from heat.

OTHER ESSENTIAL INGREDIENTS

SAKE

Sake (Japanese rice wine) is a versatile ingredient used in many Japanese dishes, so it's always a good idea to keep some in your pantry. While stores often sell both drinking sake and cooking sake, it's best to use drinking sake for cooking whenever possible, even if you go for the cheapest bottle. Drinking-grade sake has a more refined aroma and doesn't contain added salt, which ensures it won't interfere with the dish's flavor. If sake is not accessible, substitute dry white wine when small amounts of sake are called for in a recipe.

MIRIN

Mirin (sweet rice wine) is another essential ingredient in Japanese cooking. Authentic mirin, known as "hon mirin," has a deep, rich flavor that enhances many dishes. Some stores also sell "mirin-like seasoning," which contains less alcohol and has significantly less flavor. For the best results in your Japanese recipes, I recommend always keeping a bottle of "hon mirin" in your pantry.

DASHI

Dashi is the foundation of Japanese cuisine. Usually, dashi is made from dried bonito flakes (a type of fish) and kelp (a type of seaweed), and it tastes best when prepared from scratch. However, it is perfectly common for home cooks to use dashi bags (which are similar to a tea bag) or granules, both of which are great time-savers. Dashi bags are more commonly used for soups and hot pots, whereas dashi powder or granules are used in small amounts and are more suitable for seasoning.

RICE

The heart of Japanese cuisine lies in its rice, specifically a variety known as japonica rice or "uruchimai" in Japanese. While other types of rice exist worldwide, such as indica and javanica, they don't quite fit Japanese cuisine. Japonica rice stands out with its distinct characteristics: it has a rounded and slightly oval shape; when cooked, it becomes soft and fluffy with an elastic and sticky consistency; as you chew, you'll notice a subtle sweetness present in the flavor. Japonica rice is the perfect ingredient for traditional Japanese dishes like onigiri (rice balls) and sushi. Its stickiness allows the grains to hold together, while its soft texture and mild sweetness complement a wide range of ingredients.

NOODLES

Japan's noodle culture is rich and diverse, with four main types dominating the culinary landscape: udon, soba, ramen, and somen. Each of these noodles has its own unique taste, texture, and typical methods of preparation. Udon are thick, chewy wheat noodles with a mild flavor. Soba noodles are made from buckwheat flour, which gives them a distinctive nutty flavor and slightly grainy texture. Ramen, perhaps the most famous Japanese noodle internationally, are thin, wheat-based noodles typically served in a rich, flavorful broth with various toppings. Somen are very thin wheat noodles, often eaten cold with a light dipping sauce during the summer.

FLOUR & STARCH

In Japanese cooking, cake flour is the most commonly used type of flour. However, for most recipes, all-purpose flour can serve as a suitable alternative. When it comes to starch, Japanese recipes often call for potato starch. This ingredient is used for various purposes, such as thickening sauces or creating crispy coatings. If you can't find potato starch, don't worry. Depending on the dish, you can often turn to tapioca starch or cornstarch as alternatives. On the other hand, Japanese sweets often require specific flours and starch, so be a bit less cavalier with your substitutions for those preparations.

COOKING OIL

Interestingly, traditional Japanese cuisine used very little oil until foreign cooking methods were introduced. The widespread use of oil in everyday cooking didn't become common among ordinary Japanese people until the mid-Meiji period (1868–1912). This historical context explains why many classic Japanese dishes rely on cooking methods like steaming, boiling, and grilling rather than frying or sautéing. In modern Japanese kitchens, rice bran oil, canola oil, or vegetable oil are popular choices, as they have a neutral flavor that doesn't overpower the delicate tastes of traditional Japanese ingredients. When a dish calls for a fragrant oil, toasted sesame oil is the go-to choice.

TOFU

Tofu is a versatile, protein-rich food made from soybean curd. Although it originated in China, tofu was introduced to Japan centuries ago and has since evolved into a staple of the country's cuisine, developing its own unique characteristics along the way. In Japanese cooking, two main types of tofu are commonly used: silken tofu (kinu) and firm tofu (momen). Each has its own texture and is typically used for different purposes in cooking. Deep-fried abura-age or atsuage tofu is also used in a variety of dishes.

MEAT

Meat is a surprisingly recent arrival to Japanese cuisine. For nearly 1,200 years, from 675 to 1872, meat eating was officially banned in Japan due to Buddhist influences. While some people did consume meat on the sly during this period, it was technically illegal. This long abstention from meat has profoundly shaped Japanese culinary traditions. Many classic Japanese dishes rely on fish, vegetables, and plant-based proteins, reflecting this meat-free history. Since the ban was lifted in 1872, Japanese cuisine has gradually incorporated more meat, evolving to include a balanced mix of chicken, pork, and beef. However, the way meat is used in Japanese cooking often differs from Western practices. In Japan, chicken thighs are preferred over breast meat, prized for their richer flavor and juicier texture. When it comes to beef and pork, we frequently use thin slices rather than thick cuts or large chunks.

AROMATICS

When it comes to aromatics, Japanese cuisine takes a different approach compared to many Western cooking traditions. While herbs play a significant role in many cuisines around the world, Japanese dishes often rely less on a variety of herbs and more on specific aromatics. In modern Japanese cuisine, which has been influenced by international flavors, you'll often see a combination of ginger and garlic. This pairing creates a robust flavor base for many contemporary Japanese dishes.

SESAME SEEDS

Sesame seeds are a key ingredient in Japanese cooking, used in both savory dishes and sweets. White, toasted, and black sesame seeds are all common, each offering a different flavor profile. Ground sesame seeds (surigoma) and sesame paste (nerigoma) are also frequently employed.

TOPPINGS & GARNISHES

Japanese cuisine uses various toppings to enhance color and texture. Common ones include chopped green onions, kizami nori (shredded seaweed), shiso leaves, tenkasu (tempura bits), and kamaboko fish cakes made with steamed white fish. For home cooks, growing green onions and shiso in a garden or windowsill box can be a convenient means of making sure you always have a few of these essential garnishes on hand.

CHUKA INGREDIENTS

Chinese-inspired Japanese dishes often use distinct seasonings. Key ingredients include doubanjiang/tobanjan (chili bean paste), Chinese chicken bouillon (garasupu), and toasted sesame oil. Adding these to your pantry will help you create authentic flavors when cooking Chuka dishes. As for the chicken bouillon powder, it can be swapped out for granulated, Western-style chicken bouillon.

YOSHOKU INGREDIENTS

Western-inspired Japanese dishes, while originally influenced by French cuisine, have evolved to use distinctly Japanese flavors. Surprisingly, the most common seasonings in these fusion dishes are Worcestershire sauce and ketchup. These ingredients have been adapted to suit Japanese tastes and are used in ways that might seem unusual to Western diners.

FREQUENTLY USED VEGETABLES

Vegetables vary widely by region and climate, and some common Japanese vegetables may be hard to find in other areas. This section describes the characteristics of vegetables frequently used in this book and suggests possible substitutions.

NEGI

"Negi" is a complex term in Japanese cuisine, encompassing leeks, green onions, and scallions. Japanese leeks are commonly used in stews and hot pots, while green onions and scallions are essential as toppings. When chopped green onion is called for in a preparation, use green onions or scallions. If a recipe calls for Japanese leeks (thick and long), and you do not have a specialty store near you that offers them, substitute regular leeks.

ONIONS

Yellow onions are most commonly used in Japanese cooking. Use yellow onions if available, and turn to white onions as the next best option. Red onions can work, but will change the appearance of the dish—always a key consideration in Japanese cuisine.

GREEN CABBAGE

Most cabbages in Japan are green cabbage varieties. Suitable alternatives include cannonball cabbage, conehead cabbage, sweetheart cabbage, late flat Dutch cabbage, and pointed cabbage.

CUCUMBERS

Japanese cucumbers are thin, long, and crunchy. Good substitutes include hothouse cucumbers, mini cucumbers, and Persian cucumbers.

GARLIC CHIVES

Also known as Chinese chives, garlic chives are common in Chuka dishes. Regular chives are the best substitute, though their flavor profile differs slightly.

DAIKON RADISH

Useful in stews and other hearty dishes. Depending on the recipe, possible substitutes include Korean radish, turnip, and common radish.

MUSHROOMS

Common Japanese mushrooms include shiitake, enoki, shimeji, and king oyster mushrooms. Except for shiitake, which gives unique depth to dishes, feel free to substitute with local mushrooms, but avoid using any intensely flavored varieties.

EGGPLANT

Japanese cuisine features many eggplant varieties. Chinese eggplant, Globe eggplant, and Italian eggplant are suitable substitutes if they are the proper size.

BURDOCK ROOT

Popular in Japan but rarely used outside of East Asia, its unique flavor and texture make substitution challenging. Try parsnips as an alternative, or simply increase the quantity of other root vegetables in the recipe.

SPINACH

Japan often uses a native variety called nihon horenso. Water spinach, a similar species, is banned in many parts of the United States as an invasive species. Baby spinach is an easy-to-find substitute.

FREQUENTLY USED FISH

Japanese cuisine deeply values seasonality, and fish are quintessential seasonal ingredients. Here are some types of fish frequently used in Japanese cooking:

SALMON

Available year-round, the most prized wild-caught salmon in Japan is the "autumn salmon," caught during spawning season. Hokkaido is Japan's most famous salmon-producing region. Japan also imports farmed salmon from Norway and Chile.

MACKEREL

In Japan, mackerel is in season from autumn to winter. The fatty mackerel caught during this period is particularly delicious. Chub mackerel is the most common in Japanese waters, but other species like blue mackerel and Atlantic mackerel are also suitable for use in cooking Japanese dishes.

YELLOWTAIL (JAPANESE AMBERJACK)

The season for Japanese yellowtail is winter. Fat-rich yellowtail is delicious as sashimi, grilled, or simmered. Other amberjack species can easily be substituted.

TUNA

Sashimi or sushi are the premium ways to enjoy tuna. The season for domestic bluefin tuna is winter, and they are especially prized during this time—a single Oma tuna from Aomori Prefecture can fetch over a million dollars. Tuna offers a variety of cuts, from leaner red meat to the premium, fatty otoro. For sashimi or sushi, always choose the freshest tuna available.

EEL
Considered a premium fish in Japan, eel is mostly farm-raised and available year-round. It's commonly eaten in summer as kabayaki (grilled). Catfish can be an inexpensive substitute.

SEA BREAM (RED SNAPPER)
Prized for its chewy texture, light taste, and elegant flavor, sea bream is popular and versatile.

Its season in Japan arrives around spring. Overseas, tilapia is sometimes used as a substitute in grilled dishes.

PACIFIC SAURY
This fish epitomizes the taste of autumn in Japan. It's commonly enjoyed grilled in most households during the fall season.

TECHNIQUES

COOKING RICE

White rice is a cornerstone of Japanese cuisine, and its importance cannot be overstated. Most Japanese main dishes are designed to complement plain white rice, as they often feature richer seasoning than their Western counterparts.

As a result, your ability to cook rice well significantly impacts the overall dining experience. Even the most delicious, expertly prepared main dish can't compensate for poorly cooked rice.

The rice cooking process begins with rinsing. Although modern milling techniques have reduced the need for extensive washing, it's still recommended to rinse the rice two to three times before cooking. Start by placing the rice in a colander over a bowl filled with water. Discard the water used in the first rinse immediately, then refill the bowl. Use a gentle, cat's paw motion to wash the rice, taking care not to damage the grains. After three rinses, the water may still appear cloudy, which is perfectly fine. Soaking is the next crucial step. Without proper soaking, the core of the rice remains hard, which will negatively affect the desired texture. Soak the rice for 30 minutes in summer or 1 hour in winter. You'll notice the grains gradually transform from clear to cloudy white, signaling the completion of the soaking process. Once soaking is finished, drain and let the rice sit in a colander and briefly dry for better cooking results. For detailed cooking instructions, refer to the Perfect Japanese Rice recipe on page 80. Each step is essential, so avoid shortcuts. The method outlined in that recipe works equally well for stovetop cooking and rice cookers.

COOKING NOODLES

When preparing udon, soba, or ramen noodles, it's crucial to use a large quantity of water for boiling. Unlike pasta, there's no need to add salt to the water. For fresh noodles dusted with flour, an extra step is recommended after boiling. Drain the noodles in a colander, then rinse them with cold water. This process removes excess starch, preventing it from affecting the flavor and consistency of the soup. While it might seem like a small detail, this step significantly enhances the overall quality of the dish. The final preparation depends on how you plan to serve the noodles. For cold dishes, simply drain the noodles thoroughly after rinsing. For hot soups and other dishes, rinse the noodles with cold water, gently washing them by hand. Then, just before serving, pour boiling water over them to reheat.

MAKING DASHI

Dashi is a fundamental element in many Japanese dishes and is another crucial component to master. While going awry with your dashi preparation is less likely to result in a catastrophic failure compared to rice cooking, you will dramatically enhance the flavor of almost any Japanese dish by learning to make good dashi.

When making dashi, temperature control is crucial. Regardless of the ingredients used, avoid bringing the mixture to a full boil. Aim to keep the temperature around 160°F to 175°F for optimal flavor extraction. When straining the broth, resist the urge to squeeze out every last drop. This gentle approach prevents bitter flavors from entering the dashi. While the process requires patience and finesse, it's efficient to prepare a large batch at once for use in various dishes. If you're short on time, dashi packets (similar to tea bags) are a convenient alternative. Dashi granules are also available, but are best used as a seasoning to add a hint of Japanese flavor rather than as a base for simmered dishes or soups. They're useful when you need a very small amount of dashi, but their salt content makes them a less suitable substitute when larger quantities are required.

THE FIVE COOKING METHODS

Japanese cuisine has evolved over centuries, developing unique preparation methods and culinary philosophies distinct from Western and other Asian cuisines. One fundamental concept in traditional Japanese cooking is the theory of "Gogyō" (Five Elements), which originated from Chinese philosophy.

The Five Cooking Methods, known as "Goho," form the cornerstone of Japanese cuisine:

- Nama: Raw (ex: sashimi)
- Niru: Simmered or Boiled (ex: nimono)
- Yaku: Grilled or Broiled (ex: grilled fish)
- Musu: Steamed (ex: savory egg custard)
- Ageru: Deep-fried (ex: tempura)

In a traditional kaiseki meal, dishes prepared using all five methods are typically present, creating a harmonious and balanced dining experience. This balance is evident in many Japanese meals, even beyond formal kaiseki dining.

It's worth noting that while these five methods form the base, Japanese cuisine also incorporates other techniques like aemono (dressed dishes) and sunomono (vinegared dishes). Modern Japanese cooking has also embraced methods from other cuisines, such as stir-frying (itameru).

Each method not only imparts distinct flavors and textures but also contributes to the overall balance and harmony of the meal, a key principle in Japanese food culture.

DEEP-FRYING

Deep-frying may seem simple, but it's a technique with surprising depth. In Japanese cuisine, the temperature for deep-frying typically ranges between 340°F and 355°F. However, successful deep-frying involves more than just temperature control. Common issues include food not cooking through, batter peeling off, and fried foods becoming soggy. While professional cooks might rely on sight and sound to judge frying conditions, home cooks can benefit greatly from using a deep-frying thermometer. It's a worthwhile investment considering the potential cost of failed attempts. At home, I use a deep fryer with a built-in thermometer, as oil temperatures can fluctuate more than you might expect. If the oil is too hot, you'll end up with a crispy exterior but raw interior. Conversely, if it's too cool, the batter will absorb excess oil and never crisp up, even if you increase the heat later. A frequent mistake is overcrowding the pan in an attempt to rush the cooking process. I get it, but this can cause the batter to peel off and the oil temperature to drop, resulting in a soggy finish. It's far more reliable to fry in small, manageable batches, even if it takes a bit longer. And don't underestimate the importance of proper oil draining. Place fried items on a wire rack or paper towel–lined plate to drain excess oil thoroughly, as even perfectly fried food can become soggy if it reabsorbs its own oil. I personally keep several sets of stainless-steel racks ready by the stove when deep-frying for this purpose. For frying oil, choose a neutral-tasting option with a high smoke point. Canola oil is an affordable choice, while rice bran oil is

a slightly pricier recommendation. For delicate tempura, extra-virgin untoasted sesame oil is an excellent option.

CUTTING METHODS

Japanese cuisine employs a variety of cutting techniques, each serving a specific purpose in dish preparation and presentation. This book frequently uses the following methods:

Wagiri (Rounds): This technique preserves a round vegetable's shape, cutting it into slices of uniform thickness. It's commonly used for cucumbers, carrots, and daikon radishes.

Rangiri (Rough Cuts): Used for ingredients like cucumbers and carrots, this method involves rotating the vegetable while cutting at an angle, resulting in irregular yet uniformly sized pieces.

Sengiri (Julienne): Similar to the Western julienne, this technique involves layering thinly sliced or peeled vegetables and cutting them into fine strips along the grain.

Mijingiri (Finely Diced/Minced): This method involves cutting vegetables very finely. It's often used for onions, garlic, and ginger.

Nanamegiri (Diagonal): This technique involves cutting vegetables on a diagonal bias, resulting in oval slices with a wide surface area. It's widely used for leeks, green onions, carrots, burdock roots, and cucumbers.

Hangetsugiri (Half-Moon): Round vegetables are first halved lengthwise, then sliced crosswise

to a certain thickness. Alternatively, round slices can be cut in half. This method is often used with daikon radishes and carrots.

Ichogiri (Quarter Rounds): This technique takes the half-moon slice a step further by cutting it in half again. The name comes from its resemblance to a ginkgo (icho) leaf. It's commonly used for radishes, carrots, and turnips.

How to Cut Meat Thin: Many Japanese recipes call for thinly sliced meat, which is readily available in Asian countries, but can be challenging to find elsewhere. Here are some strategies to obtain this crucial ingredient. First, if possible, ask your local butcher to cut the meat into thin slices for you. Professional butchers have the skills and equipment to produce consistently thin slices, making this the ideal option when available. If that's not an option, consider investing in a quality meat slicer for your home. While it may seem extravagant, it's a game changer for Japanese cooking enthusiasts. To use a meat slicer effectively, cut your meat into manageable chunks, wrap them tightly, and freeze overnight. Before slicing, let the meat partially thaw for about an hour—this semi-frozen state is ideal for achieving thin slices. Keep in mind that while you might be tempted to try hand-slicing with a sharp knife, it's challenging to maintain consistency using this approach. A meat slicer, on the other hand, ensures uniform thickness every time. Although a meat slicer represents an initial investment, it can quickly prove to be worth it, especially if you frequently prepare Asian dishes. It's also generally more economical than regularly buying pre-sliced meat from Asian supermarkets.

TOOLS

Do you need special equipment to make Japanese food outside of Japan? Not necessarily. Many basic dishes can be prepared with tools already in your kitchen. However, there are some useful items that can enhance your Japanese cooking experience. A list follows below:

Rice Cooker: While I'll show you how to cook rice on the stovetop using a pot, a rice cooker from a Japanese manufacturer is recommended if you plan to cook Japanese food frequently. Every Japanese household has one.

Knives: A chef's knife and a paring knife can handle most tasks. For specialized tasks, you might consider a deba knife for cleaning fish, a sashimi knife for raw fish, and an usuba knife for vegetables.

Yukihira Pan: A versatile, one-handled saucepan with a pouring spout that is good for various cooking methods.

Tamagoyaki Pan: A square (Kanto region) or rectangular (Kansai region) pan used for making rolled-up omelets.

Earthenware Pot (Donabe): A traditional Japanese ceramic pot that retains heat well and is ideal for rice dishes and hot pots.

Handai/Sushi Oke: A wooden container that is essential for making vinegared sushi rice (sumeshi). It should be moistened with water before adding rice to prevent sticking. Clean it thoroughly and dry completely after using.

Saibashi: Long chopsticks used in cooking. Very useful for various cooking tasks.

Shamoji: A rice paddle used for mixing and serving rice.

Rolling Sushi Mat (Makisu): Used primarily for forming sushi rolls and tamagoyaki.

Japanese Grater: Produces a more finely grated result for ingredients like daikon, ginger, and garlic compared to Western-style graters.

Mortar and Pestle: Often used for grinding spices and sesame seeds.

Miso Strainer: Helps create smooth miso soup by straining out clumps of miso paste.

Drop Lid (Otoshibuta): Placed directly on the surface when a dish is simmering, it helps food cook evenly. Stainless-steel versions are easiest to use, just make sure to choose those that fit the sizes of your pots and pans.

Mesh Spoon or Spider Skimmer: Useful for removing fried foods from oil.

ICHIJU SANSAI: THE JAPANESE CONCEPT OF A MEAL

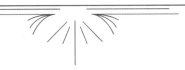

The concept of Ichiju Sansai is fundamental to traditional Japanese cuisine. It consists of:

- Gohan (rice): Freshly cooked white rice, brown rice, or mixed grains
- Main: Traditionally fish (e.g., grilled fish), but in modern times, this can be meat or fish
- Soup: Such as miso soup
- Nimono (simmered side): Dishes like nikujaga or kinpira
- Aemono (dressed side): Salads such as ohitashi

However, daily meals in modern Japanese households have evolved. They often consist of rice, soup, one main dish (meat or seafood), and a vegetable-centered side dish. This shift reflects changing societal norms.

It's not necessary to adhere strictly to this concept when preparing Japanese food at home. Few modern Japanese families follow it rigorously, but this structure was common in older generations.

The traditional story ends here. Now, let's talk more practically for our age.

For those new to Japanese cooking, I recommend starting with freshly cooked white rice and miso soup as the base of your meal, then deciding whether the main dish will be fish or meat. Many Japanese main dishes are designed quite rich and flavorful, in order to complement unseasoned, well-made white rice.

Your choice of main dish can be based on anything: the fish looked fresh today, the meat was on sale, you're in the mood for seafood—whatever motivates you. The reason doesn't matter—it's all about what appeals to you at the moment.

With white rice, soup, and a main course, you already have a standard Japanese meal. If you have more time, or if the main dish is particularly rich, you can add a simple dressed salad or some pickles for a nice contrast. When you think about it this way, it's not too difficult, is it? There's no need to be overly fussy just because it's Japanese food.

For those more familiar with Japanese cuisine, there's the concept of "five flavors, five colors, and five methods" (Gomi Goshoku Goho):

- Five Flavors: Sweet, spicy, sour, salty, and bitter
- Five Colors: Red, green, yellow, white, and black
- Five Cooking Methods: Grilling, boiling, deep-frying, steaming, and serving raw

While this concept might seem unrealistic for everyday home cooking—and it is indeed difficult to incorporate everything perfectly at home—keeping these principles in mind can make it easier to create a well-balanced menu.

For instance, a meal won't be satisfying if all the dishes are too rich or too light in flavor. Ideally, consider which dish will be the star of the meal, and use the gomi-goshoku-goho concept to guide your selection of the other dishes, considering which elements will best complement or accentuate the main dish. By understanding these principles, you can create satisfying Japanese meals that suit your taste and lifestyle, whether you're aiming for traditional authenticity or a more modern interpretation.

HOMEMADE INGREDIENTS

As many ingredients that are commonplace in Japan can be challenging to find in other parts of the world, this section is dedicated to helping you create them from scratch in your own kitchen. By learning to prepare these ingredients yourself, you'll not only ensure authenticity in your cooking, but also gain a deeper appreciation for the flavors and techniques that make Japanese food so special. Plus, you might be surprised to discover how easy it is to make many of these essential components yourself.

AWASE DASHI STOCK

YIELD: 4 CUPS / **ACTIVE TIME:** 10 MINUTES / **TOTAL TIME:** 40 MINUTES

When a Japanese recipe mentions "dashi stock," it typically refers to this preparation, which is made from a blend of dried kelp (kombu) and bonito flakes (katsuobushi). This type of dashi is a cornerstone of Japanese cuisine, offering a versatile base for a wide array of dishes. The secret to its rich flavor lies in the synergy between the inosinic acid from bonito flakes and glutamic acid from kelp, creating the profound umami taste that is fundamental to Japanese cooking. Mastering awase dashi is key to preparing various Japanese dishes and unlocking the essence of the authentic flavors. When preparing dashi, soft water (meaning lower mineral content) is ideal.

1. Place the kombu in a pot and pour the water over it. Cover the pot with a lid and allow the kombu to rehydrate for at least 30 minutes. For a deeper flavor, let the kombu soak for up to 24 hours. If opting for the longer soaking time, let the kombu soak in the refrigerator.

2. Add the bonito flakes to the pot and warm the mixture over medium-low heat. Closely monitor the temperature and remove the kombu just before the water reaches 170°F, making sure not to let it come to a boil. Once the kombu has been removed, raise the heat to high and cook the dashi for an additional minute. Remove the pan from heat.

3. Line a fine-mesh sieve with a paper towel and place it over a heatproof bowl. Carefully pour the dashi through the sieve to strain out the bonito flakes and either use immediately or let the dashi cool before storing it in the refrigerator.

INGREDIENTS:

	4-INCH SQUARE OF DRIED KOMBU
4	CUPS COLD WATER
¾	CUP BONITO FLAKES

SHOJIN DASHI STOCK

YIELD: 4 CUPS / **ACTIVE TIME**: 5 MINUTES / **TOTAL TIME**: 12 HOURS

Shojin ryori is the embodiment of traditional vegan Japanese cuisine, crafted solely from vegetables, tofu, and other plant-based components. Rooted in the traditional dietary practices of Buddhist monks, this approach showcases Japan's rich heritage of plant-based cooking. A cornerstone of this cuisine is shojin dashi, which forms the flavorful base of many dishes. Also, a good practice to start doing is reserving the kombu after using it here for another preparation, like tsukudani.

1. Place the water in a large pot. Add the kombu, mushrooms, and soybeans and weigh down the mixture with a plate so that the mushrooms remain submerged. Cover the pot with a lid and let the mixture soak overnight.

2. Remove the mushrooms from the pot and reserve them for another preparation. Add the radish and carrot peels and warm the mixture over medium heat. Closely monitor the temperature and remove the kombu just before the water comes to a boil. Reduce the heat to low and let the dashi simmer gently for 5 minutes, skimming any foam that forms on the surface to maintain a clear broth.

3. Remove the pot from heat and strain the dashi through a fine-mesh sieve. Use immediately or let the dashi cool to room temperature before storing it in the refrigerator.

INGREDIENTS:

- 4 CUPS COLD WATER
- 4-INCH SQUARE OF DRIED KOMBU
- 2 DRIED SHIITAKE MUSHROOMS
- ⅔ OZ. DRIED SOYBEANS
- PEEL OF ½ DAIKON RADISH, RINSED WELL BEFORE PEELING
- PEEL OF 1 CARROT, RINSED WELL BEFORE PEELING

MENTSUYU

YIELD: 2 CUPS / **ACTIVE TIME:** 10 MINUTES / **TOTAL TIME:** 40 MINUTES

Mentsuyu is a versatile Japanese condiment that is primarily used for noodle dishes. Made from a mixture of soy sauce, mirin, sugar, salt, and dashi stock, among other ingredients, it provides a rich, umami-filled character wherever it appears. Although it is mainly used as a dipping sauce for soba, udon, hiyamugi, and somen noodles, mentsuyu is also a popular choice for a wider range of applications. It is an excellent dipping sauce for tempura and has increasingly become a favored alternative to soy sauce.

1. Place the water in a saucepan and add the kombu. Cover the pan and let the kombu soak for 30 minutes.

2. Transfer the saucepan to the stove and warm the mixture over medium heat. Closely monitor the temperature and remove the kombu just before the water comes to a boil.

3. Let the water come to a boil and then reduce the heat to low. Stir in the bonito flakes, soy sauce, mirin, and sugar and let the mixture gently simmer for 5 minutes. Remove the pan from heat and let the mentsuyu cool slightly.

4. Strain the mentsuyu through a fine-mesh sieve. Use immediately if serving it hot. Let it cool to room temperature and then refrigerate it for a chilled version.

INGREDIENTS:

2	CUPS WATER
	2-INCH SQUARE OF DRIED KOMBU
¾	CUP BONITO FLAKES
6	TABLESPOONS SOY SAUCE
3	TABLESPOONS MIRIN
1	TABLESPOON SUGAR

PONZU SAUCE

YIELD: 1 CUP / **ACTIVE TIME:** 5 MINUTES / **TOTAL TIME:** 24 HOURS

Ponzu is a unique all-purpose Japanese condiment made with soy sauce, dashi, and citrus juice (yuzu and lemon are the most common). Its balance of salty, sour, and mild sweetness makes it an ideal everyday ingredient for dipping sauces, marinades, and general cooking. Although it goes especially well with fish, its uses extend far and wide.

1. Place the mirin in a small saucepan, bring it to a boil, and let it cook for 30 seconds to 1 minute. Remove the pan from heat and pour the mirin into a heatproof container.

2. Cut the kombu to fit the container and place it in the mirin. Add the remaining ingredients, cover the container, and let the ponzu rest in the refrigerator for at least 24 hours. If time allows, let the ponzu rest for 2 to 3 days for maximum flavor.

3. Strain the ponzu into a sterilized mason jar and either use immediately or store it in the refrigerator for up to 6 months.

INGREDIENTS:

2	TABLESPOONS MIRIN
	3 X 4–INCH SHEET OF DRIED KOMBU
6	TABLESPOONS FRESH CITRUS JUICE
2	TABLESPOONS RICE VINEGAR
½	CUP SOY SAUCE
1	CUP BONITO FLAKES

JAPANESE MAYONNAISE

YIELD: 1 CUP / **ACTIVE TIME:** 15 MINUTES / **TOTAL TIME:** 1 HOUR AND 15 MINUTES

Mayonnaise is a popular condiment in Japanese cuisine, and is typically used for dishes such as okonomiyaki, takoyaki, fried noodles, and salads. Japanese mayonnaise is typically rich and creamy, and made with egg yolks rather than whole eggs.

1. Place the egg yolks and mustard in a large, wide mixing bowl and whisk until well combined. While whisking continually, pour the canola oil down the side of the bowl a few drops at a time. It is crucial to add the oil slowly and along the side of the bowl, as adding too much at once or pouring it directly into the center of the egg mixture will cause the mayonnaise to split. Repeat until you have incorporated half of the canola oil and the mayonnaise is thick.

2. Combine the apple cider vinegar and rice vinegar in a small bowl. While whisking continually, pour the vinegar mixture along the side of the bowl a few drops at a time. Repeat until you have incorporated half of the vinegar mixture.

3. While whisking continually, pour the remaining canola oil along the side of the bowl a few drops at a time. When it has emulsified, add the remaining vinegar mixture as before, whisking continually.

4. Transfer the mayonnaise to a small blender and add the remaining ingredients. Puree until the mayonnaise is smooth, fluffy, and pale. Transfer it to a container, cover it, and store the mayonnaise in the refrigerator for 1 hour to let it thicken further before serving.

INGREDIENTS:

2	EGG YOLKS
½	TEASPOON JAPANESE MUSTARD
½	TEASPOON SMOOTH DIJON MUSTARD
¾	CUP CANOLA OIL
1	TABLESPOON APPLE CIDER VINEGAR
2	TEASPOONS RICE VINEGAR
½	TEASPOON FINE SEA SALT
½	TEASPOON FRESH LEMON JUICE
	PINCH OF WHITE PEPPER
¼	TEASPOON SUGAR

RAYU

YIELD: ¾ CUP / **ACTIVE TIME:** 15 MINUTES / **TOTAL TIME:** 15 MINUTES

Rayu is an aromatic chili oil, and a prized condiment in Chuka cuisine. This vibrant red oil, infused with the intense flavors of chile peppers and various spices, adds a thrilling kick of heat and a depth of flavor to countless dishes. While the thought of making rayu at home might seem intimidating, the truth is that it is surprisingly simple to prepare.

1. Place the canola oil and sesame oil in a large skillet and warm them to 320°F.

2. Reduce the heat to low and add the ginger, garlic, and leek to the pan. Tear the chile peppers open and drop them into the oil along with their seeds. Cook over low heat for 10 minutes, stirring occasionally.

3. Place the red chili powder in a heatproof bowl, add the water, and stir to combine.

4. Remove the pan from heat. Place a colander or fine-mesh sieve over the heatproof bowl. Carefully strain the hot oil mixture into the bowl. Stir the rayu and let it cool completely before using or storing.

INGREDIENTS:

½	CUP CANOLA OIL
½	CUP TOASTED SESAME OIL
3	SLICES OF FRESH GINGER
1	GARLIC CLOVE, CHOPPED
1	JAPANESE LEEK, GREEN PART ONLY, CHOPPED
5	DRIED RED CHILE PEPPERS
2	TABLESPOONS RED CHILI POWDER
½	TABLESPOON WATER

WAFU DRESSING

Wafu dressing is a Japanese-inspired vinaigrette that combines the nuttiness of sesame oil with a base of soy sauce and rice vinegar. My version adds citrus juice and zest, creating a refreshing and versatile dressing.

1. Rinse the yuzu well with hot water and dry them thoroughly with paper towels.

2. Grate the yuzu zest into a large bowl. Cut the yuzu in half and squeeze their juice into the bowl through a fine-mesh sieve to catch the seeds.

3. Add the remaining ingredients and whisk until the sugar and dashi powder have dissolved and the dressing is well combined. Use as desired.

INGREDIENTS:

2	YUZU, LEMONS, OR ORANGES
¼	CUP SOY SAUCE
2	TABLESPOONS RICE VINEGAR
2	TABLESPOONS SESAME OIL
2	TEASPOONS WHITE SESAME SEEDS
2	TABLESPOONS GROUND SESAME SEEDS
2	TEASPOONS SUGAR
2	TABLESPOONS WATER
	PINCH OF DASHI POWDER

GOMA DRESSING

YIELD: 16 SERVINGS / ACTIVE TIME: 10 MINUTES / TOTAL TIME: 10 MINUTES

Goma dressing is one of the most popular dressings in Japan. Its distinct nutty, tangy flavor and creamy texture allow it to transform any salad into something truly delicious.

1. Place the sesame seeds in a large, dry skillet and toast over medium-high heat until they are fragrant and lightly golden brown, shaking the pan frequently.

2. Place the toasted sesame seeds in a food processor and pulse until they are a fine powder.

3. Add the mayonnaise, rice vinegar, sugar, soy sauce, and sesame oil to the food processor and blitz for a few seconds until the dressing has emulsified. Transfer the dressing to a container and chill it in the refrigerator before serving.

INGREDIENTS:

1   CUP WHITE SESAME SEEDS

1   CUP JAPANESE MAYONNAISE (SEE PAGE 46)

2⅔   TABLESPOONS RICE VINEGAR

¼   CUP SUGAR

2⅔   TABLESPOONS SOY SAUCE

2⅔   TABLESPOONS TOASTED SESAME OIL

Wafu Dressing, see page 50

PONZU DRESSING

YIELD: 4 SERVINGS / **ACTIVE TIME:** 5 MINUTES / **TOTAL TIME:** 5 MINUTES

This is a simple and refreshing vinaigrette that utilizes the balanced salt and tang flavors of ponzu sauce, the beloved Japanese condiment.

1. Place the mirin in a small saucepan, bring it to a boil, and cook for 1 minute.

2. Pour the mirin into a heatproof bowl, add the remaining ingredients, and whisk until well combined.

3. Whisk the dressing again before pouring it over a salad to ensure the ingredients are evenly distributed.

INGREDIENTS:

2 TABLESPOONS MIRIN

½ CUP PONZU SAUCE (SEE PAGE 45)

1 TABLESPOON EXTRA-VIRGIN OLIVE OIL

1 TABLESPOON SESAME OIL

2 TEASPOONS GROUND SESAME SEEDS

2 TEASPOONS WASABI PASTE

SHISO DRESSING

YIELD: 4 SERVINGS / **ACTIVE TIME:** 5 MINUTES / **TOTAL TIME:** 5 MINUTES

Perilla leaves, known in Japanese as shiso or ooba, are an aromatic wild herb with an intense and aromatic flavor. Blending them with a soy sauce–infused vinaigrette produces a unique and refreshing salad dressing with a bold Japanese flavor. If you are making the dressing without a food processor, chop the perilla leaves with a knife on a chopping board. Cut them as finely as possible by rocking the knife in all directions, then add them to a bowl with the rest of the ingredients and whisk until combined.

1. Place all of the ingredients in a food processor and blitz until the perilla leaves are finely chopped. Use the dressing as desired.

INGREDIENTS:

1 GARLIC CLOVE, GRATED

10 PERILLA LEAVES

2 TABLESPOONS SOY SAUCE

2 TABLESPOONS RICE VINEGAR

1 TABLESPOON SUGAR

2 TABLESPOONS EXTRA-VIRGIN OLIVE OIL

ONSEN TAMAGO

YIELD: 4 SERVINGS / **ACTIVE TIME:** 5 MINUTES / **TOTAL TIME:** 25 MINUTES

Onsen tamago is a delicately cooked egg with a semi-set yolk and just-firm egg white, distinct from any other boiled egg variety. This cooking technique heats eggs in water slightly above 150°F, leveraging the temperature at which yolks and whites begin to set. The name comes from the traditional method of cooking eggs in hot spring waters, which made them a staple in hot spring resort accommodations. While Japan offers specialized gadgets for preparing onsen tamago, their scarcity abroad inspired me to refine and adapt the method, adjusting temperatures and cooking times to achieve an even better result than those found in Japanese markets.

1. Place 1¼ cups of water in a bowl and chill it in the refrigerator. Add the remaining water to a large pot and bring to a rolling boil.

2. Turn off the heat and stir in the chilled water. This will lower the water temperature to the optimal range for cooking onsen tamago, around 175°F. Carefully add the eggs, taken straight from the refrigerator, to the pot. Cover the pot with a lid and set a timer for 15 minutes.

3. After the timer goes off, remove the eggs from the pot and let them rest at room temperature for exactly 5 minutes. While the eggs are resting, prepare an ice bath.

4. Transfer the eggs to the ice bath to stop the cooking process.

5. For those who want to enjoy onsen tamago as a standalone dish, combine the dashi, soy sauce, mirin, and water in a small, microwave-safe bowl, place it in the microwave, and microwave on high for 1 minute.

6. To serve, gently crack the onsen tamago into a serving bowl and drizzle approximately 1 tablespoon of the sauce over the top.

INGREDIENTS:

7¾	CUPS COLD WATER
4	MEDIUM EGGS, REFRIGERATED
2	TABLESPOONS AWASE DASHI STOCK (SEE PAGE 38)
1½	TEASPOONS LIGHT SOY SAUCE
1	TABLESPOON MIRIN
1	TABLESPOON WATER

Shiso Dressing, see page 56

KOMBU NO TSUKUDANI

YIELD: 4 SERVINGS / **ACTIVE TIME:** 10 MINUTES / **TOTAL TIME:** 40 MINUTES

After making dashi stock, repurposing the kombu is not only eco-friendly but also deliciously practical. Kombu no tsukudani is an excellent recipe for this purpose, transforming the leftover kombu into a savory, umami-rich condiment. Whether served atop white rice, mixed into rice balls, or utilized in various other dishes, kombu no tsukudani provides a flavorful and sustainable option for those looking to maximize their ingredients.

1. Cut the kombu into thin strips and place it in a medium saucepan along with the water, sake, and rice vinegar.

2. Warm the mixture over medium heat and bring it to a rolling boil. Reduce the heat so that it gently simmers and cook until the liquid has reduced to just under half its original volume, about 20 minutes.

3. Stir in the sugar, mirin, and soy sauce, raise the heat to medium, and boil the mixture until the liquid has nearly evaporated, stirring frequently to prevent the kombu from burning. Once the kombu is glazed and the pan is nearly dry, sprinkle in the sesame seeds, stir to combine, and use as desired.

INGREDIENTS:

2	OZ. REHYDRATED KOMBU
2	CUPS WATER
2	TABLESPOONS SAKE
1	TEASPOON RICE VINEGAR
1	TABLESPOON SUGAR
1	TABLESPOON MIRIN
2	TABLESPOONS SOY SAUCE
1½	TEASPOONS WHITE SESAME SEEDS

SALMON FLAKES

YIELD: 6 SERVINGS / **ACTIVE TIME:** 5 MINUTES / **TOTAL TIME:** 15 MINUTES

Salmon flakes are a highly versatile and flavorful topping in Japanese cuisine that can be used on top of white rice, as an ingredient in rice balls, or for any purpose one likes. While commercially available in jars in Japan, making it at home is straightforward and allows for a fresher ingredient and a personalized touch.

1. Pat the salmon dry with paper towels. Rub ½ teaspoon of salt over the salmon and let it rest for 5 minutes.

2. While the salmon is resting, bring a pot of water to a boil.

3. Pat the salmon dry again. Reduce the boiling water to a simmer and carefully add the salmon. Poach for 5 minutes, adjusting the heat as necessary to maintain a gentle simmer.

4. Remove the salmon from the water and gently shake it to remove any excess. Transfer the salmon to a wide container and carefully peel off the skin. The skin can be fried until crispy and enjoyed as a snack or discarded. Using a spatula, break the salmon into small flakes, removing any bones with tweezers.

5. Place the butter in a large skillet and melt it over medium-low heat. Add the flaked salmon, sake, mirin, and remaining salt to the pan, stir to combine, and cook until the liquid has nearly evaporated.

6. Remove the pan from heat and stir in the soy sauce and sesame seeds. Use immediately or transfer the salmon flakes to a clean container and let them cool completely before storing in the refrigerator for up to 5 days.

INGREDIENTS:

2	SALMON FILLETS (EACH ABOUT 3½ OZ.)
½	TEASPOON PLUS ⅛ TEASPOON FINE SEA SALT
1	TEASPOON UNSALTED BUTTER
1½	TEASPOONS SAKE
½	TABLESPOON MIRIN
¼	TEASPOON SOY SAUCE
1	TEASPOON WHITE SESAME SEEDS

Kombu No Tsukudani, see page 60

JAPANESE CURRY POWDER

YIELD: ⅓ CUP / **ACTIVE TIME:** 10 MINUTES / **TOTAL TIME:** 10 MINUTES

Japanese curry powder is the key ingredient in making authentic Japanese-style curry rice from scratch. It's a carefully crafted blend of spices that I've perfected through extensive experimentation and numerous iterations.

1. Using a mortar and pestle or spice grinder, grind the cinnamon stick, star anise, bay leaf, chile, cardamom seeds, and cloves into a fine powder.

2. Transfer the freshly ground spices to a large skillet and add the remaining ingredients. Place the pan over medium heat. As soon as the pan is warm, stir the mixture continually.

3. As you toast the spices, you'll notice the color deepening to a beautiful, rich brown. Once the desired color is achieved and the spices are fragrant, 1 to 2 minutes, remove the pan from heat.

4. Let the curry powder cool completely in the pan, stirring occasionally to release some of the heat. When the curry powder has cooled, use immediately or store it in an airtight container.

INGREDIENTS:

1	CINNAMON STICK (1½ INCHES LONG)
1	STAR ANISE POD
1	BAY LEAF
1	DRIED RED CHILE PEPPER
	SEEDS OF 4 GREEN CARDAMOM PODS
4	WHOLE CLOVES
1	TABLESPOON TURMERIC POWDER
1½	TEASPOONS CORIANDER
1½	TEASPOONS CUMIN
1½	TEASPOONS FENUGREEK
1	TEASPOON GROUND FENNEL
1	TEASPOON GROUND GINGER
1	TEASPOON GARLIC POWDER
½	TEASPOON BLACK PEPPER
½	TEASPOON FRESHLY GRATED NUTMEG
½	TEASPOON ALLSPICE
¼	TEASPOON GROUND CARDAMOM
¼	TEASPOON CAYENNE PEPPER

NAMA PANKO

YIELD: 8 SERVINGS / **ACTIVE TIME:** 5 MINUTES / **TOTAL TIME:** 5 MINUTES

The term "panko" is made up of the Japanese words "pan" (bread) and "ko" (powder or crumb) and refers to light and flaky Japanese-style bread crumbs. Nama panko is made using fresh bread (not dried or stale), which produces larger crumbs that will result in a crispy yet light texture when deep-fried. Panko is typically used for dishes such as tonkatsu, ebi fry, and korokke. If you do not have a food processor, freeze the bread for several hours, until it is frozen all the way through, and then grate the bread using a large-hole grater.

1. Cut the bread into cubes. Remove the crusts if you prefer panko with a lighter color.

2. Place the bread in a food processor and blitz for a few seconds, until the panko is chunky. Be careful not to blitz for too long, as you don't want the panko to be too fine.

3. Use immediately or store the panko in the freezer.

INGREDIENTS:

4   SLICES OF FRESH WHITE
     BREAD

TENKASU

YIELD: 4 SERVINGS / **ACTIVE TIME:** 10 MINUTES / **TOTAL TIME:** 10 MINUTES

Tenkasu is the crispy, golden by-product of the tempura frying process. In Japan, these deep-fried bits of batter are frequently used as a condiment in soups featuring udon and soba noodles. While tenkasu is readily available for purchase in Japan, there's a certain satisfaction in making use of the leftover batter from your own homemade tempura.

1. Add canola oil to a Dutch oven until it is about 2 inches deep and warm it to 355°F.

2. Dip a balloon whisk into the batter and then hold it over the hot oil. Shake the whisk to allow the batter to drip off the whisk and into the oil. Alternatively, you can dip your hand into the batter and then shake it over the hot oil to create the tenkasu. However, using a whisk will result in finer tenkasu.

3. As the batter hits the hot oil, it will puff up and create small, irregular-shaped bits. The bits will naturally stick to each other as they fry. To ensure even cooking and to prevent the tenkasu from clumping together too much, fry only a small amount of batter at a time.

4. Fry until the tenkasu turns golden brown. Depending on the temperature of the oil, this should take about 2 minutes.

5. Once the tenkasu is golden brown, use a fine-mesh skimmer or slotted spoon to remove it from the oil. Hold the skimmer or spoon over the pot to allow any excess oil to drain back into the pot.

6. Transfer the tenkasu to a paper towel–lined plate to drain and cool. When it has cooled completely, use as desired.

INGREDIENTS:

TEMPURA OR SHOJIN-AGE
(SEE PAGE 272 OR 279)

CANOLA OIL, AS NEEDED

ABURA-AGE

YIELD: 4 SHEETS / **ACTIVE TIME:** 20 MINUTES / **TOTAL TIME:** 8 HOURS AND 20 MINUTES

Abura-age is a a type of tofu that's been transformed through a process of cutting, pressing, and deep-frying. Also known as "usuage" or "age," abura-age offers a unique texture and flavor profile that sets it apart from regular tofu.

INGREDIENTS:

14   OZ. FIRM TOFU

     CANOLA OIL, AS NEEDED

1. Cut the tofu lengthwise into four equal slices. Wrap the tofu in paper towels, and then wrap it in a clean kitchen towel. Place the tofu on a plate and put a heavy pot on top of it. Place the tofu in the refrigerator overnight.

2. Remove the pressed tofu from the refrigerator and unwrap it. Using fresh paper towels, gently pat the tofu slices dry to remove any remaining moisture.

3. Add canola oil to a Dutch oven until it is about 2 inches deep and warm it to 250°F.

4. Carefully slip the tofu into the hot oil and fry it on each side for 5 minutes. You will notice the surface of the tofu becoming puffier during this initial frying stage.

5. Use a slotted spoon or a fine-mesh skimmer to remove the fried tofu from the oil. Place the fried tofu on a wire rack to drain. While the tofu is draining, warm the frying oil to 320°F.

6. Carefully slip the tofu back into the hot oil and fry until it is lightly golden brown on each side, turning it frequently to ensure that it browns evenly.

7. Transfer the abura-age to a wire rack or paper towel–lined plate to drain and cool slightly before using as desired.

Tenkasu, see page 68

ATSUAGE TOFU

YIELD: 2 SERVINGS / **ACTIVE TIME:** 10 MINUTES / **TOTAL TIME:** 1 HOUR AND 20 MINUTES

Atsuage tofu is a versatile and flavorful form of tofu where only the outer layer is deep-fried, creating a unique combination of textures: a crispy exterior and a smooth, soft interior. Atsuage tofu can be enjoyed on its own, or incorporated into various dishes, such as hot pots.

1. Pat the tofu dry with paper towels and place it on a microwave-safe dish. Microwave on high for 2 minutes.

2. Remove the tofu from the microwave and discard any water that has accumulated in the dish. Place a paper towel over the tofu and place a weight on top. Let the tofu sit under the weight for 10 minutes to press out any excess moisture.

3. Cut the tofu into eight pieces. Add canola oil to a pan until it is about half the height of the pieces of tofu and warm it to 350°F. Carefully slip the tofu into the hot oil and fry, turning occasionally, until all of the moisture has evaporated and it is crispy and golden brown all over.

4. Remove the atsuage tofu from the pan, top it with any or all of the suggested garnishes, and serve.

INGREDIENTS:

14 OZ. FIRM TOFU

CANOLA OIL, AS NEEDED

1 TABLESPOON CHOPPED DAIKON RADISH, FOR GARNISH

1½ TEASPOONS SOY SAUCE, FOR GARNISH

1 TEASPOON CHOPPED GREEN ONION, FOR GARNISH

GYOZA WRAPPERS

YIELD: 40 WRAPPERS / **ACTIVE TIME:** 30 MINUTES / **TOTAL TIME:** 1 HOUR

Homemade gyoza wrappers will bring your dumplings to the next level—they're cheap to make, taste better than store-bought, and allow you to adjust the size to suit your needs.

1. Sift the flours into a large bowl, add the salt, and whisk to combine. Make a well in the center of the mixture and pour the boiling water into the well. Stir until the mixture comes together as a rough dough.

2. Dust a work surface with cake flour and scrape the dough onto it. Knead the dough until it is smooth, about 10 minutes. Resist the urge to add more flour to the dough during the early stages of kneading; it should become less sticky as you knead it.

3. Cover the dough with plastic wrap and let it rest at room temperature for 30 minutes.

4. Cut the dough into quarters and roll each piece into a cylinder. Working with one piece of dough at a time, cut it into 10 pieces. Roll each piece into a ball, dust them with cake flour, and then roll out until they are about 1⁄16 inch thick. Gently pinch the edge of the wrapper; this will prevent the top of the gyoza from becoming too thick when they are sealed. Stack the wrappers in an airtight container, dusting each one with cake flour to prevent them from sticking together as you go. While you are working to turn the cylinders into wrappers, make sure to keep the other cylinders covered with a kitchen towel to prevent them from drying out.

5. Use immediately or store the wrappers in the refrigerator, making sure to use them the same day you make them.

INGREDIENTS:

1	CUP CAKE FLOUR, PLUS MORE AS NEEDED
1	CUP BREAD FLOUR
½	TEASPOON FINE SEA SALT
½	CUP BOILING WATER

GOHAN
(RICE)

*R*ice is an absolutely essential component of the Japanese table. While there are standard methods for preparing rice, it's important to note that personal preferences for rice texture can vary. The basic recipe provides a starting point for achieving perfectly cooked rice. However, you may find that you prefer your rice slightly harder or softer. In this case, you can slightly adjust the amount of water used without needing to change the cooking time.

Please note that all measurements using cups refer to standard US cups (8 fluid ounces/237ml), and not Japanese rice cups (6 fluid ounces/180ml). A single portion of rice in this book is ⅓ US cup before cooking and a little over 1 cup after cooking. This measure is based on the Japanese average standard portion size of 5.8 ounces.

PERFECT JAPANESE RICE

YIELD: 6 SERVINGS / **ACTIVE TIME:** 5 MINUTES / **TOTAL TIME:** 1 HOUR

Freshly cooked Japanese short-grain white rice is an absolute essential of Japanese cuisine, offering a distinct soft and sticky texture and sweet taste that are integral to many dishes. While preparing it in a rice cooker is straightforward, cooking it on the stove can seem daunting. But fear not! With the right recipe, you can produce perfect rice time after time. Please note that this recipe is designed for gas and induction stovetops.

1. Wash the rice and let it soak for 30 minutes (1 hour in colder climates).

2. Drain the rice through a fine-mesh sieve, place it over a bowl, and let it dry for about 5 minutes.

3. Place the rice in a heavy-bottomed pot. Add the water, cover the pot with a lid, and place it on the stove. Cook the rice over medium heat. Do not remove the lid at any point during the cooking process; you need to preserve the steam and temperature throughout to ensure that the rice cooks evenly.

4. Listen for the sound of water boiling. Once you hear consistent bubbling, set a timer for 30 seconds. After 30 seconds, reduce the heat to medium-low and set a timer for 2 minutes. After 2 minutes, reduce the heat to low and let the rice simmer for 5 minutes.

5. Raise the heat to the highest possible temperature and cook the rice for 10 seconds. Turn off the heat and leave the pot covered on the warm stove, allowing the rice to steam for 10 minutes. Resist the urge to remove the lid as the rice steams.

6. Remove the lid. Using a rice paddle or a moist spoon or silicone spatula (the moisture will prevent the rice from sticking), gently stir and fold the rice. Serve immediately.

INGREDIENTS:

2   CUPS JAPANESE SHORT-GRAIN WHITE RICE

2¼ CUPS COLD WATER

JUKKOKUMAI

YIELD: 8 SERVINGS / **ACTIVE TIME:** 5 MINUTES / **TOTAL TIME:** 1 HOUR

Multigrain rice, or zakkoku-mai, combines white rice with an assortment of minor grains. While white rice is now the staple in Japanese households, minor grains have been cultivated since ancient times. In fact, until just after World War II, many Japanese relied on this multigrain rice. This recipe features 10 different minor grains, hence the name jukkoku-mai, meaning "rice with 10 grains." It offers a nutritious and flavorful alternative to plain white rice, and is rich in texture and nutrients. This recipe can also be made in a rice cooker using the regular white rice setting.

1. Place the white rice, black rice, red rice, and brown rice in a fine-mesh sieve and place it over a large bowl. Pour cold water over the rice until the bowl is full and drain it immediately. Refill the bowl with cold water. Gently swish the rice to wash it. When the water becomes cloudy, drain it. Repeat this washing process three times in total.

2. Transfer the washed rice to a bowl and cover it with cold water. Add the pearl barley, millet, and quinoa to the bowl, cover the bowl, and let the grains soak for 1 hour (up to 2 hours in colder climates).

3. Drain the rice mixture through a fine-mesh sieve, place it over a bowl, and let it dry for about 5 minutes.

4. Place the rice mixture in a heavy-bottomed pot. Add the chia seeds, sesame seeds, and water, cover the pot with a lid, and place it on the stove. Cook the rice over medium heat. Do not remove the lid at any point during the cooking process; you need to preserve the steam and temperature throughout to ensure that the rice cooks evenly.

5. Listen for the sound of water boiling. Once you hear consistent bubbling, set a timer for 30 seconds. After 30 seconds, reduce the heat to medium-low and set a timer for 2 minutes. After 2 minutes, reduce the heat to low and let the rice simmer for 5 minutes.

6. Raise the heat to the highest possible temperature and cook the rice for 10 seconds. Turn off the heat and leave the pot covered on the warm stove, allowing the rice to steam for 15 minutes. Resist the urge to remove the lid as the rice steams.

7. Remove the lid. Using a rice paddle or a moist spoon or silicone spatula (the moisture will prevent the grains from sticking), gently stir and fold the rice. Serve immediately.

INGREDIENTS:

2	CUPS JAPANESE SHORT-GRAIN WHITE RICE
1	TABLESPOON BLACK RICE
1	TABLESPOON RED RICE
1	TABLESPOON BROWN RICE
1	TABLESPOON PEARL BARLEY
1½	TEASPOONS MILLET
1½	TEASPOONS QUINOA
1	TEASPOON WHITE CHIA SEEDS
1	TEASPOON BLACK CHIA SEEDS
½	TEASPOON WHITE SESAME SEEDS
½	TEASPOON BLACK SESAME SEEDS
2½	CUPS COLD WATER

MAME GOHAN

YIELD: 4 SERVINGS / **ACTIVE TIME:** 15 MINUTES / **TOTAL TIME:** 1 HOUR AND 35 MINUTES

Mame gohan is a humble yet delicious rice dish that celebrates the simple beauty of green peas. The star ingredient here lends a subtle saltiness and rustic flavor to the fluffy cooked rice. Mame gohan is the perfect side dish, complementing a variety of main courses without overwhelming the senses.

1. Wash the rice and let it soak for 1 hour (2 hours in colder climates).

2. Drain the rice through a fine-mesh sieve, place it over a bowl, and let it dry for about 5 minutes. Remove the thin skin from the green peas (if using sweet peas, you can skip this step), wash them, and drain them in a colander.

3. Place the rice in a heavy-bottomed pot. Add the water, sake, salt, green peas, and kombu, cover the pot with a lid, and place it on the stove. Cook the rice over medium heat. Do not remove the lid at any point during the cooking process; you need to preserve the steam and temperature throughout to ensure that the rice cooks evenly.

4. Listen for the sound of water boiling. Once you hear consistent bubbling, set a timer for 30 seconds. After 30 seconds, reduce the heat to medium-low and set a timer for 2 minutes. After 2 minutes, reduce the heat to low and let the rice simmer for 5 minutes.

5. Raise the heat to the highest possible temperature and cook the rice for 10 seconds. Turn off the heat and leave the pot covered on the warm stove, allowing the rice to steam for 10 minutes. Resist the urge to remove the lid as the rice steams.

6. Remove the lid. Using a rice paddle or a moist spoon or silicone spatula (the moisture will prevent the rice from sticking), gently stir and fold the rice. Serve immediately.

INGREDIENTS:

1	CUP JAPANESE SHORT-GRAIN WHITE RICE
3½	OZ. GREEN PEAS
1	CUP WATER
2	TABLESPOONS SAKE
1	TEASPOON FINE SEA SALT
	2 X 3–INCH SHEET OF DRIED KOMBU

SEKIHAN

YIELD: 4 SERVINGS / **ACTIVE TIME:** 15 MINUTES / **TOTAL TIME:** 15 MINUTES

Sekihan is a traditional dish made with sticky rice and adzuki beans. It gets its name from its reddish hue, which is achieved through cooking in the leftover liquid from the adzuki beans. Red is considered a lucky color in Japan, and it is for this reason that sekihan is often served during special occasions.

1. Wash the adzuki beans with cold water to remove any dust or debris. If time allows, soak the beans for 1 to 3 hours to reduce the cooking time.

2. Place the beans in a pot and add 2 cups of water (or enough to cover the beans by 1 inch). Place the pot on the stove and bring to a boil over medium heat. Boil for 10 minutes, reduce the heat to low, and simmer the beans for 5 minutes.

3. Drain and return the beans to the pot. Add the remaining water and cover the pot with a lid. Bring to a boil, reduce the heat to medium-low so that the beans gently boil, and cook until they are tender enough to crush with your fingers, 40 to 50 minutes. It is important to cover the pot with a lid to prevent evaporation; if you notice the water getting too low, add more water. Be careful not to overcook the beans, remembering that they will also cook with the rice later on.

4. Remove the pot from the stove. Reserve 1½ cups of the cooking liquid and drain the beans. If the cooking liquid does not measure out to 1½ cups, add cold water as needed.

5. Remove 1½ teaspoons of the cooking liquid and replace it with the sake. Add the fine sea salt and sugar and stir until they have dissolved. Let the cooking liquid cool completely; it is important that it is not warm when you use it to cook the rice. If time allows, chill the cooking liquid in the refrigerator before using it to cook the rice.

6. Rinse the sweet rice and then transfer it to a heavy-bottomed pot. Add the cooled cooking liquid and shake the pot to evenly distribute the rice. Evenly spread the cooked beans on top of the rice and cover the pot with a lid. Do not stir the beans into the rice, as this can result in uneven cooking.

INGREDIENTS:

2½	TABLESPOONS DRIED ADZUKI BEANS
6	CUPS WATER, PLUS MORE AS NEEDED
1½	TEASPOONS SAKE
1	TEASPOON FINE SEA SALT
½	TEASPOON SUGAR
1½	CUPS SWEET RICE (MOCHI RICE)
	BLACK SESAME SEEDS, FOR GARNISH
	FLAKY SEA SALT, FOR GARNISH

7. Place the pot on the stove and bring to a boil over medium heat. Let the mixture boil for 1 minute, then reduce the heat to low and simmer for 10 minutes. Do not remove the lid at any point during the cooking process; you need to preserve the steam and temperature throughout to ensure that the rice cooks evenly.

8. Raise the heat to the highest possible temperature and cook the rice for 10 seconds. Turn off the heat and leave the pot covered on the warm stove, allowing the rice and beans to steam for 15 minutes. Resist the urge to remove the lid as the rice and beans steam.

9. Remove the lid. Using a rice paddle or a moist spoon or silicone spatula (the moisture will prevent the rice from sticking), gently stir and fold the rice. Divide the rice among the serving bowls, garnish with sesame seeds and flaky sea salt, and serve.

NATTO GOHAN

YIELD: 1 SERVING / **ACTIVE TIME:** 3 MINUTES / **TOTAL TIME:** 3 MINUTES

Natto, a traditional Japanese food made of fermented soybeans, has the power to evoke strong emotions—people either passionately love it or vehemently avoid it. In Japan, natto gohan, a simple yet iconic dish featuring natto served over steamed rice, has been a beloved breakfast staple for generations. In this recipe, I will not only guide you through the process of making traditional natto gohan, but also share my personal favorite toppings.

1. Place the rice in a serving bowl. Open the package of natto and place it in a bowl. Vigorously stir the natto until it becomes foamy and develops stringy, sticky threads.

2. Stir in the sauce that is included with the package of natto. Add the salt, Tenkasu, and sesame oil and use chopsticks to mix everything together until evenly distributed.

3. Top the rice with the natto mixture. Garnish with the avocado and green onion and enjoy.

INGREDIENTS:

1   SERVING OF PERFECT JAPANESE RICE (SEE PAGE 80)

1   PACKAGE OF NATTO

⅛   TEASPOON FINE SEA SALT

1   TABLESPOON TENKASU (SEE PAGE 68)

1   TEASPOON TOASTED SESAME OIL

FLESH OF ¼ AVOCADO, CUBED, FOR GARNISH

GREEN ONION, CHOPPED, FOR GARNISH

SATSUMAIMO GOHAN

YIELD: 4 SERVINGS / **ACTIVE TIME:** 15 MINUTES / **TOTAL TIME:** 1 HOUR AND 10 MINUTES

Satsumaimo gohan is an especially popular dish in the fall and winter, when sweet potatoes are at their peak of flavor. This dish pairs the natural sweetness and hearty texture of sweet potatoes with subtly salted rice, creating a delightful balance of flavors. The seasoning is kept light to let the natural flavors shine, making this dish a perfect alternative to plain white rice.

1. Wash the rice and let it soak for 30 minutes (1 hour in colder climates).

2. Drain the rice through a fine-mesh sieve, place it over a bowl, and let it dry for about 5 minutes.

3. Place the rice in a heavy-bottomed pot and add the water, sweet potato, salt, sake, mirin, and dashi granules. Do not stir, as this can result in uneven cooking. Cover the pot with a lid, place it on the stove, and cook over medium heat. Do not remove the lid at any point during the cooking process; you need to preserve the steam and temperature throughout to ensure that the rice cooks evenly.

4. Listen for the sound of water boiling. Once you hear consistent bubbling, set a timer for 30 seconds. After 30 seconds, reduce the heat to medium-low and set a timer for 2 minutes. After 2 minutes, reduce the heat to low and let the rice simmer for 5 minutes.

5. Raise the heat to the highest possible temperature and cook for 10 seconds. Turn off the heat and leave the pot covered on the warm stove, allowing the rice and sweet potato to steam for 10 minutes. Resist the urge to remove the lid as the rice steams.

6. Remove the lid. Using a rice paddle or a moist spoon or silicone spatula (the moisture will prevent the rice from sticking), gently stir and fold the satsumaimo gohan. Serve immediately.

INGREDIENTS:

1   CUP JAPANESE SHORT-GRAIN WHITE RICE

1   CUP WATER

1   SWEET POTATO, SKIN LEFT ON, WASHED AND DICED

½   TEASPOON FINE SEA SALT

1   TABLESPOON SAKE

1   TABLESPOON MIRIN

½   TEASPOON DASHI GRANULES

BLACK SESAME SEEDS, FOR GARNISH

OMUSUBI

YIELD: 3 OMUSUBI / **ACTIVE TIME:** 10 MINUTES / **TOTAL TIME:** 10 MINUTES

Omusubi, also known as onigiri, is a traditional Japanese fast food that has been cherished for centuries. These portable and convenient treats are crafted by shaping cooked rice into triangular, spherical, or cylindrical forms and are often wrapped in a sheet of crisp seaweed. The beauty of omusubi lies in its versatility, as it can be filled with an array of ingredients to suit various tastes and preferences.

1. Divide the rice into three equal portions and place each portion in its own bowl.

2. Add the Salmon Flakes to one bowl and stir until they are evenly distributed.

3. Add the bonito flakes, sesame seeds, and soy sauce to another bowl and stir until well combined.

4. Prepare an ice bath and add a small amount of salt to a small bowl.

5. Wash your hands thoroughly with soap and water and then submerge your hands in the ice bath for about 15 to 20 seconds. This will help keep the rice from sticking to your hands while shaping the omusubi. Remove your hands from the ice bath and rub 1 to 2 pinches of salt over your palms.

6. Take the rice with the Salmon Flakes and shape it, pressing the edges of the rice while turning it to form a firm triangle. You want to work quickly and avoid handling the rice for too long. Repeat with the rice you added the bonito flakes to.

7. Place the rice from the remaining bowl in your palm and place the Kombu Tsukudani in the center. Fold the rice over the top and shape it into a triangle.

8. To serve, wrap the bottom half of each omusubi in a piece of the nori.

INGREDIENTS:

2	CUPS PERFECT JAPANESE RICE (SEE PAGE 80)
1	TABLESPOON SALMON FLAKES (SEE PAGE 61)
1	TABLESPOON BONITO FLAKES
1	TEASPOON SESAME SEEDS
1	TEASPOON SOY SAUCE
	SALT, TO TASTE
1–2	TEASPOONS KOMBU NO TSUKUDANI (SEE PAGE 60)
1	SHEET OF NORI, CUT INTO THIRDS

ULTIMATE TAMAGO KAKE GOHAN

YIELD: 1 SERVING / **ACTIVE TIME:** 3 MINUTES / **TOTAL TIME:** 3 MINUTES

Tamago kake gohan, also known as TKG, is a cherished Japanese breakfast. It combines rice with raw egg, soy sauce, and other seasonings to create a simple yet profound dish. Contrary to its perception as a modern invention, its origins trace back to the Edo period (1603–1868), highlighting its deep-rooted history. To elevate this classic beyond its basic form—rice, soy sauce, and egg—this recipe introduces the rich, nutty aroma of sesame oil, my personal twist on tradition.

1. Carefully separate the yolk from the white of your egg. Set each part aside.

2. Place the rice in the serving bowl, add the egg white, sesame oil, soy sauce, garlic paste, and sugar, and stir until the rice is evenly coated and the flavors are well combined.

3. Create a bed of bonito flakes on top of the rice. Carefully arrange the green onion in a circle on top of the bonito flakes. Gently place the egg yolk in the center of the green onion. Enjoy, stirring the egg yolk into the rice mixture right before eating.

INGREDIENTS:

1	PASTEURIZED EGG
1	CUP PERFECT JAPANESE RICE (SEE PAGE 80)
2	TEASPOONS SESAME OIL
2	TEASPOONS SOY SAUCE
¼	TEASPOON GARLIC PASTE
⅛	TEASPOON SUGAR
1	TEASPOON BONITO FLAKES
1	TEASPOON CHOPPED GREEN ONION

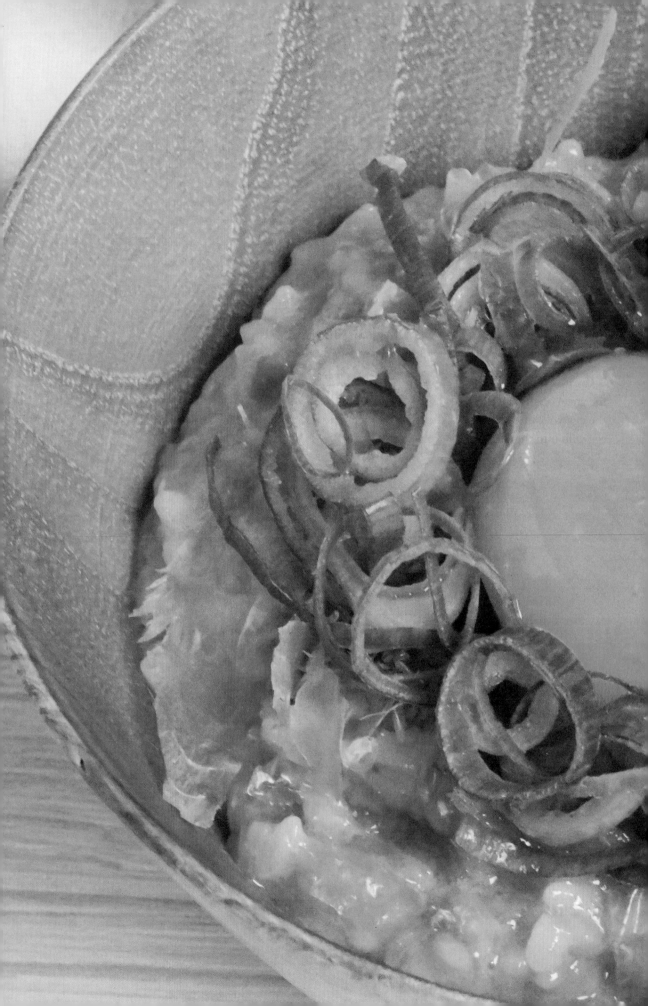

Ultimate Tamago Kake Gohan, see page 93

OKAYU

YIELD: 4 SERVINGS / **ACTIVE TIME:** 10 MINUTES / **TOTAL TIME:** 30 MINUTES

In Japan, okayu is a traditional comfort food consumed during times of illness, utilizing simple yet flavorful ingredients to create a delicious porridge.

1. Place the rice and water in a pot and bring to a boil over medium-high heat. Reduce the heat so that the mixture simmers and add the dashi granules, salt, and miso paste. Stir until the miso paste has completely dispersed and the flavors are well distributed throughout the okayu.

2. Simmer, stirring occasionally, until the okayu thickens to the desired consistency.

3. Divide it among the serving bowls, garnish each portion with Umeboshi and shiso leaves, and serve.

INGREDIENTS:

4   SERVINGS OF PERFECT JAPANESE RICE (SEE PAGE 80)

4   CUPS WATER

2   TEASPOONS DASHI GRANULES

½   TEASPOON FINE SEA SALT

4   TEASPOONS YELLOW MISO PASTE

4   UMEBOSHI (SEE PAGE 329), FOR GARNISH

    SHISO LEAVES, FOR GARNISH

CHICKEN ZOSUI

YIELD: 4 SERVINGS / **ACTIVE TIME:** 30 MINUTES / **TOTAL TIME:** 40 MINUTES

Zosui is a gentle Japanese rice soup made by simmering cooked rice with dashi stock, soy sauce, meat, and vegetables. It's perfect for cold winter days or when you're feeling under the weather.

1. Place the canola oil in a large pot and warm it over medium-low heat. Add the chicken and stir-fry until it is browned all over.

2. Add the water, dashi granules, mirin, salt, and sake to the pot, raise the heat to medium-high, and bring the mixture to a boil. Reduce the heat to medium-low and let the broth simmer.

3. Place the rice in a bowl and fill the bowl with cold water. Gently swish the rice to remove excess starch and then drain the rice. Stir the rice, carrot, leek, mushrooms, and soy sauce into the pot and cook until the carrot starts to soften, about 5 minutes.

4. Set a timer for 5 minutes.

5. After the 5 minutes is up, crack the eggs into a bowl, whisk to scramble, and then pour them around the pot. Set a timer for 30 seconds and cook, allowing the eggs to gently set, making sure not to stir.

6. Ladle the dish into bowls, garnish with green onions and sesame oil, and serve.

INGREDIENTS:

1	TEASPOON CANOLA OIL
5	OZ. BONELESS, SKIN-ON CHICKEN THIGHS, CUT INTO BITE-SIZE PIECES
1⅔	CUPS WATER
½	TEASPOON DASHI GRANULES
1	TABLESPOON MIRIN
¼	TEASPOON FINE SEA SALT
2	TABLESPOONS SAKE
1⅓	CUPS PERFECT JAPANESE RICE (SEE PAGE 80)
½	CARROT, PEELED AND JULIENNED
¼	JAPANESE LEEK, SLICED ON A BIAS
2	SHIITAKE MUSHROOMS, STEMMED AND SLICED THIN
1	CUP ENOKI MUSHROOMS, STEMMED
2	TABLESPOONS LIGHT SOY SAUCE
2	EGGS
	GREEN ONIONS, FINELY DICED, FOR GARNISH
	SESAME OIL, FOR GARNISH

SALMON OCHAZUKE

YIELD: 4 SERVINGS / **ACTIVE TIME:** 10 MINUTES / **TOTAL TIME:** 20 MINUTES

Ochazuke is a comforting dish that combines the simplicity of rice with the soothing warmth of tea. This easy-to-make recipe enhances the traditional ochazuke by incorporating salmon, a popular ingredient that adds a rich, savory flavor to the dish.

1. Pat the salmon dry with paper towels and sprinkle the salt over it. Place the canola oil in a large skillet and warm it over medium-high heat. Place the salmon in the pan, skin side down, and cook for 3 minutes. Turn the salmon over, sprinkle the sake over the top, and reduce the heat to low. Cover the pan and cook the salmon until it is cooked through, about 5 minutes.

2. Transfer the salmon to a bowl and flake it. Set the salmon aside.

3. Place the dashi and tea in a mug and steep for 1 minute. Remove the tea bags and stir the soy sauce into the tea.

4. To serve, divide the rice among the serving bowls and top each portion with equal amounts of the sesame seeds, salmon, and salmon skin. Garnish with nori, green onions, and wasabi (if desired) and serve.

INGREDIENTS:

4   **SALMON FILLETS**

1   **TEASPOON FINE SEA SALT**

1½   **TEASPOONS CANOLA OIL**

1   **TABLESPOON SAKE**

2½   **CUPS AWASE DASHI STOCK (SEE PAGE 38), WARMED TO 175°F**

2   **BAGS OF GREEN TEA**

4   **TEASPOONS LIGHT SOY SAUCE**

4   **SERVINGS OF PERFECT JAPANESE RICE (SEE PAGE 80)**

4   **TEASPOONS GROUND SESAME SEEDS**

   KIZAMI (SHREDDED) NORI, FOR GARNISH

   GREEN ONIONS, FINELY DICED, FOR GARNISH

   WASABI (SEE PAGE 500 FOR HOMEMADE), FOR GARNISH (OPTIONAL)

Salmon Ochazuke, see page 99

YAKI ONIGIRI DASHI CHAZUKE

YIELD: 4 SERVINGS / **ACTIVE TIME:** 10 MINUTES / **TOTAL TIME:** 30 MINUTES

Dashi chazuke is a variation of the traditional ochazuke, which typically involves pouring tea over rice. This recipe takes a creative twist by using grilled rice balls as the foundation of the dish.

1. Stir the sesame seeds into the rice. Divide the rice into four equal portions and shape them into tight balls. Place the rice balls on a plate and let them air-dry for about 10 minutes, turning them over halfway through.

2. While the rice balls are air-drying, place the soy sauce, mirin, sesame oil, miso paste, and garlic in a small bowl and whisk to combine.

3. Brush one half of the rice balls with the sauce. Place the butter in a large skillet and melt it over medium heat. Place the rice balls in the pan, sauce side down. Brush the top half with the sauce and fry the rice balls until they are nicely browned all over, 1 to 2 minutes, turning them over once.

4. To serve, place a rice ball in each of the serving bowls. Combine the hot water, dashi granules, and salt, pour the mixture evenly over the rice balls, and garnish with green onions and nori.

INGREDIENTS:

1   TABLESPOON WHITE SESAME SEEDS

1½ LBS. PERFECT JAPANESE RICE (SEE PAGE 80)

2   TABLESPOONS SOY SAUCE

1   TABLESPOON MIRIN

1   TEASPOON SESAME OIL

1   TEASPOON YELLOW MISO PASTE

1   TEASPOON GARLIC PASTE

1   TABLESPOON UNSALTED BUTTER

2½ CUPS HOT WATER

2   TEASPOONS DASHI GRANULES

¼   TEASPOON FINE SEA SALT

GREEN ONIONS, CHOPPED, FOR GARNISH

NORI, SHREDDED, FOR GARNISH

MAZE GOHAN WITH BAMBOO SHOOTS

YIELD: 6 SERVINGS / **ACTIVE TIME:** 20 MINUTES / **TOTAL TIME:** 20 MINUTES

Maze gohan is a versatile dish where cooked white rice is mixed with various ingredients. This method contrasts with takikomi gohan, where the rice and other ingredients are cooked together. In this recipe, bamboo shoots are incorporated to create a simple yet flavorful maze gohan.

1. Place the sesame oil in a large skillet and warm it over medium heat. Add the chicken, season it with half of the salt, and cook until it is browned all over, stirring as necessary.

2. Add the bamboo shoots, mushrooms, carrot, Abura-age, and remaining salt and cook, stirring frequently, until the carrots have softened, 5 to 7 minutes.

3. Place the remaining ingredients, except for the rice, in a small bowl and whisk to combine. Add the sauce to the skillet and stir-fry until the chicken and vegetables have absorbed it, about 5 minutes.

4. Place the chicken and vegetables in a large bowl, add the rice, and toss to combine. Serve immediately.

INGREDIENTS:

- 1 TABLESPOON SESAME OIL
- ⅓ LB. BONELESS, SKINLESS CHICKEN THIGHS, CHOPPED
- 2 PINCHES OF FINE SEA SALT
- 1 CUP BOILED BAMBOO SHOOTS, CHOPPED
- 2 SHIITAKE MUSHROOMS, STEMMED AND SLICED
- ½ CARROT, PEELED AND JULIENNED
- 2 SHEETS OF ABURA-AGE, (SEE PAGE 69), SLICED THIN
- 1½ TEASPOONS DASHI GRANULES
- 1 TABLESPOON SUGAR
- 2 TABLESPOONS LIGHT SOY SAUCE
- 2 TABLESPOONS MIRIN
- 2 TABLESPOONS SAKE
- 4½ CUPS PERFECT JAPANESE RICE (SEE PAGE 80)

Yaki Onigiri Dashi Chazuke, see page 102

TAIMESHI

YIELD: 6 SERVINGS / **ACTIVE TIME:** 15 MINUTES / **TOTAL TIME:** 1 HOUR AND 35 MINUTES

Sea bream, or snapper, and rice have been cherished staples in Japanese cuisine since ancient times, and taimeshi beautifully combines these two ingredients. In Japanese culture, sea bream is considered a lucky fish, making taimeshi a popular choice for festive occasions and celebrations.

1. Wash the rice and let it soak for 1 hour (2 hours in colder climates).

2. Prepare a gas or charcoal grill for high heat (about 500°F). Pierce both sides of the sea bream with a fork and sprinkle the salt over it. Place it on the grill and cook until the sea bream is lightly charred on both sides, turning it over once. It does not need to be cooked through on the grill, as it will continue to cook with the rice. Remove the sea bream from the grill and set it aside.

3. Drain the rice through a fine-mesh sieve, place it over a bowl, and let it dry for about 5 minutes.

4. Place the rice in a heavy-bottomed pot. Add the water, place the ginger, kombu, and sea bream on top of the rice, and pour the soy sauce, mirin, and sake over the sea bream. Do not stir.

5. Cover the pot with a lid and place it on the stove. Cook the rice over medium heat. Do not remove the lid at any point during the cooking process; you need to preserve the steam and temperature throughout to ensure that the rice cooks evenly.

6. Listen for the sound of water boiling. Once you hear consistent bubbling, set a timer for 30 seconds. After 30 seconds, reduce the heat to medium-low and set a timer for 2 minutes. After 2 minutes, reduce the heat to low and let the rice simmer for 5 minutes.

7. Raise the heat to the highest possible temperature and cook the rice for 10 seconds. Turn off the heat and leave the pot covered on the warm stove, allowing the rice to steam for 10 minutes. Resist the urge to remove the lid as the rice steams.

8. Remove the lid and carefully remove the fish, kombu, and ginger from the pot. Scrape the cooked sea bream off the bones and add it back to the pot. Gently stir the sea bream into the rice until it is evenly distributed and serve.

INGREDIENTS:

1	CUP JAPANESE SHORT-GRAIN WHITE RICE
1	SMALL WHOLE SEA BREAM, CLEANED
2	PINCHES OF FINE SEA SALT
1	CUP WATER
2	THICK SLICES OF FRESH GINGER
	4-INCH SQUARE OF DRIED KOMBU
1½	TABLESPOONS LIGHT SOY SAUCE
2	TEASPOONS MIRIN
2	TEASPOONS SAKE

SALMON TAKIKOMI GOHAN

YIELD: 6 SERVINGS / ACTIVE TIME: 30 MINUTES / TOTAL TIME: 1 HOUR AND 50 MINUTES

Takikomi gohan, a beloved Japanese rice dish, embodies the essence of comfort and seasonality in every bite. This dish is prepared by cooking an array of ingredients together with the rice, allowing the flavors to meld and infuse into each grain. This recipe can also be made in a rice cooker using the regular white rice setting and increasing the steaming time by 10 minutes.

1. Wash the rice and let it soak for 1 hour (2 hours in colder climates).

2. Drain the rice through a fine-mesh sieve, place it over a bowl, and let it dry until you are ready to prepare it.

3. Place the canola oil in a large skillet and warm it over medium heat. Add the salmon and, if using skin-on salmon fillets, place them skin side down and let the skin get crispy. Add the mushrooms, carrot, ginger, Abura-age, and salt to the pan and stir-fry until the vegetables have softened slightly and the salmon is broken up, 4 to 6 minutes. Remove the pan from heat.

4. Place the rice in a heavy-bottomed pot. Add the water, place the salmon and vegetable mixture on top of the rice, and add all of the remaining ingredients, except for the garnish. Do not stir.

5. Cover the pot with a lid and place it on the stove. Cook the rice over medium heat. Do not remove the lid at any point during the cooking process; you need to preserve the steam and temperature throughout to ensure that the rice cooks evenly.

6. Listen for the sound of water boiling. Once you hear consistent bubbling, set a timer for 2 minutes. After 2 minutes, reduce the heat to medium-low and set a timer for 3 minutes. After 3 minutes, reduce the heat to the lowest possible temperature and let the rice simmer for 5 minutes.

7. Raise the heat to the highest possible temperature and cook the rice for 10 seconds. Turn off the heat and leave the pot covered on the warm stove, allowing the rice to steam for 20 minutes. Resist the urge to remove the lid as the rice steams.

8. Remove the lid and gently stir the rice, salmon, and vegetable mixture. Garnish with green onions and serve.

INGREDIENTS:

- 1 CUP JAPANESE SHORT-GRAIN WHITE RICE
- ½ TEASPOON CANOLA OIL
- 2 SALMON FILLETS
- 2 SHIITAKE MUSHROOMS, STEMMED AND SLICED
- ¼ CARROT, PEELED AND JULIENNED
- 1 TABLESPOON MINCED FRESH GINGER
- 3 SHEETS OF ABURA-AGE (SEE PAGE 69), SLICED THIN
- ¼ TEASPOON FINE SEA SALT
- ¾ CUP WATER
- 2 TABLESPOONS LIGHT SOY SAUCE
- 2 TABLESPOONS SAKE
- 1 TABLESPOON MIRIN
- ½ TEASPOON DASHI GRANULES
- ¼ TEASPOON SUGAR
- GREEN ONIONS, FINELY DICED, FOR GARNISH

SHIRUMONO
(SOUP)

*S*hirumono is the general term for Japanese soups that are made with dashi stock. There are many varieties, including miso soup, as well as soups that are soy sauce– and salt-based.

While there are numerous options, no meal in Japanese cuisine is complete without a soup on the side. Simply adding soup to a meal is enough to elevate it, bringing one's satisfaction to another level. If you want to create a complete Japanese meal, I encourage you to choose one of these soups and pair it with rice and a main dish.

CLASSIC MISO SOUP

YIELD: 5 SERVINGS / ACTIVE TIME: 10 MINUTES / TOTAL TIME: 15 MINUTES

A classic Japanese soup made with dashi and miso paste. It's a staple in the Japanese diet, commonly served as a side dish and a convenient way to use and enjoy local ingredients. In this recipe, I have created an authentic taste by selecting only those ingredients that can inarguably be called "classic."

1. Pour the dashi into a medium saucepan and bring to a gentle simmer over medium heat. As the dashi approaches coming to a boil, gently stir in the tofu, Abura-age, leek, mushrooms, and wakame.

2. Cook until the broth is once again about to return to a boil and then reduce the heat so that the soup simmers gently. Simmer the soup until the vegetables are cooked to your liking and the tofu is warmed through, 2 to 3 minutes.

3. Turn off the heat, place the miso paste in a strainer or ladle, and submerge it in the soup. Whisk to loosen and dissolve the paste. You want to ensure that it dissolves smoothly and that no clumps remain.

4. Carefully ladle the soup into warmed bowls and serve.

INGREDIENTS:

4   CUPS AWASE DASHI STOCK (SEE PAGE 38)

5   OZ. FIRM TOFU, CUBED

½   CUP ABURA-AGE, SLICED THIN (SEE PAGE 69)

½   CUP THINLY SLICED JAPANESE LEEK (CUT ON A BIAS)

3   SHIITAKE MUSHROOMS, STEMMED AND SLICED THIN

1   TABLESPOON DRIED WAKAME

¼   CUP YELLOW MISO PASTE

PLANT-BASED MISO SOUP

YIELD: 4 SERVINGS / **ACTIVE TIME:** 10 MINUTES / **TOTAL TIME:** 40 MINUTES

It may surprise you, but meat consumption in Japan became common only around 1871. Before then, influenced by Buddhist beliefs, the government had banned the practice. As a result, the Japanese diet has a long-standing tradition of plant-based and pescatarian cuisine, developed over centuries. This recipe is a prime example of this tradition, relying on kombu and dried shiitake mushrooms for flavor.

1. Place the kombu and shiitake mushroom in a medium saucepan and cover them with the cold water. Cover the pan with a lid and let the mixture soak for at least 30 minutes, until they have rehydrated fully and released their flavors.

2. Remove the lid, place the saucepan on the stove, and warm the mixture over medium heat until it is just about to come to a boil. Carefully remove the kombu and shiitake mushroom with a slotted spoon.

3. Slice the rehydrated shiitake mushroom into matchsticks. Cut the rehydrated kombu into matchsticks until you have the same amount of it as you do of ginger. Discard the rest of the kombu or reserve it for another preparation.

4. Add the shimeji mushrooms, tofu, ginger, shiitake mushroom, and sliced kombu to the broth. Simmer until everything is warmed through and cooked to your liking.

5. Turn off the heat. Place the miso paste in a strainer or ladle and submerge it in the soup. Whisk to loosen and dissolve the paste. You want to ensure that it dissolves smoothly and that no clumps remain.

6. Carefully ladle the warmed soup into bowls, garnish with sesame seeds, and enjoy.

INGREDIENTS:

	4-INCH SQUARE OF DRIED KOMBU
1	DRIED SHIITAKE MUSHROOM
2	CUPS COLD WATER
1	CUP SHIMEJI MUSHROOMS
5	OZ. FIRM TOFU, CUBED
	2-INCH PIECE OF FRESH GINGER, PEELED AND JULIENNED
¼	CUP YELLOW MISO PASTE
	WHITE SESAME SEEDS, FOR GARNISH

ASARI MISO SOUP

YIELD: 4 SERVINGS / **ACTIVE TIME:** 30 MINUTES / **TOTAL TIME:** 1 HOUR AND 30 MINUTES

Asari is one of the most popular variations of miso soup and is made with Manila clams. The briny juice of the clams is packed with natural umami flavor, which contributes a beautiful depth to the soup.

1. Place 2 cups of water and the salt in a bowl. Rinse the clams under running water and place them in the salted water. Let them soak for 1 hour to remove any sand from them.

2. While the clams are soaking, combine the remaining water and the kombu in another bowl. Soak the kombu for 1 hour.

3. Rinse the clams again to ensure that all of the sand has been removed. Place them in a large saucepan and add the sake. Warm over medium heat until the sake begins to simmer. Reduce the heat to low, cover the pan, and let the clams steam until the majority of them start to open, about 5 minutes. Remove the clams from the pot using a slotted spoon, leaving the clam juice behind. Set the clams aside. Discard any clams that did not open.

4. Add the kombu stock to the pot and warm the broth over medium-low heat, removing the kombu just before the broth reaches a boil. Return the clams to the pot and simmer for 1 to 2 minutes.

5. Turn off the heat. Place the miso paste in a strainer or ladle and submerge it in the soup. Whisk to loosen and dissolve the paste. You want to ensure that it dissolves smoothly and that no clumps remain.

6. Ladle the soup into warmed bowls, garnish each portion with green onions, and serve.

INGREDIENTS:

6½	CUPS WATER
2	TEASPOONS KOSHER SALT
1	LB. CLAMS
	3 X 4–INCH SHEET OF DRIED KOMBU
3	TABLESPOONS SAKE
¼	CUP YELLOW MISO PASTE
	GREEN ONIONS, CHOPPED, FOR GARNISH

WHITE MISO SOUP

YIELD: 4 SERVINGS / **ACTIVE TIME:** 15 MINUTES / **TOTAL TIME:** 25 MINUTES

Miso soup made with white miso paste is a delicious wintry variation of the classic miso soup. It is a perfect choice for those who enjoy the milder flavor profile of white miso paste and the natural sweetness of root vegetables.

1. Place the canola oil in a medium saucepan and warm it over medium-low heat. Add the potato, carrot, and onion and cook, stirring occasionally, until the onion has softened, about 5 minutes.

2. Add the dashi, raise the heat to medium, and bring to a boil. Reduce the heat to medium-low, cover the pan, and let the broth simmer until the potato and carrot are fork-tender, 10 to 15 minutes.

3. Turn off the heat. Place the miso paste in a strainer or ladle and submerge it in the soup. Whisk to loosen and dissolve the paste. You want to ensure that it dissolves smoothly and that no clumps remain.

4. Stir in the soy sauce and snow peas and let the snow peas cook until they are just tender.

5. Ladle the soup into warmed bowls, garnish each portion with green onions, and serve.

INGREDIENTS:

- 1½ TEASPOONS CANOLA OIL
- 1 POTATO, PEELED AND CHOPPED
- ½ CARROT, PEELED AND CHOPPED
- ½ ONION, SLICED THIN
- 2 CUPS AWASE DASHI STOCK (SEE PAGE 38)
- 2 TABLESPOONS WHITE MISO PASTE
- ¼ TEASPOONS LIGHT SOY SAUCE
- 5 SNOW PEAS, STRINGS REMOVED

GREEN ONIONS, CHOPPED, FOR GARNISH

RED MISO SOUP

YIELD: 4 SERVINGS / **ACTIVE TIME:** 10 MINUTES / **TOTAL TIME:** 15 MINUTES

Red miso soup, or akadashi, is a distinct variant of miso soup prepared with red miso paste, particularly Hatcho miso from near Nagoya. Having grown up near the Hatcho Miso factory, I experienced akadashi as a local staple in my hometown. Unlike typical miso soups, akadashi's unique characteristic comes from soybean miso, a blend of soybeans, salt, soybean koji (a mold that grows on the soybeans), and water, offering a rich, deep flavor with a slight bitterness. Initially a specialty in traditional Japanese restaurants, akadashi became a popular home-cooked dish across Japan after the commercialization of Hatcho Miso in the mid-1950s.

1. Place the dashi in a medium saucepan and bring to a boil over medium heat. Add the dried wakame and Abura-age and bring the broth back to a boil. Reduce the heat so that the broth simmers and add the tofu.

2. Cook until the tofu is heated through, 3 to 4 minutes.

3. Turn off the heat. Place the miso in a strainer or ladle and submerge it in the soup. Whisk to loosen and dissolve the paste. You want to ensure that it dissolves smoothly and that no clumps remain.

4. Ladle the soup into warmed bowls, garnish each portion with green onions, and serve.

INGREDIENTS:

2 CUPS AWASE DASHI STOCK (SEE PAGE 38)

1½ TEASPOONS DRIED WAKAME

1 SQUARE OF ABURA-AGE (SEE PAGE 69), SLICED

2½ OZ. FIRM TOFU OR SILKEN TOFU, CUBED

2 TABLESPOONS RED MISO PASTE (HATCHO MISO PREFERRED)

GREEN ONIONS, CHOPPED, FOR GARNISH

TONJIRU

YIELD: 6 SERVINGS / ACTIVE TIME: 30 MINUTES / TOTAL TIME: 45 MINUTES

Tonjiru is a heartier version of miso soup that is enriched with pork and a variety of vegetables. Although any vegetable can be used, it's often made with root vegetables—in this case, vegetables commonly found in the US—creating a robust and satisfying dish. It's versatile enough to serve as a warming side or a substantial main.

1. Warm a large saucepan over medium heat. Add the canola oil and pork belly, season with the salt, and fry until the pork belly is lightly browned all over, turning it as necessary.

2. Add the carrot, sweet potato, and turnip and cook, stirring occasionally, until they are tender, about 10 minutes.

3. Add the cabbage and mushrooms to the pan and stir-fry for 1 to 2 minutes. Pour in the dashi and bring the soup to a boil.

4. Reduce the heat so that it simmers, partially cover the pan, and cook for 10 minutes. Add the leek and simmer until the leek is tender, about 5 minutes.

5. Turn off the heat. Place the miso in a strainer or ladle and submerge it in the soup. Whisk to loosen and dissolve the paste. You want to ensure that it dissolves smoothly and that no clumps remain.

6. Ladle the soup into warmed bowls and serve.

INGREDIENTS:

1½	TEASPOONS CANOLA OIL
⅓	LB. PORK BELLY, SLICED THIN
¼	TEASPOON KOSHER SALT
1	CARROT, PEELED AND SLICED
½	SWEET POTATO, PEELED AND CHOPPED
1	TURNIP, PEELED AND ROUGHLY CHOPPED
3	NAPA CABBAGE LEAVES, CHOPPED
3	SHIITAKE MUSHROOMS, STEMMED AND SLICED THIN
4	CUPS AWASE DASHI STOCK (SEE PAGE 38)
1	JAPANESE LEEK, SLICED ON A BIAS
¼	CUP YELLOW MISO PASTE

KENCHIN JIRU

YIELD: 4 SERVINGS / **ACTIVE TIME:** 10 MINUTES / **TOTAL TIME:** 15 MINUTES

Kenchin jiru is a traditional Japanese vegan soup with a rich history rooted in the culinary practices at Buddhist temples, and it even predates miso soup. While modern adaptations sometimes include animal products, this recipe adheres to the original plant-based specifications.

1. Warm a large saucepan over medium heat and add the sesame oil. Add the carrot, radish, mushrooms, satoimo, and Abura-age and stir-fry for 1 minute.

2. Pour the dashi into the pan and bring the broth to a simmer. Cook until the carrot and radish are fork-tender, 5 to 10 minutes. Stir in the sake, mirin, and soy sauce and let the soup simmer for another 2 to 3 minutes.

3. Add the leek and simmer until it is tender, about 5 minutes.

4. Taste the soup and adjust the seasoning as necessary. Ladle the soup into warmed bowls and serve.

INGREDIENTS:

1	TEASPOON SESAME OIL
½	CARROT, PEELED AND CHOPPED
¼	DAIKON RADISH, PEELED, CUT INTO ROUNDS, AND QUARTERED
3	SHIITAKE MUSHROOMS, STEMMED AND SLICED
5	SMALL SATOIMO (JAPANESE TARO), PEELED
2	SHEETS OF ABURA-AGE (SEE PAGE 69), SLICED THIN
2	CUPS SHOJIN DASHI STOCK (SEE PAGE 41)
2	TABLESPOONS SAKE
2	TABLESPOONS MIRIN
3	TABLESPOONS SOY SAUCE
1	JAPANESE LEEK, WHITE PART ONLY, SLICED ON A BIAS

Tonjiru, see page 124

TORIJIRU

YIELD: 6 SERVINGS / **ACTIVE TIME:** 20 MINUTES / **TOTAL TIME:** 35 MINUTES

Torijiru is a miso soup made with hearty root vegetables and tender chicken thighs. It can either be served as a main or nutritious side. This version includes crispy chicken skin as a garnish for added depth of flavor.

1. Remove the skin from the chicken thighs and place it flat in a large saucepan. Cook over low heat and slowly render the fat until the chicken skin is crispy and golden brown, about 10 minutes, turning it over halfway through.

2. While you are cooking the chicken skin, cut the chicken into bite-size pieces. Transfer the chicken skin to a paper towel–lined plate to drain. Add the chicken to the pan, raise the heat to medium, and fry until the chicken is lightly browned all over, around 5 minutes, stirring as necessary.

3. Add the onion, garlic, and ginger, season with the salt, and stir-fry until the onion has softened, 3 to 4 minutes. Add the burdock root, carrot, and radish and stir-fry for 2 to 3 minutes.

4. Stir in the mushrooms, leek, dashi, sake, and soy sauce and cook until the soup is just about to come to a boil. Reduce the heat and simmer the soup until the root vegetables are cooked to your liking, about 10 minutes.

5. Turn off the heat. Place the miso in a strainer or ladle and submerge it in the soup. Whisk to loosen and dissolve the paste. You want to ensure that it dissolves smoothly and that no clumps remain.

6. Ladle the soup into warmed bowls. Chop the crispy chicken skins into thin strips, garnish each portion with them and green onions, and serve.

INGREDIENTS:

- ⅔ LB. BONELESS, SKIN-ON CHICKEN THIGHS
- ½ YELLOW ONION, SLICED THIN
- 1 GARLIC CLOVE, MINCED
- 1-INCH PIECE OF FRESH GINGER, PEELED AND MINCED
- ¼ TEASPOON KOSHER SALT
- 5 OZ. BURDOCK ROOT, PEELED AND SLICED ON A BIAS
- 1 CARROT, PEELED AND CUT INTO THICK HALF-MOONS
- 1 LB. DAIKON RADISH, PEELED AND CUT INTO THICK HALF-MOONS
- 1 BUNCH OF ENOKI MUSHROOMS, ROOTS REMOVED
- 1 JAPANESE LEEK, SLICED ON A BIAS
- 4¼ CUPS AWASE DASHI STOCK (SEE PAGE 38)
- 1 TABLESPOON SAKE
- 1 TEASPOON SOY SAUCE
- ¼ CUP AWASE MISO PASTE
- GREEN ONIONS, CHOPPED, FOR GARNISH

SAWANIWAN

YIELD: 4 SERVINGS / **ACTIVE TIME:** 5 MINUTES / **TOTAL TIME:** 10 MINUTES

Made with julienned vegetables and pork, sawaniwan is often served for school lunches due to its light flavor and the array of nutritious ingredients.

1. Prepare an ice bath. Bring water to a boil in a large saucepan. Add the carrot, radish, and snow peas and blanch them for 30 seconds. Quickly drain the vegetables and transfer them to the ice bath.

2. Place the dashi in a clean saucepan and bring to a boil. Add the pork belly, mirin, and soy sauce and boil for 1 minute. Add the blanched vegetables and mushrooms, reduce the heat, and simmer until the pork belly is cooked through.

3. Ladle the soup into warmed bowls, garnish each portion with freshly ground pepper, and serve.

INGREDIENTS:

½ CARROT, PEELED AND JULIENNED

⅓ LB. DAIKON RADISH, PEELED AND JULIENNED

10 SNOW PEAS, SLICED THIN

3½ CUPS AWASE DASHI STOCK (SEE PAGE 38)

5 OZ. PORK BELLY, SLICED THIN

¼ CUP MIRIN

¼ CUP LIGHT SOY SAUCE

4 SHIITAKE MUSHROOMS, STEMMED AND SLICED THIN

FRESHLY GROUND BLACK PEPPER, FOR GARNISH

KAKITAMAJIRU

YIELD: 4 SERVINGS / **ACTIVE TIME:** 15 MINUTES / **TOTAL TIME:** 15 MINUTES

Kakitamajiru is a traditional Japanese soup consisting of a clear broth and fluffy ribbons of egg, producing a light yet umami-packed result.

1. Place the dashi in a large, deep saucepan, stir in the soy sauce and salt, and bring to a boil over medium heat. Add the leeks, reduce the heat, and gently simmer the soup.

2. In a small bowl, combine the cornstarch and water to create a slurry. Drizzle the slurry into the simmering soup, stirring continually to prevent lumps from forming.

3. Crack the eggs into a measuring cup and beat until they are scrambled. Raise the heat to medium and bring the soup back to a boil. Slowly drizzle in the eggs in four increments, letting the soup return to a simmer between each addition. This will give the eggs time to cook and form soft ribbons.

4. After all of the eggs have been added, gently stir the soup a few times to evenly distribute the ribbons of cooked egg.

5. Remove the pan from heat and ladle the soup into warmed bowls. Garnish each portion with green onions and shichimi togarashi and serve.

INGREDIENTS:

4 CUPS AWASE DASHI STOCK (SEE PAGE 38)

2 TEASPOONS LIGHT SOY SAUCE

1½ TEASPOONS KOSHER SALT

1 CUP SLICED JAPANESE LEEKS, WHITE PARTS ONLY, SLICED ON A BIAS

1 TABLESPOON CORNSTARCH

1 TABLESPOON WATER

4 EGGS

GREEN ONIONS, CHOPPED, FOR GARNISH

SHICHIMI TOGARASHI, FOR GARNISH

OSUIMONO

YIELD: 6 SERVINGS / ACTIVE TIME: 10 MINUTES / TOTAL TIME: 10 MINUTES

This is a light and delicate soup that focuses on simplicity, adding elegance to any Japanese meal. The light soy sauce adds a subtle saltiness, while the dark soy sauce contributes color and a richer flavor.

1. Pour the dashi into a medium saucepan, stir in the sake and mushrooms, and place the pan over medium heat. Just as the broth is about to come to a boil, reduce the heat and let it simmer gently. Let the broth simmer for 3 minutes and then turn off the heat.

2. Stir in the soy sauces and salt. Stir well to ensure the seasonings are evenly distributed throughout the soup.

3. Divide the kamaboko, mushrooms, and temari fu, if using, among the warmed serving bowls and carefully ladle the soup over the mixture.

4. Garnish each portion with yuzu peel and mitsuba and serve.

INGREDIENTS:

4   CUPS AWASE DASHI STOCK (SEE PAGE 38)

½   TEASPOON SAKE

6   SHIITAKE MUSHROOMS, STEMMED

2   TEASPOONS LIGHT SOY SAUCE

1   TEASPOON DARK SOY SAUCE

1   TEASPOON KOSHER SALT

12   SLICES OF KAMABOKO FISH CAKE

2   PIECES OF TEMARI FU (DRIED WHEAT GLUTEN; OPTIONAL)

STRIPS OF YUZU PEEL, FOR GARNISH

FRESH MITSUBA (JAPANESE WILD PARSLEY), FINELY CHOPPED, FOR GARNISH

OZONI

YIELD: 4 SERVINGS / **ACTIVE TIME:** 10 MINUTES / **TOTAL TIME:** 20 MINUTES

Ozoni is a traditional Japanese soup made with rice cakes and enjoyed during New Year's celebrations. Many regions in Japan have their own version of the dish that honors favored local ingredients.

1. Warm a large saucepan over medium heat. Add the canola oil and chicken, season with the salt, and cook until the chicken is cooked through, 6 to 8 minutes, stirring as necessary. Transfer the chicken to a bowl and set it aside.

2. Add the dashi, sake, and soy sauce to the pan and bring to a boil. Reduce the heat so that the broth simmers and add the carrot, radish, and mushroom. Simmer until the carrot and radish are fork-tender, 5 to 10 minutes.

3. Stir the chicken and any accumulated juices into the soup and simmer for an additional 2 to 3 minutes.

4. Turn off the heat. Divide the grilled kirimochi among the warmed serving bowls and arrange the carrot, daikon, and mushroom around it. Ladle the soup over the top, garnish each portion with mitsuba, and serve.

INGREDIENTS:

1½ TEASPOONS CANOLA OIL

3½ OZ. BONELESS, SKINLESS CHICKEN THIGH OR BREAST, CHOPPED

2 PINCHES OF KOSHER SALT

3 CUPS AWASE DASHI STOCK (SEE PAGE 38)

1 TABLESPOON SAKE

2 TABLESPOONS LIGHT SOY SAUCE

½ CARROT, PEELED AND SLICED INTO ROUNDS

1¼ LBS. DAIKON RADISH, PEELED, CUT INTO ROUNDS, AND QUARTERED

1 SHIITAKE MUSHROOM, STEMMED AND SLICED THIN

4 PIECES OF KIRIMOCHI (SQUARE RICE CAKES), GRILLED

FRESH MITSUBA (JAPANESE WILD PARSLEY), FINELY CHOPPED, FOR GARNISH

Osuimono, see page 134

NIRATAMA SOUP

YIELD: 4 SERVINGS / **ACTIVE TIME**: 15 MINUTES / **TOTAL TIME**: 15 MINUTES

"Nira-tama" combines the Japanese words for garlic chives (nira) and egg (tamago). Usually, this is a beloved stir-fry pairing, but this time the classic duo is deployed in a delightful soup.

1. Crack the eggs into a bowl, add the oyster sauce, sugar, salt, and pepper, and whisk until the mixture is well combined. Set the bowl near the stove.

2. Warm a large skillet or wok over high heat and add the canola oil. Add the garlic chives and stir-fry for 30 seconds. Add the cooked garlic chives to the egg mixture and stir to combine.

3. Place the water, bouillon, garlic paste, and soy sauce in a large, deep saucepan and bring to a boil over medium heat.

4. Reduce the heat slightly so that the soup simmers. Pour the egg mixture into the soup one-third at a time and wait for the soup to return to a simmer after each addition, allowing the egg mixture to cook. After the final increment of the egg mixture is added and the soup has returned to a simmer, use chopsticks to gently stir the soup, creating ribbons of egg.

5. Drizzle the sesame oil over the soup, ladle it into warmed bowls, and serve.

INGREDIENTS:

3	EGGS
½	TEASPOON OYSTER SAUCE
1	TEASPOON SUGAR
¼	TEASPOON KOSHER SALT
	PINCH OF BLACK PEPPER
1	TABLESPOON CANOLA OIL
1	CUP CHOPPED FRESH GARLIC CHIVES (CHINESE CHIVES)
3	CUPS WATER
1½	TABLESPOONS CHINESE CHICKEN BOUILLON
1	TEASPOON GARLIC PASTE
1	TEASPOON LIGHT SOY SAUCE
1	TEASPOON SESAME OIL

CORN POTAGE

YIELD: 4 SERVINGS / **ACTIVE TIME:** 25 MINUTES / **TOTAL TIME:** 40 MINUTES

This creamy corn soup is a beloved culinary staple in Japan despite its mysterious origins and French-inspired name. This soup enjoys a popularity that extends beyond restaurants to vending machines, pre-made packets, and as a cherished flavor for snacks.

1. Rinse the corn and remove the kernels from the cobs. Cut the cobs into thirds or quarters. Set the corn kernels and cobs aside.

2. Place the butter in a large saucepan and melt it over medium heat. Add the onion and cook, stirring occasionally, until it is golden brown, 8 to 10 minutes.

3. Reduce the heat to medium-low, add the milk, corn cobs, and half of the salt and pepper. Bring to a low simmer, where small bubbles are forming around the edge. Do not allow the milk to come to a boil. Turn off the heat, remove the corn cobs, and discard them.

4. Add the corn kernels along with the remaining salt and pepper to the soup and turn the heat to medium-low. Cook until small bubbles start to appear around the edge of the soup, remove the pan from heat, and let the soup cool slightly.

5. Transfer the soup to a blender and puree until it is smooth. Strain the corn potage back into the pan through a fine-mesh sieve. If you'd like it to be warmer, gently reheat the soup over low heat.

6. Ladle the soup into warmed bowls, garnish each portion with croutons and heavy cream, and serve.

INGREDIENTS:

2	EARS OF CORN, HUSKED
2	TABLESPOONS UNSALTED BUTTER
½	MEDIUM ONION, SLICED THIN
1¼	CUPS WHOLE MILK
4	PINCHES OF KOSHER SALT
4	PINCHES OF WHITE PEPPER
	HOMEMADE CROUTONS (SEE PAGE 681), FOR GARNISH
	HEAVY CREAM, FOR GARNISH

Corn Potage, see page 139

CHAWANMUSHI

YIELD: 4 SERVINGS / **ACTIVE TIME:** 30 MINUTES / **TOTAL TIME:** 40 MINUTES

Chawanmushi is a classic dish featuring egg and dashi, steamed in ramekins until silky and custard-like; however, it is regarded as a soup. Despite its complex flavor, chawanmushi is relatively simple to prepare and can be made authentically with ease.

1. Place the whole shrimp, four slices of mushroom, and the kamaboko in a bowl, cover the mixture with water, cover the bowl with aluminum foil, and set the mixture aside. These ingredients will be used as a garnish.

2. Divide the remaining shrimp and mushrooms among four ramekins and set them aside.

3. Crack the eggs into a large measuring cup or mason jar, taking note of the total volume. Lightly beat the eggs, just enough to break up the yolks. Add the salt, sake, and mirin and then add dashi until the volume of the mixture has quadrupled the volume of the eggs (e.g., if you had 3 oz. of eggs, the total volume should be 12 oz.). It is important to be precise while measuring here, as it will determine whether the chawanmushi is going to be successful or not.

4. Place a fine-mesh sieve over a mixing bowl and strain the egg mixture into the bowl to remove any lumps, using a rubber spatula to push it through if necessary. Transfer the strained mixture into a jug or measuring cup to allow for easy pouring. Divide the mixture evenly among the ramekins.

5. Bring water to a boil in a stockpot. Drain the bowl of garnishes. If your ramekins have lids, place them on top. If not, cover each one with aluminum foil. Place them in a steaming basket along with the bowl of garnishes. Place the steaming basket over the boiling water and steam for 3 minutes. Reduce the heat so that the water simmers and steam for another 10 minutes.

6. Carefully remove the foil from one ramekin and gently tilt it to see if the chawanmushi has set. If it's not fully set, continue to steam for 1 to 2 minutes. Once the chawanmushi are set, garnish each portion with some of the shrimp-and-kamaboko mixture and a leaf of mitsuba and serve.

INGREDIENTS:

- 6 SHRIMP, SHELLED AND DEVEINED; 4 LEFT WHOLE, 2 CUT INTO QUARTERS
- 2 SHIITAKE MUSHROOMS, STEMMED AND SLICED THIN
- 8 SLICES OF KAMABOKO FISH CAKE
- 2 MEDIUM EGGS
- ¼ TEASPOON KOSHER SALT
- ½ TEASPOON SAKE
- 1 TEASPOON MIRIN
- AWASE DASHI STOCK (SEE PAGE 38), AS NEEDED
- FRESH MITSUBA (JAPANESE WILD PARSLEY), FOR GARNISH.

AEMONO (DRESSED SALADS & SIDES)

*A*emono is a Japanese-style dressed salad or side dish, where ingredients are mixed with seasonings and other flavor-enhancing components. The appeal of aemono lies in its quick preparation—pretty much all you have to do is mix the ingredients together. Adding an aemono to your table will improve the overall dining experience by providing a refreshing contrast to other dishes, offering a variety of textures and flavors.

WAKAME SALAD

YIELD: 4 SERVINGS / ACTIVE TIME: 10 MINUTES / TOTAL TIME: 30 MINUTES

This simple and quick salad is a perfect accompaniment or palate cleanser, and pairs very well with fish dishes.

1. To begin preparations for the salad, place the wakame in a bowl and cover it with warm water. Soak the wakame for the time recommended by the instructions on the package, typically 5 to 10 minutes.

2. Wrap the tofu in paper towels, place it in the microwave, and microwave it on high for 1½ minutes to evaporate the excess moisture. Remove the tofu from the microwave and let it cool slightly before cutting it into cubes. Set the tofu aside.

3. To prepare the dressing, place all of the ingredients in a bowl and whisk until the sugar has dissolved. Set the dressing aside.

4. Drain the wakame and squeeze it to remove any excess water. In a mixing bowl, combine the rehydrated wakame, cucumbers, and tomatoes. Pour the dressing over the salad and gently toss to coat. Add the tofu and gently toss to incorporate, being careful not to break the tofu.

5. Cover the bowl with plastic wrap and place it in the refrigerator for 20 to 30 minutes.

6. Garnish the salad with bonito flakes and serve.

INGREDIENTS:

FOR THE SALAD

1 TABLESPOON DRIED WAKAME

6 OZ. SILKEN TOFU

⅓ CUP THINLY SLICED JAPANESE OR PERSIAN CUCUMBERS

5 CHERRY TOMATOES, HALVED

BONITO FLAKES, FOR GARNISH

FOR THE DRESSING

1 TABLESPOON WATER

⅛ TEASPOON DASHI GRANULES

1 TABLESPOON RICE VINEGAR

1½ TABLESPOONS SOY SAUCE

¼ TEASPOON SUGAR

1 TABLESPOON SESAME OIL

1 TEASPOON GINGER PASTE

½ TEASPOON GROUND SESAME SEEDS

SUNOMONO

YIELD: 5 SERVINGS / **ACTIVE TIME:** 5 MINUTES / **TOTAL TIME:** 15 MINUTES

Here's a simple side dish made with fish, shellfish, or vegetables mixed with vinegar, soy sauce, and sugar. It's cherished in traditional Japanese households for its distinctive sourness, which complements a wide range of meals.

1. Place the soy sauce, mirin, and rice vinegar in a pan and bring to a boil over medium heat. Cook for 2 minutes, remove the pan from heat, and let it cool.

2. Place the wakame in a bowl of cold water and soak until it is fully rehydrated.

3. Place the cucumbers in a mixing bowl, season with the salt, and gently massage until the cucumbers are evenly coated. Let them sit for 5 minutes.

4. Break the surimi sticks into thin shreds. Rinse the salted cucumbers under cold water and then squeeze them to remove any excess liquid. Drain the rehydrated wakame and gently squeeze it to remove any excess water. In a large bowl, combine the cucumber, wakame, and surimi sticks.

5. Pour the cooled sauce over the mixture and toss to coat. Garnish the salad with sesame seeds and serve.

INGREDIENTS:

1	TABLESPOON SOY SAUCE
1	TABLESPOON MIRIN
1	TABLESPOON RICE VINEGAR
1	TABLESPOON DRIED WAKAME
3½	OZ. JAPANESE OR PERSIAN CUCUMBERS, SLICED THIN
½	TEASPOON KOSHER SALT
3	OZ. SURIMI STICKS (IMITATION CRAB)
	SESAME SEEDS, FOR GARNISH

SHABU-SHABU SALAD .

YIELD: 4 SERVINGS / **ACTIVE TIME:** 10 MINUTES / **TOTAL TIME:** 10 MINUTES

Shabu-shabu salad is a beloved classic in Japanese cuisine, combining the delicate flavors of thinly sliced pork with the refreshing crunch of crisp vegetables.

1. Place the water, sake, and salt in a large saucepan and bring the mixture to a boil over high heat. Add the pork and cook until it is cooked through, 30 seconds to 1 minute. Use a slotted spoon or strainer to remove the pork from the pan and transfer it to a colander to drain.

2. Rinse the pork under cold water. In a serving bowl, arrange the salad greens, cucumber, and tomato, creating a bed for the pork. Place the pork on top of the salad, drizzle the dressing over it, and serve.

INGREDIENTS:

4   CUPS WATER

2   TABLESPOONS SAKE

       PINCH OF KOSHER SALT

½   LB. PORK TENDERLOIN, SLICED THIN

5   OZ. SALAD GREENS

1   JAPANESE OR PERSIAN CUCUMBER, SLICED ON A BIAS

1   TOMATO, CUT INTO WEDGES

       PONZU DRESSING (SEE PAGE 54)

NAPA CABBAGE OHITASHI

YIELD: 4 SERVINGS / **ACTIVE TIME:** 10 MINUTES / **TOTAL TIME:** 40 MINUTES

Ohitashi is a traditional Japanese technique where vegetables are immersed in dashi, enriching them with considerable depth of flavor. While originally involving a soaking process, a simpler modern adaptation includes just drizzling vegetables with soy sauce. Spinach is the typical choice for ohitashi in Japan, but this recipe features boiled napa cabbage, offering a fresh take on the classic dish.

1. Cut the cabbage into bite-size chunks.

2. Prepare an ice bath. Bring water to a boil in a large saucepan and season with the salt. Add the cabbage and boil for 3 minutes.

3. While the cabbage is boiling, combine the sesame seeds, dashi granules, and light soy sauce in a large bowl. Take 1 tablespoon of the boiling water from the pot, add it to the bowl, and whisk to fully dissolve the dashi granules.

4. Drain the cabbage and add it to the ice bath. When the cabbage has cooled, drain it again and squeeze it to remove any excess water.

5. Add the cabbage to the bowl containing the dressing and toss until evenly coated. Place the salad in the refrigerator and chill for at least 30 minutes.

6. Remove the salad from the refrigerator and transfer it to a serving dish. Top the salad with the bonito flakes and serve.

INGREDIENTS:

1	LB. NAPA CABBAGE
	PINCH OF KOSHER SALT
1	TEASPOON GROUND SESAME SEEDS
¼	TEASPOON DASHI GRANULES
1	TABLESPOON LIGHT SOY SAUCE
1	TABLESPOON BONITO FLAKES, FOR GARNISH

GREEN BEANS GOMAAE

YIELD: 4 SERVINGS / **ACTIVE TIME:** 10 MINUTES / **TOTAL TIME:** 15 MINUTES

Gomaae is a traditional Japanese side dish that features boiled greens, such as spinach, green beans, or other vegetables, dressed with a mixture of ground sesame seeds and soy sauce. Known for its distinctive sesame aroma and subtle sweetness, gomaae is a versatile accompaniment that pairs well with a wide range of Japanese dishes.

1. Prepare an ice bath. Fill a small saucepan with enough water to cover the green beans completely once they are added. Season the water generously with salt and bring to a rolling boil over high heat.

2. Add the green beans and cook until they are bright green and just tender, about 2 minutes.

3. Remove the green beans from the pan using a slotted spoon, strainer, or tongs and plunge them into the ice bath. Let the green beans cool.

4. Place the salt, soy sauce, ground sesame seeds, brown sugar, whole sesame seeds, and water in a salad bowl and whisk until well combined.

5. Drain the green beans and shake off any excess water. Add them to the salad bowl, toss to evenly coat, and serve.

INGREDIENTS:

1   CUP GREEN BEANS, TRIMMED AND HALVED

¼   TEASPOON KOSHER SALT, PLUS MORE TO TASTE

1½ TEASPOONS SOY SAUCE

2   TABLESPOONS GROUND SESAME SEEDS

1   TABLESPOON LIGHT BROWN SUGAR

1½ TEASPOONS WHITE SESAME SEEDS

1½ TEASPOONS WATER

SHRIMP & ASPARAGUS SUMISO-AE

YIELD: 4 SERVINGS / **ACTIVE TIME**: 10 MINUTES / **TOTAL TIME**: 10 MINUTES

Sumiso is a unique dish that combines the flavor of rich and salty miso with the tangy sweetness of rice vinegar. Its name comes from the Japanese words su (meaning vinegar) and miso.

1. Prepare an ice bath. Using a vegetable peeler, gently peel away the outer layer of the asparagus to remove any fibrous skin.

2. Fill a large saucepan with water and bring it to a rolling boil. Add a large pinch of salt and the asparagus and cook for 2 minutes. Using a slotted spoon, strainer, or tongs, transfer the asparagus to the ice bath and let it cool.

3. Drain the asparagus and pat it dry with paper towels. Chop the blanched asparagus and set it aside.

4. Place the miso paste, rice vinegar, sugar, and mustard in a salad bowl and whisk until well combined.

5. Add the shrimp and asparagus to the bowl and toss until they are evenly coated.

6. Serve immediately or chill the salad in the refrigerator.

INGREDIENTS:

4 ASPARAGUS STALKS, TRIMMED

SALT, TO TASTE

2 TABLESPOONS YELLOW MISO PASTE

1 TABLESPOON RICE VINEGAR

1 TEASPOON SUGAR

½ TEASPOON JAPANESE MUSTARD

1 CUP BOILED SHRIMP

CARROT PEANUT-AE

YIELD: 4 SERVINGS / ACTIVE TIME: 15 MINUTES / TOTAL TIME: 15 MINUTES

Peanut-ae is a contemporary twist on the traditional Japanese goma-ae salad, substituting sesame seeds with peanuts to create a unique blend of flavors and textures. Ready in just 15 minutes, it's one of the quickest and most delicious ways to incorporate more vegetables into your meal.

1. Use a vegetable peeler or mandoline to slice the carrots very thin lengthwise. Then, using a sharp knife, cut the carrots into even thinner "noodles."

2. Place the peanuts, soy sauce, sugar, peanut butter, and vinegar in a salad bowl and whisk vigorously until the mixture is completely smooth and free of any lumps of peanut butter.

3. Add the carrots to the bowl with the dressing and toss until they are evenly coated. Garnish with parsley and serve.

INGREDIENTS:

2	CARROTS, PEELED
½	CUP ROASTED PEANUTS, CHOPPED
4	TEASPOONS SOY SAUCE
2	TEASPOONS SUGAR
2	TEASPOONS SMOOTH PEANUT BUTTER
1	TEASPOON RICE VINEGAR
	DRIED PARSLEY, FOR GARNISH

BROCCOLI KARASHI-AE

YIELD: 4 SERVINGS / ACTIVE TIME: 10 MINUTES / TOTAL TIME: 15 MINUTES

This offers an irresistibly simple yet addictive way to enjoy the versatility of broccoli, as the harmonious blend of spicy Japanese mustard and umami-rich bonito flakes, dashi, and soy sauce creates a flavor profile that perfectly complements its crisp, fresh taste.

1. Place the broccoli in a large microwave-safe bowl and add 2 tablespoons of water. Loosely cover the bowl with plastic wrap, place it in the microwave, and microwave on high until the broccoli is fork-tender, about 3 minutes.

2. Remove the broccoli from the microwave and let it cool.

3. Place the remaining ingredients in a salad bowl and whisk until the sugar and dashi granules have completely dissolved.

4. Add the broccoli to the salad bowl, toss until it is evenly coated, and serve.

INGREDIENTS:

- 12 BROCCOLI FLORETS, RINSED WELL
- 2 TABLESPOONS LIGHT SOY SAUCE
- 1½ TEASPOONS JAPANESE MUSTARD
- 2 TABLESPOONS BONITO FLAKES
- 1½ TEASPOONS SESAME SEEDS
- ¼ TEASPOON DASHI GRANULES
- ¼ TEASPOON SUGAR

Carrot Peanut-Ae, see page 158

AVOCADO & CUCUMBER UME-GOMA-AE

YIELD: 4 SERVINGS / **ACTIVE TIME:** 5 MINUTES / **TOTAL TIME:** 5 MINUTES

Here's a dressed salad that leans on the tangy, salty taste of umeboshi and the nuttiness of sesame oil to create a perfect blend of flavors.

1. Place the Umeboshi, sesame seeds, soy sauce, sesame oil, and sugar in a salad bowl and whisk until well combined.

2. Add the avocado and cucumbers to the salad and gently toss until they are evenly coated.

3. Garnish with bonito flakes and serve.

INGREDIENTS:

5   UMEBOSHI (SEE PAGE 329), SEEDED AND MASHED INTO A PASTE

1½   TEASPOONS WHITE SESAME SEEDS

½   TEASPOON SOY SAUCE

½   TEASPOON SESAME OIL

¼   TEASPOON SUGAR

     FLESH OF 1 AVOCADO, CUBED

3½   OZ. JAPANESE OR PERSIAN CUCUMBERS, CHOPPED

     BONITO FLAKES, FOR GARNISH

CHICKEN & CUCUMBER BAINIKU-AE

YIELD: 4 SERVINGS / **ACTIVE TIME:** 10 MINUTES / **TOTAL TIME:** 20 MINUTES

Bainiku-ae, or ume-ae is a refreshing salad that incorporates umeboshi into its dressing. For this recipe, I chose to use chicken breast and cucumbers for their lightness, making it a refreshing option perfect for summer.

1. To begin preparations for the salad, pat the chicken dry with paper towels and poke it all over with a fork. Season with salt and sprinkle the cornstarch over the chicken.

2. Place the sake, bouillon, sugar, mirin, and salt in a microwave-safe bowl and whisk until well combined. Place the chicken breast in the bowl, cover it loosely with plastic wrap, and microwave it on high for 2 minutes.

3. Remove the chicken from the microwave and carefully turn it over. Loosely cover the bowl with the plastic wrap, return it to the microwave, and microwave it on high for another 2 minutes. Leave the chicken in the microwave and let it steam for 10 minutes. The residual heat will continue to gently cook the chicken, ensuring it stays moist and tender.

4. To prepare the dressing, place all of the ingredients in a salad bowl and whisk until well combined.

5. Remove the chicken from the microwave and shred it. Add the shredded chicken and 1 tablespoon of the juices to the salad bowl and toss until evenly coated.

6. Garnish with nori and serve immediately, or chill it in the refrigerator before garnishing and serving.

INGREDIENTS:

FOR THE SALAD

⅔ LB. BONELESS, SKINLESS CHICKEN BREAST

½ TEASPOON KOSHER SALT, PLUS MORE TO TASTE

1 TEASPOON CORNSTARCH

1½ TEASPOONS SAKE

1 TEASPOON CHINESE CHICKEN BOUILLON

¼ TEASPOON SUGAR

1 TEASPOON MIRIN

NORI, SHREDDED, FOR GARNISH

FOR THE DRESSING

10 SHISO LEAVES, SLICED THIN

1 TABLESPOON SESAME OIL

½ CUP SLICED CUCUMBER, CUT INTO MATCHSTICKS

1 TABLESPOON BONITO FLAKES, CRUSHED

1 TEASPOON SOY SAUCE

½ TEASPOON SUGAR

1½ TEASPOONS WHITE SESAME SEEDS

5 UMEBOSHI (SEE PAGE 329), SEEDED AND MASHED INTO A PASTE

POTATO ISO CHEESE-AE

YIELD: 4 SERVINGS / **ACTIVE TIME:** 10 MINUTES / **TOTAL TIME:** 30 MINUTES

This is a modern salad that combines Western cheeses with Japanese nori, resulting in a unique mix of flavors.

1. Place the potatoes in a large saucepan and cover them with cold water. Season with salt, bring to a boil, and cook until the potatoes are fork-tender, 15 to 20 minutes.

2. While the potatoes are cooking, place the remaining ingredients in a salad bowl and whisk until well combined.

3. Drain the potatoes, add them to the salad, and mash so that the mixture is well combined but the potatoes retain a bit of texture.

4. Serve warm or chilled.

INGREDIENTS:

2 POTATOES, PEELED AND CHOPPED

¼ TEASPOON KOSHER SALT, PLUS MORE TO TASTE

2 TABLESPOONS CREAM CHEESE, SOFTENED

1½ TABLESPOONS GRATED PARMESAN OR PECORINO CHEESE

1 TEASPOON JAPANESE MUSTARD

1 TABLESPOON SESAME OIL

1 TABLESPOON AONORI POWDER

1 TEASPOON LIGHT SOY SAUCE

¼ SHEET OF NORI, CRUSHED

Potato Iso Cheese-Ae, see page 165

OKRA & CARROT SHIRA-AE

YIELD: 4 SERVINGS / ACTIVE TIME: 10 MINUTES / TOTAL TIME: 10 MINUTES

This dish is known for its creamy texture and nuanced flavors and is highly regarded in traditional Japanese households.

1. Prepare an ice bath. Bring water to a boil in a large saucepan. Add salt, the okra, and carrot and blanch the vegetables for 1½ minutes. Drain the vegetables and place them in the ice bath.

2. Wrap the tofu in paper towels, place it in the microwave, and microwave it on high for 2 minutes. Remove the tofu from the microwave.

3. Place the tofu and remaining ingredients in a food processor and blitz until the mixture is smooth.

4. Remove the okra from the ice bath and slice it into rounds. Drain the carrot.

5. Place the okra, carrot, and tofu dressing in a salad bowl, toss until the vegetables are evenly coated, and serve.

INGREDIENTS:

	SALT, TO TASTE
8	OKRA
1	SMALL CARROT, PEELED AND SHREDDED
6	OZ. FIRM TOFU
1½	TEASPOONS WHITE MISO PASTE
1	TEASPOON SOY SAUCE
1½	TEASPOONS GROUND SESAME SEEDS
1	TEASPOON SUGAR
½	TEASPOON DASHI GRANULES

CARROT MASAGO-AE

YIELD: 4 SERVINGS / **ACTIVE TIME:** 5 MINUTES / **TOTAL TIME:** 5 MINUTES

Masago-ae refers to a group of dishes that include tarako (salted pollock roe) and vegetables. Masago means "fine sand," and it is believed that the dish was named after the appearance of the tarako when it is correctly prepared.

1. Place the canola oil in a large skillet and warm it over medium-low heat. Add the carrot and cook, stirring occasionally, for 30 seconds.

2. Add the tarako and soy sauce and gently stir to coat the tarako and carrot with the soy sauce.

3. Cook until all of the water has evaporated and the grains of tarako start to cling together. Serve warm or chilled.

INGREDIENTS:

1   TEASPOON CANOLA OIL

1   CARROT, PEELED AND JULIENNED

½   TARAKO (SALTED POLLOCK ROE), SKIN REMOVED

¼   TEASPOON LIGHT SOY SAUCE

EGGPLANT ZUNDA-AE

YIELD: 4 SERVINGS / ACTIVE TIME: 15 MINUTES / TOTAL TIME: 15 MINUTES

Zunda is a local dish from the Tohoku region, made by grinding edamame and mixing it with sugar and salt. Zunda mochi is a well-known example of this dish, but it can also be made with eggplant, as this version shows.

1. Prepare a gas or charcoal grill for high heat (about 500°F) Place the eggplants, cut sides down, on the grill and cook until they are lightly charred, about 5 minutes. Transfer the eggplants to a heat-proof container, cover them, and let them steam.

2. While the eggplants are steaming, prepare the zunda mixture. Use a mortar and pestle to grind the edamame, wasabi, dashi granules, light soy sauce, and sugar until the mixture is well combined and has some small chunks left for texture. If you prefer a smoother zunda mixture, you can use a food processor for this step.

3. When the eggplants are cool enough to handle, peel off the skins and cut each half into six strips.

4. Place the zunda mixture, eggplant strips, and shrimp in a salad bowl, gently stir to combine, and serve.

INGREDIENTS:

2   JAPANESE EGGPLANTS, HALVED LENGTHWISE

½   LB. BOILED EDAMAME, PODS AND THIN SKINS REMOVED

1½ TEASPOONS WASABI (SEE PAGE 500 FOR HOMEMADE)

½   TEASPOON DASHI GRANULES

1   TABLESPOON LIGHT SOY SAUCE

1   TEASPOON SUGAR

½   CUP CHOPPED BOILED SHRIMP

Carrot Masago-Ae, see page 170

NABESHIGI

YIELD: 4 SERVINGS / **ACTIVE TIME:** 10 MINUTES / **TOTAL TIME:** 20 MINUTES

Nabeshigi is a humble yet flavorful Japanese dish that traditionally features eggplant fried with sugar, mirin, and other seasonings. This recipe introduces a creative twist by incorporating miso, garlic, bell pepper, and chile, providing a flavor profile that would perfectly complement freshly cooked white rice.

1. To begin preparations for the eggplants, slice the eggplants in half lengthwise. Carefully score their skins in a crosshatch pattern, cut the eggplants into bite-size chunks, and place them in a bowl. Cover them with water and let them soak for 10 minutes; this will help remove any bitterness.

2. While the eggplants are soaking, prepare the sauce. Place all of the ingredients in a bowl and whisk until the sauce is completely smooth. Set it aside.

3. Drain the eggplants and pat them dry. Place the canola oil in a large skillet and warm it over medium heat. Add the eggplants, skin side down, and cook until they are just tender, turning them over once.

4. Stir in the bell pepper, chile, and sesame seeds, reduce the heat to low, and add the sauce. Stir to evenly coat the vegetables and cook until everything is warmed through.

5. Turn off the heat. Drizzle the sesame oil over the dish, garnish with the shiso leaves, and serve.

INGREDIENTS:

FOR THE EGGPLANTS

2	JAPANESE EGGPLANTS
1	TABLESPOON CANOLA OIL
1	GREEN BELL PEPPER, STEMMED, SEEDED, AND CUBED
1	TEASPOON THINLY SLICED DRIED CHILE PEPPER
1	TEASPOON SESAME SEEDS
1½	TEASPOONS SESAME OIL
1	TABLESPOON THINLY SLICED SHISO LEAVES, FOR GARNISH

FOR THE SAUCE

1½	TABLESPOONS YELLOW MISO PASTE
1½	TEASPOONS MIRIN
1½	TEASPOONS SAKE
1½	TEASPOONS SUGAR
1	TEASPOON GARLIC PASTE

UME CUCUMBER

YIELD: 4 SERVINGS / **ACTIVE TIME:** 5 MINUTES / **TOTAL TIME:** 5 MINUTES

Umeboshi and cucumbers are a classic combination that makes a refreshing side dish or snack. Smashing the cucumbers allows them to absorb more flavor, and supplies the dish with different textures.

1. Place all of the ingredients, except for the cucumbers, in a serving bowl and whisk until well combined. Set the mixture aside.

2. Rinse the cucumbers well under cold water and pat them dry. Using a heavy object such as a rolling pin, gently beat the cucumbers to lightly crush them. Cut off the ends and discard them. Roughly chop the cucumbers and add them to the bowl. Toss until the cucumbers are evenly coated and serve.

INGREDIENTS:

2   TABLESPOONS SEEDED AND MASHED UMEBOSHI (SEE PAGE 329)

2   TABLESPOONS BONITO FLAKES

2   TABLESPOONS SESAME SEEDS

½   TEASPOON LIGHT SOY SAUCE

½   TEASPOON RICE VINEGAR

1½   TEASPOONS SESAME OIL

2   JAPANESE OR PERSIAN CUCUMBERS

Ume Cucumber, *see page 175*

NIMONO
(SIMMERED DISHES)

*N*imono is a general term referring to dishes prepared by simmering. Most of these preparations feature dashi stock, and all of them can be considered staples of home cooking and comfort food in Japan. The beauty of nimono is its versatility—it can be the star of the show or serve as a flavorful side dish.

KABOCHA NO NIMONO

YIELD: 6 SERVINGS / **ACTIVE TIME:** 15 MINUTES / **TOTAL TIME:** 25 MINUTES

Here's a delightful dish that highlights the natural sweetness, unique texture, and rich flavor of the unique kabocha squash. This straightforward simmered preparation is both satisfying and nourishing, making it a cherished side dish in many Japanese households.

1. Begin by washing the squash. Cut it in half, scoop out the seeds and stringy pulp, and discard them. Cut the squash into chunks, leaving the skin on for added texture.

2. Place the kabocha pieces in a large saucepan in an even layer, skin side up.

3. Place the water in a measuring cup and stir in the dashi granules. Pour the dashi into the pot with the kabocha and cook over medium heat. When the dashi starts to boil, add the brown sugar, mirin, soy sauce, and sake and cook for 2 minutes. Reduce the heat and let the squash simmer.

4. Place a drop lid directly on the surface of the water. If you don't have a drop lid, you can place aluminum foil or parchment paper on the surface. Simmer until the squash is fork-tender, 10 to 15 minutes. Serve immediately.

INGREDIENTS:

1	LB. KABOCHA SQUASH
1	CUP WATER
1	TEASPOON DASHI GRANULES
1½	TEASPOONS LIGHT BROWN SUGAR
2	TABLESPOONS MIRIN
2	TABLESPOONS SOY SAUCE
2	TABLESPOONS SAKE

BAMBOO SHOOT OKAKA-NI

YIELD: 4 SERVINGS / **ACTIVE TIME:** 15 MINUTES / **TOTAL TIME:** 15 MINUTES

If you're looking to use something other than bamboo shoots in this preparation, taro, konnyaku, and radish are good options.

1. Place the sesame oil in a medium saucepan and warm it over medium heat. Add the bamboo shoots and stir until they are lightly coated with the sesame oil.

2. Add the remaining ingredients and stir until well combined. Cover the pan, reduce the heat to medium-low, and simmer for 10 minutes.

3. Serve warm or chilled.

INGREDIENTS:

1½	TEASPOONS SESAME OIL
3½	OZ. BOILED BAMBOO SHOOTS, CHOPPED
1	TABLESPOON SAKE
1	TABLESPOON SOY SAUCE
1	TEASPOON MIRIN
1	TEASPOON SUGAR
¼	CUP WATER
2	TABLESPOONS BONITO FLAKES

Bamboo Shoot Okaka-Ni, see page 183

KINPIRA RENKON

YIELD: 4 SERVINGS / **ACTIVE TIME:** 10 MINUTES / **TOTAL TIME:** 20 MINUTES

Kinpira is a classic Japanese side dish of stir-fried burdock and carrots in a sweet and spicy sauce. In modern Japanese cuisine, the dish has evolved to include a wider variety of root vegetables, such as lotus root, which features here.

1. If you're starting with raw lotus roots, peel them and slice them thin. Place the lotus roots in a bowl of water with a splash of vinegar and let them soak for 5 minutes.

2. Bring water to a boil in a medium saucepan. Drain the lotus roots, add them to the pan, and boil for 3 minutes. Drain the lotus roots and set them aside.

3. Place the sesame oil in a large skillet and warm it over medium heat. Add the chile and cook, stirring frequently, until it is fragrant, about 2 minutes.

4. Add the lotus roots and stir-fry for 1 minute. Stir in the sake and sugar and cook until the lotus roots have absorbed most of the sake. Add the soy sauce and cook, stirring occasionally, until the lotus roots have absorbed most of the liquid. Add the mirin and sesame seeds and stir-fry until the flavor has developed to your liking. Serve immediately.

INGREDIENTS:

- ½   LB. LOTUS ROOTS
-      RICE VINEGAR, AS NEEDED
- 1   TABLESPOON SESAME OIL
- 1   DRIED CHILE PEPPER, STEMMED, SEEDED, AND SLICED THIN
- 3   TABLESPOONS SAKE
- 1   TABLESPOON SUGAR
- 2   TABLESPOONS SOY SAUCE
- 1½   TEASPOONS MIRIN
- 1½   TEASPOONS SESAME SEEDS

SIMMERED SWEET POTATOES

YIELD: 4 SERVINGS / ACTIVE TIME: 10 MINUTES / TOTAL TIME: 15 MINUTES

Simmering sweet potatoes in dashi produces the perfect combination of sweet and savory.

1. Cut the sweet potato into ½-inch-thick rounds and soak it in a bowl of cold water.

2. Combine the dashi, soy sauce, mirin, sugar, and ginger in a small saucepan and bring to a boil over medium heat. Reduce the heat to medium-low and let the broth simmer.

3. Drain the sweet potato and add it to the pot, ensuring it is submerged in the broth. Simmer until the sweet potato is fork-tender, about 15 minutes.

4. Serve immediately or let the sweet potato cool in the broth after it is tender and reheat it before serving.

INGREDIENTS:

½ LB. SWEET POTATO, PEELED

1¼ CUPS AWASE DASHI STOCK (SEE PAGE 38)

2 TABLESPOONS SOY SAUCE

1 TABLESPOON MIRIN

1 TABLESPOON SUGAR

4 THIN SLICES OF FRESH GINGER

KIRIBOSHI DAIKON

YIELD: 6 SERVINGS / **ACTIVE TIME:** 15 MINUTES / **TOTAL TIME:** 20 MINUTES

This is a simmered side dish made with rehydrated strips of daikon radish and fresh vegetables. While this dish is not widely recognized outside of Japan, it's a staple for many Japanese families.

1. Place the daikon in a bowl of cold water and rub it to loosen any dust and debris. Drain and repeat two more times.

2. Place the daikon and water in a bowl and let the daikon soak for 20 minutes.

3. Remove the rehydrated daikon from the bowl and squeeze it to remove any excess liquid. Cut the daikon into 3-inch pieces. Reserve the soaking liquid and set it aside.

4. Place the sesame oil in a large skillet and warm it over medium heat. Add the carrot, mushrooms, and Abura-age and stir-fry for 2 to 3 minutes.

5. Add the daikon and stir-fry for 1 minute. Add the reserved soaking liquid along with the light soy sauce, mirin, and brown sugar and stir until the brown sugar has dissolved. Simmer until the liquid has evaporated, stirring occasionally.

6. Add the sake and stir-fry for 1 minute. Garnish with the sesame seeds before serving hot, warm, or chilled.

INGREDIENTS:

- 2 OZ. KIRIBOSHI DAIKON (DRIED SHREDDED DAIKON)
- 1¼ CUPS COLD WATER
- 1 TEASPOON SESAME OIL
- 1 CARROT, PEELED AND JULIENNED
- 2 SHIITAKE MUSHROOMS, STEMMED AND JULIENNED
- 2 SHEETS OF ABURA-AGE (SEE PAGE 69), SLICED THIN
- 3 TABLESPOONS LIGHT SOY SAUCE
- 3 TABLESPOONS MIRIN
- 1 TABLESPOON LIGHT BROWN SUGAR
- 1 TEASPOON SAKE
- 1 TABLESPOON WHITE SESAME SEEDS, FOR GARNISH

Kiriboshi Daikon, see page 189

ORANDANI

YIELD: 4 SERVINGS / **ACTIVE TIME:** 10 MINUTES / **TOTAL TIME:** 25 MINUTES

The term "oranda" in Japanese refers to Holland, and is a nod to the Netherlands' role in introducing culinary techniques to Japan, an exchange that is rooted in a long and significant history of trade between the two nations. Despite the name, the taste of orandani is quite traditionally Japanese, but the fried vegetables and a hint of spice make it stand out from other traditional simmered dishes in Japan.

1. Bring water to a boil in a large pot. Cut the eggplants in half lengthwise and carefully score a crosshatch pattern on their skin, taking care not to slice all the way through. Slice the eggplants into rounds, place them in a bowl, and cover with cold water. Let the eggplants soak.

2. Add canola oil to a Dutch oven until it is about 2 inches deep and warm it to 355°F. Drain the eggplants and pat them dry with paper towels. Gently slip the eggplants into the hot oil and fry until they are soft and lightly browned. Transfer the fried eggplants to a colander. Gently slip the bell pepper into the hot oil and fry until it is just tender. Add the bell pepper to the colander. Pour the boiling water over the vegetables and let them drain. This is a traditional Japanese technique to remove excess oil.

3. Place the dashi, soy sauce, mirin, sugar, and dried chile in a saucepan and bring to a boil. Reduce the heat so that the broth simmers, add the eggplants and bell pepper, and gently simmer for 15 minutes.

4. If you prefer to enjoy the dish hot, serve it immediately after simmering. For a cold version, allow the dish to cool completely and then refrigerate it before serving. Garnish the dish with bonito flakes and additional dried chile.

INGREDIENTS:

2   JAPANESE OR CHINESE EGGPLANTS

    CANOLA OIL, AS NEEDED

1   GREEN BELL PEPPER, STEMMED, SEEDED, AND SLICED

1¼   CUPS AWASE DASHI STOCK (SEE PAGE 38)

2   TABLESPOONS SOY SAUCE

2   TABLESPOONS MIRIN

2½   TABLESPOONS SUGAR

1   DRIED RED CHILE PEPPER, STEMMED, SEEDED, AND MINCED, PLUS MORE FOR GARNISH

    BONITO FLAKES, FOR GARNISH

GOMOKU MAME

YIELD: 6 SERVINGS / ACTIVE TIME: 15 MINUTES / TOTAL TIME: 1 HOUR AND 30 MINUTES

Gomoku mame has a simple appearance, yet it is very comforting. It also has the advantage of being a plant-based dish, making it suitable for vegans.

1. Place the mushrooms and kombu in a bowl and cover them with the water. Let the mixture soak for 30 minutes.

2. Remove the rehydrated kombu and mushrooms from the bowl and finely dice them. Reserve the soaking liquid and set it aside.

3. Place the canola oil in a medium saucepan and warm it over medium heat. Add the soybeans, carrots, bamboo shoots, mushrooms, and kombu to the pan and stir-fry for 1 minute. Add the reserved soaking liquid and the remaining ingredients to the pan and bring to a boil.

4. Reduce the heat to low, cover the pan with a lid, and simmer for 30 minutes.

5. Adjust the lid so that some steam can escape and simmer for an additional 15 minutes.

6. Serve immediately. However, for an even better result, let the dish cool completely and then reheat it right before serving.

INGREDIENTS:

2   DRIED SHIITAKE MUSHROOMS

    3 X 3–INCH SHEET OF DRIED KOMBU

1½   CUPS WATER

1   TEASPOON CANOLA OIL

1   CUP COOKED OR CANNED SOYBEANS

½   CARROT, PEELED AND FINELY DICED

¼   CUP BOILED BAMBOO SHOOTS, FINELY DICED

2   TABLESPOONS SOY SAUCE

2   TABLESPOONS SAKE

2   TABLESPOONS SUGAR

2   TABLESPOONS MIRIN

RED KIDNEY BEANS AMANI

YIELD: 8 SERVINGS / **ACTIVE TIME:** 10 MINUTES / **TOTAL TIME:** 24 HOURS

Amani is usually prepared using a type of kidney bean known as kintoki-mame in Japan. However, you can use common red kidney beans to make it as well. This is a very sweet side dish that is commonly used in osechi, a group of traditional Japanese dishes served around New Year.

1. Rinse the kidney beans under cold water, transfer them to a bowl, and cover with cold water. Cover the bowl and let the beans soak overnight.

2. Drain the beans and rinse them well. Place them in a saucepan and cover by 1 to 2 inches with cold water. Bring to a boil over medium heat and cook for 20 minutes.

3. Drain the beans and return them to the saucepan. Cover with water and bring to a boil.

4. Reduce the heat so that the beans simmer and place a drop lid, aluminum foil, or parchment paper on the surface. Simmer the beans until they are tender enough to be easily crushed between your fingers, 40 minutes to 1 hour.

5. Stir in the sugar and salt and simmer until most of the liquid has been reduced. Stir in the soy sauce and serve immediately.

INGREDIENTS:

¾ CUP DRIED RED KIDNEY BEANS

⅔ CUP MUSCOVADO SUGAR

½ TEASPOON FINE SEA SALT

1½ TEASPOONS SOY SAUCE

YUDOFU WITH SPICY SESAME SAUCE

YIELD: 4 SERVINGS / **ACTIVE TIME:** 10 MINUTES / **TOTAL TIME:** 40 MINUTES

A comforting side dish that is traditionally enjoyed with soy sauce and other simple condiments. However, this recipe introduces a contemporary twist, pairing it with a spicy, nutty sauce.

1. Place the kombu and water in a large saucepan. Let the kombu soak for 30 minutes.

2. Turn the heat to medium and watch the pan closely. Remove the kombu just before the water comes to a boil. Reduce the heat to low and carefully add the tofu and salt to the pan. Simmer until the tofu is warmed through.

3. Use a slotted spoon to transfer the tofu to a serving dish. Drizzle the sauce over the tofu, garnish with green onions, and serve.

INGREDIENTS:

¼ OZ. DRIED KOMBU

4 CUPS WATER

¾ LB. SILKEN TOFU, CUT INTO 4 TO 8 LARGE CUBES

¼ TEASPOON SALT

SPICY SESAME SAUCE (SEE PAGE 681)

GREEN ONIONS, FINELY CHOPPED, FOR GARNISH

CHIKUZENNI

YIELD: 5 SERVINGS / ACTIVE TIME: 30 MINUTES / TOTAL TIME: 1 HOUR AND 30 MINUTES

Chikuzenni is a regional dish from Fukuoka Prefecture, known for its hearty and flavorful profile. It features a combination of chicken, root vegetables, and konnyaku that is first stir-fried and then simmered in a sweet-and-savory sauce, a process that infuses the dish with a rich, deep flavor.

1. Place the mushrooms in a bowl, cover with the water, and let them soak for 30 minutes.

2. Drain the mushrooms and reserve the soaking liquid. Remove the stems from the mushrooms, discard them, and cut the caps into quarters. Set the mushrooms aside.

3. Place the sesame oil in a large saucepan and warm it over medium heat. Place the chicken, skin side down, in the pan and cook until it is browned all over, stirring as necessary.

4. Add the mushrooms, carrot, lotus roots, bamboo shoots, and konnyaku to the pan and stir-fry for 30 seconds.

5. Add the reserved soaking liquid, light brown sugar, and sake and place a drop lid, aluminum foil, or parchment paper on the surface. Bring the mixture to a boil, reduce the heat to medium-low, and simmer until the liquid has reduced by half, about 10 minutes.

6. Carefully pull up the lid and add the soy sauce and mirin. Do not stir. Instead, gently tilt the pan side to side to distribute them. Place the lid back on the surface and simmer until the liquid has reduced by one-third.

7. Turn off the heat and let the dish cool, with the lid on.

8. Prepare an ice bath. Bring water to a boil in a medium saucepan, add the snow peas, and blanch them for 1 minute. Drain, add the snow peas to the ice bath, and let them cool. Drain the snow peas again and slice them on a bias. Set them aside.

9. Add additional soy sauce and mirin to the pan and bring the dish to a boil over medium heat. Reduce the heat to medium-low and let it simmer for 5 minutes. Again, do not stir, but tilt the pan to move the liquid around. Top the dish with the snow peas and serve immediately.

INGREDIENTS:

3	DRIED SHIITAKE MUSHROOMS
2	CUPS WATER
1	TABLESPOON TOASTED SESAME OIL
⅔	LB. BONELESS, SKIN-ON CHICKEN THIGHS, CHOPPED
½	CARROT, PEELED AND CHOPPED
3½	OZ. BOILED LOTUS ROOTS, SLICED AND HALVED
3½	OZ BOILED BAMBOO SHOOTS, CHOPPED
1	SHEET OF KONNYAKU, CHOPPED
2	TEASPOONS LIGHT BROWN SUGAR
¼	CUP SAKE
¼	CUP SOY SAUCE, PLUS MORE TO TASTE
¼	CUP MIRIN, PLUS MORE TO TASTE
10	SNOW PEAS

NIKU DOFU

YIELD: 5 SERVINGS / **ACTIVE TIME:** 20 MINUTES / **TOTAL TIME:** 1 HOUR

This is a comforting wintry dish that combines thinly sliced beef, firm tofu, and onions, simmered in a sweet and savory broth that is reminiscent of the world-famous sukiyaki. Originating in Kyoto, this regional dish has also become a favorite across Japan for its simplicity and ease of preparation. Traditionally, niku dofu featured kujo negi—a prized vegetable local to Kyoto—but this version opts for onions, making it more accessible while maintaining its delicious essence.

1. Place the potato starch in a shallow bowl and dredge the beef in it until it is coated. Place the canola oil in a large saucepan and warm it over medium heat. Add the beef and cook until it is browned all over, turning it as necessary. Remove the beef from the pan and set it aside.

2. Add the soy sauce, sake, brown sugar, water, and dashi granules to the pan, stir until well combined, and warm until the mixture has almost come to a boil. Add the onion, tofu, mushrooms, and beef, cook until the mixture has almost come to a boil, and reduce the heat so that it simmers.

3. Place a drop lid, aluminum foil, or parchment paper on the surface and simmer for 10 minutes.

4. Turn off the heat and let the dish cool for 30 minutes to 1 hour. This resting period allows the ingredients to absorb the broth.

5. Prepare an ice bath. Bring water to a boil in a medium saucepan, add the snow peas, and blanch them for 1 minute. Drain, add the snow peas to the ice bath, and let them cool. Drain the snow peas again and slice them on a bias.

6. Warm the niku dofu over medium heat until it comes to a boil. Sprinkle the snow peas over the dish and serve.

INGREDIENTS:

1	TABLESPOON POTATO STARCH
½	LB. BEEF, SLICED THIN
1½	TEASPOONS CANOLA OIL
¼	CUP SOY SAUCE
½	CUP SAKE
3	TABLESPOONS LIGHT BROWN SUGAR
1	CUP WATER
½	TEASPOON DASHI GRANULES
1	ONION, SLICED THIN
½	LB. FIRM TOFU, CUBED
¼	LB. ENOKI MUSHROOMS, ROOTS REMOVED
10	SNOW PEAS

SOBORO DAIKON

YIELD: 6 SERVINGS / **ACTIVE TIME:** 10 MINUTES / **TOTAL TIME:** 15 MINUTES

Soboro refers to finely minced meat or seafood in Japanese cuisine, often cooked until it turns crumbly. This comforting side dish pairs sweet and savory soboro with tender radish. While you can simmer the ingredients to prepare this recipe, here I offer a modern twist and use a microwave, streamlining the process without sacrificing flavor.

1. Place all of the ingredients, except for the radish and garnishes, in a mixing bowl and stir until well combined.

2. Place the radish in an even layer in a large, microwave-safe bowl. It will act as a bed for the chicken mixture. Spread the chicken mixture evenly over the radish.

3. Cover the bowl with plastic wrap, leaving it slightly loose to allow steam to escape. Microwave on high for 10 minutes.

4. After 10 minutes, carefully check the radish to see if it is fork-tender. If it is, serve and garnish with green onions, shichimi togarashi, and sesame seeds. If it is not, gently stir the mixture, ensuring that the radish is covered again, and return the bowl to the microwave. Microwave for 1 to 3 minutes, until the radish is fork-tender.

INGREDIENTS:

¼ LB. GROUND CHICKEN

½ CUP AWASE DASHI STOCK (SEE PAGE 38)

1 TABLESPOON SOY SAUCE

1½ TEASPOONS SUGAR

1½ TEASPOONS MIRIN

1 TEASPOON YELLOW MISO PASTE

½ TEASPOON GRATED FRESH GINGER

1 TABLESPOON CORNSTARCH

1 TEASPOON SESAME OIL

10 OZ. DAIKON RADISH, PEELED AND CUT INTO ½-INCH-THICK HALF-MOONS

GREEN ONIONS, FINELY CHOPPED, FOR GARNISH

SHICHIMI TOGARASHI, FOR GARNISH

WHITE SESAME SEEDS, FOR GARNISH

Soboro Daikon, see page 203

BUTA NO KAKUNI

YIELD: 4 TO 6 SERVINGS / **ACTIVE TIME:** 20 MINUTES / **TOTAL TIME:** 3 HOURS

The dish gets it's name from the cubes (kaku) of pork (buta) that are slowly simmered (niru) and then marinated in a sauce that offers a perfect balance of sweet and savory.

1. Bring water to a boil in a large saucepan.

2. Warm a large skillet over medium-high heat. Add the pork belly and sear until it is browned all over, turning it as necessary. Transfer the pork belly to a cutting board and cut it into thick chunks.

3. Reduce the heat so that the water simmers, add the pork belly, and simmer for 10 minutes. Drain, rinse out the pan, and return the pork belly to it. Cover with fresh water and bring to a boil.

4. Cut a 2-inch piece out of the white part of the leek and set it aside. Cut the rest of the leek into large pieces and place them in the pan along with the ginger. When the water starts to boil, reduce the heat, and simmer for 1 hour, turning the pork over halfway through. Check occasionally to make sure that the pork is always submerged and add water as necessary.

5. Cut the reserved piece of leek lengthways to the center and then separate the layers. Cut the layers into thin strips to make shiraganegi, which you will use to garnish the dish. Place the leek in a bowl, add salt, and cover with water. Let the shiraganegi soak until you are going to serve the dish.

6. Transfer 2 cups of the broth from cooking the pork belly to a large saucepan. Add the soy sauce, lager, honey, and light brown sugar and bring to a boil. Reduce the heat and let the mixture simmer. Add the pork belly and place a drop lid, aluminum foil, or parchment paper on the surface. Simmer for 30 minutes.

7. Turn off the heat and let the pork cool in the marinade.

8. If desired, add the soft-boiled eggs to the broth. Place the pan in the refrigerator and let the dish marinate for 1 hour.

9. Place the pan on the stove and reheat the dish over medium heat for 15 minutes. If using, remove the eggs once they're warmed through to keep from overcooking the yolks.

10. Garnish the dish with the shiraganegi and serve with the mustard and blanched greens.

INGREDIENTS:

1½ LBS. PORK BELLY

1 LARGE JAPANESE LEEK

4-INCH PIECE OF FRESH GINGER, PEELED AND SLICED

SALT, TO TASTE

½ CUP SOY SAUCE

½ CUP LAGER

1 TABLESPOON HONEY

2 TABLESPOONS LIGHT BROWN SUGAR

4 SOFT-BOILED EGGS (OPTIONAL)

JAPANESE KARASHI MUSTARD, FOR SERVING

GREENS, BLANCHED, FOR SERVING

NIKUJAGA

YIELD: 4 TO 6 SERVINGS / **ACTIVE TIME:** 20 MINUTES / **TOTAL TIME:** 1 HOUR

Nikujaga is a classic homestyle dish that combines meat (niku) and potatoes (jagaimo). Although its origins are unclear, some say that it was inspired by British beef stew and was recreated using local Japanese ingredients and condiments.

1. Place the potatoes in a bowl, cover with cold water, and let them soak for 10 minutes.

2. Place the canola oil in a medium saucepan and warm it over medium heat. Add the beef and cook until it is browned all over, stirring as necessary. Add the onion and stir-fry for 1 minute.

3. Drain the potatoes and add them to the pan along with the carrot, water, and dashi granules. Bring to a boil, gently stir in the brown sugar, mirin, sake, and light soy sauce, and reduce the heat so that the dish simmers. Place a drop lid, aluminum foil, or parchment paper on the surface and gently simmer for 30 minutes.

4. Prepare an ice bath. Bring water to a boil in a medium saucepan, add the snow peas, and blanch them for 1 minute. Drain, add the snow peas to the ice bath, and let them cool. Set them aside.

5. Remove the lid and add the dark soy sauce to the pot. Avoid stirring the dish from this point on. Instead, tilt the pan from side to side to distribute the dark soy sauce. Place the lid back on the surface and simmer for 5 minutes.

6. Divide the nikujaga among the serving bowls, sprinkle the snow peas over the top of each portion, and serve.

INGREDIENTS:

2	WAXY POTATOES, PEELED AND CHOPPED
1	TEASPOON CANOLA OIL
½	LB. THINLY SLICED BEEF, CUT INTO BITE-SIZE PIECES
½	ONION, CUT INTO WEDGES
1	MEDIUM CARROT, PEELED AND CHOPPED
1⅔	CUPS WATER
½	TEASPOON DASHI GRANULES
1	TABLESPOON LIGHT BROWN SUGAR
3	TABLESPOONS MIRIN
3	TABLESPOONS SAKE
2	TABLESPOONS LIGHT SOY SAUCE
½	CUP SNOW PEAS, STRINGS REMOVED AND CUT ON A BIAS INTO THIRDS
1½	TEASPOONS DARK SOY SAUCE

JIBU-NI

YIELD: 4 SERVINGS / **ACTIVE TIME**: 20 MINUTES / **TOTAL TIME**: 20 MINUTES

Jibu-ni is a beloved regional dish from Ishikawa Prefecture with a rich history dating back to the Edo period. This homestyle dish is frequently served at weddings and celebratory events and was traditionally made with duck meat, reflecting the abundance of ducks in the region. Nowadays, many contemporary recipes substitute chicken thighs for the duck, making it more accessible.

1. Make diagonal incisions over the surface of the leek. Cut it into 2-inch pieces and set it aside.

2. Place the dashi, sake, mirin, soy sauce, and brown sugar in a saucepan and bring to a boil over medium heat. Reduce the heat to medium-low. Add the bamboo shoots, mushrooms, carrot, and leek and gently simmer for 5 minutes.

3. Place the flour in a shallow bowl. Dredge the duck breasts in it until they are lightly coated. Carefully add the duck to the pan and simmer until it is cooked through and the vegetables are tender, 5 to 10 minutes. Serve immediately.

INGREDIENTS:

1	JAPANESE LEEK
2½	CUPS AWASE DASHI STOCK (SEE PAGE 38)
¼	CUP SAKE
¼	CUP MIRIN
¼	CUP LIGHT SOY SAUCE
2	TABLESPOONS LIGHT BROWN SUGAR
1	CUP CHOPPED BOILED BAMBOO SHOOTS
4	SHIITAKE MUSHROOMS, STEMMED
1	CARROT, PEELED AND SLICED
2	TABLESPOONS ALL-PURPOSE FLOUR
½	LB. DUCK BREASTS OR CHICKEN THIGHS, SLICED THIN

SIMMERED TARO & SQUID

YIELD: 4 SERVINGS / **ACTIVE TIME:** 10 MINUTES / **TOTAL TIME:** 1 HOUR

This timeless Japanese stew showcases the harmonious marriage of two seemingly disparate ingredients. While many simmered dishes in Japan rely on the umami-rich depth of dashi, this particular recipe takes a different approach, opting for water and allowing the natural flavor of the squid to take center stage.

1. Place all of the ingredients, except for the snow peas, in a medium saucepan and bring to a boil over medium heat, stirring occasionally.

2. Reduce the heat to medium-low. Place a drop lid, aluminum foil, or parchment paper on the surface and simmer until the liquid has reduced to one-quarter of its original volume.

3. Remove the pot from heat and let the mixture cool slightly with the lid on.

4. Prepare an ice bath. Bring water to a boil in a medium saucepan, add the snow peas, and blanch them for 1 minute. Drain, add the snow peas to the ice bath, and let them cool. Drain the snow peas again and slice them on a bias. Set them aside.

5. Remove the lid from the surface of the dish and return the pan to the stove. Cook over medium heat until everything is warmed through.

6. Top the dish with the snow peas and serve.

INGREDIENTS:

⅔   LB. TARO ROOTS, PEELED AND PARBOILED

5   OZ. CLEANED SQUID, SLICED

2   SLICES OF FRESH GINGER

2   TABLESPOONS SOY SAUCE

2   TABLESPOONS MIRIN

2   TABLESPOONS SAKE

1   TABLESPOON SUGAR

1½   CUPS WATER

8   SNOW PEAS

BEEF SHIGURENI

YIELD: 4 SERVINGS / **ACTIVE TIME:** 15 MINUTES / **TOTAL TIME:** 30 MINUTES

Shigureni is a savory Japanese side dish, traditionally simmering shellfish or beef in a soy sauce-and-sugar mixture spiked with ginger. Originating from the Edo period, this version alters the classic preparation slightly by substituting white wine and light brown sugar for the sake and sugar, adding a nice depth.

1. Peel the burdock root and slice it very thin on a bias. Place it in a bowl, cover with cold water, and stir in the rice vinegar. Set the burdock root aside. Place the ginger in a separate bowl, cover it with cold water, and set it aside.

2. Chop the beef into 1-inch pieces and prepare an ice bath. Bring water to a boil in a medium saucepan. Turn off the heat and add the beef. Let it cook for about 30 seconds; it should still be a little pink. Drain and quickly transfer the beef to the ice bath. When it is cool, drain and set it aside.

3. Place the sesame oil in a large skillet and warm it over medium heat. Drain the burdock root, add it to the pan, and cook for 2 minutes, stirring occasionally. Drain the ginger and add it to the pan along with the white wine, soy sauce, brown sugar, and mirin. Stir and simmer over medium heat until the liquid has reduced by two-thirds.

4. Add the beef, raise the heat to medium-high, and stir-fry until the liquid has almost completely evaporated.

5. Garnish with green onions and sesame seeds and serve.

INGREDIENTS:

5	OZ. BURDOCK ROOT
	DASH OF RICE VINEGAR
	1-INCH PIECE OF FRESH GINGER, PEELED AND JULIENNED
10	OZ. BEEF (PREFERABLY WITH MARBLING FAT), SLICED THIN
1½	TEASPOONS SESAME OIL
¼	CUP WHITE WINE
3	TABLESPOONS SOY SAUCE
2	TABLESPOONS LIGHT BROWN SUGAR
1	TABLESPOON MIRIN
	GREEN ONIONS, FINELY DICED, FOR GARNISH
	SESAME SEEDS, FOR GARNISH

Beef Shigureni, see page 211

BURI DAIKON

YIELD: 4 SERVINGS / **ACTIVE TIME:** 15 MINUTES / **TOTAL TIME:** 50 MINUTES

This beloved winter dish features yellowtail (also known as Japanese amberjack), taking advantage of the fish's seasonal peak, as it is known for its rich flavor and optimal fat content during colder months. Unlike many other Japanese simmered dishes that rely on dashi for their base, buri daikon uniquely uses only kombu. This choice ensures that the deliciously natural broth produced by the yellowtail retains its full glory.

1. Season the yellowtail with the salt and set it aside.

2. Place the radish in a medium saucepan, cover with water, and bring to a simmer. Cook for 30 minutes.

3. Prepare an ice bath. Place the yellowtail in a heatproof bowl and pour some of the hot water from cooking the radish over it. After 10 seconds, transfer the yellowtail to the ice bath. Drain, pat it dry with paper towels, and set it aside.

4. Drain the radish and set it aside.

5. Place the water, sake, light brown sugar, radish, and yellowtail in a clean saucepan and bring the mixture to a boil over medium heat. Reduce the heat to medium-low and add the soy sauce, mirin, chile, and kombu. Place a drop lid, aluminum foil, or parchment paper on the surface and simmer for 15 minutes.

6. Remove the lid, raise the heat to high, and cook for 2 minutes. Turn off the heat and let the dish cool.

7. Reheat the dish, garnish with the ginger, and serve.

INGREDIENTS:

½ LB. YELLOWTAIL FILLETS, CHOPPED

¼ TEASPOON KOSHER SALT

½ LB. DAIKON RADISH, CUT INTO THICK HALF-MOONS

½ CUP WATER

¼ CUP SAKE

1 TABLESPOON LIGHT BROWN SUGAR

1½ TABLESPOONS SOY SAUCE

1 TABLESPOON MIRIN

1 DRIED RED CHILE PEPPER

2-INCH SQUARE OF DRIED KOMBU

1-INCH PIECE OF FRESH GINGER, PEELED AND CUT INTO FINE MATCHSTICKS, FOR GARNISH

FISH

*T*hese dishes are the essence of Japanese cuisine, as the country abstained from eating meat for a long period of its history, a stretch that has fostered 1,200 years of expertise in pescatarian dietary practices. If you cannot find the specific fish mentioned in a recipe in your area, I strongly encourage you to try substituting one of your local fish varieties, as this willingness to adapt aligns powerfully with the Japanese culinary philosophy of using fresh, local, and seasonal ingredients.

BAKED SHIOZAKE

YIELD: 4 SERVINGS / **ACTIVE TIME**: 10 MINUTES / **TOTAL TIME**: 3 HOURS AND 15 MINUTES

A traditional dish that is typically served with rice and miso soup. It is made with fresh salmon fillets and seasoned very simply with salt. If you have visited a ryokan in Japan, you have likely seen it served for breakfast.

1. Thoroughly pat the salmon dry with paper towels and place it in a container with a lid. Season the salmon all over with the salt and then gently massage the salt into it. Cover the container and chill the salmon in the refrigerator for at least 3 hours. For optimal flavor infusion, let the salmon chill overnight.

2. Preheat the oven to 480°F. Line a baking sheet with parchment paper. Remove the salmon from the refrigerator and pat it dry with paper towels. Arrange the salmon on the pan, skin side up, and lightly sprinkle the sake over it.

3. Place the salmon on the lower rack in the oven and bake for 10 minutes.

4. Remove the salmon from the oven and, if desired, serve with wedges of sudachi.

INGREDIENTS:

4 SKIN-ON SALMON FILLETS

1 TEASPOON KOSHER SALT

2 TEASPOONS SAKE

SUDACHI OR PREFERRED CITRUS, CUT INTO WEDGES, FOR SERVING (OPTIONAL)

SABA NO SHIOYAKI

YIELD: 4 SERVINGS / *ACTIVE TIME*: 15 MINUTES / **TOTAL TIME**: 25 MINUTES

Mackerel is a very popular fish in Japan and the most delicious and easiest way to enjoy it is "salt grilling," known as shioyaki in Japan. If you don't have a grill or don't feel like grilling, you can also broil the mackerel in your oven.

1. Rinse the mackerel under cold running water and place it in a container with a lid. Pour the sake over the mackerel and rub it into the fish. Cover the container and chill the mackerel in the refrigerator for 15 minutes. If time allows, chill for 30 minutes.

2. Prepare a grill for medium-high heat (450°F). Coat the rack lightly with nonstick cooking spray.

3. Remove the mackerel from the refrigerator and pat both sides dry with paper towels. Make three shallow, diagonal incisions on the skin side of each fillet. Generously season the fish with salt—sprinkling from a height will help distribute it evenly.

4. Place the mackerel on the grill, skin side down, and cook for 4 minutes. Carefully turn the mackerel over and grill until the mackerel is cooked through, about 3 minutes. Please keep in mind that the exact cooking time will vary depending on the heat of your grill and the thickness of the fish.

5. Remove the mackerel from the grill. Either serve with the sudachi and daikon, or drizzle soy sauce over the daikon.

INGREDIENTS:

4	SKIN-ON MACKEREL FILLETS
2	TABLESPOONS SAKE
	SALT, TO TASTE
2	SUDACHI OR PREFERRED CITRUS, HALVED, FOR SERVING (OPTIONAL)
¼	CUP GRATED DAIKON RADISH, FOR SERVING
	SOY SAUCE, TO TASTE (OPTIONAL)

Saba No Shioyaki, see page 221

SANMA NO SHIOYAKI

YIELD: 4 SERVINGS / **ACTIVE TIME:** 20 MINUTES / **TOTAL TIME:** 30 MINUTES

The Pacific saury, also known as mackerel pike, is typically enjoyed in the fall, when it is in season. In addition to the ubiquitous miso soup and rice, this dish is typically served with pickles.

1. Wash the fish in a bowl of cold water, gently rubbing it to remove any blood or debris from the surface. Drain the water, pat the fish dry, and generously season with salt. Rub the salt into the fish and let it rest for 5 minutes.

2. Place the water and sake in the bowl and wash the fish again. Remove it from the bowl and pat it dry with paper towels. Generously season with salt, rub the salt into the fish, and let it rest for 5 to 10 minutes.

3. Prepare a grill for medium-high heat (450°F). Coat the rack lightly with nonstick cooking spray.

4. Place the fish on the grill, directly over the heat source. Grill until it is cooked through, 5 to 7 minutes on each side.

5. Either serve with the sudachi and daikon, or drizzle soy sauce over the daikon.

INGREDIENTS:

4 WHOLE PACIFIC SAURY

SALT, TO TASTE

1 CUP WATER

6 TABLESPOONS SAKE

2 SUDACHI OR PREFERRED CITRUS, HALVED, FOR SERVING (OPTIONAL)

¼ CUP GRATED DAIKON RADISH, FOR SERVING

SOY SAUCE, TO TASTE (OPTIONAL)

FISH TERIYAKI

YIELD: 4 SERVINGS / **ACTIVE TIME:** 10 MINUTES / **TOTAL TIME:** 15 MINUTES

Although many people might associate teriyaki with chicken, in Japan fish is often the preferred choice for this cooking method. One of the most popular options is yellowtail, but this recipe is versatile and can be made with various types of fish, such as salmon, tuna, and cod.

1. Season the fish with the salt and let it sit for 15 minutes.

2. While the fish is resting, bring water to a boil in a large saucepan and prepare an ice bath. After 15 minutes, gently slip the fish into the boiling water for 10 seconds and then, using tongs, quickly transfer it to the ice bath.

3. After a few minutes, remove the fish from the ice bath and pat it dry with paper towels. Lightly dust the fish all over with the cornstarch.

4. Place the canola oil in a large skillet and warm it over medium heat. Place the fish in the pan, skin side down, and cook for 2 minutes. Carefully turn the fish over and cook until it is just about cooked through, about 2 minutes.

5. While the fish is cooking, quickly combine the soy sauce, mirin, sake, and sugar to make the teriyaki sauce.

6. Raise the heat to high and pour the teriyaki sauce over the fish. Cook for 30 seconds, allowing the sauce to bubble and thicken. Turn the fish over and cook until the interior is flaky and the outside is beautifully glazed with the teriyaki sauce, about 30 seconds. Serve immediately.

INGREDIENTS:

4	SKIN-ON FILLETS OF PREFERRED FISH
1	TEASPOON KOSHER SALT
2	TABLESPOONS CORNSTARCH
1	TABLESPOON CANOLA OIL
¼	CUP SOY SAUCE
¼	CUP MIRIN
¼	CUP SAKE
2	TEASPOONS SUGAR

Sanma No Shioyaki, see page 224

SABA NO MISONI

YIELD: 4 SERVINGS / ACTIVE TIME: 10 MINUTES / TOTAL TIME: 30 MINUTES

Here is one of the most common mackerel dishes in Japan, marrying the rich flavors of this particular fish with an equally robust sauce.

1. Bring water to a boil and prepare an ice bath. Make shallow cuts across the skin of the mackerel and place it in a baking dish. Pour the boiling water over it for 10 seconds and then use tongs to quickly transfer the mackerel to the ice bath.

2. Drain the mackerel and pat it dry with paper towels.

3. Place the water, sake, mirin, sugar, and ginger in a medium saucepan and bring to a boil over medium heat. Reduce the heat so that the mixture gently simmers. Carefully place the mackerel, skin side up, and mushrooms in the pan. Spoon the cooking liquid over the mackerel for 1 to 2 minutes. Place a drop lid, aluminum foil, or parchment paper on the surface and simmer for 10 minutes.

4. In a small bowl, combine the yellow miso paste and ¼ cup of the hot cooking liquid to create a loose miso mixture. Adjust the consistency with more cooking liquid if desired.

5. Remove the lid and arrange the eggplant and leek around the mackerel. Gently pour the miso mixture into the pan and simmer until the liquid has been reduced by half, occasionally spooning the cooking liquid over the mackerel to help it absorb more flavor.

6. To serve, divide the mackerel and vegetables among the serving plates, drizzle the reduced cooking liquid over each portion, and garnish with shiraganegi.

INGREDIENTS:

4	SKIN-ON MACKEREL FILLETS
¾	CUP WATER
½	CUP SAKE
1	TEASPOON MIRIN
2	TABLESPOONS SUGAR
4	SLICES OF FRESH GINGER
4	SHIITAKE MUSHROOMS, STEMMED
¼	CUP YELLOW MISO PASTE
1	JAPANESE EGGPLANT, CUT INTO STRIPS
	2-INCH PIECE OF JAPANESE LEEK, CHOPPED
	SHIRAGANEGI (SEE PAGE 206), FOR GARNISH

BAKED COD SAIKYO-YAKI

YIELD: 4 SERVINGS / **ACTIVE TIME:** 15 MINUTES / **TOTAL TIME:** 1 TO 2 DAYS

Saikyo-yaki is a traditional dish where fish gets marinated in Saikyo Miso, a sweet white miso paste originating from Kyoto, and then grilled. This oven-baked version of saikyo-yaki simplifies the cooking process, making it almost impossible to go awry.

1. Sprinkle the salt and sugar over the cod and let it sit for 30 minutes. This process helps to remove any fishy odor.

2. While the cod is resting, place the white miso, sake, and mirin in a container large enough to hold the cod and stir to combine.

3. Rinse the cod under cold water and pat it dry with paper towels.

4. Place the cod in the marinade and turn to ensure it is completely coated. Marinate the cod in the refrigerator for at least 1 day. If time allows, marinate the cod for 2 days.

5. Preheat the oven to 390°F. Line a baking sheet with parchment paper. Remove the cod from the marinade and rinse it under cold water. Pat the cod dry with paper towels and place it on the baking sheet.

6. Place the baking sheet on the lower rack in the oven and bake for 7 minutes. Transfer the pan to the upper rack and bake for another 3 minutes. These cook times are estimates, and can vary depending on the thickness of your cod and the efficiency of your oven.

7. Remove the cod from the oven and serve immediately.

INGREDIENTS:

½	TEASPOON KOSHER SALT
½	TEASPOON SUGAR
4	COD FILLETS
⅓	CUP WHITE MISO PASTE
1½	TABLESPOONS SAKE
1½	TABLESPOONS MIRIN

SAKANA NO NITSUKE

YIELD: 4 SERVINGS / **ACTIVE TIME:** 10 MINUTES / **TOTAL TIME:** 45 MINUTES

This recipe can work with all kinds of whitefish, so it's a must-try for seafood lovers.

1. Bring some water to a boil. Prepare an ice bath. Season the fish with salt and let it rest for 10 minutes.

2. Using a sharp knife, cut a shallow cross on the fish's skin. Pour the boiling water into a heatproof bowl and, using tongs, place the fish in it for 5 seconds. Transfer the fish to the ice bath, drain, and pat it dry. Set the fish aside.

3. Bring water to a boil in a large saucepan. Prepare another ice bath. Place the water, sake, mirin, and sugar in a medium saucepan and warm over medium heat, stirring until the sugar dissolves. Add the ginger and fish, skin side up, and bring the broth to a gentle boil. Reduce the heat so that it simmers and place a drop lid, aluminum foil, or parchment paper on the surface. Simmer for 3 minutes.

4. Remove the lid and pour the soy sauce over the fish 1 tablespoon at a time, spooning the broth over the fish to incorporate the soy sauce. Place the lid back on the surface and simmer for 10 minutes.

5. Add the bok choy to the boiling water and cook for 1 minute. Drain and transfer it to the ice bath to cool. Drain, squeeze the bok choy to remove any excess water, and cut it into 2-inch pieces. Set the bok choy aside.

6. Remove the lid from the surface of the broth and cook until the broth has reduced to one-third of its original volume, basting the fish as the broth reduces.

7. Divide the fish among the serving plates and top each portion with some of the ginger and a few tablespoons of the reduced broth. Squeeze the bok choy once again to remove any excess water from it and serve it alongside the fish.

INGREDIENTS:

4	SKIN-ON FILLETS OF PREFERRED FISH
	SALT, TO TASTE
⅓	CUP WATER
⅓	CUP SAKE
3	TABLESPOONS MIRIN
3	TABLESPOONS SUGAR
2	TABLESPOONS SLICED FRESH GINGER
3	TABLESPOONS SOY SAUCE
2	BOK CHOY

YELLOWTAIL YUAN-YAKI

YIELD: 4 SERVINGS / ACTIVE TIME: 10 MINUTES / TOTAL TIME: 50 MINUTES

The base of yuan-ji is sake, soy sauce, mirin, and yuzu, though other citrus fruits are usually added to give it a uniquely fresh aroma.

1. Prepare a grill for medium-high heat (about 450°F). Season the yellowtail with salt and let it sit for 10 minutes.

2. Combine the sake, mirin, soy sauce, and yuzu in a resealable plastic bag large enough to hold the yellowtail. Pat the yellowtail dry with paper towels and place it in the marinade, making sure it is completely coated. Seal the bag and marinate the yellowtail in the refrigerator for 30 minutes.

3. Place the yellowtail on the grill, skin side up, and grill for 8 minutes. Carefully turn the yellowtail over and cook until it is cooked through, about 2 minutes. Serve immediately.

INGREDIENTS:

4	SKIN-ON YELLOWTAIL FILLETS
½	TEASPOON KOSHER SALT
2	TABLESPOONS SAKE
2	TABLESPOONS MIRIN
2	TABLESPOONS SOY SAUCE
1	YUZU OR PREFERRED CITRUS, SLICED

MACKEREL UME-NI

YIELD: 4 SERVINGS / **ACTIVE TIME:** 10 MINUTES / **TOTAL TIME:** 45 MINUTES

U me-ni is a distinctive simmered dish that incorporates the unique flavor of umeboshi into its base. Typically prepared with sardines or chicken, this variation uses mackerel, which is an excellent choice due to umeboshi's ability to neutralize the fish's pungent odor.

1. Season the mackerel with the salt and let it rest in the refrigerator for 30 minutes.

2. Place the water and kombu in a medium saucepan and let the kombu soak for 30 minutes.

3. Pat the mackerel dry with paper towels and add it to the pan along with the Umeboshi, ginger, sake, mirin, soy sauce, and sugar. Place the pan over medium heat and bring the mixture to a boil. Remove the kombu and reduce the heat to medium-low. Cover the pan and let the dish simmer for 15 minutes.

4. Carefully transfer the mackerel to a serving dish. Top it with the cooked Umeboshi, garnish with the shiso leaves, and serve.

INGREDIENTS:

4	MACKEREL FILLETS
¼	TEASPOON KOSHER SALT
1	CUP WATER
	3 X 4–INCH SHEET OF DRIED KOMBU
10	UMEBOSHI (SEE PAGE 329), LIGHTLY CRUSHED BY HAND
4	THIN SLICES OF FRESH GINGER
¼	CUP SAKE
¼	CUP MIRIN
2	TABLESPOONS SOY SAUCE
1½	TEASPOONS SUGAR
6	SHISO LEAVES, SLICED THIN, FOR GARNISH

SALMON NANBAN-YAKI

YIELD: 4 SERVINGS / **ACTIVE TIME:** 10 MINUTES / **TOTAL TIME:** 20 MINUTES

Salmon nanban yaki is a simple dish made with salmon fillets topped with a sweet and tangy sauce. To create a slight twist on the traditional nanban sauce, I used grated radish instead of leeks or chile pepper to create a sauce with a slight pungency. In addition, the salmon is covered with cornstarch before cooking to make it crispy, creating an enjoyable contrast to the sauce.

1. To begin preparations for the salmon, season the salmon with salt and let it sit for 10 minutes.

2. While the salmon is resting, prepare the sauce. Place all of the ingredients in a bowl and whisk to combine. Set the sauce aside.

3. Place the cornstarch in a shallow bowl and dredge the salmon in the cornstarch until it is lightly coated.

4. Place the canola oil in a large skillet and warm it over medium heat. Add the salmon, skin side down, and cook for 8 minutes. Carefully turn the salmon over and cook for 2 minutes.

5. Pour the sauce over the salmon and carefully turn it so that every bit of its surface comes into contact with the sauce. Let the sauce simmer for 30 seconds to 1 minute. Transfer the salmon to a serving dish, pour any remaining sauce from the pan over the top, and serve.

INGREDIENTS:

FOR THE SALMON

4	SKIN-ON SALMON FILLETS
¼	TEASPOON KOSHER SALT
2	TABLESPOONS CORNSTARCH
1	TABLESPOON CANOLA OIL

FOR THE SAUCE

¼	CUP GRATED DAIKON RADISH
¼	CUP LIGHT SOY SAUCE
¼	CUP MIRIN
1	TABLESPOON RICE VINEGAR
1½	TEASPOONS DARK SOY SAUCE

SALMON CHAN CHAN-YAKI

YIELD: 4 SERVINGS / **ACTIVE TIME:** 20 MINUTES / **TOTAL TIME:** 30 MINUTES

Salmon chan chan-yaki is a regional dish from Hokkaido featuring succulent salmon caught in the fall and winter, alongside an assortment of seasonal vegetables. The rich, umami-packed sauce harmonizes well with freshly cooked white rice.

1. To begin preparations for the salmon, season the salmon with the salt and pepper. Place half of the canola oil in a large skillet and warm it over medium heat. Add the salmon and cook until it is lightly browned on both sides, turning it over once. Remove the salmon from the pan and place it on a plate.

2. Add the remaining canola oil and warm it over medium heat. Add the onion and carrot and cook, stirring occasionally, until they start to soften, about 5 minutes.

3. Add the mushrooms and cabbage and cook, stirring occasionally, until the cabbage starts to soften, 5 to 8 minutes.

4. While the vegetables are cooking, prepare the sauce. Place all of the ingredients in a bowl and whisk to combine.

5. Return the salmon to the pan, placing it on top of the vegetables. Add the butter, pour the sauce over the salmon and vegetables, and reduce the heat to low. Cover the pan and steam the salmon and vegetables until they are cooked to your liking, about 5 minutes.

6. Uncover the pan, season the dish with pepper, and serve.

INGREDIENTS:

FOR THE SALMON

4	SKINLESS SALMON FILLETS
¼	TEASPOON KOSHER SALT
¼	TEASPOON BLACK PEPPER, PLUS MORE TO TASTE
2	TABLESPOONS CANOLA OIL
1	ONION, SLICED
1	CARROT, PEELED AND JULIENNED
2	KING OYSTER MUSHROOMS, CHOPPED
4	CUPS CHOPPED GREEN CABBAGE
1	TABLESPOON UNSALTED BUTTER

FOR THE SAUCE

5	TABLESPOONS YELLOW MISO PASTE
1	TABLESPOON SUGAR
1	TABLESPOON MIRIN
¼	CUP SAKE
2	TABLESPOONS FINELY CHOPPED GREEN ONION
	BLACK PEPPER, TO TASTE

MEAT

While vegetarian and seafood dishes form the foundation of Japanese cuisine, recipes built around meat are the epitome of modern Japanese cuisine, a claim that is supported by the reality that many of the dishes known worldwide as staples of Japanese cuisine are meat-based. In this section, I will introduce recipes using mainly chicken, pork, and beef. Notably, chicken and pork are often interchangeable in many of these recipes, allowing you to adapt them to your own tastes and preferences.

TERIYAKI CHICKEN

YIELD: 4 SERVINGS / **ACTIVE TIME:** 10 MINUTES / **TOTAL TIME:** 15 MINUTES

Did you know that in Japan "teriyaki" refers not to a sauce or marinade but to a cooking technique? This cooking method involves pan-frying food while coating it with a sweet-and-savory sauce made with soy sauce, mirin, sake, and sugar. This teriyaki chicken recipe follows the 1:1:1:0.5 ratio that is known as the golden teriyaki ratio in Japan.

1. Place the chicken on a cutting board, skin side down. Make horizontal incisions in the thickest parts of the chicken, creating small flaps. Gently pull these flaps outward to even out the thickness of the chicken. If large skin-on, boneless chicken thighs similar to that featured in the photo on pages 242–243 are not available, cut the chicken into bite-size pieces.

2. Flip the chicken over and pierce the skin all over with a fork. Pat the chicken dry with paper towels. Combine the salt, pepper, and cornstarch, dust the chicken with the mixture until it is completely coated, and shake off any excess.

3. Place the canola oil in a large skillet and place the chicken in the pan, skin side down. If the pan is too small to accommodate all of the chicken, it's best to cook it in two batches. Gently move the chicken in a circular motion to coat the skin and the pan with the canola oil.

4. Set the heat to medium and fry the chicken for 7 minutes, occasionally rotating it to ensure that the skin browns evenly.

5. While the chicken is cooking, prepare the teriyaki sauce by placing the soy sauce, mirin, sake, and sugar in a small bowl and whisking until well combined.

6. Turn the chicken over and cook for 2 minutes. If there's excess fat in the pan, carefully dab it away with a paper towel. Raise the heat to medium-high and pour the teriyaki sauce into the pan. Continually spoon the sauce over the chicken and cook until the sauce becomes thick and glossy.

7. Remove the chicken from the pan and let it rest for a few minutes. Cut the chicken into strips, drizzle any teriyaki sauce left in the pan over it, and serve.

INGREDIENTS:

2½	LBS. BONELESS, SKIN-ON CHICKEN THIGHS
	PINCH OF KOSHER SALT
	PINCH OF BLACK PEPPER
¼	CUP CORNSTARCH
1	TABLESPOON CANOLA OIL
6	TABLESPOONS SOY SAUCE
6	TABLESPOONS MIRIN
6	TABLESPOONS SAKE
3	TABLESPOONS SUGAR

SHOGAYAKI

YIELD: 4 SERVINGS / **ACTIVE TIME:** 10 MINUTES / **TOTAL TIME:** 15 MINUTES

Despite its name, which translates to "fried ginger," shogayaki typically refers to Japanese-style ginger pork. This quick recipe, ready in just 15 minutes, captures the authentic taste one might expect at a traditional Japanese teishoku-ya.

1. Place the ginger, apple, garlic, soy sauce, sake, mirin, honey, salt, pepper, and flour in a mixing bowl and stir until well combined.

2. Add the pork and stir until it is completely coated. If you're looking for a more intensely flavored shogayaki, marinate the pork in the refrigerator for 10 to 20 minutes.

3. Place the canola oil and red pepper flakes in a large skillet and warm over medium heat. Add the pork and the marinade and stir-fry over medium heat, using chopsticks to break up the pork as it cooks. Cook until the pork is browned all over.

4. Add the onions to the pan and stir-fry until they have softened to your liking.

5. Raise the heat to high and stir-fry until most of the moisture in the pan has evaporated and the sauce has thickened and is clinging to the pork and onions. Serve immediately.

INGREDIENTS:

- 3 TABLESPOONS GRATED FRESH GINGER
- 2 TABLESPOONS GRATED APPLE
- 2 GARLIC CLOVES, GRATED
- ¼ CUP SOY SAUCE
- ¼ CUP SAKE
- ¼ CUP MIRIN
- 2 TEASPOONS HONEY
- PINCH OF KOSHER SALT
- PINCH OF BLACK PEPPER
- 1 TABLESPOON CAKE FLOUR
- 1½ LBS. PORK LOIN, SLICED THIN AND CHOPPED
- 1 TABLESPOON CANOLA OIL
- 2 TEASPOONS RED PEPPER FLAKES
- 2 MEDIUM ONIONS, CUT INTO WEDGES

Teriyaki Chicken, see page 240

TONTEKI

YIELD: 4 SERVINGS / **ACTIVE TIME:** 15 MINUTES / **TOTAL TIME:** 20 MINUTES

Tonteki is a Japanese pork steak, offering an exquisite taste experience with its rich and dark Worcestershire-based sauce and crispy fried garlic. This dish, a fusion of "ton" (pork) and "teki" (steak), is often served with rice and miso soup.

1. To prepare the sauce, place all of the ingredients in a bowl and whisk until well combined. Place the sauce by the stove for later.

2. To begin preparations for the pork, cut three to four slits, each about ½ inch apart, all the way through the fatty edges of the pork chops. Season both sides of the pork chops with salt and pepper.

3. Place the canola oil in a large skillet and warm it over medium heat. Add the garlic and pork chops, cover the pan, and cook for 3 minutes.

4. Reduce the heat slightly, turn the pork chops over, and cover the pan. Cook until the pork is cooked through, about 3 minutes. If your pork chops are very thick, they may require additional cooking time. You want the interior to be around 145°F.

5. Uncover the pan and pour the sauce over the pork chops. Cook, stirring occasionally, until the sauce has nicely coated the pork and garlic. Serve alongside shredded green cabbage.

INGREDIENTS:

FOR THE SAUCE

- ¼ CUP WORCESTERSHIRE SAUCE
- 2 TABLESPOONS SOY SAUCE
- 2 TABLESPOONS MIRIN
- 1½ TEASPOONS HONEY
- 1½ TEASPOONS SUGAR
- 2 TEASPOONS UNSALTED BUTTER, MELTED
- 1½ TEASPOONS GARLIC PASTE

FOR THE PORK

- 4 THICK BONELESS PORK CHOPS
- SALT AND PEPPER, TO TASTE
- 2 TABLESPOONS CANOLA OIL
- 8 GARLIC CLOVES, PEELED AND CUT INTO THIRDS LENGTHWAYS
- GREEN CABBAGE, SHREDDED, FOR SERVING

MISO-MARINATED BEEF STEAKS

YIELD: 2 SERVINGS / **ACTIVE TIME:** 15 MINUTES / **TOTAL TIME:** 25 HOURS

This dish is a celebration of the country's iconic flavors, marrying the rich umami of miso, the depth of sake, and the delicate sweetness of mirin and sugar.

1. Place the yellow miso, sugar, sake, mirin, ginger, and garlic in a bowl and whisk to combine. Spread half of the marinade evenly over the bottom of a container that is large enough to hold the steaks and mushrooms.

2. Place the steaks and mushrooms on top of the marinade and pour the remaining marinade over them, making sure that they are well coated.

3. Place a piece of plastic wrap directly on the surface of the steaks and mushrooms, cover the container with more plastic wrap, and let the steaks and mushrooms marinate in the refrigerator for 1 day.

4. Remove the steaks and mushrooms from the marinade and use paper towels to wipe off any excess marinade, as any residue left behind may burn quickly during cooking.

5. Place the canola oil in a large skillet and warm it over medium-high heat. Carefully place the steaks and mushrooms in the pan, immediately reduce the heat to low, and cook until the steaks and mushrooms are browned on one side. To prevent them from burning, keep the heat on low throughout the cooking process.

6. Turn the steaks and mushrooms over and cook until they are browned and cooked to your liking. Remove them from the pan, wrap them in aluminum foil, and let them rest for 5 minutes.

7. Slice the steaks and serve them alongside the mushrooms.

INGREDIENTS:

3	TABLESPOONS YELLOW MISO PASTE
2	TABLESPOONS SUGAR
2	TABLESPOONS SAKE
1	TEASPOON MIRIN
1	TEASPOON GRATED FRESH GINGER
1	TEASPOON GRATED GARLIC
2	BEEF STEAKS
4	SHIITAKE MUSHROOMS, STEMMED
1	TABLESPOON CANOLA OIL

CHICKEN NANBAN

YIELD: 4 SERVINGS / **ACTIVE TIME**: 30 MINUTES / **TOTAL TIME**: 30 MINUTES

A delicious dish from Miyazaki Prefecture that is considered soul food there. Enjoy this with a simple salad.

1. To begin preparations for the chicken, pierce it all over with a fork. Slice it, transfer the chicken to a bowl or container, and season with the salt and pepper. Set the chicken aside.

2. To prepare the sauce, place all of the ingredients in a saucepan and bring to a boil over medium heat, stirring occasionally. Reduce the heat and let the sauce simmer for 30 seconds. Remove the pan from heat and set the sauce aside.

3. Place each of the eggs in a separate bowl. Place the cake flour in another bowl. Place the chicken in the bowl containing one of the eggs and let it sit.

4. Add canola oil to a large, deep skillet until it is about ½ inch deep and warm it to 340°F.

5. Dredge the chicken in the flour until it is lightly coated, dip it into the other bowl containing an egg, and then gently slip it into the hot oil. Fry until the chicken is golden brown, crispy, and cooked through, about 6 minutes, turning it over halfway through.

6. Transfer the chicken to a wire rack and let it drain.

7. Dip the fried chicken into the nanban sauce and arrange it on a serving dish. Spoon the Tartar Sauce over the chicken and serve.

INGREDIENTS:

FOR THE CHICKEN

1⅓	LBS. BONELESS, SKINLESS CHICKEN BREASTS
¼	TEASPOON KOSHER SALT
⅛	TEASPOON FRESHLY GROUND BLACK PEPPER
2	EGGS
⅓	CUP CAKE FLOUR
	CANOLA OIL, AS NEEDED

FOR THE SAUCE

1½	TABLESPOONS DARK SOY SAUCE
1	TABLESPOON LIGHT SOY SAUCE
2	TABLESPOONS SUGAR
3	TABLESPOONS RICE VINEGAR
1	TEASPOON MIRIN
⅛	TEASPOON SHICHIMI TOGARASHI
⅛	TEASPOON DASHI GRANULES
	TARTAR SAUCE (SEE PAGE 680), FOR SERVING

Chicken Nanban, see page 247

CHICKEN HAMBAGU WITH UME-AN SAUCE

YIELD: 4 SERVINGS / ACTIVE TIME: 30 MINUTES / TOTAL TIME: 30 MINUTES

Although Western-inspired hambagu made with beef or pork is the most common type in Japan, Japanese-flavored hambagu is usually made with ground chicken.

1. To begin preparations for the hambagu, place half of the canola oil in a large skillet and warm it over medium heat. Add the mushrooms and onion, season with the salt and pepper, and cook, stirring occasionally, until the onion starts to brown, about 8 minutes. Transfer the mixture to a bowl and let it cool.

2. To prepare the sauce, place the Umeboshi, dashi, rice vinegar, and soy sauce in a medium saucepan and bring to a boil over medium heat. Place the tapioca starch and water in a small bowl and whisk to combine. While whisking continually, add the slurry to the pan and cook until the sauce has thickened. Remove the pan from heat and set the sauce aside.

3. Place the chicken, tapioca starch, soy sauce, mirin, sugar, shiso leaves, mayonnaise, miso paste, and mushroom mixture in a mixing bowl and work the resulting mixture until it is well combined. Form the mixture into four to eight patties, depending on your preferred hambagu size.

4. Place the remaining canola oil in a clean large skillet and warm it over medium heat. Add the hambagu and cook until they are lightly browned on both sides, turning them over once.

5. Reduce the heat to low, cover the pan, and let the hambagu cook for 3 minutes. Turn them over and cook until the hambagu are cooked through, about 2 minutes.

6. Divide the hambagu among the serving plates, pour the sauce over each portion, garnish with additional shiso leaves, and serve.

INGREDIENTS:

FOR THE HAMBAGU

1   TABLESPOON CANOLA OIL

2   SHIITAKE MUSHROOMS, STEMMED AND FINELY DICED

1   ONION, FINELY DICED

¼   TEASPOON KOSHER SALT

⅛   TEASPOON BLACK PEPPER

1   LB. GROUND CHICKEN

2   TABLESPOONS TAPIOCA STARCH

1   TABLESPOON SOY SAUCE

1   TABLESPOON MIRIN

1   TEASPOON SUGAR

10 SHISO LEAVES, SLICED THIN, PLUS MORE FOR GARNISH

2   TABLESPOONS JAPANESE MAYONNAISE (SEE PAGE 46)

2   TEASPOONS YELLOW MISO PASTE

FOR THE SAUCE

5   UMEBOSHI (SEE PAGE 329), SEEDED AND MASHED

¾   CUP AWASE DASHI STOCK (SEE PAGE 38)

1   TABLESPOON RICE VINEGAR

1   TABLESPOON SOY SAUCE

2   TEASPOONS TAPIOCA STARCH

2   TEASPOONS WATER

LEMON TERIYAKI PORK

YIELD: 2 SERVINGS / **ACTIVE TIME:** 15 MINUTES / **TOTAL TIME:** 20 MINUTES

In Japan, the teriyaki method is most commonly used for cooking fish and chicken, but it is a versatile technique that works well with many ingredients. This recipe offers a refreshing twist on classic teriyaki, coating pork chops in a tangy lemon glaze that is sweetened with a touch of honey.

---

1. Place the pork chops on a cutting board and make a series of shallow cuts in their thick fatty edges. This will prevent the pork chops from curling during cooking. Season the pork chops with the salt and set them aside.

2. Warm a large skillet over medium-low heat. Add the canola oil and garlic and stir-fry until the garlic is golden brown and crispy. Carefully remove the garlic chips from the pan and place them on a paper towel–lined plate to drain.

3. Raise the heat to medium-high, add the pork chops, and sear until golden brown, 1½ to 2 minutes. Turn the pork chops over, reduce the heat to medium-low, and cover the pan. Cook until they are just about cooked through (the interior is 135°F), 3 to 4 minutes, making sure not to overcook them.

4. Place the soy sauce, mirin, sake, and honey in a bowl and whisk until well combined.

5. Add the mushroom and sauce to the pan and cook, stirring frequently, until the mushroom is tender and the sauce thickens slightly.

6. Add the lemon to the pan and raise the heat to medium. Cook until the sauce is syrupy and the pork chops are well coated with it.

7. Transfer the pork chops to the serving plates and let them rest for 3 minutes.

8. Top the pork chops with the lemon, mushroom, garlic chips, and any remaining sauce and serve.

INGREDIENTS:

2	THICK PORK CHOPS
2	PINCHES OF KOSHER SALT
1	TABLESPOON CANOLA OIL
1	GARLIC CLOVE, SLICED THIN
2	TABLESPOONS SOY SAUCE
2	TABLESPOONS MIRIN
2	TABLESPOONS SAKE
1½	TEASPOONS HONEY
1	KING OYSTER MUSHROOM, FINELY DICED
4	LEMON SLICES

CHICKEN DRUMSTICK SAPPARI-NI

YIELD: 4 SERVINGS / ACTIVE TIME: 20 MINUTES / TOTAL TIME: 40 MINUTES

The term sappari means "refreshing," and this dish embodies this concept beautifully, as the vinegar-rich seasoning imparts a bright and invigorating flavor.

1. Place half of the sesame oil in a large skillet and warm it over medium heat. Add the drumsticks and cook until they are browned all over, turning them as necessary. Remove the drumsticks from the pan and set them aside.

2. Add the remaining sesame oil to the pan and warm it over medium heat. Add the garlic and ginger and cook, stirring frequently, for 2 minutes.

3. Add the water, vinegar, sugar, soy sauce, and sake and bring to a boil. Reduce the heat to low, return the browned drumsticks to the pan, add the eggs, and place a drop lid, aluminum foil, or parchment paper on the surface. Simmer for 10 minutes.

4. Stir the dish, remove the drop-lid, and simmer for another 10 minutes.

5. Remove the eggs, place them in a bowl of cold water, and let them sit for 10 minutes.

6. Peel the eggs, halve them, and divide them and the sappari-ni among the serving plates. Garnish with shiraganegi and serve.

INGREDIENTS:

1	TABLESPOON SESAME OIL
8	CHICKEN DRUMSTICKS
1	GARLIC CLOVE, SLICED
4	SLICES OF FRESH GINGER
1	CUP WATER
½	CUP RICE VINEGAR
2	TABLESPOONS SUGAR
3	TABLESPOONS SOY SAUCE
3	TABLESPOONS SAKE
4	EGGS, IN THEIR SHELLS
	SHIRAGANEGI (SEE PAGE 206), FOR GARNISH

BAKED CHICKEN KATSU

YIELD: 2 SERVINGS/ **ACTIVE TIME**: 15 MINUTES / **TOTAL TIME**: 40 MINUTES

Although katsu dishes are typically associated with the crispy, golden delights born from a deep fryer, baking them in the oven is also possible, as this lighter but still flavorful preparation shows.

1. Preheat the oven to 430°F. Set a wire rack in a baking sheet. Warm a dry skillet over medium heat. Add the panko and toast, stirring frequently, until it is nicely browned. Transfer the toasted panko to a bowl and let it cool until it is comfortable to handle.

2. Using a fork, pierce the chicken all over. Season it with the salt and pepper, transfer the chicken to a bowl, and lightly dust it with the flour. Add the mayonnaise and stir until the chicken is completely coated. Set the chicken aside.

3. Dredge the chicken in the panko until it is completely coated and place it on the wire rack.

4. Place the chicken on the lower rack in the oven and bake for 10 minutes.

5. Remove the chicken from the oven and carefully turn it over. Return the chicken to the oven and bake until it is crispy, golden brown, and cooked through (the interior is 165°F), about 15 minutes.

6. While the chicken is in the oven, place the remaining ingredients in a bowl and whisk to combine.

7. Remove the chicken from the oven and serve it with the sauce.

INGREDIENTS:

- ¾ CUP NAMA PANKO (SEE PAGE 66)
- 1 LB. BONELESS, SKINLESS CHICKEN BREASTS, CUT INTO ½-INCH SLICES
- PINCH OF KOSHER SALT
- PINCH OF BLACK PEPPER
- 1 TABLESPOON ALL-PURPOSE FLOUR
- 2 TABLESPOONS JAPANESE MAYONNAISE (SEE PAGE 46)
- 2 TABLESPOONS TOASTED SESAME SEEDS, GROUND
- 2 TEASPOONS SOY SAUCE
- 2 TEASPOONS WORCESTERSHIRE SAUCE
- 1 TABLESPOON KETCHUP
- 1 TEASPOON SUGAR
- 4 TEASPOONS WATER

Baked Chicken Katsu, see page 255

CHICKEN MISO YUAN-YAKI

YIELD: 4 SERVINGS / **ACTIVE TIME:** 10 MINUTES / **TOTAL TIME:** 45 MINUTES

This recipe features a twist on the traditional Japanese marinade yuan-ji, incorporating miso paste, an addition that adds depth and complexity while still retaining the original blend's aromatic notes of citrus notes.

1. Using a fork, pierce the chicken all over. Place the yuzu, soy sauces, sake, mirin, and white miso in a bowl and stir to combine. Transfer the marinade to a resealable plastic bag and add the chicken, making sure it is completely coated. Seal the bag and let the chicken marinate in the refrigerator for 30 minutes.

2. Preheat the oven to 390°F. Line a baking sheet with parchment paper.

3. Remove the chicken from the marinade and place it on the baking sheet, skin side up. Reserve the marinade. If using shishito peppers, place them alongside the chicken. Place the pan on the lower rack of the oven and bake for 10 minutes.

4. Remove the pan from the oven and brush the chicken with some of the leftover marinade. Place the pan on the upper rack in the oven and bake until the chicken is cooked through (the interior is 165°F), 5 to 10 minutes.

5. Remove the pan from the oven and transfer the chicken and peppers to a serving dish. Garnish with strips of yuzu peel and grated radish and serve.

INGREDIENTS:

4 BONELESS, SKIN-ON CHICKEN THIGHS

1 YUZU, SLICED

1½ TABLESPOONS LIGHT SOY SAUCE

1½ TABLESPOONS DARK SOY SAUCE

3 TABLESPOONS SAKE

3 TABLESPOONS MIRIN

3 TABLESPOONS WHITE MISO PASTE

8 SHISHITO PEPPERS (OPTIONAL)

STRIPS OF YUZU PEEL, FOR GARNISH

DAIKON RADISH, GRATED, FOR GARNISH

PORK RIKYU-YAKI

YIELD: 4 SERVINGS / **ACTIVE TIME:** 10 MINUTES / **TOTAL TIME:** 50 MINUTES

This dish pays tribute to renowned tea master Sen no Rikyu and his love for sesame seeds. Although this recipe uses pork, the sesame-spiked sauce can also be used with whitefish.

1. Place the sake, mirin, soy sauce, and sesame paste in a bowl and stir to combine. Transfer the marinade to a resealable plastic bag, add the pork chops, seal the bag, and massage the marinade into the pork chops, making sure they are completely coated. Let the pork chops marinate in the refrigerator for 30 minutes.

2. Preheat the oven to 425°F. Line a baking sheet with parchment paper.

3. Remove the pork chops from the marinade, place them on the baking sheet, and sprinkle the sesame seeds over the top. If using the shishito peppers, place them alongside the pork. Place the pan on the upper rack in the oven and bake until the pork is cooked through (the interior is 145°F), about 15 minutes.

4. Remove the pan from the oven and let the pork chops rest for 2 minutes before serving.

INGREDIENTS:

2	TABLESPOONS SAKE
2	TABLESPOONS MIRIN
2	TABLESPOONS SOY SAUCE
1	TABLESPOON SESAME PASTE
4	PORK CHOPS
¼	CUP SESAME SEEDS
8	SHISHITO PEPPERS (OPTIONAL)

SOY-GLAZED ROASTED CHICKEN LEGS

YIELD: 4 SERVINGS / **ACTIVE TIME:** 10 MINUTES / **TOTAL TIME:** 1 HOUR

The addition of citrus adds a zesty, festive flavor to this recipe, which is popular around Christmastime—though it is a versatile dish that can be enjoyed year round.

1. Pat the chicken legs dry with paper towels. Turn them over and cut along each side of the bones. Find the joints where the drumsticks and thighs are connected and cut through them. Pierce the chicken all over with a fork.

2. Place the chicken in a resealable plastic bag and add the yuzu zest, yuzu juice, soy sauce, sake, and mirin, season with salt and pepper, seal the bag, and massage the marinade into the chicken. Marinate the chicken in the refrigerator for 30 minutes to 1 hour. Be careful not to let it marinate for too long, as the flavor can become overpowering.

3. Preheat the oven to 390°F. Line a baking sheet with parchment paper.

4. Remove the chicken from the marinade and place it on the baking sheet. Place the marinade in a small saucepan. Place the pan on the lower rack in the oven and roast until the chicken is almost cooked through (the interior is 160°F), about 18 minutes.

5. While the chicken is in the oven, bring the marinade to a boil, reduce the heat to medium-low, and stir in the sugar. Simmer until the mixture is glossy and has thickened. Remove the pan from heat and set the glaze aside.

6. Remove the chicken from the oven and brush it with the glaze. Return it to the oven, this time on the upper rack, and roast for 1 minute. Remove the chicken from the oven and brush it with the glaze once again. Return it to the upper rack in the oven and roast for another minute. Remove the chicken from the oven, wrap the exposed bones with aluminum foil so that you can hold it, and serve.

INGREDIENTS:

4	SKIN-ON CHICKEN LEG QUARTERS
	ZEST AND JUICE OF 2 YUZU
¼	CUP SOY SAUCE
3	TABLESPOONS SAKE
2	TABLESPOONS MIRIN
	SALT AND PEPPER, TO TASTE
1	TABLESPOON SUGAR

Soy-Glazed Roasted Chicken Legs, see page 261

GOYA CHAMPURU

YIELD: 4 SERVINGS / **ACTIVE TIME:** 20 MINUTES / **TOTAL TIME:** 25 MINUTES

This is a homestyle dish from Okinawa that is typically enjoyed in the summer. The star of this simple stir-fry is the bitter melon, a seasonal vegetable known in Japanese as goya, which is prized for its distinctive flavor.

1. Cut the bitter melons in half lengthwise, scoop out the seeds, and discard them. Cut the melons into thick slices and place them in a bowl. Add the salt and sugar and massage them over the melons until they are evenly covered. Let the melons sit for 10 minutes. Rinse them under cold water and set them aside.

2. Drain the tofu and wrap it in paper towels, place it on a plate, place it in the microwave, and microwave on high for 1½ minutes to evaporate any excess moisture. Remove the tofu from the microwave, let it cool for a few minutes, and cut it into large cubes.

3. Place the canola oil in a large skillet and warm it over medium heat. Add the tofu and cook until it is browned all over, turning it as necessary. Transfer the tofu to a plate and set it aside.

4. Add the pork belly, season with salt and the pepper, and cook until it is seared on both sides, turning it over once. Return the browned tofu to the pan, add the melons, dashi granules, miso paste, sake, oyster sauce, and soy sauce, stir to incorporate, and cook for 2 to 3 minutes.

5. Pour the eggs into the pan and cook, not mixing the dish, until the eggs are just set.

6. Divide the dish among the serving plates, garnish with bonito flakes, and serve.

INGREDIENTS:

2	GOYA (OKINAWAN BITTER MELONS)
1	TEASPOON KOSHER SALT, PLUS MORE TO TASTE
½	TEASPOON SUGAR
14	OZ. FIRM TOFU
2	TABLESPOONS CANOLA OIL
⅔	LB. PORK BELLY, SLICED THIN
2	PINCHES OF BLACK PEPPER
1	TEASPOON DASHI GRANULES
1½	TEASPOONS YELLOW MISO PASTE
1	TABLESPOON SAKE
1½	TEASPOONS OYSTER SAUCE
1½	TEASPOONS SOY SAUCE
2	EGGS, BEATEN
	BONITO FLAKES, FOR GARNISH

MISO STIR-FRY

YIELD: 4 SERVINGS / **ACTIVE TIME:** 15 MINUTES / **TOTAL TIME:** 15 MINUTES

This dish showcases the beautiful combination of pork, eggplant, and green bell pepper. The rich umami flavor of miso paste forms the base of this simple yet flavorful stir-fry, perfectly complementing the succulent pork and the vegetables' natural sweetness.

1. To prepare the sauce, place all of the ingredients in a bowl and whisk to combine. Set the sauce aside.

2. Place half of the canola oil in a large skillet or wok and warm it over medium heat. Add the garlic and ginger and cook, stirring frequently, for 2 minutes. Raise the heat to medium-high, add the pork belly, and stir-fry until it is evenly browned on all sides.

3. Add the eggplants, pepper, onion, and remaining canola oil to the pan and raise the heat to high. Stir-fry until the vegetables have softened slightly.

4. Pour the sauce into the pan and stir-fry until most of the liquid has evaporated and the sauce has thickened.

5. Remove the pan from heat, garnish with the sesame oil, green onions, and sesame seeds, and serve.

INGREDIENTS:

FOR THE SAUCE

⅓ CUP AWASE DASHI STOCK (SEE PAGE 38)

2½ TABLESPOONS YELLOW MISO PASTE

1 TABLESPOON SAKE

1½ TEASPOONS SOY SAUCE

1½ TEASPOONS SUGAR

1 TEASPOON CHILI BEAN PASTE

FOR THE STIR-FRY

2 TABLESPOONS CANOLA OIL

2 GARLIC CLOVES, MINCED

1½ TEASPOONS MINCED FRESH GINGER

1 LB. PORK BELLY OR PORK SHOULDER, SLICED THIN AND CUT INTO 1½-INCH-LONG PIECES

3 JAPANESE OR CHINESE EGGPLANTS, CUT INTO THICK STRIPS

1 GREEN BELL PEPPER, STEMMED, SEEDED, AND JULIENNED

½ ONION, SLICED

1 TEASPOON SESAME OIL, FOR GARNISH

GREEN ONIONS, FINELY CHOPPED, FOR GARNISH

SESAME SEEDS, FOR GARNISH

Miso Stir-Fry, see page 265

AGEMONO

*A*gemono is a Japanese term meaning "deep-fried dishes." However, many Japanese households nowadays substitute shallow frying for deep-frying, and many of the recipes presented here can also be made using the former method. If you choose to shallow fry, adjust the cooking time accordingly. For everyday cooking, rice bran oil is recommended due to its neutral flavor and high smoke point. For more delicate dishes such as tempura, untoasted extra-virgin sesame oil is favored among chefs.

TEMPURA

YIELD: 4 SERVINGS / **ACTIVE TIME:** 40 MINUTES / **TOTAL TIME:** 1 HOUR AND 30 MINUTES

Tempura might seem simple at first glance, but it's actually quite a challenge to perfect. The art of tempura lies in creating a light, crisp coating that doesn't absorb excess oil, enhancing rather than masking the natural flavors of the ingredients. This recipe has been carefully developed to ensure success in making an authentic tempura batter.

1. To begin preparations for the tempura, measure out the still water and sparkling water and chill them in the refrigerator for 20 to 30 minutes. Combine the cornstarch and flour in a bowl and chill it in the freezer for 20 to 30 minutes.

2. While waiting for the waters and flour mixture to chill, prepare the ingredients you are going to fry: the prawns, shiso leaves, peppers, mushrooms, pumpkin, nori, and eggplant. Pat them dry using paper towels and set them aside.

3. To prepare the sauce, combine the dashi, mirin, and soy sauce in a small saucepan and bring to a boil. Cook for 2 minutes, remove the pan from heat, and let the sauce cool. Transfer the cooled sauce to a container, cover it, and chill it in the refrigerator.

4. Add sesame oil to a Dutch oven until it is 2 inches deep and warm it to 355°F. Place a wire rack in a rimmed baking sheet.

5. Combine the chilled still water, chilled sparkling water, and ice cubes in a large bowl. Crack the egg into the bowl and whisk gently to combine. If any foam forms while mixing, scoop it out with a spoon.

6. Working in three increments, alternate between sifting the chilled flour mixture and adding the baking powder to the batter. Use chopsticks to gently incorporate the dry ingredients, drawing crosses through the mixture and making sure not to overmix. You don't need a smooth batter for tempura, it is normal to have a few lumps.

7. Test the hot oil's temperature by dropping a small amount of batter into it. If the batter sizzles and floats, the oil is hot enough.

8. Working in batches to prevent the pot from becoming overcrowded, coat the prawns, shiso leaves, peppers, mushrooms, pumpkin, nori, and eggplant in a light layer of flour, dip them into the batter until completely coated, and immediately place them in the hot oil. Fry until the ingredients are crispy but before they become golden brown.

9. Transfer the tempura to the wire rack to drain. When everything has been fried, serve the tempura with the chilled sauce.

INGREDIENTS:

FOR THE TEMPURA

¾ CUP WATER

¼ CUP SPARKLING WATER

¼ CUP CORNSTARCH

¾ CUP CAKE FLOUR, PLUS MORE AS NEEDED

8 PRAWNS, SHELLS REMOVED, DEVEINED

8 SHISO LEAVES

4 SHISHITO PEPPERS

4 SHIITAKE MUSHROOMS

FLESH OF ¼ PUMPKIN, SEEDED AND SLICED

1 SHEET OF SUSHI NORI, CUT INTO 4 STRIPS AND HALVED

1 JAPANESE EGGPLANT, QUARTERED

EXTRA-VIRGIN SESAME OIL OR RICE BRAN OIL, AS NEEDED

5 ICE CUBES

1 SMALL EGG, CHILLED

½ TEASPOON BAKING POWDER

FOR THE SAUCE

½ CUP AWASE DASHI STOCK (SEE PAGE 38)

1½ TABLESPOONS MIRIN

1½ TABLESPOONS SOY SAUCE

KANI KURIMU KOROKKE

YIELD: 4 SERVINGS / **ACTIVE TIME:** 45 MINUTES / **TOTAL TIME:** 1 HOUR AND 30 MINUTES

A Japanese-style croquette made with tender crabmeat and sweet onions bound together by a creamy béchamel sauce.

1. To begin preparations for the croquettes, place the butter in a small saucepan and warm it over medium-low heat. Add the onions and cook until they have softened, about 5 minutes. Stir in the crabmeat and ketchup, sprinkle the flour over the mixture, and stir until well combined. While stirring continually, add the milk in three increments, making sure to scrape the bottom and side of the pan as you stir.

2. Add the salt, pepper, nutmeg, and cheddar, reduce the heat to low, and continue to stir until the mixture has the consistency of mashed potatoes. Transfer the mixture to a wide container, spread it as thin as possible, and let it cool. Using multiple containers will speed up the cooling process. Once the mixture is cool to the touch, cover the container, and chill the mixture in the freezer for 30 minutes, making sure it does not solidify.

3. Add rice bran oil to a Dutch oven until it is about 2 inches deep and warm it to 355°F. Place a wire rack in a rimmed baking sheet.

4. To prepare the breading, place the water, egg, and flour in a bowl and whisk until the mixture comes together as a smooth batter. Place some flour in a shallow bowl. Place the panko in a separate shallow bowl.

5. Remove the crab mixture from the freezer and divide it into 16 equal pieces. Form each piece into a cylinder and then divide them into batches. The number of batches should be determined by the size of your Dutch oven. Work with one batch at a time and chill the others in the freezer.

6. Dredge the croquettes in the flour, dip them into the batter until completely coated, and then dredge them in the panko until they are generously coated. Gently slip the croquettes into the hot oil and fry until they are crispy and golden brown. Transfer the fried croquettes to the wire rack and repeat with the remaining batches of croquettes.

7. When all of the croquettes have been fried, prepare the sauce. Place the ketchup and Worcestershire sauce in a bowl and stir to combine. Either drizzle the sauce over the croquettes or serve it on the side.

INGREDIENTS:

FOR THE CROQUETTES

¼	CUP UNSALTED BUTTER
2	ONIONS, FINELY DICED
8½	OZ. CANNED WHITE CRABMEAT, DRAINED
2	TEASPOONS KETCHUP
½	CUP ALL-PURPOSE FLOUR, SIFTED
1⅔	CUPS WHOLE MILK
½	TEASPOON KOSHER SALT
⅛	TEASPOON BLACK PEPPER
	LARGE PINCH OF FRESHLY GRATED NUTMEG
¼	CUP GRATED CHEDDAR CHEESE
	RICE BRAN OIL, AS NEEDED

FOR THE BREADING

½	CUP COLD WATER
1	LARGE EGG
6	TABLESPOONS ALL-PURPOSE FLOUR, PLUS MORE AS NEEDED
2½	CUPS NAMA PANKO (SEE PAGE 66)

FOR THE SAUCE

¼	CUP KETCHUP
2	TABLESPOONS WORCESTERSHIRE SAUCE

Tempura, see page 272

TORITEN

YIELD: 4 SERVINGS / **ACTIVE TIME:** 15 MINUTES / **TOTAL TIME:** 45 MINUTES

Toriten is a variation of tempura made with marinated chicken. This dish comes from Oita, which is famous for its chicken dishes and locally grown kabosu (sour mandarins).

1. To begin preparations for the toriten, place the chicken in a baking dish, add the soy sauce, ginger, garlic, sake, and sesame oil, and stir until the chicken is evenly coated. Cover the dish with plastic wrap and let the chicken marinate in the refrigerator for 30 minutes.

2. Measure out the water and refrigerate it for 30 minutes.

3. Add sesame oil to a Dutch oven until it is 2 inches deep and warm it to 340°F. Place a wire rack in a rimmed baking sheet.

4. Crack the eggs into a bowl and whisk until scrambled. Add the chilled water and whisk gently to prevent too many air bubbles from forming. Sift the flour and potato starch into the bowl and mix until all of the flour has been incorporated. It's OK if there are small lumps in the batter.

5. Working in batches to keep from overcrowding the pot, dip the chicken into the batter until it is completely coated and gently slip it into the hot oil. Fry until it is crispy and cooked through, about 8 minutes. Transfer the fried chicken to the wire rack to drain.

6. When all of the chicken has been fried, prepare the sauce. Combine the juice, soy sauce, and rice vinegar in a small bowl and serve it alongside the toriten.

INGREDIENTS:

FOR THE TORITEN

1¾   LBS. BONELESS, SKINLESS CHICKEN BREASTS, CUT INTO BITE-SIZE PIECES

¼   CUP SOY SAUCE

     1-INCH PIECE OF FRESH GINGER, PEELED AND GRATED

3   GARLIC CLOVES, GRATED

2   TEASPOONS SAKE

2   TEASPOONS EXTRA-VIRGIN SESAME OIL, PLUS MORE AS NEEDED

½   CUP WATER

2   EGGS

½   CUP ALL-PURPOSE FLOUR

6   TABLESPOONS POTATO STARCH

FOR THE SAUCE

2   TEASPOONS FRESH KABOSU, YUZU, OR LEMON JUICE

2   TABLESPOONS SOY SAUCE

2   TEASPOONS RICE VINEGAR

SHOJIN-AGE

YIELD: 4 SERVINGS / **ACTIVE TIME:** 40 MINUTES / **TOTAL TIME:** 1 HOUR AND 30 MINUTES

Shojin-age is a lesser-known gem in Japanese cuisine, a traditional plant-based tempura that showcases the ingenuity and deliciousness of vegan cooking. Unlike conventional tempura, which relies on egg-based batter, shojin-age sets itself apart by employing an egg-free batter to effortlessly fry an assortment of fresh, seasonal vegetables.

1. Measure out the still water and sparkling water and chill them in the refrigerator for 20 to 30 minutes. Combine the cornstarch and flour in a bowl and chill it in the freezer for 20 to 30 minutes.

2. While waiting for the waters and flour mixture to chill, prepare the ingredients you are going to fry: the sweet potato, lotus root, mushroom, asparagus, and bamboo. Pat them dry using paper towels and set them aside.

3. Place the salt and matcha powder in a small bowl and whisk to combine. Set the matcha salt aside.

4. Add sesame oil to a Dutch oven until it is 2 inches deep and warm it to 355°F. Place a wire rack in a rimmed baking sheet.

5. Combine the chilled still water, chilled sparkling water, and ice cubes in a large bowl. Add the rice vinegar to the bowl.

6. Working in three increments, alternate between sifting the chilled flour mixture and adding the baking powder to the batter. Use chopsticks to gently incorporate the dry ingredients, drawing crosses through the mixture and making sure not to overmix. You don't need a perfectly smooth batter for shojin age, it is normal to have a few lumps.

7. Test the hot oil's temperature by dropping a small amount of batter into it. If the batter sizzles and floats, the oil is hot enough.

8. Work in batches to avoid crowding the pot. Pat the vegetables dry with paper towels again, coat them in a light layer of flour, and dip them into the batter until completely coated. Gently slip the battered vegetables into the hot oil and fry until they are crispy but before they become golden brown.

9. Transfer the shojin age to the wire rack and let it drain. When all of the vegetables have been fried, serve with the matcha salt.

INGREDIENTS:

¾ CUP WATER

¼ CUP SPARKLING WATER

¼ CUP CORNSTARCH

¾ CUP CAKE FLOUR, PLUS MORE AS NEEDED

1 SWEET POTATO, SLICED

1 SMALL BOILED LOTUS ROOT, SLICED

1 KING OYSTER MUSHROOM, SLICED

6 ASPARAGUS STALKS, TRIMMED AND HALVED

3½ OZ BOILED BAMBOO SHOOTS, CHOPPED

1½ TEASPOONS KOSHER SALT

½ TEASPOON MATCHA POWDER

EXTRA-VIRGIN SESAME OIL, AS NEEDED

3 ICE CUBES

1 TABLESPOON RICE VINEGAR

½ TEASPOON BAKING POWDER

TORI NO KARAAGE

YIELD: 4 SERVINGS / **ACTIVE TIME:** 25 MINUTES / **TOTAL TIME:** 1 HOUR

Tori no karaage is one of the most-loved Japanese dishes and can be found everywhere from homes and specialty shops to izakayas, street food stalls, supermarkets, and convenience stores across Japan.

1. Place the chicken on a cutting board, skin side down. Make incisions in the thickest parts of the chicken, creating small flaps. Gently pull these flaps outward to even out the thickness of the chicken and cut it into large, bite-sized pieces (each piece should weigh about 1½ oz.). Season the chicken generously with salt and pepper.

2. Place the chicken, soy sauce, sake, oyster sauce, sesame oil, garlic, ginger, and sugar in a resealable plastic bag, seal the bag, and then massage the marinade into the chicken. Let the chicken marinate in the refrigerator for 30 minutes.

3. Remove the chicken from the refrigerator, add the egg white and 1 tablespoon of cornstarch, and seal the bag. Massage the egg white and cornstarch into the chicken.

4. Add rice bran oil to a Dutch oven until it is 2 inches deep and warm it to 320°F. Use a thermometer to get this temperature exact. Place a wire rack in a rimmed baking sheet.

5. Place the rice flour and remaining cornstarch in a shallow bowl and whisk to combine. Working in batches to avoid overcrowding the pot, dredge the chicken in the mixture until it is completely coated and gently slip it into the hot oil. Fry for 3 minutes, transfer the fried chicken to the wire rack, and let it rest for 3 minutes.

6. Heat the oil to 365°F. Gently slip the chicken into the hot oil a second time and fry until it is golden brown all over, 1 to 2 minutes. Return the fried chicken to the wire rack and let it drain before serving.

INGREDIENTS:

1	LB. BONELESS, SKIN-ON CHICKEN THIGHS
	SALT AND PEPPER, TO TASTE
2	TABLESPOONS LIGHT SOY SAUCE
2	TABLESPOONS SAKE
1	TABLESPOON OYSTER SAUCE
1	TABLESPOON SESAME OIL
1½	TEASPOONS GRATED GARLIC
1½	TEASPOONS GRATED FRESH GINGER
½	TEASPOON SUGAR
1	EGG WHITE
6	TABLESPOONS CORNSTARCH
	RICE BRAN OIL, AS NEEDED
5	TABLESPOONS RICE FLOUR

CITRUSY CHICKEN KARAAGE

YIELD: 4 SERVINGS / **ACTIVE TIME:** 25 MINUTES / **TOTAL TIME:** 1 HOUR

This recipe is a game changer for those who prefer chicken breasts over thighs. If you're looking for a lighter version of the famous Japanese fried chicken, this is a great option.

1. Slice the chicken into strips, keeping in mind that the width of these pieces will determine the final size of your pieces of fried chicken. Use a fork to pierce the chicken pieces all over. Using a sharp knife, cut the chicken on a bias into large bite-size pieces. Cutting the chicken on a bias will create a larger surface area and, in turn, ensure a crispier end result.

2. Place the chicken in a mixing bowl, crack the egg over it, and stir until the chicken is evenly coated.

3. Place the sake, sugar, ginger, garlic, salt, and sesame oil in a small bowl, whisk to combine, and add this to the chicken mixture. Stir until well combined, add 3 tablespoons of tapioca starch, and stir until the chicken is evenly coated. Cover the bowl with plastic wrap and marinate in the refrigerator for 30 minutes.

4. Place the remaining tapioca starch, lemon juice, and lemon zest in a bowl and work the mixture with a fork until combined, breaking up the large clumps caused by the moisture of the lemon juice. Work the mixture with your hands until it is fine and powdery.

5. Add rice bran oil to a Dutch oven until it is 2 inches deep and warm it to 320°F. Use a thermometer to get this temperature exact. Place a wire rack in a rimmed baking sheet.

6. Working in batches to avoid overcrowding the pot, dredge the chicken in the lemon-and-tapioca starch mixture until it is evenly coated and gently slip it into the hot oil. Fry for 3 minutes, transfer the fried chicken to the wire rack, and let it rest for 3 to 5 minutes.

7. Heat the oil to 360°F. Gently slip the chicken into the hot oil a second time and fry until it is golden brown and crispy all over, 1 to 2 minutes. Return the fried chicken to the wire rack and let it drain before serving.

INGREDIENTS:

1	LB. BONELESS, SKIN-ON CHICKEN BREAST
1	EGG
3	TABLESPOONS SAKE
½	TEASPOON SUGAR
1½	TEASPOONS GRATED FRESH GINGER
1½	TEASPOONS GRATED GARLIC
1	TEASPOON SEA SALT
1	TEASPOON SESAME OIL
½	CUP PLUS 3 TABLESPOONS TAPIOCA STARCH
2	TABLESPOONS FRESH LEMON JUICE
1½	TEASPOONS LEMON ZEST
	RICE BRAN OIL, AS NEEDED

TONKATSU

YIELD: 4 SERVINGS / **ACTIVE TIME:** 15 MINUTES / **TOTAL TIME:** 30 MINUTES

Tonkatsu is an iconic dish made with meaty yet tender pork cutlets coated in a crispy layer of panko. This well-loved dish is often sliced into strips and served with cabbage, rice, miso soup, and the tangy tonkatsu sauce featured here.

1. To begin preparations for the tonkatsu, add rice bran oil to a Dutch oven until it is 2 inches deep and warm it to 340°F. Place a wire rack in a rimmed baking sheet.

2. Place the pork on a cutting board and use the point of a sharp knife to make incisions along the muscle to keep it from curling as it fries. Pound the pork until each tenderloin is ¾ inch thick and season it with salt and pepper.

3. Place the flour in a shallow bowl and the panko in another shallow bowl. Place the egg, milk, and rice bran oil in a bowl and whisk to combine. Dredge the pork in the flour and gently pat it to remove any excess. Dip it into the egg mixture until completely coated and then dredge it in the panko, gently pressing down on the bread crumbs to secure them.

4. Working in batches if necessary to avoid overcrowding the pot, slip the breaded pork into the hot oil and fry until it is cooked through and golden brown, about 8 minutes, turning it over halfway through. Transfer the tonkatsu to the wire rack.

5. To prepare the sauce, place all of the ingredients in a bowl and whisk to combine. Serve the sauce alongside the tonkatsu and shredded cabbage.

INGREDIENTS:

FOR THE TONKATSU

2   TEASPOONS RICE BRAN OIL, PLUS MORE AS NEEDED

1½   LBS. PORK TENDERLOINS

     SALT AND PEPPER, TO TASTE

¼   CUP ALL-PURPOSE FLOUR

2   CUPS NAMA PANKO (SEE PAGE 66)

1   LARGE EGG

2   TABLESPOONS WHOLE MILK

2   CUPS SHREDDED CABBAGE, FOR SERVING

FOR THE SAUCE

¼   CUP WORCESTERSHIRE SAUCE

2   TABLESPOONS KETCHUP

2   TABLESPOONS SOY SAUCE

⅛   TEASPOON LIGHT BROWN SUGAR

2   TABLESPOONS TOASTED WHITE SESAME SEEDS

MENCHI KATSU

YIELD: 4 SERVINGS / **ACTIVE TIME:** 20 MINUTES / **TOTAL TIME:** 1 HOUR

Menchi katsu is a type of deep fried "cutlet" that features a filling of minced pork or beef that has been shaped into patties.

1. To begin preparations for the katsu, place the butter in a large skillet and warm it over medium heat. Add the onion and cook, stirring occasionally, until it has softened and is lightly golden brown. Stir in the mirin and Worcestershire sauce and cook until the liquid has nearly evaporated. Remove the pan from heat and let the mixture cool to room temperature.

2. Place 3 tablespoons of panko and the milk in a bowl, stir to combine, and let the panko soak.

3. Place the pork and beef in a mixing bowl, season with the salt and pepper, and stir to combine. Add the soaked panko, ketchup, sugar, nutmeg, and onion mixture and work the mixture until it is well combined. Form the mixture into eight round or oval patties. Place the patties on a plate, cover with plastic wrap, and let them firm up in the refrigerator for 30 minutes.

4. Add rice bran oil to a Dutch oven until it is 2 inches deep and warm it to 320°F. Place a wire rack in a rimmed baking sheet.

5. Place the flour in a shallow bowl and the remaining panko in another shallow bowl. Place the egg in a bowl and whisk until scrambled. Dredge the patties in the flour, dip them into the egg mixture until completely coated, and then dredge them in the panko, gently pressing down on the bread crumbs to secure them.

6. Working in batches if necessary to avoid crowding the pot, slip the breaded patties into the hot oil and fry until they are cooked through and golden brown, about 4 minutes, turning them over halfway through. Transfer the katsu to the wire rack and let them drain.

7. Heat the oil to 355°F. Return the katsu to the oil and fry until they are golden brown, 1 to 2 minutes. Transfer the katsu patties to the wire rack to drain.

8. While the katsu are draining, prepare the sauce. Place all of the ingredients in a bowl, whisk to combine, and serve the sauce alongside the katsu.

INGREDIENTS:

FOR THE KATSU
1   TEASPOON UNSALTED BUTTER
½   ONION, FINELY DICED
1½ TEASPOONS MIRIN
1   TABLESPOON WORCESTERSHIRE SAUCE
1½ CUPS PLUS 3 TABLESPOONS NAMA PANKO (SEE PAGE 66)
1½ TABLESPOONS WHOLE MILK
½   LB. GROUND PORK
2½ OZ. THINLY SLICED BEEF, MINCED
    PINCH OF KOSHER SALT
    PINCH OF BLACK PEPPER
½   TEASPOON KETCHUP
1   TEASPOON SUGAR
    PINCH OF FRESHLY GRATED NUTMEG
    RICE BRAN OIL, AS NEEDED
½   CUP ALL-PURPOSE FLOUR
1   LARGE EGG

FOR THE SAUCE
1   TABLESPOON KETCHUP
1   TABLESPOON WORCESTERSHIRE SAUCE
1   TEASPOON OYSTER SAUCE
⅛   TEASPOON EXTRA-VIRGIN OLIVE OIL
⅛   TEASPOON RICE VINEGAR

KUSHIAGE

YIELD: 4 SERVINGS / **ACTIVE TIME:** 30 MINUTES / **TOTAL TIME:** 30 MINUTES

Kushiage features bite-sized morsels of seafood, meat, or vegetables skewered and deep-fried to golden perfection. This type of dish has evolved into a cherished tradition across eastern, central, and western Japan, with each region boasting its own unique flair. However, it is Osaka's kushiage that has garnered the most fame and adoration.

1. To prepare the sauce, place all of the ingredients in a saucepan and bring to a boil over medium heat, stirring occasionally. Reduce the heat to low and let the sauce simmer for 1 minute. Remove the pan from heat and let the sauce cool.

2. To begin preparations for the kushiage, place the flour, water, and egg in a bowl and whisk until the mixture comes together as a smooth batter. Place the panko in a separate bowl.

3. Add rice bran oil to a Dutch oven until it is 2 inches deep and warm it to 340°F. Place a wire rack in a rimmed baking sheet.

4. Thread one or two pieces of each of the lotus root, eggplant, quail eggs, mushrooms, shrimp, Camembert cheese, pork, and chicken onto skewers, keeping the depth of the hot oil in mind when assembling the skewers. Dip the skewers into the batter until completely coated and then roll them in the panko, pressing gently to make sure the bread crumbs adhere.

5. Working in batches to prevent the pot from becoming over-crowded, gently slip the skewers into the hot oil. Fry until they are golden brown and crispy, about 3 minutes. The cooking time may vary depending on the size of the pieces on the skewers.

6. Using a slotted spoon or a strainer, remove the fried skewers from the oil and place them on the wire rack to drain.

7. To serve, dip each skewer into the sauce, making sure to coat it thoroughly, and enjoy.

INGREDIENTS:

FOR THE SAUCE

⅓ CUP WORCESTERSHIRE SAUCE

¼ CUP WATER

1 TABLESPOON SUGAR

1 TABLESPOON MIRIN

1 TABLESPOON RED WINE

1 TEASPOON KETCHUP

¼ TEASPOON DASHI GRANULES

FOR THE KUSHIAGE

1¼ CUPS CAKE FLOUR

1 CUP COLD WATER

1 EGG

3 CUPS NAMA PANKO (SEE PAGE 66)

RICE BRAN OIL, AS NEEDED

4 SLICES OF LOTUS ROOT

8 SLICES OF EGGPLANT

8 BOILED QUAIL EGGS

4 SHIITAKE MUSHROOMS, STEMMED

8 SHRIMP, SHELLS REMOVED, DEVEINED

4 PIECES OF CAMEMBERT CHEESE

2 PORK CHOPS, CHOPPED

⅔ LB. BONELESS, SKINLESS CHICKEN BREAST, SLICED

AGEDASHI TOFU

YIELD: 4 SERVINGS / **ACTIVE TIME:** 25 MINUTES / **TOTAL TIME:** 25 MINUTES

Agedashi tofu is a beloved dish that exemplifies the elegant simplicity of Japanese cuisine.

1. To begin preparations for the tofu, pat the tofu dry with paper towels to remove any excess moisture. Place the potato starch in a bowl and set it near the oven.

2. Add rice bran oil to a large, deep skillet until it is about ½ inch deep and warm it to 335°F. Line a wire rack with paper towels.

3. Dredge the tofu in the potato starch until it is completely coated and immediately slip it into the hot oil. Fry the tofu until it is crispy all over, about 30 seconds on each side. Aim to keep the tofu as white as possible, avoiding any browning. Transfer the fried tofu to a paper towel–lined rack.

4. To prepare the sauce, place the dashi, mirin, soy sauces, and sake in a saucepan and bring to a boil over medium heat. Place the water and potato starch in a bowl and whisk to combine. While whisking continually, add the slurry to the pan and cook until the sauce thickens. Remove the pan from heat and stir in the radish.

5. To serve, divide the fried tofu among the serving plates, generously spoon the sauce over each piece, and garnish with green onions and shichimi togarashi.

INGREDIENTS:

FOR THE TOFU

¾   LB. FIRM TOFU, DRAINED AND CUBED

¼   CUP POTATO STARCH

    RICE BRAN OIL, AS NEEDED

    GREEN ONIONS, CHOPPED, FOR GARNISH

    SHICHIMI TOGARASHI, FOR GARNISH

FOR THE SAUCE

½   CUP AWASE DASHI STOCK (SEE PAGE 38)

1   TABLESPOON MIRIN

1   TABLESPOON DARK SOY SAUCE

1   TEASPOON LIGHT SOY SAUCE

1   TABLESPOON SAKE

1   TABLESPOON WATER

1   TEASPOON POTATO STARCH

2   TABLESPOONS GRATED DAIKON RADISH

EBI FURAI

YIELD: 4 SERVINGS / **ACTIVE TIME:** 30 MINUTES / **TOTAL TIME:** 1 HOUR

Ebi furai is a popular deep-fried dish made with large prawns coated in a thick, crispy layer of golden panko. One thing to keep in mind before you start: make sure you have skewers that are longer than the prawns

1. Place the bamboo skewers in a glass of water and let them soak. This will make removing the prawns easier after frying.

2. Remove the shells from the prawns, leaving the tails intact, and devein them. Place them in a bowl and sprinkle the salt and cornstarch over them. Rub the mixture into the prawns and rinse them under cold water.

3. Place the prawns on their sides on a cutting board and trim the tails horizontally. Turn the prawns so that their bellies are facing up and make shallow diagonal incisions along the entire length of their bodies. Dip the skewers in rice bran oil and thread the prawns onto them, making sure the skewers go straight through.

4. Add rice bran oil to a large, deep skillet until it is about 2 inches deep and warm it to 370°F. Place a wire rack in a rimmed baking sheet.

5. Place the flour in a shallow bowl and the panko in another shallow bowl. Place the eggs in a bowl and whisk until scrambled. Pat the prawns dry with paper towels, dredge them in the flour until coated, and tap the skewers to remove any excess. Dip the prawns into the eggs until completely coated and then dredge them in the panko. Repeat with the eggs and panko and gently slip the prawns into the hot oil.

6. Fry until they are golden brown, crispy, and cooked through, about 5 minutes. Transfer the fried prawns to the wire rack to drain.

7. Carefully remove the skewers, twisting to help them come out. Serve with Tangy Tartar Sauce and lemon wedges.

INGREDIENTS:

12 BAMBOO SKEWERS

12 BLACK TIGER PRAWNS

¼ TEASPOON KOSHER SALT

2 TEASPOONS CORNSTARCH

RICE BRAN OIL, AS NEEDED

½ CUP ALL-PURPOSE FLOUR

2 CUPS NAMA PANKO (SEE PAGE 66)

2 EGGS

TANGY TARTAR SAUCE (SEE PAGE 680), FOR SERVING

4 LEMON WEDGES, FOR SERVING

SALMON FRY

YIELD: 4 SERVINGS / **ACTIVE TIME:** 15 MINUTES / **TOTAL TIME:** 30 MINUTES

Salmon fry is a beloved autumn dish in Japan that showcases the delicious combination of fatty salmon and crispy, golden brown bread crumbs.

1. Place the salmon in a bowl and sprinkle the sake over it, making sure it is evenly distributed. Cover the bowl with plastic wrap and chill it in the refrigerator for 15 minutes.

2. Remove the salmon from the refrigerator and pat it dry with a paper towel. Sprinkle the salt and 1 tablespoon of flour over the salmon, coating it thinly and evenly.

3. Place the remaining flour, the water, and egg in a bowl and whisk until the mixture comes together as a smooth batter. Place the panko in a separate shallow bowl.

4. Add rice bran oil to a Dutch oven until it is about 2 inches deep and warm it to 355°F. Place a wire rack in a rimmed baking sheet.

5. Dip the salmon in the batter and allow any excess batter to drip off. Dredge the salmon in the panko, pressing gently to ensure the bread crumbs adhere well.

6. Gently slip the breaded salmon into the hot oil and fry until it is crispy and cooked through, about 4 minutes, turning it over halfway through.

7. Using a slotted spoon or a strainer, remove the fried salmon from the hot oil and transfer it to the wire rack.

8. To serve, divide the salmon among the serving plates, pour some of the tartar sauce over each portion, and garnish with dried parsley.

INGREDIENTS:

4	SALMON FILLETS
2	TABLESPOONS SAKE
1	TEASPOON KOSHER SALT
¼	CUP ALL-PURPOSE FLOUR
⅓	CUP WATER
1	EGG
1	CUP NAMA PANKO (SEE PAGE 66)
	RICE BRAN OIL, AS NEEDED
	TANGY TARTAR SAUCE (SEE PAGE 680), FOR SERVING
	DRIED PARSLEY, FOR GARNISH

BIFUKATSU

YIELD: 4 SERVINGS / **ACTIVE TIME:** 20 MINUTES / **TOTAL TIME:** 20 MINUTES

Bifukatsu showcases the exquisite combination of tender, juicy beef steak, and a crisp, golden breading. While beef cutlets can be found throughout Japan, the city of Kobe, which historically had a strong beef-eating culture, is particularly famous for this dish.

1. To begin preparations for the bifukatsu, pierce the steaks all over with a fork, pat them dry with paper towels, and season with the salt and pepper. Place the flour in a shallow bowl and the panko in another bowl. Dredge the steaks in the flour until they are lightly coated and then gently pat them to remove any excess flour. Place the egg and milk in a bowl and whisk until smooth. Dip the steaks into the egg mixture until completely coated and then dredge them in the panko, gently pressing down on the bread crumbs to secure them.

2. Add rice bran oil to a Dutch oven until it is 2 inches deep and warm it to 355°F. Place a wire rack in a rimmed baking sheet.

3. While the rice bran oil is warming, prepare the sauce. Combine all of the ingredients in a saucepan and bring to a simmer over medium-low heat, stirring occasionally. Cook until the sauce thickens slightly, remove the pan from heat, and set the sauce aside.

4. Working in batches if necessary to avoid overcrowding the pot, gently slip the breaded steaks into the hot oil and fry until they are cooked to your liking and golden brown, about 2 minutes, turning them over halfway through. Transfer the bifukatsu to the wire rack and let it drain for 3 minutes.

5. Transfer the steaks to a cutting board and slice them into strips that are approximately ½ inch thick.

6. Arrange the steaks on a serving dish, drizzle the sauce over them, and serve.

INGREDIENTS:

FOR THE BIFUKATSU

4	BEEF STEAKS
4	PINCHES OF KOSHER SALT
4	PINCHES OF BLACK PEPPER
¼	CUP ALL-PURPOSE FLOUR
1	LARGE EGG
2	TABLESPOONS WHOLE MILK
¾	CUP NAMA PANKO (SEE PAGE 66)
	RICE BRAN OIL, AS NEEDED

FOR THE SAUCE

1	TABLESPOON UNSALTED BUTTER
1	TABLESPOON SUGAR
2	TABLESPOONS SOY SAUCE
2	TABLESPOONS WORCESTERSHIRE SAUCE
2	TABLESPOONS RED WINE
¼	CUP KETCHUP

Bifukatsu, see page 295

SQUID KARAAGE

YIELD: 4 SERVINGS / **ACTIVE TIME:** 10 MINUTES / **TOTAL TIME:** 40 MINUTES

Karaage is most known as a chicken dish, but it is just as delicious when prepared with seafood—squid and octopus being the best choices if you elect to go this route.

1. Place the squid in a resealable plastic bag. Add the soy sauce, sake, pepper, garlic, and ginger to the bag, seal it, and rub the ingredients together to ensure the squid is thoroughly coated with the marinade. Let the squid marinate in the refrigerator for 30 minutes.

2. Add rice bran oil to a Dutch oven until it is about 2 inches deep and warm it to 355°F.

3. Add the tapioca starch to the resealable plastic bag, seal it, and rub the squid until it is evenly coated with the starch.

4. Working in batches if necessary to avoid overcrowding the pot, gently slip the squid into the hot oil and fry until it is a dark golden brown, 2 to 3 minutes.

5. Transfer the fried squid to a paper towel–lined plate to drain. Serve with lemon wedges.

INGREDIENTS:

⅔ LB. CLEANED SQUID, CHOPPED

1 TABLESPOON SOY SAUCE

1 TABLESPOON SAKE

⅛ TEASPOON BLACK PEPPER

1½ TEASPOONS GRATED GARLIC

1 TEASPOON GRATED FRESH GINGER

RICE BRAN OIL, AS NEEDED

6 TABLESPOONS TAPIOCA STARCH

LEMON WEDGES, FOR SERVING

CHIKUWA NO ISOBE-AGE

YIELD: 4 SERVINGS / **ACTIVE TIME:** 10 MINUTES / **TOTAL TIME:** 10 MINUTES

Isobe-age is a type of tempura that is much simpler and easier to make than traditional tempura. The batter doesn't contain any salt, so you can fully enjoy the unique taste of the aonori seaweed and the subtle flavor of chikuwa.

1. Place the flour, tapioca starch, aonori, and katsuobushi in a bowl and stir to combine. Pour in the sparkling water and gently stir until the batter just comes together.

2. Add sesame oil to a Dutch oven until it is about 2 inches deep and warm it to 355°F. Place a wire rack in a rimmed baking sheet.

3. Dip the chikuwa in the batter until they are evenly coated. Gently slip them into the hot oil and fry until they are golden brown, about 2 minutes, turning them over halfway through.

4. Transfer the fried chikuwa to a paper towel–lined plate and let them drain before serving.

INGREDIENTS:

2   TABLESPOONS CAKE FLOUR

2   TABLESPOONS TAPIOCA STARCH

1   TABLESPOON AONORI

1   TEASPOON KATSUOBUSHI (DRIED BONITO FLAKES), CRUSHED

¼   CUP SPARKLING WATER

    EXTRA-VIRGIN SESAME OIL, AS NEEDED

4   CHIKUWA FISH CAKES, HALVED LENGTHWISE AND THEN CROSSWISE

KAWARI AGE

YIELD: 4 SERVINGS / **ACTIVE TIME:** 20 MINUTES / **TOTAL TIME:** 35 MINUTES

Kawari age is a playful Japanese concept that involves frying unusual or unexpected ingredients. In this recipe, we'll explore the delightful crunch and texture that spring rolls bring to the batter-frying process.

1. Place the shrimp and cod in a resealable plastic, add the soy sauce and sake, seal the bag, and toss to coat. Let the seafood marinate in the refrigerator for 15 minutes.

2. Add rice bran oil to a Dutch oven until it is about 2 inches deep and warm it to 355°F. Place a wire rack in a rimmed baking sheet.

3. Remove the seafood from the bag and place it on a plate or in a shallow bowl. Pat it dry with paper towels and set it aside.

4. Place the flour and water in a small bowl and stir until the mixture comes together as a thick, glue-like batter. Spread a thin layer of the batter on each shrimp and cod fillet, taking care not to apply too much.

5. Place each shrimp and piece of cod on a piece of spring roll. Working in batches if necessary to avoid crowding the pot, wrap the spring roll tightly around the seafood and gently slip it into the hot oil. Fry until they turn golden brown and crispy, about 3 minutes.

6. Using a slotted spoon or a strainer, transfer the kawari age to the wire rack to drain.

7. To prepare the sauce, place all of the ingredients in a bowl and stir to combine. Serve the sauce alongside the kawari age.

INGREDIENTS:

FOR THE KAWARI AGE

8   SHRIMP, SHELLS REMOVED, DEVEINED

2   COD FILLETS, CHOPPED

1½   TEASPOONS SOY SAUCE

1½   TEASPOONS SAKE

    RICE BRAN OIL, AS NEEDED

¼   CUP CAKE FLOUR

¼   CUP WATER

10   SPRING ROLL WRAPPERS, CUT INTO ¼-INCH STRIPS

FOR THE SAUCE

3   TABLESPOONS JAPANESE MAYONNAISE (SEE PAGE 46)

1   TEASPOON JAPANESE CURRY POWDER (SEE PAGE 65)

1   TEASPOON SOY SAUCE

¼   TEASPOON SUGAR

TSUKEMONO
(PICKLES)

The history of pickles in Japan is long and rich, dating back to the Jomon period (circa 13,000 BCE to the fourth century BCE), when vegetable peels were already being preserved in salt. This extensive history has led to the development of diverse pickling traditions across Japan. Today, regional pickle varieties exist in every part of the country, with an estimated 600 or more different types.

NUKAZUKE-STYLE PICKLES

YIELD: 6 SERVINGS / ACTIVE TIME: 5 MINUTES / TOTAL TIME: 26 HOURS

Traditionally, nukazuke is a pickle made with rice bran, and known for its unique flavor and texture. However, the traditional process can be time-consuming, involving careful maintenance of a fermented rice bran bed and specialized containers. This innovative recipe offers a shortcut that produces a similar taste with less time and effort. The secret ingredient? Yogurt.

1. Wash and peel the vegetables. Slice them into approximately ⅓-inch-thick pieces. The shape of the slices can be tailored to your preference, such as rounds, half-moons, or batons.

2. Place the sliced vegetables in a large bowl. Sprinkle the salt over the vegetables and gently massage it into them using your hands, making sure the salt gets evenly distributed. Let the salted vegetables sit in the bowl for 1 hour; this will allow the salt to draw out excess moisture.

3. Wash your hands and squeeze the vegetables to remove as much water as possible from them. Discard any liquid.

4. Combine the miso paste and yogurt in a large resealable plastic bag. Add the vegetables and seal the bag, making sure to remove as much air from it as possible. Using your hands, gently massage the miso-and-yogurt mixture into the vegetables, ensuring they are evenly coated.

5. Place the vegetables in the refrigerator and let them pickle for 24 hours.

6. Remove the vegetables from the bag and place them in a fine-mesh sieve. Rinse the vegetables under cold water and shake the sieve to remove excess water. Serve or refrigerate until ready to serve.

INGREDIENTS:

1	CARROT
1	JAPANESE OR PERSIAN CUCUMBER
¼	DAIKON RADISH
1	TEASPOON KOSHER SALT
¼	CUP YELLOW MISO PASTE
3	TABLESPOONS PLAIN YOGURT

FUKUJINZUKE

YIELD: 12 SERVINGS / **ACTIVE TIME:** 30 MINUTES / **TOTAL TIME:** 12 HOURS AND 30 MINUTES

Fukujinzuke is a popular sweet and tangy pickle that is most commonly served alongside Japanese curry. It is believed that it gets its name from the Seven Lucky Gods "Shichi Fukujin" because it is traditionally made with seven or more different vegetables. Store-bought versions are often notable for their vibrant red appearance, but homemade fukujinzuke is typically more of an ochre.

1. Fill a large bowl with cold water. Peel the daikon, eggplant, and cucumber and then cut them into pieces that are no larger than ½-inch cubes, place them in the cold water, and let them soak.

2. Peel and finely dice the ginger, then drain the water from the bowl of vegetables and add the ginger and salt. Mix thoroughly and let the mixture sit for 20 minutes.

3. Bring water to a rolling boil in a large saucepan. Peel and thinly slice the lotus root, then cut each piece into sixths. Add the lotus root to the boiling water and cook for 1 minute. Drain and let the lotus root cool.

4. Place the soy sauce, water, dashi granules, red wine, brown sugar, and vinegar in a small saucepan and bring to a boil over medium heat. Let the mixture boil for 2 to 3 minutes, remove the pan from heat, and let the brine cool.

5. After 20 minutes, the vegetables you added the salt to will have released some of their liquid. Drain the mixture through a fine-mesh sieve and squeeze the vegetables to remove as much liquid as possible.

6. Transfer the vegetables, lotus root, brine, and kombu to a resealable plastic bag and seal it, making sure to remove as much air from it as possible.

7. Let the vegetables pickle in the refrigerator for 12 hours before serving.

INGREDIENTS:

⅔ LB. DAIKON RADISH

1 EGGPLANT

1 JAPANESE OR PERSIAN CUCUMBER

1½-INCH PIECE OF FRESH GINGER

2 TABLESPOONS KOSHER SALT

3 OZ. LOTUS ROOT

3 TABLESPOONS SOY SAUCE

2 TABLESPOONS WATER

PINCH OF DASHI GRANULES

3 TABLESPOONS RED WINE

3 TABLESPOONS LIGHT BROWN SUGAR

1 TABLESPOON RICE VINEGAR

3-INCH PIECE OF DRIED KOMBU

HAKUSAI NO ASAZUKE

YIELD: 8 SERVINGS / **ACTIVE TIME:** 10 MINUTES / **TOTAL TIME:** 24 HOURS

Here's a quick and refreshing pickle made with salted napa cabbage flavored with the delicate citrus flavors of yuzu with a hint of heat from the chile. Also, other citrus fruits, like lemon or orange, can be used in place of yuzu.

1. Wash the napa cabbage and shake it thoroughly to remove excess water. Cut it into 1- to 2- inch squares and place them in a large resealable plastic bag.

2. Cut the yuzu peel into thin strips. Cut the kombu into thin slices that are approximately the size of matchsticks.

3. Add the yuzu juice, yuzu peels, and kombu to the plastic bag. Add the salt, sugar, chile, and light soy sauce and rub them into the cabbage until it is evenly coated.

4. Seal the bag, making sure to remove as much air from it as possible. Place the bag on a baking sheet and weigh it down with something heavy such as a large canned good. Let the cabbage pickle in the refrigerator for 24 hours before serving.

INGREDIENTS:

⅔	LB. NAPA CABBAGE
	PEEL AND JUICE OF ½ YUZU
	3-INCH SQUARE OF DRIED KOMBU
1½	TEASPOONS KOSHER SALT
½	TEASPOON SUGAR
1	TEASPOON MINCED DRIED RED CHILE PEPPER
¼	TEASPOON LIGHT SOY SAUCE

Fukujinzuke, see page 310

BENISHOGA

YIELD: 16 SERVINGS / **ACTIVE TIME:** 20 MINUTES / **TOTAL TIME:** 1 DAY

A vibrant red pickle made with young ginger root, benishoga's bright color and tangy refreshing flavor make it a popular accompaniment for rich or oily dishes such as gyudon beef bowl or yakisoba fried noodles. Preparing it is also well worth the investment, as it will keep in the refrigerator for up to 6 months.

1. Thoroughly wash the ginger. Cut it into pieces that are about 2 inches long and slice these thin. Place the slices in a bowl of water.

2. Bring water to a rolling boil in a large saucepan. Add the ginger and cook for 1 minute. Drain and rinse the ginger under cold water. Transfer it to a bowl, add the salt, and rub the salt into the ginger until it is evenly coated. Place a clean plate on top of the ginger, place a heavy object on top of the plate, and let the ginger rest for 1 hour.

3. Squeeze the ginger to remove as much liquid as possible and discard it. If time allows, arrange the ginger on a bamboo tray and let it air-dry in a well-ventilated area for 2 to 3 hours. If you do not have 2 to 3 hours, pat the ginger dry with paper towels.

4. Once the ginger is dry, cut each piece into matchsticks and place them in a sterilized jar. Pour the vinegar over the ginger until it is completely submerged and add the sugar. Seal the jar and shake it to combine.

5. Let the ginger pickle in the refrigerator for 1 to 2 days before serving.

INGREDIENTS:

- 3½ OZ. FRESH YOUNG GINGER OR COMMON GINGER
- ½ TEASPOON KOSHER SALT
- ½ CUP RED UME PLUM VINEGAR
- 1½ TEASPOONS SUGAR

BETTARAZUKE

YIELD: 6 SERVINGS / **ACTIVE TIME**: 15 MINUTES / **TOTAL TIME**: 49 HOURS

I t's name—bettara means "sticky" in Japanese—is due to the mildly sticky surface created by the amazake, a traditional Japanese drink made from fermented rice.

1. Cut the radish in half lengthwise. If it is particularly thick, cut it into quarters lengthwise. Place the radish in a large resealable plastic bag, add half of the salt, and massage it into the radish. Seal the bag, making sure to remove as much air from it as possible, and place it in the refrigerator overnight.

2. Remove the radish from the bag and pat it dry. Discard the liquid that has accumulated in the bag and rinse out the bag. Cut the radish into approximately ¼-inch-thick slices.

3. Place the chile and kombu in the bag along with the radish. Add the amazake, sugar, and remaining salt and seal the bag, making sure to remove as much air from it as possible. Massage the ingredients until well combined and let the mixture pickle in the refrigerator overnight before serving.

INGREDIENTS:

¼ DAIKON RADISH, PEELED

2 TABLESPOONS KOSHER SALT

1 DRIED RED CHILE PEPPER, STEMMED, SEEDED, AND SLICED THIN

   2-INCH SQUARE OF DRIED KOMBU, SLICED THIN

½ CUP AMAZAKE

1 TABLESPOON SUGAR

SHIBAZUKE

YIELD: 8 SERVINGS / **ACTIVE TIME:** 30 MINUTES / **TOTAL TIME:** 3 DAYS

This popular pickle originated in Kyoto. Traditionally, it gets its bright purple color by pickling the vegetables together with purple shiso leaves. However, a lighter color of the same shade can be achieved through using red plum vinegar alone.

1. Fill a bowl with cold water and add a pinch of salt. Cut off both ends of the eggplants and then cut them in half lengthwise. If the eggplants are thick, cut them into quarters lengthwise. Cut each piece into ⅛-inch-thick slices, place them in the salted water, and let them soak for 20 minutes.

2. Bring water to a rolling boil in a small saucepan and slice the ginger thin. Add the ginger to the pan and cook for 30 seconds. Drain and rinse the ginger under cold water. When it is cool enough to touch, cut the ginger into thin matchsticks.

3. Cut off the ends of the cucumber and then cut it in half lengthwise. Scoop out the seeds and then slice it into pieces that have a similar thickness as the eggplants. Trim the ends of the myoga and then slice it thin. Cut the shiso leaves into thin shreds.

4. Drain the eggplants and place them in a clean bowl. Add the rest of the vegetables and the shiso leaves and sprinkle the salt over the mixture. Rub the salt into the vegetables until it is evenly distributed, place plastic wrap directly on the surface of the vegetables, and weigh the mixture down with a plate and something heavy like a bag of sugar or a large canned good. Place the mixture in the refrigerator and let it sit overnight.

5. Squeeze the vegetables to remove any excess liquid and discard it. Place the vegetables in a resealable plastic bag and add the vinegar and sugar. Massage them into the vegetables. Seal the bag, making sure to remove as much air from it as possible, and place it on the baking sheet. Let the vegetables pickle in the refrigerator for 2 days, turning the bag over once or twice a day.

6. Strain the vegetables and discard the pickling liquid. Squeeze the vegetables to remove any excess liquid, transfer them to a sterile airtight jar, and either serve or store it in the refrigerator.

INGREDIENTS:

- 1½ TEASPOONS COARSE SEA SALT, PLUS MORE TO TASTE
- 2 JAPANESE OR CHINESE EGGPLANTS (ABOUT 7 OZ.)
- 1-INCH PIECE OF FRESH GINGER, PEELED (ABOUT ¼ OZ.)
- 1 JAPANESE OR PERSIAN CUCUMBER (ABOUT 3½ OZ.)
- 3 MYOGA (JAPANESE GINGER) (ABOUT 1.7 OZ)
- 5 SHISO LEAVES
- 3 TABLESPOONS RED PLUM VINEGAR
- 1 TABLESPOON SUGAR

TAKUAN

YIELD: 12 SERVINGS / **ACTIVE TIME:** 15 MINUTES / **TOTAL TIME:** 3 DAYS

Takuan is a vibrant yellow pickled dish made with daikon radish. It is often eaten as a side dish or at the end of meals and is believed to aid digestion. You will also see it used in sushi rolls and bentos. Traditionally, takuan would take weeks of drying and months of pickling, but this quicker version allows you to enjoy the sweet flavor of takuan in just a few days. If you don't have access to dried gardenia fruit, you can simply add a few drops of yellow food coloring before the final pickling

1. Wash the radish, peel it, cut it in half lengthwise, and slice it into thick half-moons. If you intend to use the takuan for sushi rolls, cut it into long matchsticks.

2. Place the radish in a large resealable plastic bag, add the salt, and massage it into the radish. Seal the bag, making sure to remove as much air from it as possible, and place it on a baking sheet. Place a 1 lb. weight atop the bag and chill it in the refrigerator for 3 hours. If time allows, chill the radish overnight.

3. Drain the radish in a colander and shake it to remove any excess moisture. Return the daikon to the plastic bag, add the sugar and vinegar, and rub them into the radish.

4. Pierce the gardenia fruit a few times with a fork to help it release its color. Place it in the bag along with the kombu and chile. Seal the bag, making sure to remove as much air from it as possible, and place it on the baking sheet. Let the radish pickle in the refrigerator for 2 days, turning the bag over once or twice a day.

5. Strain the radish and discard the pickling liquid. Transfer the takuan to a sterile airtight jar and either serve or store it in the refrigerator.

INGREDIENTS:

1	LB. DAIKON RADISH
2	TEASPOONS COARSE SEA SALT
⅓	CUP LIGHT BROWN CANE SUGAR
4	TEASPOONS RICE VINEGAR
1	DRIED GARDENIA FRUIT
	2-INCH SQUARE OF DRIED KOMBU
1	DRIED RED CHILE PEPPER

CUCUMBER MISOZUKE

YIELD: 8 SERVINGS / **ACTIVE TIME:** 10 MINUTES / **TOTAL TIME:** 1 DAY 10 MINUTES

Japan has a wide variety of cucumber pickles, each with its own distinctive flavor profile. This recipe is unique because it uses savory miso paste to create an easy-to-eat pickle with a subtle garlic flavor.

1. Place the cucumbers in a bowl and rub them with the salt, making sure to evenly coat them. Let the salted cucumbers sit for 10 minutes.

2. Rinse the cucumbers under cold water to remove the salt, pat them dry with paper towels, and set them aside.

3. Place all of the remaining ingredients in a large resealable plastic bag. Place the cucumbers in the bag and seal it tightly, make sure to remove as much air from it as possible. Gently massage the marinade into the cucumbers, making sure they are evenly coated.

4. Let the cucumbers pickle in the refrigerator for 24 hours before serving.

INGREDIENTS:

- 3 JAPANESE OR PERSIAN CUCUMBERS, HALVED
- 1 TEASPOON KOSHER SALT
- 2 TABLESPOONS YELLOW MISO PASTE
- 1 TEASPOON GARLIC PASTE
- 1 TEASPOON TOASTED SESAME OIL
- ½ DRIED RED CHILE PEPPER, FINELY DICED
- ½ TEASPOON SUGAR
- ½ TEASPOON DASHI GRANULES

DAIKON AMAZU-ZUKE

YIELD: 8 SERVINGS / **ACTIVE TIME:** 10 MINUTES / **TOTAL TIME:** 24 HOURS

Amazu-zuke is a pickle recipe featuring a sweet-and-tangy, vinegar-based brine. This recipe features daikon radish, but the versatile pickling method can be applied to a wide variety of vegetables.

1. Wash the radish, peel it, cut it in half lengthwise, and slice it into thin half-moons. Place it in a large bowl, add the salt, and massage it into the radish. Let the radish sit for 10 minutes.

2. Squeeze the radish to remove any excess liquid. Discard the liquid and place the radish in a large resealable plastic bag. Add all of the remaining ingredients and seal the bag, making sure to remove as much air from it as possible. Gently massage the radish until it is completely coated.

3. Let the radish pickle in the refrigerator for 24 hours before serving.

INGREDIENTS:

¼	DAIKON RADISH
½	TEASPOON KOSHER SALT
2	TABLESPOONS SUGAR
2	TABLESPOONS RICE VINEGAR
2	TABLESPOONS WATER
½	TABLESPOON LIGHT SOY SAUCE
1	DRIED RED CHILE PEPPER
	3-INCH SQUARE OF DRIED KOMBU

NANBANZUKE

YIELD: 4 SERVINGS / ACTIVE TIME: 20 MINUTES / TOTAL TIME: 3 HOURS AND 20 MINUTES

Nanbanzuke is a popular dish that consists of fried fish or meat that is then soaked in a sweet vinegar marinade. In Japan, horse mackerel is the most popular choice, but this preparation is versatile enough to allow for other whitefish or salmon to be used.

1. Sprinkle the salt over the mackerel and let it sit for 10 minutes.

2. Place the dashi, vinegar, soy sauce, mirin, sugar, and chile in a small saucepan and bring the mixture to a boil. Add the onion, reduce the heat to low, and simmer for 3 minutes. Remove the pan from heat, add the pepper and carrot, and let the mixture rest.

3. Add rice bran oil to a Dutch oven until it is about 2 inches deep and warm it to 320°F. Pat the mackerel dry with paper towels and coat it with the tapioca starch. Gently slip the mackerel into the hot oil and fry until it is golden brown and cooked through, about 6 minutes. Transfer the fried mackerel to a paper towel–lined plate to drain.

4. Transfer the brine and vegetables to a large mason jar. Add the fried mackerel, making sure that it is completely submerged. Seal the mason jar and let the mackerel and vegetables pickle in the refrigerator for 3 hours before serving.

INGREDIENTS:

¼   TEASPOON KOSHER SALT

⅔   LB. HORSE MACKEREL FILLETS, CHOPPED

1   CUP AWASE DASHI STOCK (SEE PAGE 38)

3½   TABLESPOONS RICE VINEGAR

2   TABLESPOONS LIGHT SOY SAUCE

1½   TABLESPOONS MIRIN

1   TABLESPOON SUGAR

½   TEASPOON MINCED DRIED CHILE PEPPER

½   ONION, SLICED THIN

½   GREEN BELL PEPPER, JULIENNED

½   CARROT, PEELED AND JULIENNED

RICE BRAN OIL, AS NEEDED

2   TABLESPOONS TAPIOCA STARCH

KOHAKU NAMASU

YIELD: 6 SERVINGS / **ACTIVE TIME:** 15 MINUTES / **TOTAL TIME:** 12 HOURS 15 MINUTES

This vibrant dish is made with shreds of daikon radish and carrots pickled in a refreshing blend of vinegar and citrus juice. The colors resemble a red-and-white obi string called mizuhiki, which is commonly used to decorate gifts and is considered good luck. Due to its auspicious connotations, kohaku namasu is often served as part of Osechi Ryori, the Japanese New Year spread.

1. Wash the radish and carrot and cut off their rounded edges to make them into block shapes. Slice them thin and then julienne until the radish and carrots are matchsticks. Place them in a large bowl, add ½ teaspoon of salt, and massage it into the vegetables. Let them sit for 15 minutes.

2. Place the vinegar, water, sugar, yuzu juice, soy sauce, yuzu peel, kombu, and remaining salt in a resealable plastic bag, seal it, and work the mixture with your hands to combine.

3. Squeeze the radish and carrot to remove any excess liquid. Discard the liquid and place the radish and carrot in the resealable bag. Seal the bag, making sure to remove as much air from it as possible. Place the bag in a baking dish, place it in the refrigerator, and let the radish and carrot pickle overnight before serving.

INGREDIENTS:

7 OZ. DAIKON RADISH

3½ OZ. CARROT, PEELED

¾ TEASPOON KOSHER SALT

2 TABLESPOONS RICE VINEGAR

3 TABLESPOONS WATER

2 TABLESPOONS SUGAR

1 TABLESPOON YUZU OR LEMON JUICE

¼ TEASPOON SOY SAUCE

1 TABLESPOON SLICED YUZU, LEMON, OR ORANGE PEEL, PLUS MORE FOR SERVING

4-INCH SQUARE OF DRIED KOMBU

Nanbanzuke. see page 324

BEER-PICKLED CUCUMBERS

YIELD: 8 SERVINGS / **ACTIVE TIME:** 5 MINUTES / **TOTAL TIME:** 12 HOURS

Cucumber pickles hold a special spot in Japanese cuisine for their home-friendly preparation methods and endless variations. This robustly flavored pickle pairs perfectly as a snack with your favorite drink or as a zesty side to a bowl of rice. And for those preferring an alcohol-free option, nonalcoholic beer makes an excellent substitute.

1. Place the cucumbers in a resealable plastic bag, add the remaining ingredients, and seal the bag, making sure to remove as much air from it as possible. Gently massage the mixture until well combined.

2. Let the cucumbers pickle in the refrigerator for 12 hours before serving.

INGREDIENTS:

3   JAPANESE OR PERSIAN CUCUMBERS (ABOUT 1 LB.), SLICED ON A BIAS

½   CUP LAGER OR NONALCOHOLIC BEER

½   CUP SUGAR

1   TEASPOON MINCED DRIED CHILE PEPPER

1   TABLESPOON KOSHER SALT

1   TEASPOON JAPANESE MUSTARD

UMEBOSHI

YIELD: 20 SERVINGS / **ACTIVE TIME:** 30 MINUTES / **TOTAL TIME:** 4 TO 6 MONTHS

Umeboshi are one of the most popular pickles in Japan. Made with fragrant Japanese plums, they are known for their vibrant red color and strong sour and salty flavor.

1. To begin preparations for the plums, inspect the plums and discard any that are bruised or damaged. Place them in a bowl and fill the bowl with cold water. Gently rub the plums to clean them and remove the small stems with a toothpick. Dry them individually with paper towels and place them on a clean plate.

2. Pour the shochu into a small bowl and roll each plum in it before placing them in a large resealable plastic bag.

3. Add the salt and massage it into the plums until they are evenly covered. Seal the bag, making sure to remove all of the air from it. Place the bag in a wide container dish and lay the plums out flat in one layer.

4. Place another container on top of the plums and weigh it down with a 2 lb. weight. Let the plums rest in a cool, dark place for 3 to 7 days, turning the bag over once or twice a day. During this time, the plums will release juices known as "umesu" or plum vinegar.

5. Once the plums have released enough vinegar to be fully submerged, begin preparations for the shiso leaves. Put on a pair of gloves, place the shiso leaves in a large bowl, and wash them. Drain, sprinkle half of the salt over them, and massage the salt into the shiso leaves to get them to release the foamy, astringent water inside. Drain the shiso leaves, repeat the process with the remaining salt, and drain.

6. Place the shiso leaves in a glass bowl and pour in about ½ cup of the plum vinegar that has accumulated in the bag containing the plums. Stir to combine, pour the shiso mixture into the bag of plums, and gently massage the bag to evenly distribute the mixture. Alternatively, transfer the plums and vinegar to a sterilized glass jar and add the shiso leaves and juices. Tightly seal the container and store the plums in a cool, dark place for 1 to 4 weeks, tilting the container occasionally.

7. When the weather is forecast to be bright and sunny for 3 consecutive days, remove the plums and shiso leaves from the vinegar and arrange them on a large, flat bamboo strainer. Reserve the vinegar.

Continued

INGREDIENTS:

FOR THE PLUMS

20	RIPE JAPANESE PLUMS (ABOUT 1 LB.)
2	TABLESPOONS SHOCHU, SAKE, OR VODKA
2.4–2.8	OZ. COARSE SEA SALT (15 TO 18 PERCENT OF THE WEIGHT OF THE PLUMS)

FOR THE SHISO LEAVES

2.4	OZ. PURPLE SHISO LEAVES
1	TABLESPOON COARSE SEA SALT

8. Cover the strainer with a net to protect it from insects and animals, then place it outside directly in the sun from morning to mid-afternoon. Bring the plums in overnight and return them to the vinegar to intensify their color. Leave the shiso leaves on the tray. Repeat for 3 days in total.

9. Once dried, the shiso leaves can be ground in a food processor and used to season rice. At this point, the umeboshi are ready for long-term storage.

10. Return them to the vinegar for an intensely red, juicy and sour umeboshi. Alternatively, store them in a sterilized mason jar without the vinegar for a paler and milder umeboshi.

11. The leftover vinegar can be used for pickles and sauces. Store the umeboshi in a cool, dark place for at least 3 months before eating, though 6 to 12 months is preferred, as the umeboshi will have a much better flavor.

DONBURI
(RICE BOWLS)

*D*onburi is a Japanese cooking style where rice and a main dish are served together in a single bowl, combining convenience with delicious flavors. An important aspect of donburi dishes is the amount of rice used. On average, the cooked rice portions for donburi are as follows: small is 1 cup, regular is 1½ cups, and large is 2 cups. I recommend starting with the regular portion and adjusting according to your preference.

OYAKO DON

YIELD: 2 SERVINGS / **ACTIVE TIME:** 20 MINUTES / **TOTAL TIME:** 25 MINUTES

This is a comforting rice bowl featuring chicken and onions simmered in a savory broth, then gently blanketed with egg. Its name, "oyako," means parent and child in Japanese, referring to the chicken and egg. This recipe streamlines the traditional method, focusing on perfecting the texture of each component. When combined, the ingredients create a symphony of flavors, offering a simple yet satisfying dining experience.

1. Place the chicken in a bowl, sprinkle the flour and salt over it, and stir until it is evenly coated.

2. Place the canola oil in a large skillet and warm it over medium heat. Add the chicken in a single layer, skin side down, and cook until it is crispy. Turn the chicken over, brown it on that side, and transfer it to a plate.

3. Add the water, mirin, sugar, and dashi granules to the pan and stir to combine. Add the onion, bring to a simmer over medium-low heat, and cook until the onion has softened, about 5 minutes.

4. Return the chicken to the pan and stir in the soy sauce.

5. Divide the egg whites and yolks into separate bowls and lightly whisk each until it is just scrambled. Pour the egg whites into the pan, cover it, and cook for 1 minute.

6. Drizzle the egg yolks over the mixture in the pan, cover it again, and cook until the chicken is cooked through and the eggs are cooked to your liking.

7. Divide the rice among the serving bowls, top each portion with some of the chicken mixture, garnish with broccoli sprouts, and serve.

INGREDIENTS:

½ LB. BONELESS, SKIN-ON CHICKEN THIGHS, CUT INTO BITE-SIZE PIECES

1 TABLESPOON ALL-PURPOSE FLOUR

   PINCH OF KOSHER SALT

1 TEASPOON CANOLA OIL

½ CUP WATER

3 TABLESPOONS MIRIN

2 TEASPOONS SUGAR

1 TEASPOON DASHI GRANULES

½ ONION, CUT INTO WEDGES

2 TABLESPOONS LIGHT SOY SAUCE

3 EGGS

3 CUPS PERFECT JAPANESE RICE (SEE PAGE 80)

   BROCCOLI SPROUTS, FOR GARNISH

GYUDON

YIELD: 4 SERVINGS / **ACTIVE TIME:** 15 MINUTES / **TOTAL TIME:** 20 MINUTES

Gyudon has been a beloved dish since the late 1800s, featuring tender beef and onions simmered in a sweet soy sauce and served over rice. Renowned as a quick and satisfying meal, this "fast food" classic can easily be recreated at home. For the beef, short plate, short ribs, brisket, skirt steak, or similar cuts are good options.

1. To begin preparations for the bowls, place the beef and sake in a bowl, stir to combine, and let the beef marinate.

2. To prepare the sauce, place all of the ingredients in a saucepan and bring to a boil over medium-high heat. Reduce the heat to medium-low and let the sauce simmer for 2 minutes. Remove the pan from heat and set the sauce aside.

3. Place the beef tallow in a large skillet and warm it over medium heat. Add the onion and cook, stirring occasionally, until it starts to soften. Remove the beef from the sake and add it to the pan.

4. Pour the sauce into the pan and bring to a boil. Reduce the heat to medium-low and simmer the beef and onion until the beef is cooked through, about 10 minutes.

5. Divide the rice among the serving bowls and spoon the beef, onion, and sauce over the top of each portion. Garnish with Benishoga and green onions and serve.

INGREDIENTS:

FOR THE BOWLS

1	LB. BEEF, SLICED THIN
¼	CUP SAKE
2	TABLESPOONS BEEF TALLOW
1	ONION, CUT INTO WEDGES
6	CUPS PERFECT JAPANESE RICE (SEE PAGE 80)
	BENISHOGA (SEE PAGE 315), FOR GARNISH
	GREEN ONIONS, FINELY CHOPPED, FOR GARNISH

FOR THE SAUCE

2	CUPS AWASE DASHI STOCK (SEE PAGE 38)
6	TABLESPOONS SAKE
6	TABLESPOONS SOY SAUCE
6	TABLESPOONS MIRIN
2	TABLESPOONS WHITE WINE
3	TABLESPOONS LIGHT BROWN SUGAR
2	GARLIC CLOVES, GRATED
1	TABLESPOON GRATED FRESH GINGER

Gyudon, see page 337

PORK KATSUDON

YIELD: 2 SERVINGS / ACTIVE TIME: 15 MINUTES / TOTAL TIME: 20 MINUTES

Katsudon consists of a bowl of rice topped with a deep-fried pork cutlet (tonkatsu), onions, and silky eggs simmered in a soy sauce–based broth.

1. Place the water, dashi granules, mirin, sugar, and sake in a large skillet and stir to combine. Add the onion to the pan and cook over medium heat until the onion has softened, about 5 minutes.

2. Stir in the soy sauce and then gently lay the Tonkatsu over the onion.

3. Divide the egg whites and yolks into separate bowls and lightly whisk each until it is just scrambled. Pour the egg whites around the edge of the pan, cover it, and cook for 1 minute.

4. Drizzle the egg yolks just inside the layer of egg whites, cover the pan again, and turn off the heat. Let the residual heat cook the eggs until they are cooked to your liking.

5. Divide the rice among the serving bowls and top each portion with some of the Tonkatsu, onion, and eggs. Garnish with mitsuba and serve.

INGREDIENTS:

⅔	CUP WATER
1	TEASPOON DASHI GRANULES
3	TABLESPOONS MIRIN
1	TEASPOON SUGAR
1	TABLESPOON SAKE
½	ONION, CUT INTO WEDGES
2	TABLESPOONS SOY SAUCE
2	TONKATSU (SEE PAGE 284)
4	EGGS
3	CUPS PERFECT JAPANESE RICE (SEE PAGE 80)
	MITSUBA (JAPANESE WILD PARSLEY), FOR GARNISH

BUTADON

YIELD: 4 SERVINGS / **ACTIVE TIME:** 15 MINUTES / **TOTAL TIME:** 20 MINUTES

Butadon is a dish from the Tokachi region of Hokkaido. It is usually prepared by grilling over charcoal, which gives it a unique smoky flavor. However, this recipe includes a specially crafted sauce that mimics the flavor supplied by charcoal grilling, making it possible to achieve a similar result in the standard home kitchen.

1. Cut the pork into slices that are just under ¼ inch thick and set it aside.

2. Place the turbinado sugar and water in a small saucepan and warm the mixture over medium heat, stirring until the sugar has fully dissolved. Stop stirring and swirl the pan occasionally until the mixture has turned into caramel.

3. Reduce the heat to medium-low and carefully add the soy sauce, sake, mirin, and honey to the caramel. Be very careful adding when adding liquid to hot caramel, as it can spatter and potentially cause severe burns. Stir until well combined and cook the mixture until it has a thin, syrupy consistency. Remove the pan from heat and set the caramel sauce aside.

4. Place the canola oil in a large skillet and warm it over medium-high heat. Add the pork in a single layer and cook until it is golden brown on one side. Turn the pork over and pour the caramel sauce over it. Gently move the pork around in the sauce, allowing the sauce to thicken and glaze the pork. Continue cooking until the pork is fully glazed and the sauce has thickened.

5. Divide the rice among the serving bowls and top each portion with some of the glazed pork. Garnish with edamame and green onions and serve.

INGREDIENTS:

1⅓	LBS. PORK BELLY OR PORK SHOULDER
2	TABLESPOONS TURBINADO SUGAR
½	CUP WATER
¼	CUP SOY SAUCE
2	TEASPOONS SAKE
2	TEASPOONS MIRIN
2	TEASPOONS HONEY
1	TABLESPOON CANOLA OIL
6	CUPS PERFECT JAPANESE RICE (SEE PAGE 80)
¼	CUP COOKED SHELLED EDAMAME, FOR GARNISH
¼	CUP FINELY CHOPPED GREEN ONIONS, FOR GARNISH

SOBORO DON

YIELD: 4 SERVINGS / **ACTIVE TIME:** 20 MINUTES / **TOTAL TIME:** 25 MINUTES

Soboro is the Japanese word for "ground meat" and can be used to refer to both meat or fish. Soboro is typically seasoned with Japanese condiments such as soy sauce and mirin, creating a harmonious blend of salty and sweet. This is also a perfect dish to serve in a bento box.

1. Prepare an ice bath and bring water to a boil in a small saucepan.

2. To prepare the eggs, place all of the ingredients, except for the canola oil, in a bowl and whisk until combined. Place the canola oil in a large skillet and warm it over medium heat. Pour in the egg mixture and let the eggs cook undisturbed until the edges begin to set. Gently scramble the eggs and cook until they are done to your liking. Transfer the eggs to a plate and set them aside. Wipe out the pan.

3. To begin preparations for the pork, place the canola oil in the pan and warm it over medium heat. Add the pork and cook until it starts to brown, about 5 minutes, breaking it up with a wooden spoon. Stir in the soy sauce, sake, mirin, ginger paste, and sugar and cook, stirring frequently, until the liquid has evaporated and the meat is cooked through, evenly coated by the sauce, and fragrant.

4. While the pork is cooking, add the snow peas to the boiling water and blanch for 1 minute. Drain and immediately plunge them into the ice bath until they are cool. Slice the snow peas on a bias.

5. Divide the rice among the serving bowls, top each portion with some of the eggs, pork, and snow peas, and serve.

INGREDIENTS:

FOR THE EGGS

6	EGGS
1	TEASPOON DASHI GRANULES
2	TABLESPOONS SAKE
¼	TEASPOON KOSHER SALT
1	TEASPOON CANOLA OIL

FOR THE PORK

1	TEASPOON CANOLA OIL
⅔	LB. GROUND PORK
2	TABLESPOONS SOY SAUCE
2	TABLESPOONS SAKE
1½	TABLESPOON MIRIN
1½	TEASPOONS GINGER PASTE
1½	TABLESPOONS SUGAR
15	SNOW PEAS
6	CUPS PERFECT JAPANESE RICE (SEE PAGE 80)

STAMINA DON

YIELD: 4 SERVINGS / **ACTIVE TIME:** 10 MINUTES / **TOTAL TIME:** 40 MINUTES

Stamina-don, affectionately called suta-don, is a popular Japanese fast food dish that combines hearty rice with succulent stir-fried pork. This pork is generously coated in a rich, garlic-infused soy sauce, the component that influenced the name, embodying the belief in Japan that garlic boosts stamina. The dish's crowning glory is the silky egg yolk, which, when mixed with the pork, creates a sublime experience.

1. Place the miso paste, soy sauce, sake, mirin, honey, chicken bouillon, oyster sauce, and water in a bowl and stir to combine. Cut the pork belly into 2-inch-long pieces and add it to the bowl. Stir until it is thoroughly coated and marinate the pork in the refrigerator for 30 minutes.

2. Place the sesame oil in a large skillet and warm it over medium heat. Add the garlic, garlic chives, and chile and stir-fry for 30 seconds. Add the onion to the pan and stir-fry until it is just tender, 3 to 5 minutes.

3. Add the pork and marinade to the pan and stir-fry until the pork is cooked through.

4. Divide the rice among the serving bowls and top each portion with some of the kizami nori and pork mixture. Garnish with the egg yolks, green onions, sesame seeds, and chili oil and serve.

INGREDIENTS:

2	TABLESPOONS YELLOW MISO PASTE
2	TABLESPOONS SOY SAUCE
2	TABLESPOONS SAKE
2	TABLESPOONS MIRIN
1	TABLESPOON HONEY
2	TEASPOONS CHINESE CHICKEN BOUILLON
2	TEASPOONS OYSTER SAUCE
¼	CUP WATER
1¼	LBS. PORK BELLY, SLICED THIN
1	TABLESPOON SESAME OIL
6	GARLIC CLOVES, MINCED
1	CUP CHOPPED GARLIC CHIVES (CHINESE CHIVES)
2	TEASPOONS MINCED DRIED CHILE PEPPER
1	ONION, CUT INTO WEDGES
6	CUPS PERFECT JAPANESE RICE (SEE PAGE 80)
¼	CUP SHREDDED KIZAMI NORI
4	PASTEURIZED EGG YOLKS OR ONSEN TAMAGO (SEE PAGE 57), FOR GARNISH
¼	CUP CHOPPED GREEN ONIONS, FOR GARNISH
4	TEASPOONS WHITE SESAME SEEDS, FOR GARNISH
2	TEASPOONS CHILI OIL, FOR GARNISH

YAKINIKU DON

YIELD: 4 SERVINGS / **ACTIVE TIME:** 15 MINUTES / **TOTAL TIME:** 15 MINUTES

Authentic yakiniku sauce is the result of blending a variety of ingredients to achieve a signature sweet and rich flavor. This recipe aims to replicate the complex flavor of the sauce found in specialty yakiniku restaurants while using fewer ingredients.

1. Prepare a grill for high heat (about 500°F). Place the beef on the grill and cook until it is cooked to your liking. Remove the beef from the grill and let it rest for 2 minutes.

2. Place the rice in a serving dish, arrange the beef on top, and pour the sauce over the top. Serve and garnish each portion with green onions and if, desired, an Onsen Tamago.

INGREDIENTS:

1⅓ LB. BEEF OR PORK, SLICED INTO ⅕-INCH-THICK PIECES

6 CUPS PERFECT JAPANESE RICE (SEE PAGE 80)

   YAKINIKU SAUCE (SEE PAGE 679)

   GREEN ONIONS, CHOPPED, FOR GARNISH

4 ONSEN TAMAGO (SEE PAGE 57; OPTIONAL)

Stamina Don, see page 346

TENDON

YIELD: 4 SERVINGS / **ACTIVE TIME:** 5 MINUTES / **TOTAL TIME:** 25 MINUTES

This is a decadent dish consisting of tempura and rice, all of it drizzled with a special sweet sauce.

1. To prepare the sauce, place the mirin, sake, soy sauce, light brown sugar, and dashi granules in a saucepan and bring to a simmer over medium-low heat. Cook for 3 to 4 minutes, remove the pan from heat, and let the sauce cool.

2. If you are planning to use freshly made Tempura, this is an ideal time to start preparing it.

3. Divide the rice among the serving bowls, sprinkle some Tenkasu over the rice, then lightly drizzle some of the tendon sauce over it.

4. Top each portion with some of the Tempura, pour the remaining sauce over the top, and serve.

INGREDIENTS:

FOR THE SAUCE

¼ CUP MIRIN

3 TABLESPOONS SAKE

3 TABLESPOONS SOY SAUCE

1 TABLESPOON LIGHT BROWN SUGAR

1 TEASPOON DASHI GRANULES

FOR THE BOWLS

4 SHRIMP TEMPURA (SEE PAGE 272)

4 EGGPLANT TEMPURA

4 NORI TEMPURA

4 SHIITAKE MUSHROOM TEMPURA

4 SHISO LEAF TEMPURA

4 SHISHITO PEPPER TEMPURA

6 CUPS PERFECT JAPANESE RICE (SEE PAGE 80)

TENKASU (SEE PAGE 68), TO TASTE

PONZU CHICKEN DONBURI

YIELD: 4 SERVINGS / **ACTIVE TIME:** 25 MINUTES / **TOTAL TIME:** 1 HOUR

This recipe takes the humble chicken thigh to a whole new level thanks to the zest and tang of ponzu sauce. This dish balances sourness, sweetness, and crispiness perfectly, thanks to meticulous seasoning adjustments and a unique weighted crisping technique.

1. To begin preparations for the bowls, place the chicken on a cutting board, skin side down. Make horizontal incisions in the thickest parts of the chicken, creating small flaps. Gently pull these flaps outward to even out the thickness of the chicken. Flip the chicken over so the skin side is facing up and stretch the skin to cover the edges of the chicken, ensuring a snug fit.

2. Turn the chicken over and place plastic wrap on the meat side. Turn it over and place it in a container with the skin side up. Pat the skin dry with paper towels to remove excess moisture. Chill the chicken, uncovered, in the refrigerator for about 30 minutes to dry out the skin.

3. Place the canola oil in a large skillet. Remove the plastic wrap from the chicken and season it with the salt and pepper. Place the chicken in the pan, skin side down, and cover the pan with aluminum foil. Place a large pot filled halfway with water on top of the foil to weigh down the chicken. This will ensure that the chicken skin crisps up beautifully.

4. Place the pan over medium-low heat. Once you hear the chicken sizzling, cook it for 10 minutes.

5. Remove the weight and foil and baste the chicken with the rendered fat and juices for 2 to 3 minutes. Turn the chicken over and cook until the chicken is cooked through, 1 to 2 minutes. Transfer the chicken to a cutting board.

6. Pour out the excess fat and juices, leaving just a little in there for frying. Warm them over medium heat, add the bok choy and mushrooms, and season with salt and pepper. Cook, stirring occasionally, until the vegetables are tender, 8 to 10 minutes. Remove the pan from heat and set the vegetables aside.

7. To prepare the sauce, place the ponzu, mirin, sake, brown sugar, and honey in a small saucepan and bring to a boil. Combine the water and potato starch in a small bowl, pour the slurry into the saucepan, and cook until the sauce thickens slightly.

8. Slice the chicken into strips. Divide the rice among the serving bowls and top each portion with some of the chicken and vegetables. Drizzle the sauce over the top and serve.

INGREDIENTS:

FOR THE BOWLS

1½   LBS. BONELESS, SKIN-ON CHICKEN THIGHS

2   TABLESPOONS CANOLA OIL

2   PINCHES OF KOSHER SALT, PLUS MORE TO TASTE

2   PINCHES OF BLACK PEPPER, PLUS MORE TO TASTE

2   BOK CHOY, TRIMMED AND CHOPPED

7   OZ. MUSHROOMS, CHOPPED

4½   CUPS PERFECT JAPANESE RICE (SEE PAGE 80)

FOR THE SAUCE

6   TABLESPOONS PONZU SAUCE (SEE PAGE 45)

2   TABLESPOONS MIRIN

2   TABLESPOONS SAKE

2   TEASPOONS LIGHT BROWN SUGAR

1   TEASPOON HONEY

1   TABLESPOON COLD WATER

1   TEASPOON POTATO STARCH

Tendon, see page 350

TERIYAKI BEEF DONBURI

YIELD: 4 SERVINGS / **ACTIVE TIME:** 10 MINUTES / **TOTAL TIME:** 10 MINUTES

The addition of fiery wasabi is key here, as it adds a spicy kick and pairs perfectly with the beef.

1. To prepare the sauce, place all of the ingredients in a bowl and whisk to combine. Keep in mind that while this amount of wasabi might seem like a lot, the flavor gets softened when cooked. Set the bowl beside the stove.

2. To begin preparations for the bowls, cut the steaks into bite-size pieces and season them with salt and pepper. Warm a large skillet over high heat. Lightly coat the steaks with the potato starch.

3. Add the canola oil to the pan and swirl it around to evenly coat the bottom. Add the steaks, sear them, and turn them over. Cook until the steaks are cooked to your liking.

4. Add the sauce and stir-fry until it becomes glossy and thickens slightly. Remove the pan from heat.

5. Divide the rice among the serving bowls and top each portion with some of the cabbage and the teriyaki beef. Garnish with green onions and sesame seeds and serve.

INGREDIENTS:

FOR THE SAUCE

2	TABLESPOONS WASABI (SEE PAGE 500 FOR HOMEMADE)
¼	CUP SOY SAUCE
¼	CUP SAKE
¼	CUP MIRIN
4	TEASPOONS SUGAR
2	TEASPOONS HONEY

FOR THE BOWLS

2	LBS. BEEF STEAKS (EACH APPROXIMATELY ¾ TO 1 INCH THICK)
	SALT AND PEPPER, TO TASTE
1	TABLESPOON POTATO STARCH
1	TABLESPOON CANOLA OIL
6	CUPS PERFECT JAPANESE RICE (SEE PAGE 80)
1	CUP SHREDDED CABBAGE
	GREEN ONIONS, FINELY CHOPPED, FOR GARNISH
	SESAME SEEDS, FOR GARNISH

SUKIYAKI DONBURI

YIELD: 4 SERVINGS / **ACTIVE TIME:** 10 MINUTES / **TOTAL TIME:** 20 MINUTES

Sukiyaki donburi takes all of the best elements of sukiyaki hot pot and presents them in the form of a rice bowl. One of the highlights of this particular recipe is the silky steamed egg, which soaks up the rich flavors of the sauce.

1. Separate the pasteurized eggs, pouring the whites into a large mixing bowl and the yolks into a smaller bowl. Set the pasteurized yolks aside.

2. Crack the standard eggs into the bowl with the pasteurized egg whites and whisk until combined. Set the mixture by the stove.

3. Place the dashi granules, soy sauce, sake, mirin, and sugar in a large skillet and whisk until the sugar has dissolved. Add the mushroom stems and caps to the sauce and cook them over medium-low heat.

4. When the sauce begins to bubble, add the beef and simmer until it is cooked to your liking. Remove the beef and mushrooms from the pan and transfer them to a warm plate.

5. Add the leeks and garland chrysanthemums to the sauce and cook until they have softened slightly. Pour the egg mixture evenly around the pan and cover it with a lid. Steam until the eggs are cooked to your liking.

6. Divide the rice among the serving bowls and top each portion with some of the steamed eggs, leek mixture, mushroom stems, and beef. Garnish with a shiitake cap, pasteurized egg yolk, and Benishoga and serve.

INGREDIENTS:

8	EGGS (4 PASTEURIZED, 4 STANDARD)
1	TEASPOON DASHI GRANULES
¼	CUP SOY SAUCE
¼	CUP SAKE
¼	CUP MIRIN
3	TABLESPOONS SUGAR
4	SHIITAKE MUSHROOMS, STEMS TRIMMED AND SLICED THIN, CAPS LEFT WHOLE
1	LB. BEEF, SLICED THIN
2	JAPANESE LEEKS, WHITE PARTS ONLY, SLICED THIN ON A BIAS
1	BUNCH OF GARLAND CHRYSANTHEMUM, CUT INTO 2-INCH PIECES
6	CUPS PERFECT JAPANESE RICE (SEE PAGE 80)
	BENISHOGA (SEE PAGE 315), FOR GARNISH

MABO DOFU DON

YIELD: 4 SERVINGS / **ACTIVE TIME:** 20 MINUTES / **TOTAL TIME:** 25 MINUTES

Mabo dofu, a dish that originated in China's Sichuan Province, has evolved into a beloved staple in Japanese households and Chinese restaurants in Japan.

1. To begin preparations for the bowls, place the pork in a large skillet, season it with the salt and pepper, and cook over medium heat until it is browned all over, breaking the pork up with a wooden spoon. Add the onion and cook, stirring occasionally, until it has softened slightly. Drizzle in the sake and soy sauce, add the miso paste, and stir until they are evenly distributed and coating the pork.

2. Push the pork to one side of the pan. On the empty side, pour in the sesame oil, chili bean sauce, and garlic. Cook for 30 seconds to 1 minute, until the mixture fragrant, and then stir the mixture into the pork. Remove the pan from heat.

3. To begin preparations for the sauce, pour the hot water into the pan and sprinkle in the chicken stock powder. Add the tofu and bring the mixture to a boil, stirring occasionally.

4. Add the sake, soy sauce, oyster sauce, and pepper and stir to incorporate. Reduce the heat so that the sauce simmers and cook until it has reduced by about half, stirring occasionally.

5. Combine the cold water and cornstarch in a small bowl, pour the slurry into the pan, and stir until the sauce thickens and becomes glossy. Remove the pan from heat.

6. Divide the rice among the serving bowls and top each portion with some of the pork mixture. Garnish with the green onions, chili oil, and, if desired, chili threads and serve.

INGREDIENTS:

FOR THE BOWLS

½	LB. GROUND PORK
	PINCH OF KOSHER SALT
	PINCH OF BLACK PEPPER
1	ONION, FINELY DICED
1	TEASPOON SAKE
1	TEASPOON SOY SAUCE
1	TABLESPOON YELLOW MISO PASTE
1	TABLESPOON SESAME OIL
1	TABLESPOON CHILI BEAN SAUCE
4	GARLIC CLOVES, GRATED
6	CUPS PERFECT JAPANESE RICE (SEE PAGE 80)
2	TEASPOONS CHILI OIL, FOR GARNISH
¼	CUP FINELY CHOPPED GREEN ONION, FOR GARNISH
1	TABLESPOON CHILI THREADS (OPTIONAL), FOR GARNISH

FOR THE SAUCE

2	CUPS HOT WATER
4	TEASPOONS CHINESE CHICKEN BOUILLON
20	OZ. FIRM TOFU
2	TABLESPOONS SAKE
1	TEASPOON SOY SAUCE
1	TABLESPOON OYSTER SAUCE
½	TEASPOON BLACK PEPPER
¼	CUP COLD WATER
4	TEASPOONS CORNSTARCH

Sukiyaki Donburi, see page 356

TERIYAKI TOFU DONBURI

YIELD: 4 SERVINGS / **ACTIVE TIME:** 15 MINUTES / **TOTAL TIME:** 20 MINUTES

This plant-based meal is easy to customize to your personal tastes and always hits the spot.

1. Wrap the tofu with paper towels and place it on a microwave-safe plate. Microwave on high for 2 minutes to evaporate any excess moisture. Remove the tofu from the microwave and let it cool.

2. Coat a large skillet with canola oil and warm it over medium heat. Add the pepper and leek and cook, stirring once or twice, until they are nicely browned all over. Transfer the vegetables to a plate and leave them by the stove.

3. Place the potato starch, salt, and pepper in a shallow bowl and whisk to combine. When the tofu is cool enough to handle, cut it into large bite-size cubes. Add a generous drizzle of canola oil to the pan and warm it over medium heat. Dredge the tofu in the potato starch mixture, place it in the pan, and fry until it is golden brown all over, turning it as necessary.

4. Place the soy sauce, mirin, sake, sugar, and garlic in a bowl and whisk to combine. Return the pepper and leek to the pan, pour in the sauce, and cook until the sauce becomes thick and glossy, gently stirring so that everything gets evenly coated by the sauce. Remove the pan from heat.

5. Divide the rice among the serving bowls and top each portion with the tofu mixture. Garnish with sesame seeds, green onions, and chili oil and serve.

INGREDIENTS:

1½ LBS. FIRM TOFU

CANOLA OIL, AS NEEDED

1 GREEN BELL PEPPER, STEMMED, SEEDED, AND CUBED

½ JAPANESE LEEK, WHITE PART ONLY, SLICED THIN ON A BIAS

6 TABLESPOONS POTATO STARCH

PINCH OF KOSHER SALT

PINCH OF BLACK PEPPER

¼ CUP SOY SAUCE

¼ CUP MIRIN

¼ CUP SAKE

4 TEASPOONS SUGAR

3 GARLIC CLOVES, GRATED

6 CUPS PERFECT JAPANESE RICE (SEE PAGE 80)

SESAME SEEDS, FOR GARNISH

GREEN ONIONS, FINELY CHOPPED, FOR GARNISH

CHILI OIL, FOR GARNISH

CHUKA DON

YIELD: 4 SERVINGS / **ACTIVE TIME**: 20 MINUTES / **TOTAL TIME**: 40 MINUTES

Chuka don, which translates to "Chinese rice bowl," is a beloved dish in Japanese Chinese cuisine, featuring fluffy rice topped with a savory mixture resembling Chinese babaocai.

1. To begin preparations for the bowls, place the mushrooms in a bowl and cover them with the water. Let the mushrooms soak until they are soft and pliable, about 20 minutes.

2. Place the pork, sake, and grated ginger in a bowl and stir until well combined. Set the mixture aside.

3. Drain the mushrooms and reserve the soaking liquid for another preparation. Remove and discard the stems. Slice the mushroom caps into thin pieces and set them aside.

4. Place the canola oil in a large wok or deep skillet and warm it over medium-high heat. Add the julienned ginger and garlic and stir-fry for 30 seconds. Add the pork mixture and seafood mixture to the pan and stir-fry until the pork is browned on the outside.

5. Add the mushrooms, carrot, bok choy, and cabbage and stir-fry until the carrot and cabbage have softened.

6. To prepare the sauce, place all of the ingredients in a bowl and whisk to combine.

7. Add the sauce and quail eggs to the pan and stir-fry until the sauce thickens and has coated everything, 2 to 3 minutes. Remove the pan from heat and stir in a drizzle of canola oil.

8. Divide the rice among the serving bowls, top each portion with some of the mixture in the pan, and serve.

INGREDIENTS:

FOR THE BOWLS

2	DRIED SHIITAKE MUSHROOMS
1	CUP WATER
⅔	LB. PORK BELLY, SLICED THIN
1	TABLESPOON SAKE
1	TEASPOON GRATED FRESH GINGER
1	TABLESPOON CANOLA OIL, PLUS MORE AS NEEDED
	2-INCH PIECE OF FRESH GINGER, PEELED AND JULIENNED
2	GARLIC CLOVES, FINELY DICED
⅓	LB. SEAFOOD MIXTURE (THAWED IF FROZEN)
½	CARROT, PEELED AND JULIENNED
1	BOK CHOY, TRIMMED AND CHOPPED
⅛	NAPA CABBAGE, CHOPPED
8	BOILED QUAIL EGGS, PEELED
6	CUPS PERFECT JAPANESE RICE (SEE PAGE 80)

FOR THE SAUCE

1½	TEASPOONS CHINESE CHICKEN BOUILLON
1½	TABLESPOON LIGHT SOY SAUCE
2	TABLESPOONS SAKE
½	TABLESPOON OYSTER SAUCE
½	TABLESPOON SUGAR
1	TABLESPOON POTATO STARCH

Teriyaki Tofu Donburi,
see page 360

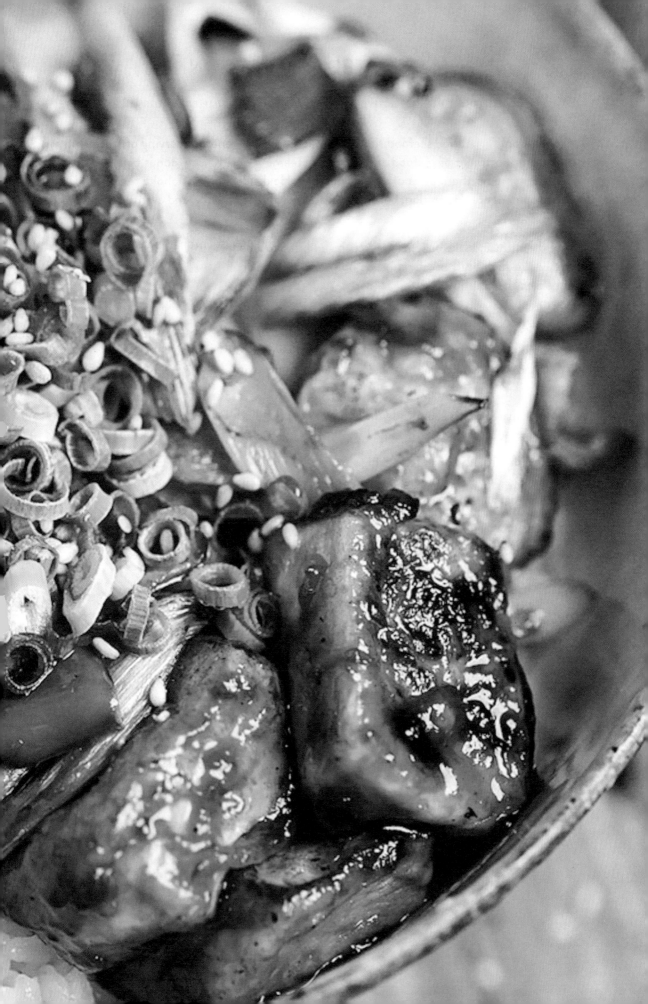

MARINATED KAISEN-DON

YIELD: 4 SERVINGS / **ACTIVE TIME:** 20 MINUTES / **TOTAL TIME:** 50 MINUTES

Kaisen-don is a beloved seafood rice bowl that features a generous serving of fresh sashimi and an assortment of seafood atop a bed of steaming rice. Kaisen-don is believed to have originated in the northern parts of Japan, including Hokkaido and the Tohoku region, and with the development of refrigeration, became available across the country, and eventually the world.

1. Place the mirin and sake in a small saucepan and bring to a boil over medium-high heat. Let the mixture boil for 1 minute and then turn off the heat.

2. Add the soy sauce to the saucepan and swirl the pan to incorporate it. Pour the marinade into a wide, shallow container and let it cool to room temperature. To speed up the cooling process, you can place the container of marinade over a bowl filled with ice water.

3. When the marinade has cooled, add the kombu to the container, making sure it is submerged in the liquid.

4. Dip the fish into the marinade, making sure that both sides are coated. Arrange the pieces in a single layer in the container, making sure they are flat and do not overlap.

5. Place plastic wrap directly on the surface of the fish. This will help prevent oxidation and ensures even marination. Place the container in the refrigerator and let the fish marinate for 30 minutes.

6. Divide the rice among the serving bowls and top each portion with some of the seafood. Drizzle some of the leftover marinade over the top, garnish with wasabi, and serve.

INGREDIENTS:

¼ CUP MIRIN

¼ CUP SAKE

¼ CUP SOY SAUCE

1 SMALL PIECE OF DRIED KOMBU

1⅓ LBS. SASHIMI-GRADE FISH OR SEAFOOD

6 CUPS PERFECT JAPANESE RICE OR SUMESHI (SEE PAGE 80 OR 484)

WASABI (SEE PAGE 500 FOR HOMEMADE), FOR GARNISH

SALMON & IKURA OYAKODON

YIELD: 4 SERVINGS / **ACTIVE TIME:** 10 MINUTES / **TOTAL TIME:** 10 MINUTES

While oyakodon is typically known as a rice bowl with chicken and eggs, the narrative shifts a little bit in Hokkaido. In this northern region of Japan, oyakodon is often a combination of salmon and salmon roe.

1. Place the rice, shiso leaves, Salmon Flakes, sesame seeds, and sesame oil in a large bowl and gently stir to combine. Divide the seasoned rice among the serving bowls.

2. Create a bed of kizami nori and broccoli sprouts atop each portion. Top with some of the salmon and spoon a generous amount of the ikura over the salmon.

3. Garnish with cucumber, wasabi, and any other toppings you like and serve.

INGREDIENTS:

4 CUPS PERFECT JAPANESE RICE (SEE PAGE 80)

6 SHISO LEAVES, SLICED THIN, PLUS MORE FOR GARNISH

¼ CUP SALMON FLAKES (SEE PAGE 61)

1 TABLESPOON SESAME SEEDS

1 TABLESPOON TOASTED SESAME OIL

¼ CUP BROCCOLI SPROUTS

¼ CUP SHREDDED KIZAMI NORI

¾ LB SASHIMI-GRADE SALMON, SLICED THIN

½ CUP IKURA (SEE PAGE 510)

CUCUMBER, SLICED ON A BIAS, FOR GARNISH

WASABI (SEE PAGE 500 FOR HOMEMADE) FOR GARNISH

UNAJU / UNADON

YIELD: 4 SERVINGS / **ACTIVE TIME:** 30 MINUTES / **TOTAL TIME:** 40 MINUTES

Here's a luxurious dish featuring grilled eel with a sweet and savory unagi sauce. When served over rice in a bowl, it's called unadon. When presented in a lacquered box (jyuubako) with rice, it's known as unaju.

1. To prepare the sauce, place the turbinado sugar in a saucepan and warm it over medium-high heat. When the sugar starts to melt, add the sake and mirin, bring the mixture to a boil, and cook for 1 to 2 minutes, stirring occasionally. Add the soy sauce, reduce the heat to low, and simmer until the sauce thickens slightly, about 10 minutes, swirling the pan occasionally to prevent the sugar from burning. Remove the pan from heat and let the sauce cool.

2. To begin preparations for the bowls, prepare a grill for medium-high heat (about 450°F). Line the grate with aluminum foil. Rinse the eels under cold water. Place a piece of plastic wrap over a cutting board and lay the eels on it. Cut each eel into 2 to 3 pieces (the size will depend on the size of your serving bowls) by pressing a sharp knife into the desired cutting area and gently pushing the eel back and forth over the plastic wrap while keeping the knife still. As eel is slippery, this is the safest way to cut it.

3. Place the eels in a large skillet, skin side down, and add the sake.

4. Turn the heat to medium and cover the pan with a lid. Steam the eel for 5 minutes.

5. Remove the pan from heat and transfer the eels, skin side down, to the foil-lined grill and cook for 6 minutes. Flip the eels over and grill for 5 minutes. Generously brush the cooled unagi sauce over the eels and grill for 30 seconds. Turn the eels over and apply the sauce to the other side. Grill for 30 seconds. Repeat the brushing and grilling process on each side two more times, for a total of three times on each side.

6. Divide the rice among the serving bowls and brush the top of the rice with the leftover unagi sauce. Top each portion with some of the grilled eel, garnish with ground sansho, and serve.

INGREDIENTS:

FOR THE SAUCE

6 TABLESPOONS TURBINADO SUGAR

½ CUP SAKE

½ CUP MIRIN

½ CUP SOY SAUCE

FOR THE BOWLS

1⅓ LBS. EEL FILLETS

¼ CUP SAKE

6 CUPS PERFECT JAPANESE RICE (SEE PAGE 80)

SANSHO PEPPER, GROUND, FOR GARNISH

RAMEN

*R*amen is a modern Japanese dish that has garnered immense popularity worldwide in recent years. This section introduces recipes for homemade toppings and various soups, allowing you to customize your ramen to your own preferences. As such, almost all of the recommendations for toppings are exactly that—feel free to swap in whatever accompaniments you like. It's also worth noting that a serving of ramen noodles typically weighs about 5 oz. to 7 oz. before boiling. If you favor a noodle-rich bowl, you're more than welcome to increase the amount.

HOMEMADE RAMEN NOODLES

YIELD: 4 SERVINGS / **ACTIVE TIME:** 45 MINUTES / **TOTAL TIME:** 25 HOURS AND 45 MINUTES

When it comes to crafting the perfect bowl of ramen at home, the quality and types of noodles you use can make all the difference. In Japan, fresh ramen noodles are readily available at supermarkets, but for those living outside of Japan, finding fresh ramen noodles can be a challenge. While it may be tempting to reach for a package of dried instant ramen as a substitute for fresh noodles, I strongly advise against it. Instant noodles and authentic ramen noodles are worlds apart in terms of taste, texture, and overall quality. In this recipe, I will demystify the process of making genuine homemade ramen noodles from scratch, helping you create noodles that rival those found in the very best ramen restaurants.

1. Place the water, kansui powder, and salt in a bowl and stir until the kansui powder and salt have dissolved and the mixture is well combined.

2. Sift the bread flour into a large bowl. Gradually add the water mixture to the flour, using your hands or chopsticks to incorporate each addition. Continue incorporating the water mixture until a crumbly dough forms. Transfer the dough to a resealable plastic bag and seal it, taking care to get all the air out of it. Let the dough rest at room temperature for 1 hour.

3. Place the bag with the dough on the floor and step on it with your foot to spread the dough evenly. Continue stepping on the dough until it evenly fills the bag. Remove the dough from the bag and fold it into thirds, as you would a letter to put into an envelope. Place the folded dough back into the bag, seal it, and step on it again. Repeat the process of folding the dough into thirds and kneading it with your feet for 15 minutes. After the last round, make sure the bag is sealed and let the dough rest at room temperature for 24 hours.

4. Remove the dough from the bag and place it on a flour-dusted work surface. Using a rolling pin, roll the dough out into a thin rectangle. Cut the rolled-out dough into quarters so that each piece will fit through the rollers on a pasta machine.

5. Set a pasta machine to the widest setting and run the dough through the machine once to flatten it. Adjust the pasta machine to the next widest setting and run the dough through again. Continue adjusting the machine to narrower settings and running the dough through each time. After running the dough through the fifth-narrowest setting, cut each piece of dough in half to make the noodles shorter. Lightly dust the pieces with flour to prevent sticking.

INGREDIENTS:

½   CUP WATER

½   TEASPOON KANSUI POWDER OR BAKING SODA

½   TEASPOON KOSHER SALT

10½   OZ. BREAD FLOUR, PLUS MORE AS NEEDED

6. Attach the spaghetti cutting blade to the pasta machine and run the thin sheets of dough through it to create the ramen noodles.

7. To cook the ramen noodles, bring a pot of water to a rolling boil. Add the noodles to the boiling water and cook for 1 minute. Pour the cooked noodles into a colander and drain them. Rinse the noodles with cold water to remove excess starch. Pour hot water over the rinsed noodles to warm them through before serving.

SPAGHETTI RAMEN HACK

YIELD: 4 SERVINGS / **ACTIVE TIME:** 5 MINUTES / **TOTAL TIME:** 10 MINUTES

This quick ramen hack will help you use spaghetti to create a ramen-esque experience. By adding baking soda to the water, the spaghetti takes on a chewy, ramen-like texture that gets closer to approximating fresh ramen noodles than instant varieties do. While not identical to real ramen, this is a great alternative for those who lack access to fresh ramen noodles or don't have time to make their own from scratch.

1. Fill a large pot with the water and bring to a rolling boil.

2. Add the salt and baking soda and stir until they have dissolved. Let the water return to a boil, add the spaghetti, and cook for 2 minutes longer than the time stated on the packaging.

3. Drain the spaghetti and rinse it under hot water if you're serving it hot, and cold water if you're serving it cold. Enjoy with your favorite ramen broth and toppings.

INGREDIENTS:

12   CUPS WATER

1½   TEASPOONS KOSHER SALT

2   TABLESPOONS BAKING SODA

¾   LB. SPAGHETTI

CLASSIC PORK CHASHU

YIELD: 6 SERVINGS / **ACTIVE TIME:** 20 MINUTES / **TOTAL TIME:** 14 HOURS AND 20 MINUTES

Chashu is a dish made with pork belly that has been slow-cooked, marinated, and braised to produce a succulent, melt-in-the-mouth ramen topping. Although this recipe originated from the Cantonese preparation char siu, the Japanese version uses different cooking methods and is typically finished with a teriyaki-like glaze. Feel free to add soft-boiled eggs to the marinade for easy ramen eggs. Also, the end pieces of the pork belly can be shredded and used for donburi or fried rice.

1. Using a fork, poke holes all over the pork belly and pat it dry with paper towels. Roll up the pork belly and secure it with butcher's twine. Place the rolled pork belly in a large pot and cover it with cold water.

2. Place the pot on the stove and bring to a boil over medium-high heat, skimming to remove any impurities that rise to the surface. Reduce the heat so that the pork simmers and add the leek, ginger, garlic, onion, and vinegar. Place a drop lid, aluminum foil, or parchment paper on the surface and simmer for 2 hours, turning the pork belly halfway through and occasionally skimming any impurities that rise to the surface. If the water gets too low while the pork belly is simmering, add more so that it is always submerged.

3. Remove the pork belly from the broth and let it cool completely.

4. Pour 1 cup of the pork broth into a saucepan and add the sake, mirin, sugar, and soy sauce. Bring to a boil and let the mixture bubble for 1 minute before removing the pan from heat. Let it cool completely.

5. Place the pork belly in a resealable plastic bag and add the marinade. Seal the bag and marinate the pork belly in the refrigerator overnight.

6. Remove the pork belly from the bag and set aside ½ cup of marinade. Warm a large skillet over medium-high heat and add the pork belly. Sear until the outside of the pork belly is caramelized, turning it as necessary. Transfer the pork belly to a plate and pour the ½ cup of marinade into the pan. Cook until it has thickened, return the pork belly to the pan, and cook, turning it frequently, to coat the surface with the glaze.

7. Remove the glazed pork belly from the pan and let it rest for 5 to 10 minutes.

8. Cut the butcher's twine, slice the pork belly thin, and use it in bowls of ramen.

INGREDIENTS:

1½	LBS. SKINLESS PORK BELLY
1	JAPANESE LEEK, GREEN PART ONLY
2	OZ. FRESH GINGER
3	GARLIC CLOVES
½	ONION, CHOPPED
1	TEASPOON RICE VINEGAR
¼	CUP SAKE
2	TABLESPOONS MIRIN
2½	TABLESPOONS SUGAR
⅔	CUP SOY SAUCE

CHICKEN BREAST CHASHU

YIELD: 4 SERVINGS / **ACTIVE TIME:** 15 MINUTES / **TOTAL TIME:** 1 HOUR AND 20 MINUTES

Chicken chashu is an excellent choice if you're looking to add chicken as a topping to your ramen. This version is incredibly easy to prepare, essentially requiring you to do nothing more than set it and forget it. Don't let this flavorful broth go to waste either—it is a fantastic way to enhance a number of dishes.

1. Using a fork, poke holes all over the chicken, season with the salt, and rub the salt into it. Cover it in plastic wrap and let the chicken rest at room temperature for 20 minutes.

2. Remove the plastic wrap and pat the chicken dry with paper towels.

3. Place all of the remaining ingredients in a medium saucepan and bring to a boil over medium heat. Reduce the heat to low, gently slip the chicken into the pan, and simmer for 15 minutes.

4. Turn off the heat, cover the pan, and let the chicken sit in the broth for 30 minutes.

5. Remove the chicken from the broth, slice it, and use it in bowls of ramen.

INGREDIENTS:

¾ LB. BONELESS, SKINLESS CHICKEN BREASTS

1 TEASPOON KOSHER SALT

⅓ CUP SAKE

⅓ CUP MIRIN

½ CUP SOY SAUCE

1 TABLESPOON SUGAR

1 TABLESPOON HONEY

1 TABLESPOON RICE VINEGAR

1 TEASPOON GRATED FRESH GINGER

1 GARLIC CLOVE, GRATED

1 TEASPOON DASHI GRANULES

2½ CUPS WATER

1 JAPANESE LEEK, GREEN PART ONLY

AJITAMA

YIELD: 4 SERVINGS / **ACTIVE TIME:** 10 MINUTES / **TOTAL TIME:** 8 HOURS

Ajitama, a seasoned soft-boiled egg, stands as an essential topping in the world of ramen, adding richness and depth to the dish. Making your own ajitama at home can significantly improve your DIY ramen, providing a delicious and authentic touch with minimal effort.

1. Fill a pot with water and bring it to a boil. Set a timer for 7 minutes. Gently slip the eggs into the boiling water, start the timer, and cook for 7 minutes.

2. While the eggs are boiling, combine the soy sauce, mirin, sake, sugar, and garlic paste in a small saucepan and bring to a simmer. Cook for 2 minutes and remove the pan from heat.

3. After 7 minutes, immediately transfer the eggs to a bowl of cold water to stop the cooking process. Peel the eggs once they are cool enough to handle.

4. Transfer the soy sauce mixture to a resealable plastic bag. When the peeled eggs are completely cool, add them and the kombu to the bag, seal it, and let the eggs marinate in the refrigerator overnight before using them in bowls of ramen.

INGREDIENTS:

4	EGGS
3	TABLESPOONS SOY SAUCE
3	TABLESPOONS MIRIN
1	TABLESPOON SAKE
1	TABLESPOON SUGAR
1	TEASPOON GARLIC PASTE
	2-INCH SQUARE OF DRIED KOMBU

FRAGRANT PORK MINCE

YIELD: 4 SERVINGS / **ACTIVE TIME:** 10 MINUTES / **TOTAL TIME:** 10 MINUTES

I f you don't have time to make chashu, you can substitute it with this preparation, which pairs especially well with miso ramen.

1. Place the butter in a large skillet and melt it over medium heat. Add garlic, ginger, and leek and cook, stirring occasionally, until the mixture is fragrant, 1 to 2 minutes.

2. Add the pork and stir-fry until it is cooked through, about 8 minutes.

3. Stir in the soy sauce, mirin, oyster sauce, and chili bean sauce and simmer until almost all of the liquid has evaporated.

4. Remove the pan from heat and use the pork in your bowls of ramen.

INGREDIENTS:

1	TEASPOON UNSALTED BUTTER
4	GARLIC CLOVES, MINCED
1	TABLESPOON MINCED FRESH GINGER
2	TABLESPOONS FINELY DICED JAPANESE LEEK, WHITE PART ONLY
6	OZ. GROUND PORK
1	TEASPOON SOY SAUCE
1	TEASPOON MIRIN
1	TEASPOON OYSTER SAUCE
½	TEASPOON CHILI BEAN SAUCE

OVEN-ROASTED CHASHU

YIELD: 4 SERVINGS / **ACTIVE TIME:** 10 MINUTES / **TOTAL TIME:** 9 HOURS

While traditional chashu pork requires hours of simmering for its signature melt-in-the-mouth texture, this recipe offers a simplified alternative that retains the core flavors and elements of classic chashu but streamlines the process significantly.

1. Using a fork, poke holes all over the pork belly. Place it in a resealable plastic bag, add the remaining ingredients, seal the bag, and massage the marinade into the pork belly. Let it marinate in the refrigerator overnight.

2. Preheat the oven to 400°F. Line a roasting pan with parchment paper. Place the marinated pork belly in the the center of the pan and place it on the lower rack of the oven. Roast for 10 minutes. Reduce the oven's temperature to 285°F and roast for 1 hour.

3. Remove the pork belly from the oven and double-check that it is cooked through (the interior is 145°F).

4. Let the pork belly rest for 10 to 15 minutes before slicing it and using it in bowls of ramen.

INGREDIENTS:

- 1 LB. SKINLESS PORK BELLY
- 1 JAPANESE LEEK, GREEN PART ONLY
- 1½ TEASPOONS GRATED FRESH GINGER
- 1½ TEASPOONS GRATED GARLIC
- 3 TABLESPOONS SOY SAUCE
- 1 TABLESPOON HONEY
- 2 TABLESPOONS SAKE
- 1 TEASPOON YELLOW MISO PASTE
- 1 TABLESPOON SUGAR
- 2 TABLESPOONS MIRIN
- 1½ TEASPOONS OYSTER SAUCE

MENMA-STYLE BAMBOO SHOOTS

YIELD: 6 SERVINGS / **ACTIVE TIME:** 10 MINUTES / **TOTAL TIME:** 20 MINUTES

Menma is a popular ramen topping made from a particular kind of bamboo shoot. However, finding this specific bamboo and fermenting it at home can be extremely challenging and time-consuming. To address this issue, this recipe provides an easy-to-follow guide for a "menma-like" topping using regular bamboo shoots.

1. Slice the bamboo shoots thin and then cut them into pieces that are about ¾ inch wide.

2. Place half of the sesame oil in a large skillet and warm it over medium heat. Add the bamboo shoots, season with the pepper, and cook, gently stirring, for 1 minute.

3. Stir in the water, soy sauce, sake, mirin, oyster sauce, chicken bouillon, and chile and cook until all of the liquid has evaporated.

4. Add the remaining sesame oil, stir until it evenly coats the bamboo shoots, and use them in your bowls of ramen.

INGREDIENTS:

½	LB. BOILED BAMBOO SHOOTS
1	TABLESPOON SESAME OIL
⅛	TEASPOON BLACK PEPPER
¾	CUP WATER
1	TABLESPOON SOY SAUCE
1	TABLESPOON SAKE
1	TABLESPOON MIRIN
1½	TEASPOONS OYSTER SAUCE
1	TEASPOON CHINESE CHICKEN BOUILLON
1	TEASPOON MINCED DRIED RED CHILE PEPPER

Oven-Roasted Chashu, *see page 382*

CRISPY GARLIC CHIPS

YIELD: 6 SERVINGS / **ACTIVE TIME:** 15 MINUTES / **TOTAL TIME:** 15 MINUTES

These garlic chips are full of punchy flavor, and can be perfect for topping bowls of ramen noodles, fried rice, salads, and rice bowls. Plus, any leftover garlic-infused oil is great when used in fried rice and stir-fries.

1. Peel the garlic, trim it, and slice it thin. Place it in a bowl, cover it with water, and let it sit for 5 minutes.

2. Drain the garlic and pat it dry with paper towels.

3. Place the garlic and rice bran oil in a small skillet and warm over medium-low heat. When bubbles start to form in the oil, reduce the heat to the lowest setting.

4. Gently fry the garlic until it is golden brown, 10 to 15 minutes, stirring occasionally. Strain the fried garlic and use it in your bowls of ramen.

INGREDIENTS:

1	GARLIC BULB
¼	CUP RICE BRAN OIL

SEASONED BEAN SPROUTS

YIELD: 4 SERVINGS / ACTIVE TIME: 2 MINUTES / TOTAL TIME: 3 MINUTES

Boiled bean sprouts are one of the most popular ramen toppings. With this recipe, you can add more layers of flavor and texture to your ramen.

1. Place all of the ingredients, except for the bean sprouts, in a bowl and stir to combine. Set the dressing aside.

2. Fill a medium saucepan with water and bring to a boil. Add the bean sprouts to the boiling water and cook for 1 minute. Drain the bean sprouts and shake the strainer to remove any excess water.

3. Add the drained bean sprouts to the dressing, toss to coat, and use the bean sprouts in your bowls of ramen.

INGREDIENTS:

1   TEASPOON CHINESE CHICKEN BOUILLON

1   TEASPOON SESAME OIL

⅛   TEASPOON SHICHIMI TOGARASHI

⅛   TEASPOON BLACK PEPPER

½   TEASPOON SUGAR

1   TEASPOON RICE VINEGAR

3½   OZ. BEAN SPROUTS

SPICY NEGI

YIELD: 4 SERVINGS / **ACTIVE TIME:** 5 MINUTES / **TOTAL TIME:** 10 MINUTES

Negi is a classic ramen topping, and this spicy version is certain to supply yours with an extra kick.

1. Prepare an ice bath. Cut the leek into 2-inch pieces. Carefully slice each piece lengthwise until you reach the center. Separate the layers and discard the core. Flatten the outer layers of the leeks on a cutting board and cut them into very thin strips, slicing in the direction of the fibers. Transfer the pieces to the ice bath and let them soak for 5 minutes.

2. Place all of the remaining ingredients in a separate bowl, stir to combine, and set the mixture aside.

3. Drain the leek and shake the strainer to remove any excess water. Stir the leek into the sesame oil mixture and use it in your bowls of ramen.

INGREDIENTS:

1	JAPANESE LEEK, WHITE PART ONLY
½	TEASPOON CHILI BEAN PASTE
½	TEASPOON CHINESE CHICKEN BOUILLON
1	TABLESPOON SESAME OIL
	PINCH OF KOSHER SALT
	PINCH OF BLACK PEPPER
⅛	TEASPOON SHICHIMI TOGARASHI

SHOYU RAMEN

YIELD: 4 SERVINGS / **ACTIVE TIME:** 10 MINUTES / **TOTAL TIME:** 15 MINUTES

Shoyu ramen is a Japanese classic. This recipe simplifies the soy sauce–based soup, offering the authentic taste in just 15 minutes.

1. Place the soy sauce, oyster sauce, sugar, chicken bouillon, duck fat, and garlic paste in a container and stir until well combined. Divide the tare among the serving bowls.

2. Place the dashi in a saucepan and bring it to a boil.

3. Cook the noodles according to the directions on the package or in the recipe and drain them.

4. Divide the dashi among the serving bowls and gently stir. Divide the noodles among the bowls, top each portion with your preferred toppings, and serve immediately.

INGREDIENTS:

6   TABLESPOONS SOY SAUCE

4   TEASPOONS OYSTER SAUCE

1   TEASPOON SUGAR

2   TABLESPOONS CHINESE CHICKEN BOUILLON

4   TEASPOONS DUCK FAT

4   TEASPOONS GARLIC PASTE

6   CUPS AWASE DASHI STOCK (SEE PAGE 38)

4   SERVINGS OF RAMEN NOODLES (SEE PAGE 372 FOR HOMEMADE)

PORK CHASHU (SEE PAGE 376 OR 382), FOR TOPPING

AJITAMA (SEE PAGE 378), FOR TOPPING

MENMA-STYLE BAMBOO SHOOTS (SEE PAGE 383), FOR TOPPING

GREEN ONIONS, CHOPPED, FOR TOPPING

NORI SEAWEED, FOR TOPPING

CRISPY GARLIC CHIPS (SEE PAGE 386), FOR TOPPING

SHIO RAMEN

YIELD: 4 SERVINGS / **ACTIVE TIME:** 15 MINUTES / **TOTAL TIME:** 20 MINUTES

Shio ramen is known for its refreshing, light broth, which offers a pleasant contrast to other ramen styles. Traditionally made with chicken carcasses or seafood, this recipe is simplified as much as possible, using duck fat to deliver the requisite deep flavor.

1. Place the duck fat in a saucepan and melt it over low heat. Add the leek and garlic and cook until they just start to change color, taking care not to let them brown. Turn off the heat and set the mixture aside.

2. Place the dashi, chicken bouillon, sesame oil, soy sauce, salt, and rice vinegar in a container and stir until well combined. Divide the tare among the serving bowls.

3. Cook the noodles according to the directions on the package or in the recipe and drain them.

4. Divide the boiling water and duck fat mixture among the serving bowls and stir to combine. Divide the noodles among the bowls, top each portion with your preferred ramen toppings, and serve immediately.

INGREDIENTS:

2	TABLESPOONS DUCK FAT
¼	CUP FINELY DICED JAPANESE LEEK, WHITE PART ONLY
4	GARLIC CLOVES, FINELY DICED
4	TEASPOONS DASHI GRANULES
4	TEASPOONS CHINESE CHICKEN BOUILLON
4	TEASPOONS TOASTED SESAME OIL
4	TEASPOONS LIGHT SOY SAUCE
1	TEASPOON KOSHER SALT
1	TEASPOON RICE VINEGAR
6	CUPS BOILING WATER
4	SERVINGS OF RAMEN NOODLES (THIN TO REGULAR RECOMMENDED; SEE PAGE 372 FOR HOMEMADE)
	CHICKEN BREAST CHASHU (SEE PAGE 377), FOR TOPPING
	GREEN ONIONS, CHOPPED, FOR TOPPING
	SOFT-BOILED EGGS, FOR TOPPING
	MENMA-STYLE BAMBOO SHOOTS (SEE PAGE 383), FOR TOPPING
	SHICHIMI TOGARASHI, FOR TOPPING

MISO RAMEN

YIELD: 4 SERVINGS / **ACTIVE TIME:** 13 MINUTES / **TOTAL TIME:** 15 MINUTES

Miso ramen is believed to have originated in Sapporo, Hokkaido. Thanks to miso's already umami-packed flavor, miso ramen is one of the easiest types of ramen to prepare authentically.

1. Place the butter in a large skillet and melt it over medium heat. Add the garlic, ginger, and leek and stir-fry for 30 seconds. Add the pork and stir-fry until it is cooked through, about 8 minutes.

2. Stir in the soy sauce, mirin, oyster sauce, and chili bean sauce and let the pork simmer until the liquid has almost completely evaporated. Remove the pan from heat and set the pork aside.

3. Place the boiling water, chicken bouillon, and peanut butter in a container and whisk to combine. Pour the broth into the pan with the pork and bring to a boil. Turn off the heat, place the miso paste in a strainer or ladle, and submerge it in the broth. Whisk to loosen and dissolve the paste. You want to ensure that it dissolves smoothly and that no clumps remain.

4. Stir in the bean sprouts and let them cook in the residual heat.

5. Cook the noodles according to the directions on the package or in the recipe, adding the spinach during the last minute of cooking. Drain and rinse them with hot water.

6. Divide the noodles, spinach, pork, and broth among the serving bowls. Top each portion with the corn, green onion, an Ajitama, nori, an additional dab of butter, and any of your other preferred toppings, and serve.

INGREDIENTS:

- 2 TEASPOONS UNSALTED BUTTER, PLUS MORE FOR TOPPING
- 8 GARLIC CLOVES, FINELY DICED
- 2 TABLESPOONS MINCED FRESH GINGER
- ¼ CUP FINELY DICED LEEK, WHITE PART ONLY
- ¾ LB. GROUND PORK
- 2 TEASPOONS SOY SAUCE
- 2 TEASPOONS MIRIN
- 2 TEASPOONS OYSTER SAUCE
- 1 TEASPOON CHILI BEAN SAUCE
- 4 CUPS BOILING WATER
- 2 TEASPOONS CHINESE CHICKEN BOUILLON
- 2 TABLESPOONS CREAMY PEANUT BUTTER
- 3 TABLESPOONS AWASE MISO PASTE
- 7 OZ. BEAN SPROUTS, FOR TOPPING
- 4 SERVINGS OF RAMEN NOODLES (SEE PAGE 372 FOR HOMEMADE)
- 2 OZ. SPINACH, FOR TOPPING
- 4 TEASPOONS SWEET CORN KERNELS, FOR TOPPING
- 4 TEASPOONS FINELY CHOPPED GREEN ONION, GREEN PART ONLY, FOR TOPPING
- 4 AJITAMA (SEE PAGE 378) OR SOFT-BOILED EGGS, FOR TOPPING
- 4 SHEETS OF NORI, FOR TOPPING

TONKOTSU-STYLE RAMEN HACK

YIELD: 4 SERVINGS / ACTIVE TIME: 10 MINUTES / TOTAL TIME: 10 MINUTES

The rich and creamy broth featured in tonkotsu ramen is loved by many, but as it is produced by simmering pork bones for hours, it can be challenging to replicate at home. This recipe solves that problem, allowing you to create a tonkotsu-style soup in just 10 minutes.

1. Combine the water, soy milk, chicken bouillon, lard, garlic paste, oyster sauce, soy sauce, and dashi granules in a large saucepan and warm over low heat, stirring occasionally and never letting the broth come to a boil. It is crucial to maintain low heat throughout the cooking process, as too much heat can cause the soy milk to curdle.

2. While the broth is warming up, cook the noodles according to the directions on the package or in the recipe.

3. Drain the noodles and divide them among the serving bowls. Ladle the hot broth over the noodles, top each portion with your preferred ramen toppings, and serve.

INGREDIENTS:

2⅔ CUPS WATER

2⅔ CUPS SOY MILK

¼ CUP CHINESE CHICKEN BOUILLON

2 TABLESPOONS LARD

4 TEASPOONS GARLIC PASTE

4 TEASPOONS OYSTER SAUCE

4 TEASPOONS SOY SAUCE

2 TEASPOONS DASHI GRANULES

4 SERVINGS OF RAMEN NOODLES (THICKER NOODLES RECOMMENDED; SEE PAGE 372 FOR HOMEMADE)

PORK CHASHU (SEE PAGE 376), FOR TOPPING

BOILED WOOD EAR MUSHROOMS, SLICED THIN, FOR TOPPING

BENISHOGA (SEE PAGE 315), FOR TOPPING

GREEN ONION, CHOPPED, FOR TOPPING

SESAME SEEDS, GROUND, FOR TOPPING

MENMA-STYLE BAMBOO SHOOTS (SEE PAGE 383), FOR TOPPING

AJITAMA (SEE PAGE 378), FOR TOPPING

NORI, FOR TOPPING

Miso Ramen, see page 396

NAGOYA'S TAIWAN RAMEN

YIELD: 4 SERVINGS / ACTIVE TIME: 20 MINUTES / TOTAL TIME: 20 MINUTES

Despite its name, Taiwan ramen proudly hails from Nagoya, Japan. This Taiwanese-inspired dish has carved its own unique identity within the diverse landscape of Japanese cuisine with its bold and fiery flavor profile.

1. Place the sesame oil in a large skillet and warm it over medium heat. Add the garlic and ginger and stir-fry until they are fragrant, about 30 seconds. Add the pork and stir-fry until it is cooked through, about 8 minutes.

2. Stir in the chili bean sauce, chiles, water, and 1½ teaspoons of chicken bouillon, bring to a simmer, and cook until almost all of the liquid has evaporated, stirring occasionally.

3. While the pork mixture is simmering, place the dashi, soy sauce, oyster sauce, salt, sugar, and remaining chicken bouillon in a medium saucepan and bring to a boil, stirring occasionally. Turn off the heat and set the broth aside.

4. Cook the ramen noodles according to the directions on the package or in the recipe. Drain, rinse them under very hot water, and divide the noodles among the serving bowls.

5. Ladle the broth over the noodles, top each portion with some of the pork and garlic chives, and serve.

INGREDIENTS:

- 2 TEASPOONS TOASTED SESAME OIL
- 4 GARLIC CLOVES, MINCED
- 2 TEASPOONS MINCED FRESH GINGER
- 7 OZ. GROUND PORK
- 1 TABLESPOON CHILI BEAN SAUCE
- 8 DRIED RED CHILE PEPPERS, CRUSHED
- 1 CUP WATER
- 2 TABLESPOONS PLUS 1½ TEASPOONS CHINESE CHICKEN BOUILLON
- 4 CUPS AWASE DASHI STOCK (SEE PAGE 38)
- 2 TABLESPOONS SOY SAUCE
- 2 TEASPOONS OYSTER SAUCE
- ½ TEASPOON KOSHER SALT
- ½ TEASPOON SUGAR
- 4 SERVINGS OF RAMEN NOODLES (SEE PAGE 372 FOR HOMEMADE)
- 1 BUNCH OF GARLIC CHIVES (CHINESE CHIVES), CHOPPED, FOR TOPPING

NAGASAKI CHAMPON

YIELD: 4 SERVINGS / **ACTIVE TIME:** 20 MINUTES / **TOTAL TIME:** 30 MINUTES

This is a signature dish of Nagasaki, celebrated as the region's soul food. It stands out from other ramen varieties due to its rich and hearty composition, featuring a diverse mix of pork, seafood, and a vibrant medley of vegetables.

1. Place the lard in a wok or large skillet and warm it over medium heat. Add the pork belly and sear it on both sides. Add the seafood mixture, season with the salt and pepper, and cook until the seafood starts to brown.

2. Add the kamaboko, onion, cabbage, corn, carrot, and shiitakes to the pan and stir-fry until the cabbage has softened and the pork and seafood are cooked through. Turn off the heat and set the mixture aside.

3. Place the dashi, soy sauce, garlic paste, ginger paste, and oyster sauce in a medium saucepan and bring to a simmer over medium heat. Stir in the chicken bouillon and turn off the heat. Stir in the milk and set the broth aside.

4. Cook the noodles according to the directions on the package or in the recipe. When they have 2 minutes left to cook, gently reheat the broth, making sure it does not come to a boil.

5. Drain the noodles and divide them among the serving bowls. Ladle the hot broth over the noodles and top each portion with some of the pork-and-seafood mixture. Garnish with wood ear mushrooms and serve.

INGREDIENTS:

- 1½ TEASPOONS LARD OR CANOLA OIL
- 7 OZ. PORK BELLY, SLICED THIN
- 2 CUPS SEAFOOD MIXTURE (THAWED IF FROZEN)
- ¼ TEASPOON KOSHER SALT
- ¼ TEASPOON GROUND BLACK PEPPER
- 16 SLICES OF KAMABOKO FISH CAKE
- ½ ONION, SLICED THIN
- ¼ GREEN CABBAGE, CHOPPED
- ½ CUP SWEET CORN KERNELS
- ¼ CARROT, PEELED AND JULIENNED
- 2 SHIITAKE MUSHROOMS, STEMMED AND SLICED
- 2⅔ CUPS AWASE DASHI STOCK (SEE PAGE 38)
- 1 TABLESPOON SOY SAUCE
- 1 TABLESPOON GARLIC PASTE
- 1 TABLESPOON GINGER PASTE
- 1 TABLESPOON OYSTER SAUCE
- 2 TABLESPOONS CHINESE CHICKEN BOUILLON
- 1⅓ CUPS WHOLE MILK
- 4 SERVINGS OF RAMEN NOODLES (SEE PAGE 372 FOR HOMEMADE)
- BOILED WOOD EAR MUSHROOM, SHREDDED, FOR GARNISH

TANTANMEN

YIELD: 4 SERVINGS / **ACTIVE TIME:** 10 MINUTES / **TOTAL TIME:** 15 MINUTES

Tantanmen is a fiery and flavorful Japanese adaptation of the classic Sichuan dish dàndàn miàn. Though it has diverged from its original form, it has secured a beloved spot in Chinese restaurants and ramen restaurants throughout Japan. In a delicious twist, this recipe substitutes the traditional sesame paste with peanut butter, not for the sake of accessibility, but for a richer, more nuanced flavor that I passionately prefer.

1. Place the canola oil in a large skillet and warm it over medium heat. Add the pork, season with the salt and pepper, and stir-fry until the pork is cooked through, about 8 minutes.

2. Stir in the onion, sugar, ⅛ teaspoon of soy sauce, the ginger, garlic, and chili bean paste and cook until the liquid has reduced by half and the mixture is fragrant, stirring occasionally. Turn off the heat and cover the pan to keep the mixture warm.

3. Place the water in a medium saucepan and bring to a boil. Stir in the chicken bouillon until it has dissolved.

4. Divide the remaining soy sauce, the sesame seeds, chili oil, vinegar, and peanut butter among the serving bowls and stir to combine. Ladle the broth into each bowl and stir to combine it with the tare.

5. Cook the noodles according to the instructions on the package or in the recipe, adding the bok choy during the last minute of cooking. Drain and rinse them with hot water. Chop the bok choy into bite-size pieces.

6. Divide the noodles among the bowls and top each portion with some of the pork mixture and bok choy. Season the ramen with red pepper flakes and additional chili oil, garnish with the green onions, and serve.

INGREDIENTS:

1	TEASPOON CANOLA OIL
½	LB. GROUND PORK
	PINCH OF KOSHER SALT
	PINCH OF BLACK PEPPER
½	ONION, FINELY DICED
	PINCH OF SUGAR
¼	CUP PLUS ⅛ TEASPOON SOY SAUCE
1	TABLESPOON GRATED FRESH GINGER
2	GARLIC CLOVES, GRATED
2	TABLESPOONS CHILI BEAN PASTE
5	CUPS WATER
8	TEASPOONS CHINESE CHICKEN BOUILLON
4	TEASPOONS GROUND SESAME SEEDS
4	TEASPOONS CHILI OIL, PLUS MORE TO TASTE
1	TEASPOON RICE VINEGAR
½	CUP CREAMY PEANUT BUTTER
4	SERVINGS OF RAMEN NOODLES (SEE PAGE 372 FOR HOMEMADE)
2	BABY BOK CHOY, TRIMMED
	RED PEPPER FLAKES, TO TASTE
¼	CUP FINELY CHOPPED GREEN ONIONS, FOR GARNISH

ABURA SOBA

YIELD: 4 SERVINGS / **ACTIVE TIME:** 5 MINUTES / **TOTAL TIME:** 15 MINUTES

Abura soba is also known as "soupless ramen." It is made with a rich sauce that is placed at the bottom of the bowl and then mixed with the cooked noodles.

1. Cook the noodles according to the directions on the package or in the recipe.

2. While the noodles are cooking, place the water, lard, oyster sauce, soy sauce, chicken bouillon, dashi granules, garlic paste, rice vinegar, ground sesame seeds, sesame oil, and sugar in a mason jar or heatproof container. Cover with plastic wrap, place the container in the microwave, and microwave on high for 1 minute.

3. Remove the sauce from the microwave and divide it among the serving bowls. Drain the noodles, divide them among the bowls, and add your preferred ramen toppings. Stir to thoroughly combine everything and serve.

INGREDIENTS:

4   SERVINGS OF RAMEN NOODLES (SEE PAGE 372 FOR HOMEMADE)

2   TABLESPOONS WATER

2   TABLESPOONS LARD

3   TABLESPOONS OYSTER SAUCE

3   TABLESPOONS SOY SAUCE

2   TEASPOONS CHINESE CHICKEN BOUILLON

2   TEASPOONS DASHI GRANULES

2   TEASPOONS GARLIC PASTE

2   TABLESPOONS RICE VINEGAR, PLUS MORE FOR TOPPING

2   TABLESPOONS GROUND SESAME SEEDS

2   TABLESPOONS TOASTED SESAME OIL, PLUS MORE FOR TOPPING

2   TEASPOONS SUGAR

    AJITAMA (SEE PAGE 378), FOR TOPPING

    KIZAMI NORI, SHREDDED, FOR TOPPING

    KATSUOBUSHI, FOR TOPPING

    GREEN ONIONS, CHOPPED, FOR TOPPING

    WHOLE SESAME SEEDS, FOR TOPPING

    CHILI OIL, FOR TOPPING

HIYASHI CHUKA

YIELD: 4 SERVINGS / **ACTIVE TIME**: 20 MINUTES / **TOTAL TIME**: 20 MINUTES

Hiyashi chuka is a popular summer dish that consists of cooked ramen noodles served cold, topped with a refreshing assortment of toppings. This recipe is especially flavorful due to its rich sesame sauce, which adds a nutty and savory depth.

1. Place the sesame seeds, mayonnaise, rice vinegar, sugar, soy sauce, sesame oil, and chili oil in a small bowl and whisk until the sugar has dissolved. Chill the sauce in the refrigerator.

2. Divide the noodles among the serving plates. Top each portion with some of the ham, vegetables, and Kinshi Tamago and drizzle the sauce over the top. Garnish with Benishoga and serve.

INGREDIENTS:

¼	CUP GROUND SESAME SEEDS
¼	CUP JAPANESE MAYONNAISE (SEE PAGE 46)
2	TEASPOONS RICE VINEGAR
1	TABLESPOON SUGAR
2	TEASPOONS SOY SAUCE
2	TEASPOONS SESAME OIL
½	TEASPOON CHILI OIL
4	SERVINGS OF COOKED RAMEN NOODLES, CHILLED
1	CUP COOKED HAM, CUT INTO THIN STRIPS
1	JAPANESE OR PERSIAN CUCUMBER, CUT INTO THIN STRIPS
1	TOMATO, SLICED THIN
½	CARROT, PEELED AND CUT INTO THIN STRIPS
1	CUP KINSHI TAMAGO (SEE PAGE 521)
	BENISHOGA (SEE PAGE 315), FOR GARNISH

Abura Soba, see page 404

TSUKEMEN

YIELD: 4 SERVINGS / ACTIVE TIME: 15 MINUTES / TOTAL TIME: 20 MINUTES

Tsukemen is a unique dish where ramen noodles are served alongside a soup, rather than in it. The soup is thicker and richer than standard ramen noodle soups, which allows it to adhere to the noodles when they are dipped into it, supplying maximum flavor.

1. Place the lard, water, dashi granules, chicken bouillon, rice vinegar, soy sauce, oyster sauce, brown sugar, sesame seeds, ginger paste, and garlic paste in a medium saucepan and bring to a boil over medium heat. Reduce the heat to low and simmer the broth for 1 minute, stirring continually. Turn off the heat and set the broth aside.

2. Add the soy milk, miso paste, and green onions to the pan and stir until everything is well combined and the broth is smooth. Set it aside.

3. Cook the noodles according to the directions on the package or in the recipe. Drain, rinse them under hot water, and place them in a mixing bowl. Add the sesame oil, toss to coat, and divide the noodles among the serving bowls that you are using for the noodles.

4. Gently reheat the broth over low heat, making sure it does not come to a boil. Divide the broth among the serving bowls you are using for the broth and toppings. Top each portion with your preferred ramen toppings and serve alongside the noodles.

INGREDIENTS:

1	TABLESPOON LARD
1	CUP WATER
1	TABLESPOON DASHI GRANULES
1½	TEASPOONS CHINESE CHICKEN BOUILLON
1	TEASPOON RICE VINEGAR
1½	TEASPOONS SOY SAUCE
1½	TEASPOONS OYSTER SAUCE
1½	TEASPOONS LIGHT BROWN SUGAR
1	TABLESPOON GROUND SESAME SEEDS
1	TEASPOON GINGER PASTE
1	TEASPOON GARLIC PASTE
⅓	CUP SOY MILK
1½	TABLESPOONS YELLOW MISO PASTE
2	TABLESPOONS FINELY CHOPPED GREEN ONIONS
4	SERVINGS OF RAMEN NOODLES (SEE PAGE 372 FOR HOMEMADE)
1	TABLESPOON SESAME OIL
¼	CUP KIZAMI (SHREDDED) NORI, FOR TOPPING
8	SLICES OF NARUTOMAKI FISH CAKE, FOR TOPPING
¼	CUP MENMA-STYLE BAMBOO SHOOTS (SEE PAGE 383), FOR TOPPING
4	AJITAMA (SEE PAGE 378), HALVED, FOR TOPPING
	CHASHU (SEE PAGE 376 OR 377), FOR TOPPING

UDON & SOBA

*U*don and soba are two of Japan's traditional noodle dishes. It's not uncommon for restaurants to offer both, and in most cases, they are interchangeable, and are often served in the same soup. In terms of portion sizing, a serving of udon noodles typically weighs about 3½ oz. for dried noodles and 4½ oz. for fresh noodles before boiling. For soba, a serving of 4 oz. to 5 oz. for both dried and fresh noodles should be about right.

HOMEMADE UDON NOODLES

YIELD: 4 SERVINGS / **ACTIVE TIME:** 50 MINUTES / **TOTAL TIME:** 3 HOURS AND 30 MINUTES

Udon are a thick, chewy noodles made with wheat flour. They can be served hot or cold and most often appear in soups, though they are also wonderful served alongside a dipping sauce. Also, since udon noodles don't contain eggs, they are suitable for plant-based diets.

1. Place the salt and water in a container and stir until the salt has fully dissolved.

2. Place the flour in a large resealable plastic bag, add the salted water, and seal the bag. Shake the bag until the mixture comes together in small clumps, about 3 minutes. Reseal the bag to make sure it is completely closed and let the mixture rest at room temperature for 30 minutes.

3. Knead the mixture through the bag until it comes together as a dough. Place the bag on the floor and spread the dough out by stepping on it. When the dough is fully stretched and evenly fills the bag, remove it and fold it into thirds, as you would a letter. Place the dough back in the bag and seal it. Continue the process of stepping on the dough and folding it until the dough becomes smooth, about 15 minutes.

4. Reseal the bag to make sure it is completely closed and let the dough rest at room temperature for 2 hours.

5. Remove the dough from the bag and place it on a flour-dusted work surface. Use a rolling pin to roll the dough out into a thin rectangle. Cut the dough in half lengthwise so that it will fit through the rollers on a pasta machine.

6. Set a pasta machine to the widest setting and run the dough through the machine once to flatten it. Adjust the pasta machine to the next widest setting and run the dough through twice. Continue adjusting the machine to narrower settings and running the dough through each time. After running the dough through the fourth- or fifth-narrowest setting and getting it to your preferred thickness, cut each piece of dough in half to make the noodles shorter. Lightly dust the pieces with flour to keep them from sticking.

7. Attach the trenette cutting blade to the pasta machine and run the thin sheets of dough through it to create udon noodles. If you prefer, you can also fold the pieces of dough and cut them into ⅛-inch-wide strips.

8. To cook the udon noodles, bring a pot of water to a rolling boil. Add the noodles to the boiling water and cook for 11 minutes. Drain the cooked noodles in a colander. Rinse the noodles with cold water to remove excess starch. Pour hot water over the rinsed noodles to warm them through before serving.

INGREDIENTS:

2　TEASPOONS SEA SALT

5　TABLESPOONS LUKEWARM, SOFT WATER (90°F)

7　OZ. ALL-PURPOSE FLOUR, PLUS MORE AS NEEDED

UDON NOODLE BROTH

YIELD: 5 SERVINGS / **ACTIVE TIME:** 5 MINUTES / **TOTAL TIME:** 5 MINUTES

Mastering this basic udon broth is the key to unlocking a variety of dishes, allowing you to customize numerous variations that are entirely tailored to your preferences.

1. Place the dashi in a large saucepan, stir in the soy sauce and mirin, and bring to a boil over medium-high heat.

2. Let the broth bubble for 1 minute, turn off the heat, and gently stir in the salt until it has dissolved. Serve with udon noodles and your preferred accompaniments.

INGREDIENTS:

4	CUPS AWASE DASHI STOCK (SEE PAGE 38)
5	TABLESPOONS SOY SAUCE
2	TABLESPOONS MIRIN
¼	TEASPOON KOSHER SALT

KAMAAGE UDON

YIELD: 4 SERVINGS / ACTIVE TIME: 10 MINUTES / TOTAL TIME: 15 MINUTES

This is the ultimate way to enjoy the true flavor of udon noodles, as it allows you to experience their authentic taste and mouthfeel.

1. Fill a large pot with water and bring to a boil over high heat. Add the noodles to the pot and cook them for one minute less than the time specified on the package or in the recipe.

2. While the udon noodles are boiling, warm the Mentsuyu over medium heat. Keep the mentsuyu warm until you are ready to serve.

3. Use tongs or a strainer to divide the noodles among the serving bowls. Ladle the hot, starchy cooking water from the pot over the noodles, making sure that they are fully submerged.

4. Pour the heated Mentsuyu into four cups, one for each serving. Enjoy the Mentsuyu alongside the udon noodles, green onions, ginger, and sesame seeds.

INGREDIENTS:

4   SERVINGS OF UDON NOODLES (SEE PAGE 414 FOR HOMEMADE)

2   CUPS MENTSUYU (SEE PAGE 42)

GREEN ONIONS, CHOPPED, FOR SERVING

FRESH GINGER, GRATED, FOR SERVING

SESAME SEEDS, FOR SERVING

HOMEMADE SOBA NOODLES

YIELD: 4 SERVINGS / **ACTIVE TIME:** 30 MINUTES / **TOTAL TIME:** 30 MINUTES

Soba is a type of Japanese noodle with a long history. Traditionally, it was made with buckwheat flour only and steamed due to its brittle nature. These days, however, it's more commonly made with a mixture of buckwheat and wheat flour, which makes it more suitable for boiling.

1. Combine the buckwheat flour and bread flour in a bowl and then sift the mixture into a large mixing bowl. Place the bowl on top of a damp kitchen towel to keep it from moving, then wet your hands with a small amount of the water and mix it into the flour mixture, moving your hands in a circular motion. Repeat this process, wetting your hands with a little water at a time and incorporating it, until no more dry flour remains and the mixture forms clumps that are about the size of a grain of rice. Be careful not to add too much water to the dough during the mixing process.

2. Press the clumps together and form the dough into a ball. Knead the dough by folding the edges into the middle and pressing them down until the dough is smooth. If the dough is flaky or cracks easily, incorporate a little more water by wetting your hands as you knead. Roll the smooth dough into a cone and press down on the point to form the dough into a thick disk.

3. Place the dough on a clean, dry work surface and roll it out until it is about ⅛ inch thick. Cut it into eight pieces narrow enough to fit through the rollers on a pasta machine.

4. Set a pasta machine to the widest setting and run the dough through the machine once to flatten it. Adjust the pasta machine to the next widest setting and run the dough through again. Continue adjusting the machine to narrower settings and running the dough through each time. After running the dough through the third-narrowest setting, cut each piece of dough in half to make the noodles shorter. Lightly dust the pieces with flour to keep them from sticking.

5. Attach the spaghetti cutting blade to the pasta machine and run the thin sheets of dough through it to create soba noodles.

6. To cook the soba noodles, bring a pot of water to a rolling boil. Add the noodles to the boiling water and cook for 1 minute and 45 seconds. Drain the cooked noodles in a colander. Rinse the noodles with cold water to remove excess starch. Pour hot water over the rinsed noodles to warm them through if you are serving them hot.

INGREDIENTS:

9   OZ. BUCKWHEAT FLOUR

2½   OZ. BREAD FLOUR

5   OZ. WATER

SOBA NOODLE BROTH

YIELD: 4 SERVINGS / **ACTIVE TIME**: 5 MINUTES / **TOTAL TIME**: 5 MINUTES

This broth is sweeter than the broth for udon noodles, a quality that complements the delicate flavor of soba noodles exceptionally well. With this foundational knowledge, you're encouraged to customize your soba dishes with a variety of toppings and ingredients of your choice. Popular choices include sliced green onions, kamaboko fish cakes, wakame seaweed, grated daikon radish, or tempura.

1. Place the dashi in a large saucepan, stir in the mirin and sake, and bring to a boil over medium-high heat.

2. Reduce the heat to medium-low or low, stir in the soy sauces, and let the broth simmer for 2 to 4 minutes. Serve with soba noodles and your preferred accompaniments.

INGREDIENTS:

4   CUPS AWASE DASHI STOCK (SEE PAGE 38)

7   TABLESPOONS MIRIN

1½   TEASPOONS SAKE

2½   TABLESPOONS DARK SOY SAUCE

2½   TABLESPOONS LIGHT SOY SAUCE

Soba Noodle Broth, see page 421

KITSUNE UDON/SOBA

YIELD: 4 SERVINGS / **ACTIVE TIME:** 15 MINUTES / **TOTAL TIME:** 1 HOUR AND 30 MINUTES

Kitsune is abura-age simmered in a flavorful mixture of traditional Japanese condiments, and it's a popular topping for udon and soba dishes.

1. Bring water to a boil in a large pot and prepare a bowl of cold water. Add the salt and stir until it has dissolved. Add the Abura-age and place a drop lid, aluminum foil, or parchment paper on the surface. Boil for 3 minutes, transfer the Abura-age to the bowl of cold water, and swish them around to wash them. Drain and squeeze the Abura-age to remove any excess water.

2. Place the dashi, sugar, sake, and mirin in a medium saucepan and warm over medium heat, stirring until the sugar has dissolved. Add the soy sauce and then reduce the heat to low just before the mixture starts to boil. Add the Abura-age, place a drop lid, aluminum foil, or parchment paper on the surface, and simmer until the liquid has reduced by one-third, turning the Abura-age over halfway through.

3. Transfer the Abura-age to a container and let it cool. When it is cool enough to touch, cover the container and chill the Abura-age in the refrigerator for 1 to 2 hours. If time allows, refrigerate it overnight.

4. Cook the noodles according to the directions on the package or in the recipe. Prepare the broth.

5. Drain the noodles and divide them and the broth among the serving bowls. Cut the Abura-age (it is now kitsune tofu) in half diagonally to make triangles and top each portion with it, the green onions, and kamaboko.

INGREDIENTS:

- 1 TEASPOON KOSHER SALT
- 4 SHEETS OF ABURA-AGE (SEE PAGE 69)
- 1 CUP AWASE DASHI STOCK (SEE PAGE 38)
- ¼ CUP SUGAR
- 2 TABLESPOONS SAKE
- ¼ CUP MIRIN
- 3 TABLESPOONS LIGHT SOY SAUCE
- 4 SERVINGS OF UDON OR SOBA NOODLES (SEE PAGE 414 OR 420 FOR HOMEMADE)
- 4 CUPS UDON NOODLE BROTH OR SOBA NOODLE BROTH (SEE PAGE 417 OR 421)
- ¼ CUP CHOPPED GREEN ONIONS
- 8–12 SLICES OF KAMABOKO FISH CAKE

KAKIAGE UDON/SOBA

YIELD: 4 SERVINGS / **ACTIVE TIME:** 40 MINUTES / **TOTAL TIME:** 1 HOUR AND 30 MINUTES

Kakiage is a type of tempura where small pieces of seafood or vegetables are mixed with tempura batter and deep-fried. You can enjoy it on its own, seasoned with salt, or as it is presented in this recipe.

1. Prepare the ingredients you are going to fry: the onion, carrot, shrimp, and green beans. Pat them dry with paper towels, lightly coat them with the flour, and set them aside.

2. Add rice bran oil to a small skillet until it is about 1 inch deep and warm it to 355°F.

3. Add the batter to the bowl containing the vegetables and shrimp. Using a slotted spoon, scoop some of the coated vegetables and shrimp from the bowl and gently slip them into the hot oil. You don't want to fill the ladle with batter, only the ingredients coated in batter. Fry for about 1 minute on each side and transfer the fried vegetables and shrimp to a wire rack to drain. Repeat until all of the vegetables and shrimp have been fried.

4. Cook the noodles according to the directions on the package or in the recipe. Prepare the broth.

5. Drain the noodles and divide them and the broth among the serving bowls. Top each portion with some of the kakiage, garnish with green onions, and serve immediately.

INGREDIENTS:

½	ONION, SLICED THIN
½	CARROT, PEELED AND JULIENNED
6	POACHED SHRIMP, CUT INTO SMALL CHUNKS
5	GREEN BEANS, HALVED LENGTHWISE
1	TABLESPOON CAKE FLOUR
	TEMPURA BATTER (SEE PAGE 272)
	RICE BRAN OIL, AS NEEDED
4	SERVINGS OF UDON OR SOBA NOODLES (SEE PAGE 414 OR 420 FOR HOMEMADE)
4	CUPS UDON NOODLE BROTH OR SOBA NOODLE BROTH (SEE PAGE 417 OR 421)
	GREEN ONIONS, CHOPPED, FOR GARNISH

ZARU UDON/SOBA

YIELD: 4 SERVINGS / **ACTIVE TIME**: 5 MINUTES / **TOTAL TIME**: 15 MINUTES

Z aru udon and zaru soba are two classic summer dishes in Japanese cuisine, both perfect ways to beat the heat and allow the quality and texture of the noodles to take center stage.

1. Cook the noodles according to the directions on the package or in the recipe. Drain, rinse the noodles under cold water, drain them again, and place the strainer over a bowl. Add a few ice cubes to the noodles so that they get extra cold.

2. Place each serving of chilled noodles in a zaru (bamboo sieve). If you don't have a zaru, you can use a bamboo sushi mat placed on a plate. Serve each portion with a cup of chilled Mentsuyu for dipping.

3. Serve with the green onions, Tenkasu, daikon radish, shichimi togarashi, and wasabi, placing the condiments on small plates so that everyone can add them to their Mentsuyu as they prefer.

INGREDIENTS:

4   SERVINGS OF UDON OR SOBA NOODLES (SEE PAGE 414 OR 420 FOR SERVING)

2   CUPS MENTSUYU (SEE PAGE 42), CHILLED

GREEN ONIONS, CHOPPED, FOR SERVING

TENKASU (SEE PAGE 68), FOR SERVING

DAIKON RADISH, GRATED, FOR SERVING

SHICHIMI TOGARASHI, FOR SERVING

WASABI (SEE PAGE 500 FOR HOMEMADE) FOR SERVING

HIYASHI TANUKI UDON/SOBA

YIELD: 4 SERVINGS / **ACTIVE TIME:** 10 MINUTES / **TOTAL TIME:** 10 MINUTES

Tanuki udon and tanuki soba are noodle dishes known for their abundant use of tempura flakes, which provide a satisfying crunch and flavor. This recipe presents a chilled variation of these popular dishes, ideal for a refreshing meal on a hot summer's day.

1. Cook the noodles according to the directions on the package or in the recipe. Drain, rinse the noodles under cold water, drain them again, and place the strainer over a bowl. Add a few ice cubes to the noodles so that they get extra cold.

2. Divide the chilled noodles among the serving plates and drizzle the Mentsuyu over each portion. Garnish with Tenkasu, cucumber, wakame, green onions, and wasabi and serve.

INGREDIENTS:

- 4 SERVINGS OF UDON OR SOBA NOODLES (SEE PAGE 414 OR 420 FOR HOMEMADE)

- 1 CUP MENTSUYU (SEE PAGE 42)

- TENKASU (SEE PAGE 68), FOR GARNISH

- 1 JAPANESE OR CHINESE CUCUMBER, JULIENNED, FOR GARNISH

- REHYDRATED WAKAME, FOR GARNISH

- GREEN ONIONS, CHOPPED, FOR GARNISH

- WASABI (SEE PAGE 500 FOR HOMEMADE) FOR GARNISH

KYOTO-STYLE UDON

YIELD: 4 SERVINGS / ACTIVE TIME: 10 MINUTES / TOTAL TIME: 20 MINUTES

In Japan, Kyoto-style udon, known as kyo udon or kyofu udon, includes all udon dishes enjoyed in the ancient capital city. Although there's no strict definition, Kyoto-style udon is famous for its elegantly simple composition.

1. To begin preparations for the udon, cut the Abura-age into bite-size pieces. Place them in a colander and pour boiling water over them to rinse any excess oil from the surface.

2. Place the Abura-age, dashi, sugar, mirin, and soy sauce in a medium saucepan and bring to a boil over medium heat. Reduce the heat and simmer until most of the liquid has been absorbed by the Abura-age. Remove the pan from heat and set it aside.

3. Cook the noodles according to the directions on the package or in the recipe.

4. While the noodles are cooking, begin preparations for the broth. Place all of the ingredients, except for the potato starch and water, in a medium saucepan and bring to a boil over medium heat. Reduce the heat to medium-low and let the broth simmer.

5. Combine the potato starch and water in a small bowl. While stirring continually, add the slurry to the simmering broth and cook until the broth thickens slightly.

6. Drain the noodles and divide them among the serving bowls. Ladle the broth over the noodles and top each portion with the Abura-age. Garnish with green onions and shichimi togarashi and serve.

INGREDIENTS:

FOR THE UDON

4	ABURA-AGE (SEE PAGE 69)
½	CUP AWASE DASHI STOCK (SEE PAGE 38)
1½	TABLESPOONS SUGAR
½	TABLESPOON MIRIN
1½	TABLESPOONS LIGHT SOY SAUCE
4	SERVINGS OF UDON NOODLES (SEE PAGE 414 FOR HOMEMADE)

FOR THE BROTH

4	CUPS AWASE DASHI STOCK
¼	CUP LIGHT SOY SAUCE
3	TABLESPOONS MIRIN
1½	TEASPOONS GRATED FRESH GINGER
½	TEASPOON KOSHER SALT
1½	TABLESPOONS POTATO STARCH
1½	TABLESPOONS WATER
	SHICHIMI TOGARASHI, FOR GARNISH
	GREEN ONIONS, CHOPPED, FOR GARNISH

Hiyashi Tanuki Udon/Soba, see page 430

BEEF NIKU UDON

YIELD: 4 SERVINGS / ACTIVE TIME: 10 MINUTES / TOTAL TIME: 20 MINUTES

Niku udon is a hearty beef or pork udon soup that offers a simple yet deeply satisfying meal. The soup itself is a highlight, absorbing the rich flavors of the meat and creating a broth that is both rich in flavor and fragrance.

1. To prepare the marinade, place all of the ingredients in a container large enough to fit the beef and stir to combine.

2. To begin preparations for the soup, add the beef to the marinade and stir until it is evenly coated. Let the beef marinate at room temperature for 10 minutes.

3. Place the dashi in a medium saucepan and stir in the soy sauce, mirin, and sugar. Bring the mixture to a boil over medium heat and let it boil for 2 minutes. Turn off the heat but leave the pan on the stove to keep it warm.

4. Begin cooking the noodles according to the directions on the package or in the recipe.

5. Place the canola oil in a large skillet and warm it over medium heat. Add the onion, season it with the salt, and cook, stirring occasionally, until it has softened.

6. Add the beef and marinade to the pan and stir-fry until the beef is cooked through. Remove the pan from heat.

7. Drain the noodles, rinse them under very hot water to remove excess starch, and divide them and the broth among the serving bowls. Top each portion with some of the beef and onion and drizzle any sauce remaining in the pan over the top. Garnish with green onions and shichimi togarashi and serve.

INGREDIENTS:

FOR THE MARINADE

2	TABLESPOONS SOY SAUCE
2	TABLESPOONS MIRIN
2	TEASPOONS OYSTER SAUCE
1	TEASPOON SUGAR
1	TEASPOON GRATED FRESH GINGER
⅓	CUP WATER
1	TEASPOON KOSHER SALT

FOR THE SOUP

¾	LB. BEEF, SLICED THIN
4	CUPS AWASE DASHI STOCK (SEE PAGE 38)
2	TABLESPOONS LIGHT SOY SAUCE
2	TABLESPOONS MIRIN
2	TEASPOONS SUGAR
2	SERVINGS OF UDON NOODLES (SEE PAGE 414 FOR HOMEMADE)
1	TEASPOON CANOLA OIL
½	ONION, SLICED
	PINCH OF KOSHER SALT
	GREEN ONIONS, FINELY CHOPPED, FOR GARNISH
	SHICHIMI TOGARASHI, FOR GARNISH

CURRY UDON

YIELD: 4 SERVINGS / **ACTIVE TIME:** 15 MINUTES / **TOTAL TIME:** 35 MINUTES

Curry udon blends the comforting texture of udon noodles with a curry-flavored broth, showcasing an early fusion of foreign flavors.

1. Place the canola oil in a large saucepan and warm it over medium heat. Add the pork belly and fry until it is nicely seared on both sides, turning it over once.

2. Add the dashi, soy sauce, mirin, and sugar and stir until well combined. Bring the mixture to a boil and then reduce the heat so that the broth simmers.

3. Combine the curry powder and potato starch in a small bowl. Add the water and stir to create a thin curry paste, aiming for the consistency of pancake batter.

4. Gradually pour the curry paste into the broth, whisking continually to ensure that no clumps form.

5. Add the leek and mushrooms to the pot. If you're including the kamaboko and Abura-age, add them at this stage.

6. Let the soup simmer until it has thickened to your liking, 10 to 15 minutes, stirring occasionally.

7. While the soup is simmering, cook the noodles according to the directions on the package or in the recipe. Drain the noodles, rinse them under hot water to remove excess starch, and divide them among the serving bowls.

8. Ladle the curry over the noodles, garnish with the green onions and shichimi togarashi, and serve.

INGREDIENTS:

1½	TEASPOONS CANOLA OIL
¾	LB. PORK BELLY, SLICED THIN
1½	CUPS AWASE DASHI STOCK (SEE PAGE 38)
6	TABLESPOONS SOY SAUCE
¼	CUP MIRIN
2	TEASPOONS SUGAR
6	TABLESPOONS JAPANESE CURRY POWDER (SEE PAGE 65)
2	TABLESPOONS POTATO STARCH
¾	CUP COLD WATER
1	JAPANESE LEEK, SLICED ON A BIAS
6	SHIITAKE MUSHROOMS, STEMMED AND SLICED THIN
8	SLICES OF KAMABOKO FISH CAKE (OPTIONAL)
4	ABURA-AGE (SEE PAGE 69; OPTIONAL), SLICED THIN
4	SERVINGS OF UDON NOODLES (SEE PAGE 414 FOR HOMEMADE)
¼	CUP FINELY CHOPPED GREEN ONIONS, FOR GARNISH
	SHICHIMI TOGARASHI, FOR GARNISH

MISO NIKOMI UDON

YIELD: 4 SERVINGS / **ACTIVE TIME:** 15 MINUTES / **TOTAL TIME:** 20 MINUTES

This is a beloved dish in Aichi Prefecture, a heartwarming and comforting bowl of stewed udon noodles that perfectly captures the essence of the local cuisine. The earthenware pot in which the dish is traditionally prepared lends a rustic charm and helps to retain heat and allow the flavors to meld harmoniously.

1. Place the canola oil in a large skillet and warm it over medium heat. Add the chicken and cook until it is browned all over, turning it as necessary. Set the chicken aside.

2. Place the dashi in a large saucepan and warm it over medium heat until the dashi is almost boiling. Add the sugar and mirin and stir until the sugar has dissolved.

3. Place ¼ cup of miso paste in a strainer or ladle and submerge it in the soup. Whisk to loosen and dissolve the paste. You want to ensure that it dissolves smoothly and that no clumps remain.

4. Cook the noodles for 5 minutes less than the time suggested on the package or in the recipe. Drain and rinse the noodles under hot water to remove excess starch.

5. Add the noodles, chicken, leek, mushrooms, Abura-age, and kamaboko (if using) to the broth and cook for 3 minutes. Reduce the heat to low and add the remaining miso paste, using the same method as before to incorporate it into the broth.

6. Crack the eggs into the pan, making sure to space them apart. Cover the pan with a lid and cook until the eggs are cooked to your liking.

7. Ladle the soup into warmed bowls and serve.

INGREDIENTS:

1 TEASPOON CANOLA OIL

1 LB. BONELESS, SKINLESS CHICKEN THIGHS, CHOPPED

4½ CUPS AWASE DASHI STOCK (SEE PAGE 38)

1 TABLESPOON SUGAR

1 TABLESPOON MIRIN

6 TABLESPOONS HATCHO RED MISO PASTE

4 SERVINGS OF UDON NOODLES (SEE PAGE 414 FOR HOMEMADE)

1 JAPANESE LEEK, GREEN PART ONLY, SLICED

4 SHIITAKE MUSHROOMS, STEMMED

4 ABURA-AGE (SEE PAGE 69), SLICED

8 KAMABOKO FISH CAKES (OPTIONAL)

4 EGGS

NIKU BUKKAKE UDON

YIELD: 4 SERVINGS / **ACTIVE TIME:** 5 MINUTES / **TOTAL TIME:** 20 MINUTES

This popular udon dish is made by pouring a strong dashi-based broth over the noodles, topping it with green onions and grated daikon radish, and mixing everything together.

1. To begin preparations for the udon, place the canola oil in a skillet and warm it over medium heat. Add the beef and cook until it starts to brown. Add the sake, soy sauce, mirin, and sugar to the pan and cook until the beef has absorbed most of the liquid. Remove the pan from heat and set it aside.

2. Cook the noodles according to the directions on the package or in the recipe.

3. While the noodles are cooking, prepare the broth. Place all of the ingredients in a medium saucepan and bring to a boil over medium-high heat. Reduce the heat to medium-low and let the broth simmer for 1 minute. Turn off the heat.

4. Drain the noodles. Divide the broth among the serving bowls. Add some noodles to each bowl, top each portion with some of the beef and your preferred toppings, and stir everything together before serving.

INGREDIENTS:

FOR THE UDON

1	TEASPOON CANOLA OIL
⅔	LB. BEEF, SLICED THIN
2	TABLESPOONS SAKE
2	TABLESPOONS SOY SAUCE
2	TABLESPOONS MIRIN
2	TEASPOONS SUGAR
4	SERVINGS OF UDON NOODLES (SEE PAGE 414 FOR HOMEMADE)

FOR THE BROTH

2	CUPS AWASE DASHI STOCK (SEE PAGE 38)
6	TABLESPOONS DARK SOY SAUCE
⅓	CUP LIGHT SOY SAUCE
¼	CUP MIRIN
1	TABLESPOON SUGAR

TENKASU (SEE PAGE 68), FOR TOPPING

GREEN ONIONS, CHOPPED, FOR TOPPING

PASTEURIZED EGG YOLKS OR ONSEN TAMAGO (SEE PAGE 57), FOR TOPPING

DAIKON RADISH, GRATED, FOR TOPPING

FRESH GINGER, GRATED, FOR TOPPING

TORORO TSUKIMI UDON

YIELD: 4 SERVINGS / **ACTIVE TIME:** 10 MINUTES / **TOTAL TIME:** 15 MINUTES

In Japan, Chinese yam, known as nagaimo, is a beloved ingredient, particularly in its grated form (tororo). Tororo tsukimi, a dish that combines this grated yam with noodles and raw egg yolk, has garnered a devoted following among food enthusiasts.

1. Cook the noodles according to the directions on the package or in the recipe.

2. While the noodles are cooking, peel the yam and grate it, working around the yam rather than across it. Set the yam aside.

3. Drain the noodles and rinse them under cold water. Divide the noodles among the serving bowls and pour the Mentsuyu over each portion. Top the noodles with a generous amount of the grated yam and carefully place an egg yolk on top of the grated yam.

4. Garnish with the Umeboshi, kizami nori, and green onions, stir everything together, and serve.

INGREDIENTS:

4   SERVINGS OF UDON NOODLES (SEE PAGE 414 FOR HOMEMADE)

¼   CHINESE YAM

6   TABLESPOONS MENTSUYU (SEE PAGE 42)

4   PASTEURIZED EGG YOLKS

4   UMEBOSHI (SEE PAGE 329), FOR GARNISH

    KIZAMI (SHREDDED) NORI, FOR GARNISH

    GREEN ONIONS, CHOPPED, FOR GARNISH

HIYASHI MENTAIKO UDON

YIELD: 4 SERVINGS / **ACTIVE TIME**: 10 MINUTES / **TOTAL TIME**: 10 MINUTES

Mentaiko udon dishes come in various forms, but this recipe uses chilled udon noodles and simplifies matters in order to highlight the spicy seafood flavor that is the signature of this collection of preparations.

1. Place the mentaiko, dashi granules, light soy sauce, sesame oil, and mayonnaise in a bowl and stir the mixture until well combined.

2. Add the noodles and toss to combine. Divide the dressed noodles among the serving bowls, garnish each bowl with bonito flakes, kizami nori, and shiso leaves, and serve.

INGREDIENTS:

⅓ CUP MENTAIKO, SKINS REMOVED

2 TEASPOONS DASHI GRANULES

2 TEASPOONS LIGHT SOY SAUCE

2 TABLESPOONS TOASTED SESAME OIL

2 TEASPOONS JAPANESE MAYONNAISE (SEE PAGE 46)

4 SERVINGS OF COOKED UDON NOODLES (SEE PAGE 414 FOR HOMEMADE), CHILLED

BONITO FLAKES, FOR GARNISH

KIZAMI (SHREDDED) NORI, FOR GARNISH

SHISO LEAVES, FOR GARNISH

KAMO NANBAN SOBA

YIELD: 4 SERVINGS / **ACTIVE TIME**: 10 MINUTES / **TOTAL TIME**: 15 MINUTES

Kamo nanban, also known as kamo nanba soba, is a traditional dish that features buckwheat noodles served in a hot broth, enriched with succulent duck and Japanese leek.

1. Place the duck and dark soy sauce in a bowl and let the duck marinate.

2. Brown the leek in a pan or on the grill until it is slightly charred and tender. Set the leek aside.

3. Add the tapioca starch to the bowl containing the duck and stir until it is coated.

4. Place the dashi in a medium saucepan and bring it to a boil. Reduce the heat so that the dashi simmers and add the light soy sauce, mirin, sake, ginger paste, salt, browned leek, and duck. Simmer until the duck is cooked to your liking.

5. Divide the noodles among the servings bowls and ladle the soup over the top. Garnish with green onions and shichimi togarashi and serve.

INGREDIENTS:

⅔	LB. DUCK BREAST, SLICED
1	TABLESPOON DARK SOY SAUCE
1	JAPANESE LEEK, CUT INTO 2-INCH PIECES
1	TABLESPOON TAPIOCA STARCH
4	CUPS AWASE DASHI STOCK (SEE PAGE 38)
¼	CUP LIGHT SOY SAUCE
⅓	CUP MIRIN
2	TABLESPOONS SAKE
1½	TEASPOONS GINGER PASTE
½	TEASPOON KOSHER SALT
4	SERVINGS OF COOKED SOBA NOODLES (SEE PAGE 420 FOR HOMEMADE)
	GREEN ONIONS, CHOPPED, FOR GARNISH
	SHICHIMI TOGARASHI, FOR GARNISH

Kamo Nanban Soba, see page 445

PORK NIKU SOBA

YIELD: 4 SERVINGS / **ACTIVE TIME:** 15 MINUTES / **TOTAL TIME:** 15 MINUTES

This hot soba soup takes a unique approach by using a salt-based broth instead of the traditional soy sauce base. This gives the soup a crisp and more pronounced flavor. The dish is topped with juicy stir-fried pork belly covered in a delicious garlic salt sauce that complements and contrasts with the broth.

1. To begin preparations for the soba, cook the noodles according to the directions on the package or in the recipe. Drain and rinse the noodles under hot water to remove excess starch.

2. Place the dashi, mirin, and salt in a medium saucepan and bring to a boil. Reduce the heat so that the broth simmers and cook for 1 to 2 minutes. Remove the pan from heat.

3. Place the canola oil in a large skillet and warm it over medium heat. Add the pork belly and cook until it is browned all over, turning it as necessary.

4. While the pork is cooking, prepare the sauce. Place all of the ingredients in a bowl and whisk to combine.

5. Pour the prepared sauce over the pork belly and cook until most of the moisture has evaporated, turning the pork in the glaze to ensure it gets evenly coated.

6. Divide the noodles among the serving bowls. Ladle the broth over the noodles and top each portion with some of the glazed pork belly. Garnish with green onions and serve.

INGREDIENTS:

FOR THE SOBA

4	SERVINGS OF SOBA NOODLES (SEE PAGE 420 FOR HOMEMADE)
4	CUPS AWASE DASHI STOCK (SEE PAGE 38)
¼	CUP MIRIN
1	TABLESPOON KOSHER SALT
1	TEASPOON CANOLA OIL
¾	LB. PORK BELLY, SLICED THIN
	GREEN ONIONS, FINELY CHOPPED, FOR GARNISH

FOR THE SAUCE

½	JAPANESE LEEK, WHITE PART ONLY, FINELY DICED
2	TABLESPOONS FINELY DICED GARLIC
2	TEASPOONS CHINESE CHICKEN BOUILLON
¼	CUP SAKE
1	TABLESPOON SESAME OIL
1	TEASPOON SUGAR
1	TEASPOON KOSHER SALT
¼	TEASPOON BLACK PEPPER
1½	TEASPOONS SESAME SEEDS

TORI NANBAN SOBA

YIELD: 4 SERVINGS / **ACTIVE TIME:** 20 MINUTES / **TOTAL TIME:** 30 MINUTES

This dish combines the earthy flavor of buckwheat noodles, a savory broth, tender chicken, and naganegi (Japanese leeks). The latter ingredient is the key to the dish, and fittingly is the reason that "nanban" appears in the name.

1. Cook the noodles according to the directions on the package or in the recipe. Drain the noodles and rinse them under hot water to remove excess starch.

2. Place the canola oil in a large saucepan and warm it over medium heat. Add the chicken, skin side down, and leek and cook until the chicken is golden brown. Turn the chicken over and brown it on the other side. While the chicken is browning, turn the leek occasionally so that its surface gets evenly browned.

3. Add the dashi and bring to a boil. Reduce the heat so that the broth simmers and stir in the chicken bouillon, soy sauce, sake, mirin, and salt. Add the Abura-age and simmer for a few minutes.

4. Combine the water and cornstarch in a small bowl and pour the slurry into the broth, stirring continually. Simmer until the broth has slightly thickened, 2 to 3 minutes, making sure not to let the broth become too thick.

5. Divide the noodles among the serving bowls and ladle the broth over them. Garnish with shimichi togarashi and serve.

INGREDIENTS:

4   SERVINGS OF SOBA NOODLES (SEE PAGE 420 FOR HOMEMADE)

1   TABLESPOON CANOLA OIL

1   LB. BONELESS, SKIN-ON CHICKEN THIGHS, CHOPPED

1   JAPANESE LEEK, CUT INTO 2-INCH PIECES

4   CUPS AWASE DASHI STOCK (SEE PAGE 38)

2   TEASPOONS CHINESE CHICKEN BOUILLON

3   TABLESPOONS LIGHT SOY SAUCE

2   TABLESPOONS SAKE

2   TABLESPOONS MIRIN

½   TEASPOON KOSHER SALT

4   ABURA-AGE (SEE PAGE 69), SLICED THIN

2   TABLESPOONS WATER

2   TEASPOONS CORNSTARCH

   SHICHIMI TOGARASHI, FOR GARNISH

OROSHI SOBA

YIELD: 4 SERVINGS / **ACTIVE TIME:** 10 MINUTES / **TOTAL TIME:** 15 MINUTES

Oroshi soba is a popular dish from Fukui Prefecture consisting of cold soba noodles served with mentsuyu, grated daikon, chopped green onion, and bonito flakes.

1. Cook the noodles according to the directions on the package or in the recipe. Drain and rinse them under cold water.

2. Divide the noodles evenly among the serving plates. Generously top each portion with the radish, green onions, and bonito flakes. Drizzle the Mentsuyu over the top, mix everything together, and serve.

INGREDIENTS:

- 4 SERVINGS OF SOBA NOODLES (SEE PAGE 420 FOR HOMEMADE)
- ¼ DAIKON RADISH, GRATED
- ½ CUP CHOPPED GREEN ONIONS
- ½ CUP BONITO FLAKES
- 2 CUPS MENTSUYU (SEE PAGE 42), CHILLED

Oroshi Soba, see page 451

COLD SOBA SALAD

YIELD: 4 SERVINGS / ACTIVE TIME: 10 MINUTES / TOTAL TIME: 15 MINUTES

Made with chilled buckwheat noodles, seasonal vegetables, and a delicious miso-spiked sauce, this dish is perfect for summer, easy to make, refreshing, and irresistible.

1. Cook the noodles according to the directions on the package or in the recipe. Drain and rinse them under cold water. Spread the noodles out on a baking sheet and scatter some ice over them so that they cool quickly.

2. Wash the tomato, eggplant, okra, and haricots verts and pat them dry with paper towels. Thinly slice the tomato, chop the eggplant, cut the okra into thick slices, and cut the haricots verts into thirds.

3. Place the sesame oil in a large skillet and warm it over medium heat. Add the pork and cook until it is browned all over, breaking it up with a wooden spoon as it cooks.

4. Add the eggplant and stir-fry until it has softened slightly but still retains some bite. Stir in the soy sauce, mirin, miso paste, and haricots verts, making sure the miso paste gets evenly distributed.

5. Add the okra and stir-fry until the pork is cooked through and the sauce has reduced slightly and thickened.

6. Divide the chilled soba noodles among the serving plates and spoon the pork and vegetables over the top. Arrange the sliced tomatoes alongside the noodles, garnish with green onions and additional sesame oil, and serve.

INGREDIENTS:

4	SERVINGS OF SOBA NOODLES (SEE PAGE 420 FOR HOMEMADE)
1	TOMATO
1	SMALL EGGPLANT
8	OKRA
8	HARICOTS VERTS
1½	TEASPOONS SESAME OIL, PLUS MORE FOR GARNISH
½	LB. GROUND PORK
3	TABLESPOONS SOY SAUCE
¼	CUP MIRIN
2	TABLESPOONS YELLOW MISO PASTE
	GREEN ONIONS, FINELY CHOPPED, FOR GARNISH

AE SOBA WITH CANNED TUNA

YIELD: 4 SERVINGS / **ACTIVE TIME:** 10 MINUTES / **TOTAL TIME:** 10 MINUTES

Learning to make use of chilled soba noodles is a great way to enjoy a satisfying meal in the summertime while keeping your house cool.

1. Cook the noodles according to the directions on the package or in the recipe. Drain and rinse them under cold water.

2. Place the sesame oil in a large skillet and warm it over medium-low heat. Add the leeks and salt and cook, stirring frequently, until the leeks are fragrant, 2 to 3 minutes. Remove the pan from heat and set the leeks aside.

3. Place the cucumbers, Mentsuyu, wasabi, sesame seeds, and tuna in a bowl and stir until well combined. Add the noodles, season with pepper, and toss to combine.

4. Divide the noodle mixture among the serving plates and top each portion with some of the leeks. Garnish with kizami nori, garlic chips, and shiso leaves and serve.

INGREDIENTS:

4   SERVINGS OF SOBA NOODLES (SEE PAGE 420 FOR HOMEMADE)

6   TABLESPOONS TOASTED SESAME OIL

2   JAPANESE LEEKS, WHITE PARTS ONLY, SLICED THIN

¼   TEASPOON KOSHER SALT

2   JAPANESE OR PERSIAN CUCUMBERS, JULIENNED

¾   CUP MENTSUYU (SEE PAGE 42)

1   TABLESPOON WASABI (SEE PAGE 500 FOR HOMEMADE)

6   TABLESPOONS GROUND BLACK SESAME SEEDS

10   OZ. TUNA IN OLIVE OIL, DRAINED

    BLACK PEPPER, TO TASTE

    KIZAMI (SHREDDED) NORI, FOR GARNISH

    CRISPY GARLIC CHIPS (SEE PAGE 386), FOR GARNISH

    SHISO LEAVES, SLICED THIN, FOR GARNISH

SOMEN WITH HOMEMADE DIPPING SAUCE

YIELD: 4 SERVINGS / **ACTIVE TIME:** 5 MINUTES / **TOTAL TIME:** 15 MINUTES

Considered the cousin of udon and soba, somen noodles are thin wheat noodles and typically eaten during the humid Japanese summer. They are usually served chilled and dipped in mentsuyu, but this recipe shows you how to make a sour dipping sauce that is guaranteed to refresh you during the dog days.

1. Prepare an ice bath. Place all of the ingredients, except for the noodles, in a bowl and whisk to combine. Chill the dipping sauce in the refrigerator while you cook the noodles.

2. Cook the noodles according to the directions on the package. Typically, somen noodles require about 2 minutes of boiling. Drain, rinse them under cold water, and plunge them into the ice bath until completely chilled.

3. Divide the noodles among the serving plates. Place the sauce in individual containers and serve them alongside the noodles.

INGREDIENTS:

1⅔	CUPS AWASE DASHI STOCK (SEE PAGE 38)
3	TABLESPOONS RICE VINEGAR
4	TABLESPOONS LIGHT SOY SAUCE
1	TABLESPOON SESAME SEEDS
1	TABLESPOON SESAME OIL
¼	CUP FINELY CHOPPED GREEN ONION
4	SERVINGS OF SOMEN NOODLES

Ae Soba with Canned Tuna, see page 456

NABEMONO
(HOT POTS)

*N*abemono, or simply nabe, refers to Japanese hot pots, which are traditionally enjoyed by groups gathered around a large pot, though modern adaptations now include individual-sized pots for solo diners. The key feature of nabemono is the interactive component: instead of being fully cooked and served, the pot is placed on a portable stovetop in the center of the table, allowing diners to cook and enjoy the meal at their own leisure.

BEEF SUKIYAKI

YIELD: 5 SERVINGS / **ACTIVE TIME:** 20 MINUTES / **TOTAL TIME:** 1 HOUR

Sukiyaki is a festive Japanese dish featuring thinly sliced Wagyu beef simmered in a rich broth of soy sauce, sugar, and sake. Accompanied by leeks, shungiku, and firm tofu, this dish is celebrated for its luxurious, deep flavors. Traditionally enjoyed during New Year's celebrations, sukiyaki symbolizes togetherness for families and relatives, embodying the festive, indulgent spirit of modern Japan.

1. Place the tallow in a wide, shallow cast-iron pot and warm it over medium heat, tilting the pot so that the tallow coats it evenly. Add the leeks and cook, stirring occasionally, until they are slightly browned, about 6 minutes.

2. Push the leeks to one side. Place a few slices of beef in the pot and cook until they are browned. Pour the Warishita Sauce over the beef. Remove the browned beef from the pot; as the beef added at this stage is only to add flavor, either eat it or discard it. Add the tofu, cabbage, mushrooms, and carrot, bring the mixture to a boil, and then reduce the heat so that it simmers.

3. Create an empty space in the pot and add more of the beef, ensuring that it's submerged in the sauce. Add the shungiku, cover the pot, and simmer the sukiyaki until the beef and vegetables are cooked to your liking, 5 to 15 minutes, depending on the thickness of the ingredients. Turn the vegetables and beef occasionally as they simmer.

4. To serve, you can present the sukiyaki family style, allowing each person to take items from the pot as they cook, and adding more ingredients to the pot as needed to ensure that everyone gets their fill. Or you can provide each diner with a bowl and a raw pasteurized egg. Guests can crack the egg into their bowl, whisk it, and use it as a dipping sauce for an authentic Japanese sukiyaki experience.

5. After removing all of the ingredients from the pot, serve the remaining broth with udon noodles.

INGREDIENTS:

- 1 TABLESPOON BEEF TALLOW OR LARD
- 2 JAPANESE LEEKS, WHITE PARTS ONLY, SLICED ON A BIAS INTO 2-INCH PIECES
- 1 LB. BEEF, SLICED THIN

  WARISHITA SAUCE (SEE PAGE 679)
- 1 LB. FIRM TOFU, CHOPPED INTO LARGE CUBES
- 4 NAPA CABBAGE LEAVES, CHOPPED
- 8 SHIITAKE MUSHROOMS, STEMMED AND CHOPPED
- ¼ LB. ENOKI MUSHROOMS, ROOTS REMOVED
- 1 CARROT, PEELED AND SLICED
- 1 BUNCH OF SHUNGIKU (EDIBLE CHRYSANTHEMUM)
- 4 PASTEURIZED EGGS (OPTIONAL)
- 4 SERVINGS OF COOKED UDON NOODLES (SEE PAGE 414 FOR HOMEMADE), FOR SERVING

SHIO LEMON NABE

YIELD: 4 SERVINGS / **ACTIVE TIME:** 10 MINUTES / **TOTAL TIME:** 1 HOUR MINUTES

Shio lemon nabe is a variation on chicken hot pot distinguished by its light and zesty broth.

1. Place the water in a large pot, add the kombu, and let it soak for 30 minutes.

2. Place the pot over medium-low heat. Just before the water comes to a boil, turn off the heat and remove the kombu. Stir in the salt, sake, mirin, and chicken bouillon and layer the cabbage and leek in the bottom of the pot.

3. Add the chicken and garlic and top them with a layer of the bean sprouts. Place the lemon on top of the bean sprouts, drizzle the sesame oil over the dish, and season with the black pepper. If the pot you are using isn't large enough to comfortably hold all the ingredients, consider dividing the broth and ingredients into two parts and cooking the dish in batches.

4. Cover the pot with a lid and simmer over medium heat until everything is cooked through, about 20 minutes. If you'd like to follow the Japanese tradition for the dish, enjoy the meat and vegetables and then add ramen or udon noodles to the remaining broth.

INGREDIENTS:

4½	CUPS WATER
	4-INCH SQUARE OF DRIED KOMBU
1	TABLESPOON KOSHER SALT
¼	CUP SAKE
3	TABLESPOONS MIRIN
1½	TEASPOONS CHINESE CHICKEN BOUILLON
¼	NAPA CABBAGE, CHOPPED
1	JAPANESE LEEK, SLICED ON A BIAS
1	LB. BONELESS, SKINLESS CHICKEN THIGHS, CHOPPED
1	GARLIC CLOVE, GRATED
1	LEMON, SLICED
½	LB. BEAN SPROUTS
1	TABLESPOON SESAME OIL
¼	TEASPOON BLACK PEPPER
4	SERVINGS OF COOKED RAMEN OR UDON NOODLES (SEE PAGE 372 OR 414 FOR HOMEMADE; OPTIONAL)

PORK & GARLIC NABE

YIELD: 4 SERVINGS / **ACTIVE TIME:** 20 MINUTES / **TOTAL TIME:** 1 HOUR

In Japanese-style hot pots, soy sauce–based broths are the most common choice, offering a deep, umami-rich foundation that complements a wide range of ingredients. This particular recipe modifies this classic broth by integrating the succulent flavor of pork belly and aromatic garlic, creating a blend that captivates the palate.

1. Place the water in a large pot, add the kombu, and let it soak for 30 minutes.

2. While the kombu is soaking, cut half of the garlic into thin slices and finely dice the other half. Set the garlic aside.

3. Place the sesame oil in a large skillet and warm it over medium heat. Add the pork belly, season with the salt and pepper, and fry until it is browned all over, turning it as necessary. Add the garlic and leek and stir-fry for 1 minute. Remove the pan from heat and set the pork mixture aside.

4. Place the pot over medium heat. Just before the water comes to a boil, turn off the heat and remove the kombu. Stir in the soy sauce, mirin, sake, ground sesame seeds, chicken bouillon, and oyster sauce and then layer the cabbage, silken tofu, and carrot in the broth.

5. In the center of the pot, add the pork mixture, including any rendered fat. Sprinkle the whole sesame seeds over the top, cover the pot, and simmer until everything is cooked through, about 20 minutes.

6. Enjoy the meat, tofu, and vegetables and then add ramen or udon noodles to the remaining broth for the final course.

INGREDIENTS:

4	CUPS WATER
	4-INCH SQUARE OF DRIED KOMBU
4	GARLIC CLOVES
1½	TEASPOONS SESAME OIL
⅔	LB. PORK BELLY, SLICED THIN AND CHOPPED
⅛	TEASPOON KOSHER SALT
⅛	TEASPOON BLACK PEPPER
1	JAPANESE LEEK, FINELY DICED
2	TABLESPOONS LIGHT SOY SAUCE
2	TABLESPOONS MIRIN
1	TABLESPOON SAKE
1	TABLESPOON GROUND SESAME SEEDS
1	TABLESPOON CHINESE CHICKEN BOUILLON
1	TEASPOON OYSTER SAUCE
¼	NAPA CABBAGE, CHOPPED
¾	LB. SILKEN TOFU, CUBED
1	CARROT, PEELED AND SLICED
1	TABLESPOON WHOLE SESAME SEEDS
4	SERVINGS OF COOKED RAMEN OR UDON NOODLES (SEE PAGE 372 OR 414 FOR HOMEMADE)

Shio Lemon Nabe, see page 466

SOY MILK TANTAN NABE

YIELD: 4 SERVINGS / ACTIVE TIME: 20 MINUTES / TOTAL TIME: 1 HOUR

Tantan nabe takes inspiration from the beloved tantanmen, transforming it into a delicious one-pot dish that merges the richness of a creamy sesame broth with the heat of spicy pork.

1. To begin preparations for the nabe, place the water in a large pot, add the kombu, and let it soak for 30 minutes.

2. While the kombu is soaking, prepare the pork. Place the sesame oil in a large skillet and warm it over medium heat. Add the garlic, ginger, and chiles and stir-fry for 1 minute. Add the pork, season with the salt and pepper, and stir in the chili bean paste. Cook until the pork is cooked through, 8 to 10 minutes, breaking it up with a wooden spoon. Remove the pan from heat and set the pork aside.

3. Place the pot over medium heat. Just before the water comes to a boil, remove the kombu and reduce the heat to medium-low. Stir in the sake, garlic, chili bean paste, chicken bouillon, cabbage, and tofu, cover the pot, and simmer for 20 minutes.

4. Turn off the heat and wait for the mixture in the pot to stop bubbling. Stir in the miso paste, sesame seeds, garlic chives, bean sprouts, soy milk, Rayu, and sesame oil. Gently arrange the pork on top of the dish and gently reheat the soup over low heat, making sure it does not come to a boil.

5. Enjoy the meat, tofu, and vegetables and then add ramen noodles to the remaining broth for the final course.

INGREDIENTS:

FOR THE NABE

3	CUPS WATER
	4-INCH SQUARE OF DRIED KOMBU
1	TABLESPOON SAKE
1	GARLIC CLOVE, GRATED
1½	TEASPOONS CHILI BEAN PASTE
1	TABLESPOON CHINESE CHICKEN BOUILLON
2	CUPS CHOPPED GREEN CABBAGE
¾	LB. SILKEN TOFU, CUT INTO SMALL CUBES
2	TABLESPOONS YELLOW MISO PASTE
3	TABLESPOONS GROUND SESAME SEEDS
½	CUP CHOPPED GARLIC CHIVES (2-INCH-LONG PIECES)
2	CUPS BEAN SPROUTS
1	CUP SOY MILK
1½	TEASPOONS RAYU (SEE PAGE 49)
1	TABLESPOON SESAME OIL
4	SERVINGS OF COOKED RAMEN NOODLES (SEE PAGE 372 FOR HOMEMADE)

FOR THE PORK

1	TEASPOON SESAME OIL
2	GARLIC CLOVES, GRATED
1½	TEASPOONS GRATED FRESH GINGER
4	DRIED CHILE PEPPERS, SLICED
4	OZ. GROUND PORK
	PINCH OF KOSHER SALT
	PINCH OF BLACK PEPPER
1½	TEASPOONS CHILI BEAN PASTE

MOTSUNABE

YIELD: 4 SERVINGS / ACTIVE TIME: 15 MINUTES / TOTAL TIME: 20 MINUTES

Motsunabe is a hot pot beloved in the Hakata ward of Fukuoka City. This iconic dish is made with beef or pork offal, known in Japanese as horumon or motsu, that gets cooked in a fragrant soy- or miso-based broth. Beef offal is favored for its fatty, tender, and sweet characteristics.

1. Bring a large pot of water to a boil.

2. While you wait for the water to come to a boil, place the beef intestines in a fine-mesh strainer set over a large heatproof bowl and fill the bowl with fresh cold water. Swish the beef intestines around and then drain them. Repeat once more.

3. When the water is boiling, submerge the strainer with the beef intestines in it for 10 seconds. Lift the strainer out of the boiling water and shake it well. Place the beef intestines back into the bowl, refill it with cold water, and set it aside.

4. Fill another bowl with cold water. Wash and peel the burdock root and then cut it into thin slices on a bias. Place it in the cold water and let it soak for 5 minutes.

5. Place the dashi, chicken bouillon, soy sauces, mirin, sake, oyster sauce, garlic, ginger, and brown sugar in a large pot, stir until well combined, and bring to a boil over medium heat.

6. Reduce the heat so that the broth simmers, drain the beef intestines and burdock root, and add them to the broth along with the cabbage and tofu. If your pot is not big enough to hold everything, divide the ingredients and cook them in multiple batches. Cook until the vegetables are cooked to your liking.

7. Sprinkle the garlic chives, chiles, garlic chips, and whole sesame seeds on top of the dish.

8. Divide the ground sesame seeds among the serving bowls and ladle the soup into the bowls. Enjoy and then add ramen noodles to the remaining broth for the final course.

INGREDIENTS:

1   LB. BEEF INTESTINES, CUT INTO BITE-SIZE PIECES

1   BURDOCK ROOT

6¾ CUPS AWASE DASHI STOCK (SEE PAGE 38)

¼   CUP CHINESE CHICKEN BOUILLON

½   CUP LIGHT SOY SAUCE

¼   CUP DARK SOY SAUCE

6   TABLESPOONS MIRIN

¼   CUP SAKE

2   TEASPOONS OYSTER SAUCE

4   GARLIC CLOVES, GRATED

    1-INCH PIECE OF FRESH GINGER, PEELED AND GRATED

2   TEASPOONS LIGHT BROWN SUGAR

½   GREEN CABBAGE, CHOPPED

¾   LB. MEDIUM-FIRM TOFU, CUBED

7   OZ. GARLIC CHIVES (CHINESE CHIVES), CUT INTO 3-INCH PIECES

2–4 DRIED RED CHILE PEPPERS, SLICED THIN

2   TABLESPOONS CRISPY GARLIC CHIPS (SEE PAGE 386)

2   TEASPOONS TOASTED WHOLE SESAME SEEDS

4   TEASPOONS GROUND SESAME SEEDS

4   SERVINGS OF COOKED AND RINSED RAMEN NOODLES (SEE PAGE 372 FOR HOMEMADE)

Soy Milk Tantan Nabe,
see page 470

ODEN

YIELD: 4 SERVINGS / **ACTIVE TIME:** 45 MINUTES / **TOTAL TIME:** 3 HOURS

Oden is a classic Japanese winter dish. It is made by simmering various ingredients in a dashi and soy sauce–based broth. In the spirit of "the more the merrier," you can add a variety of different ingredients to deepen the flavor, so just take what's listed here as suggestions rather than commands.

1. Bring a pot of water to a boil. Add the beef tendon and boil for a few minutes to remove any excess fat.

2. Drain the beef tendon and rinse it thoroughly under cold water. Refill the pot with about 4 cups of water (or enough to cover the beef tendon) and bring to a boil.

3. While waiting for the water to boil, cut the beef tendon into strips.

4. Reduce the heat to simmer. Add the leek, ginger, and beef tendon to the pot and simmer for 1 hour, adding water as necessary to keep the beef submerged.

5. Remove the beef tendon from the pot and let it cool. Remove the leek and ginger and discard them. Simmer the broth until it has reduced by one-third. When the beef tendon is cool enough to handle, thread it onto skewers.

6. While you are simmering the broth, bring water to a boil in a medium saucepan. Score one side of each piece of radish with a cross that is about ½ inch deep, place it in the pan, and cook until the radish is fork-tender, 10 to 15 minutes.

7. Cut the rice cakes in half. Cut one end of each Abura-age. Stuff a piece of rice cake into each Abura-age, replace the ends that you cut off, and secure them with a toothpick. Set them aside.

8. Place the dashi in a large saucepan and stir in ½ cup of the broth created by boiling the beef tendon. Add the sake, sugar, mirin, soy sauce, and oyster sauce, bring to a boil, and cook for 2 to 3 minutes.

9. Reduce the heat so that the broth simmers and add the daikon, boiled eggs, and skewered beef tendon. At this point, add any other firm ingredients you have elected to use, such as the carrot and potatoes. Simmer for 30 minutes.

10. Add the fish cakes, stuffed Abura-age, Atsuage Tofu, and any other soft ingredients you have elected to use. Simmer for another 15 minutes.

11. Serve the nabe with Japanese mustard.

INGREDIENTS:

1	LB. BEEF TENDON (SINEW)
1	JAPANESE LEEK, GREEN PART ONLY
3	SLICES OF FRESH GINGER
¼	DAIKON RADISH, SLICED INTO THICK ROUNDS
2	KIRIMOCHI RICE CAKES
4	ABURA-AGE (SEE PAGE 69)
4	CUPS AWASE DASHI STOCK (SEE PAGE 38)
2	TABLESPOONS SAKE
1½	TEASPOONS SUGAR
3	TABLESPOONS MIRIN
5	TABLESPOONS SOY SAUCE
1	TABLESPOON OYSTER SAUCE
4	BOILED EGGS, PEELED
½	CARROT, PEELED AND SLICED
2	POTATOES, CHOPPED
8	SLICES OF KAMABOKO FISH CAKES
4	PIECES OF ATSUAGE TOFU (SEE PAGE 73)
5	OZ. CLEANED SQUID, SLICED
4	CHIKUWA FISH CAKES, HALVED
8	SMOKED SAUSAGES
	JAPANESE MUSTARD, FOR SERVING

SALMON MISO NABE

YIELD: 4 SERVINGS / **ACTIVE TIME:** 10 MINUTES / **TOTAL TIME:** 1 HOUR

Miso-based hot pots pair well with the flavors of the sea. While salmon and scallops are suggested here, feel free to substitute whatever seafood is fresh locally.

1. Place the water in a large pot, add the kombu, and let it soak for 30 minutes.

2. Place the pot over medium-low heat. Just before the water comes to a boil, turn off the heat and remove the kombu. Add the miso paste, soy sauce, mirin, and sugar and stir until the miso paste and sugar have dissolved.

3. Add all of the remaining ingredients, except for the noodles, cover the pot, and simmer over medium heat for 20 minutes.

4. Ladle the stew into the bowls. Enjoy and then add ramen noodles to the remaining broth for the final course.

INGREDIENTS:

4½	CUPS WATER
	4-INCH SQUARE OF DRIED KOMBU
5	TABLESPOONS YELLOW MISO PASTE
1	TABLESPOON SOY SAUCE
1	TABLESPOON MIRIN
1	TABLESPOON SUGAR
3	SKIN-ON SALMON FILLETS
1	CUP SCALLOPS
¼	NAPA CABBAGE, CHOPPED
½	CUP SLICED ABURA-AGE (SEE PAGE 69)
1	JAPANESE LEEK, SLICED ON A BIAS
4	SHIITAKE MUSHROOMS, STEMMED
1	GARLIC CLOVE, GRATED
1	TABLESPOON UNSALTED BUTTER
1	TABLESPOON SWEET CORN KERNELS
4	SERVINGS OF COOKED RAMEN NOODLES (SEE PAGE 372 FOR HOMEMADE)

Salmon Miso Nabe, see page 475

CHANKO NABE

YIELD: 4 SERVINGS / **ACTIVE TIME:** 15 MINUTES / **TOTAL TIME:** 1 HOUR

Chanko refers to any meal prepared by or for sumo wrestlers, encompassing a broad range of dishes beyond the hot pot. Each sumo stable might craft its version with unique broths and diverse ingredients, but the underlying principle remains constant: the dish must be rich in both meat and vegetables, ensuring a balanced, filling meal that supports the wrestlers' substantial energy requirements.

1. To begin preparations for the nabe, place the water in a large saucepan, add the kombu, and let it soak for 30 minutes.

2. While the kombu is soaking, prepare the meatballs. Place all of the ingredients in a mixing bowl and work the mixture until well combined. Chill the mixture in the refrigerator.

3. Place the sesame oil in a large pot and warm it over medium heat. Add the chicken, garlic, and onion, season with 1 teaspoon of salt and the pepper, and cook, stirring occasionally, until the onion is tender, about 8 minutes.

4. Add the water, kombu, sake, chicken bouillon, mirin, garlic paste, ginger paste, remaining salt, and the sugar and cook until the nabe is just about to come to a boil. Remove the kombu and then reduce the heat so that the nabe simmers.

5. Gently scrape spoonfuls of the meatball mixture into the simmering broth. Add the remaining ingredients, cover the pot, and simmer for 20 minutes. If your pot cannot accommodate all of the vegetables at once, add them in two batches, adding the second portion after serving the first batch.

6. Taste the nabe, adjust the seasoning as necessary, and serve.

INGREDIENTS:

FOR THE NABE

4	CUPS WATER
	4 X 6–INCH PIECE OF DRIED KOMBU
1½	TEASPOONS SESAME OIL
⅔	LB. BONELESS, SKINLESS CHICKEN THIGHS, CHOPPED
2	GARLIC CLOVES, FINELY DICED
¼	ONION, SLICED
2½	TEASPOONS KOSHER SALT
⅛	TEASPOON BLACK PEPPER
2	TABLESPOONS SAKE
1	TABLESPOON CHINESE CHICKEN BOUILLON
2	TABLESPOONS MIRIN
1	TEASPOON GARLIC PASTE
1	TEASPOON GINGER PASTE
1½	TEASPOONS SUGAR
2	CUPS BEAN SPROUTS
¼	NAPA CABBAGE, CHOPPED
½	CARROT, PEELED AND SLICED
1	JAPANESE LEEK, SLICED ON A BIAS
2	SHIITAKE MUSHROOMS, STEMMED AND SLICED
2	ABURA-AGE (SEE PAGE 69), SLICED

FOR THE MEATBALLS

½	LB. GROUND CHICKEN
1	SMALL EGG
1½	TEASPOONS YELLOW MISO PASTE
½	TEASPOON GINGER PASTE
½	TEASPOON GARLIC PASTE
1½	TEASPOONS CORNSTARCH

JOYA NABE

YIELD: 4 SERVINGS / **ACTIVE TIME**: 15 MINUTES / **TOTAL TIME**: 45 MINUTES

Joya translates to "every night" in Japanese, suggesting that this dish is so tasty, one could enjoy it daily without ever growing weary of it.

1. Place the water in a large pot, add the kombu, ginger, and sake and let the mixture soak for 30 minutes.

2. Place the pot over medium heat. Just before the water comes to a boil, remove the kombu and ginger. Reduce the heat slightly, add the pork belly, spinach, and tofu, cover, and simmer until the pork belly is cooked through, 15 to 20 minutes.

3. While the ingredients are simmering, divide the ponzu into individual portions. Garnish with the green onions and shichimi togarashi and set them aside.

4. To serve, dip the pork belly, spinach, and tofu into the ponzu. After enjoying these, bring the remaining broth to a boil, add the noodles, and cook according to the directions on the package or in the recipe. Enjoy the cooked noodles with any remaining ponzu.

INGREDIENTS:

4	CUPS WATER
	4-INCH SQUARE OF DRIED KOMBU
3	SLICES OF FRESH GINGER
¼	CUP SAKE
1	LB. PORK BELLY, SLICED THIN
½	LB. SPINACH
1½	LBS. SILKEN TOFU, DICED
	PONZU SAUCE (SEE PAGE 45)
	GREEN ONIONS, CHOPPED, FOR GARNISH
	SHICHIMI TOGARASHI, FOR GARNISH
4	SERVINGS OF UDON NOODLES (SEE PAGE 414 FOR HOMEMADE)

SUSHI & SASHIMI

*S*ushi and sashimi stand as the most globally recognized Japanese dishes, so much so that in many people's minds they are synonymous with Japanese cuisine. Their long-standing popularity has led to numerous international variations, such as the California roll, resulting in slight differences between Japanese and global interpretations of "sushi." This section provides a comprehensive guide to authentic Japanese sushi and sashimi making, from perfect sushi rice to traditional rolls. One thing to keep in mind, many of these preparations include numerous filling options. These are only suggestions, and you should feel free to include as many or as few as you like.

SUMESHI

YIELD: 6 SERVINGS / ACTIVE TIME: 10 MINUTES / TOTAL TIME: 1 HOUR

For authentic sushi dishes, such as hosomaki, gunkanmaki, futomaki, nigiri, chirashizushi, and so on, the key ingredient is vinegared rice—not just any regular cooked white rice. This essential component imparts a distinctive tang and subtly sweet flavor, foundational to the sushi experience. This recipe provides you with the knowledge to create perfect vinegared rice, whether you have a rice cooker or not.

1. Wash the rice and transfer it to a pot with a tight-fitting lid. Add the cold water and kombu and let the rice soak for 30 minutes (1 hour in colder climates).

2. Cover the pot and cook it over medium heat. Listen for the sound of water boiling. Once you hear consistent bubbling, set a timer for 30 seconds. After 30 seconds, reduce the heat to medium-low and set a timer for 2 minutes. After 2 minutes, reduce the heat to low and let the rice simmer for 5 minutes.

3. Raise the heat to the highest possible temperature and cook the rice for 10 seconds. Turn off the heat and leave the pot covered on the warm stove, allowing the rice to steam for 10 minutes. Resist the urge to remove the lid as the rice steams.

4. While the rice is steaming, place the vinegar, sugar, and salt in a small bowl and stir until the sugar and salt have dissolved.

5. Wet the surface of a sushi oke (sushi rice tub) or a wide, shallow container. Remove the lid from the pot. Using a rice paddle or a moist spoon or silicone spatula (the moisture will prevent the rice from sticking), gently stir and fold the rice. Transfer it to the container and pour the vinegar mixture over the rice, gently folding it in with a rice paddle while fanning it to cool it down. Spread the rice into a thin, even layer so that it will cool down quickly.

6. When the sushi rice is around body temperature, it is ready to use for making sushi rolls. If not using right away, it can be covered with a damp kitchen towel to prevent it from drying out. Ideally, you want to use the rice within 2 hours.

INGREDIENTS:

2   CUPS JAPANESE SHORT-GRAIN RICE

2   CUPS COLD WATER

    2-INCH SQUARE OF DRIED KOMBU

2½   TABLESPOONS RICE VINEGAR

1½   TEASPOONS SUGAR

1   TEASPOON KOSHER SALT

HOSOMAKI

YIELD: 6 ROLLS / ACTIVE TIME: 30 MINUTES / TOTAL TIME: 30 MINUTES

Hosomaki is a rolled sushi known for its thin shape and use of 1 to 2 fillings. The most popular variations of hosomaki include kappa maki (cucumber), tekka maki (tuna), and kanpyo maki (strips of dried gourd), but many variations exist. This roll is perfect for beginners looking for a simple, yet tasty, option to start their sushi-making journey.

1. Cut the cucumber, Kanpyo, and tuna to the same length as the nori. Fold the nori in half and tear or cut it along the fold.

2. Prepare a bowl of water so that you can easily wet your hands when handling the rice.

3. Lay a bamboo sushi mat on a flat surface, making sure the bamboo is horizontal in relation to you. Place a half-sheet of nori on the sushi mat, rough side facing up, lining up the bottom of the nori with the bottom of the mat. Lightly wet your hands and shape approximately ½ cup of sushi rice into a cylinder. Place the rice down on the nori and spread it out evenly, leaving a finger-width border along the top. Pinch the top edge of the rice, lifting it slightly to make a ridge.

4. For the cucumber and tuna rolls, spread wasabi over the middle of the rice and place the filling on top of it. For the rolls with Kanpyo, leave the rice plain and lay the pieces of Kanpyo along the center.

5. Lift the bottom of the bamboo mat and carefully roll it so that the edges of the rice meet, then lift the mat slightly and roll it so that the empty border wraps around the outside and closes up the seam. There is no need to wet it down, as the moisture from the warm rice will help the nori stick together. Press firmly on the bamboo mat to shape the roll.

6. Repeat until all of your rice, nori, and fillings are used up, then use a sharp knife to cut each cylinder into 4 to 6 equal pieces using a quick sawing motion. Wipe the knife off each time to ensure clean cuts. Serve the kanpyo rolls on their own, and the cucumber-and-tuna rolls with soy sauce.

INGREDIENTS:

½ JAPANESE OR PERSIAN CUCUMBER, HALVED LENGTHWISE

10–12 STRIPS OF KANPYO (SEE PAGE 520)

2 STRIPS OF SASHIMI-GRADE TUNA

3 SHEETS OF NORI

3 CUPS SUMESHI (SEE PAGE 484)

WASABI (SEE PAGE 500), TO TASTE

SOY SAUCE, FOR SERVING

Sumeshi, see page 484

FUTOMAKI

YIELD: 6 ROLLS / **ACTIVE TIME:** 40 MINUTES / **TOTAL TIME:** 40 MINUTES

Futomaki is a thick-rolled sushi filled with four or more ingredients. It's fun and easy to customize, making it an ideal dish for parties and gatherings. One special type of futomaki is ehomaki, which is known to contain seven fillings and believed to ward off bad luck. Ehomaki is served uncut, and is eaten during the bean throwing festival Setsubun on February 3. There are a number of options listed for filling here—for best results, choose at least four and as many as seven for your rolls. And, of course, if you would prefer to add another filling to the options mentioned here, feel free to do so.

1. Prepare your fillings by cutting them to the same length as the nori, if possible. If the pieces are too short, multiple pieces can be lined up in one roll. Fold the nori in half and tear or cut it along the fold.

2. Set up your rolling station: a plate of your chosen fillings, the nori, the Sumeshi in a bowl covered with a damp kitchen towel to prevent it from drying out, a bamboo sushi mat, and a bowl of water so you can easily wet your hands when handling rice.

3. Lay the bamboo sushi mat on a flat surface, making sure the bamboo is horizontal. Place a half-sheet of nori on the sushi mat, rough side facing up, lining up the bottom of the nori with the bottom of the mat. Lightly wet your hands and shape approximately 1 cup of sushi rice into a cylinder. Place the rice down on the nori and spread it out evenly, leaving a finger-width border along the top. Pinch the top edge of the rice, lifting it up slightly to make a ridge.

4. Spread Wasabi (if using) through the middle of the rice and place your desired fillings on top. Futomaki should be thick, with each roll containing at least 3 or 4 different fillings, depending on the thickness of the ingredients. If using leafy ingredients—like shiso leaves—place them on the very top of the fillings. This will help hold the other ingredients in place.

5. Lift the bottom of the bamboo mat and carefully roll it so that the edges of the rice meet, then lift the mat slightly and roll it so that the empty border wraps around the outside and closes up the seam. There is no need to wet it down, as the moisture from the warm rice will help the nori stick together. Press firmly on the bamboo mat to shape the roll.

6. Repeat until all of your rice, nori, and fillings are used up, then use a sharp knife to cut each cylinder into 4 to 6 equal pieces using a quick sawing motion. Wipe the knife off each time to ensure clean cuts. Serve with soy sauce, Gari, and additional Wasabi.

INGREDIENTS:

CUCUMBER, CUT INTO LONG STRIPS

DASHIMAKI TAMAGO (SEE PAGE 517), CUT INTO LONG STRIPS

SASHIMI-GRADE SEAFOOD (SALMON, TUNA, YELLOW-TAIL, SQUID, ETC.), CUT INTO LONG STRIPS

KANPYO (SEE PAGE 520), CUT TO THE LENGTH OF THE NORI

BUTTERFLIED SHRIMP (SEE PAGE 513)

IMITATION CRAB

SHISO LEAVES

IKURA (SEE PAGE 510)

AVOCADO, FINELY DICED

SAKURA DENBU (SEE PAGE 516)

TAKUAN (SEE PAGE 318)

WASABI (SEE PAGE 500), PLUS MORE FOR SERVING

6   SHEETS OF NORI

6   CUPS SUMESHI (SEE PAGE 484)

SOY SAUCE, FOR SERVING

GARI (SEE PAGE 499), FOR SERVING

TEMAKIZUSHI

YIELD: 4 SERVINGS / **ACTIVE TIME:** 40 MINUTES / **TOTAL TIME:** 40 MINUTES

Temakizushi is a fun, interactive type of sushi often enjoyed during family gatherings or parties. It involves rolling your own sushi using a sheet of nori, a layer of sushi rice, and various fillings. The beauty of temakizushi lies in its versatility; there are no strict rules about what ingredients to use, allowing everyone to customize their sushi to their liking.

1. Wet your hands and place about 1 oz. of sushi rice on each piece of nori. Spread the rice out and shape it into a right triangle, leaving the one upper corner of the nori empty.

2. If you are using Wasabi, spread a thin layer of it diagonally across the rice triangle.

3. Place your chosen fillings on top of the Wasabi or rice. To form the cone, bring the bottom left corner of the nori to the center, making sure the short sides of the rice triangle meet. Roll the remaining nori over to form a cone, trying to align the points for a smoother and more aesthetically pleasing roll. Serve with soy sauce.

INGREDIENTS:

4   CUPS SUMESHI (SEE PAGE 484)

8   SHEETS OF NORI, HALVED

    WASABI (SEE PAGE 500; OPTIONAL)

½   LB. SASHIMI-GRADE SEAFOOD (TUNA, SALMON, SHRIMP, ETC.), CUT INTO STRIPS

⅓   LB. NEGITORO (SEE PAGE 512)

⅓   LB. VEGETABLES (CUCUMBER, AVOCADO, ETC.), CUT INTO STRIPS

    DASHIMAKI TAMAGO (SEE PAGE 517), CUT INTO STRIPS

    SHISO LEAVES

    SOY SAUCE, FOR SERVING

INARIZUSHI

YIELD: 4 SERVINGS / **ACTIVE TIME:** 40 MINUTES / **TOTAL TIME:** 1 HOUR AND 40 MINUTES

Inarizushi is a sushi that consists of sweet and savory deep-fried tofu pouches stuffed with vinegared rice. It was beloved as an affordable and delicious food by the common people during the Edo period.

1. Roll out the Abura-age until they are flat. Bring a small pot of water to a boil, add the Abura-age, and place a drop lid, aluminum foil, or parchment paper on the surface. Boil for 2 minutes, drain, and rinse the Abura-age under cold water. Squeeze out any excess water and lay them on a chopping board. Cut a slit into one edge of each Abura-age to create an opening for the filling.

2. Place the soy sauce, dashi, mirin, and turbinado sugar in a small saucepan and bring to a boil. Add the Abura-age, reduce the heat so that the sauce simmers, and place the drop lid, aluminum foil, or parchment paper on the surface. Simmer until the sauce has reduced to about one-third of its original volume.

3. Transfer the Abura-age and sauce to a container and let it cool. Cover the container and let the Abura-age marinate in the refrigerator for at least 1 hour. If time allows, let the Abura-age marinate overnight.

4. Remove the Abura-age from the refrigerator. Lightly wet your hands. Divide the sushi rice into eight equal portions and shape these into barrels. Carefully open the Abura-age and push a rice barrel inside of each one, pressing it down with a spoon and taking care not to rip the tofu.

5. Close the Abura-age up, flip them over to hide the seams, and serve.

INGREDIENTS:

8   ABURA-AGE (SEE PAGE 69)

2   TABLESPOONS LIGHT SOY SAUCE

1   CUP AWASE DASHI STOCK (SEE PAGE 38)

1   TABLESPOON MIRIN

2   TABLESPOONS TURBINADO SUGAR

2¼   CUPS SUMESHI (SEE PAGE 484)

Temakizushi, see page 490

TEMARIZUSHI

YIELD: 4 SERVINGS / **ACTIVE TIME:** 45 MINUTES / **TOTAL TIME:** 45 MINUTES

This variation of sushi is inspired by temari, a traditional Japanese handball made with the fabric leftover from making kimonos. Despite its impressive appearance, temarizushi is very easy to make and shape, making it an ideal choice for parties and celebrations.

1. If using, place the cucumber in a bowl, cover it with water, and add salt. Let the cucumber soak for 15 minutes. Drain the cucumber, pat it dry with paper towels, and place it on a large plate with your other chosen fillings.

2. Lightly wet your hands. Roll the sushi rice into small balls. Each ball should weigh about 1 oz. Place the rice balls on a plate or in a container and cover them with a damp kitchen towel to keep them from drying out.

3. Place the filling of your choice in the center of a piece of plastic wrap, with the side you want to be showing facing down. Place a rice ball on top and tightly wrap up the plastic wrap, twisting to make it as tight as possible. Unwrap the rice ball, transfer it to a serving platter, and repeat with the remaining rice balls and fillings. Reuse the plastic wrap for similar ingredients and experiment with different cuts and ingredient combinations to create your own unique display.

4. Arrange the temarizushi on a plate and decorate with edible flowers. Serve with soy sauce and Wasabi.

INGREDIENTS:

1	OZ. CUCUMBER, SLICED THIN INTO STRIPS OR ROUNDS
	SALT, TO TASTE
6½	CUPS SUMESHI (SEE PAGE 484)
12	SLICES OF SASHIMI-GRADE FISH
8	BOILED SCALLOPS
4	BUTTERFLIED SHRIMP (SEE PAGE 513)
1	LEMON SLICE, QUARTERED
4	TEASPOONS IKURA (SEE PAGE 510)
4	SHISO LEAVES
¼	CUP KINSHI TAMAGO (SEE PAGE 521), COOLED
	EDIBLE FLOWERS, FOR GARNISH
	SOY SAUCE, FOR SERVING
	WASABI (SEE PAGE 500), FOR SERVING

CHIRASHIZUSHI

YIELD: 4 SERVINGS / **ACTIVE TIME**: 30 MINUTES / **TOTAL TIME**: 1 HOUR

Chirashizushi is a colorful kind of sushi that involves sprinkling a variety of ingredients over vinegared rice. The name means "to scatter," and this dish is usually served in bowls rather than shaped into rolls.

1. Place the mushrooms and water in a bowl and let the mushrooms soak until they are fully rehydrated, about 30 minutes.

2. Remove the mushrooms from the water and slice them thin. Strain the soaking liquid into a small saucepan, add the mushrooms, carrot, Abura-age, sake, sugar, mirin, and soy sauce and stir to combine. Cook over medium heat, stirring occasionally, until all of the liquid has evaporated, making sure that the mixture does not burn. Remove the pan from heat.

3. Add the cooked mixture to the sushi rice and gently fold until it is evenly distributed. Cover the rice with a damp kitchen towel immediately to keep it from drying out.

4. Divide the rice mixture among the serving bowls, top it with your preferences among the remaining ingredients, and serve.

INGREDIENTS:

- 3   DRIED SHIITAKE MUSHROOMS
- 1   CUP COLD WATER
- ½   CARROT, PEELED AND JULIENNED
- 3   ABURA-AGE (SEE PAGE 69), SLICED THIN
- 1   TABLESPOON SAKE
- 1   TABLESPOON SUGAR
- 2   TABLESPOONS MIRIN
- 2   TABLESPOONS SOY SAUCE
- 4   CUPS SUMESHI (SEE PAGE 484)
- 3   OZ. SCALLOPS, BOILED OR STEAMED
- 3   OZ. MARINATED TUNA SASHIMI (SEE PAGE 507), CUBED
- 1   DASHIMAKI TAMAGO (SEE PAGE 517), CUBED
-   FLESH OF 1 AVOCADO, CUBED
- 10   SNOW PEAS, BLANCHED AND CUT ON A BIAS

GARI

YIELD: 14 SERVINGS / **ACTIVE TIME:** 30 MINUTES / **TOTAL TIME:** 1 DAY 30 MINUTES

Gari, young ginger pickled in sweet vinegar, is a simple yet essential accompaniment to sushi. Its role goes beyond mere garnish; it serves to cleanse the palate between bites, removing any lingering taste of fish. To achieve the perfect balance of tender texture and mild flavor in your gari, it is crucial to use young ginger, which can be identified by its white-and-pink color, rather than mature ginger.

1. Using a spoon, carefully scrape off the thin skin from the ginger. Cut off any pink parts from the ginger and set them aside. Cut the remaining ginger into 2-inch-long pieces, slice these thin, and place them in a bowl. Cover the ginger with water and let it soak.

2. Place the water, rice vinegar, brown sugar, soy sauce, and kombu in a small saucepan and warm over medium heat until the mixture is just about to come to a boil.

3. Turn off the heat and let the brine cool to room temperature.

4. Bring water to a boil in a medium pot. Drain the ginger pieces you are soaking and add them to the pot along with the pink parts of the ginger. Cook for 1 minute, drain, and sprinkle the salt over the ginger. Let it cool.

5. When the ginger is cool enough to handle, squeeze it to remove any excess moisture.

6. Remove the kombu from the cooled brine and discard the kombu. Place the ginger and brine in a large container, making sure the ginger is fully submerged. Cover the container with a tight-fitting lid and place it in the refrigerator. Let the ginger pickle in the refrigerator for at least 24 hours before using.

INGREDIENTS:

¾	LB. YOUNG GINGER
1	CUP WATER
½	CUP RICE VINEGAR
⅓	CUP LIGHT BROWN SUGAR
1	TEASPOON LIGHT SOY SAUCE
1	PIECE OF DRIED KOMBU
1	TEASPOON KOSHER SALT

WASABI

YIELD: 8 SERVINGS / **ACTIVE TIME:** 5 MINUTES / **TOTAL TIME:** 5 MINUTES

Wasabi is a plant deeply rooted in Japanese history and cuisine, revered for its medicinal properties since ancient times. This precious herb is notoriously challenging to cultivate, requiring a delicate balance of environmental factors to thrive. True wasabi demands cool and constant water temperature, a steady supply of water, well-draining soil, and gentle sunlight. As a result, genuine wasabi paste, crafted by grating the fresh wasabi root, is a rare and coveted condiment. The taste of authentic wasabi paste is a revelation compared to the store-bought varieties commonly found today, offering a nuanced, rather than overwhelming, flavor profile.

1. Thoroughly rinse the wasabi root under cold water and remove any dirt or debris. Using your hands, gently remove the top stems from the wasabi root.

2. Inspect the wasabi root for any black or discolored parts. If present, use a scrub brush to gently remove them, or carefully scrape them off with a knife. Unlike many other vegetables, wasabi root's skin should not be completely peeled off, as the area around the peel contains the compounds responsible for wasabi's distinctive aroma and flavor.

3. Use a microplane or an oroshigane (a traditional sharkskin grater) to grate the wasabi root, working slowly and gently moving the wasabi root in a circular motion. You want to keep from applying too much force, as this will result in a coarse texture and diminish the wasabi's flavor.

4. For an extra-smooth texture, transfer the grated wasabi to a cutting board and use a sharp knife to chop it further, working the knife in a rocking motion. Use as desired.

INGREDIENTS:

1   FRESH WASABI ROOT

SASHIMI PLATTER

YIELD: 4 SERVINGS / **ACTIVE TIME:** 15 MINUTES / **TOTAL TIME:** 15 MINUTES

A sashimi platter, known as otsukuri in Japanese, is a stunning display of the finest cuts of raw fish and seafood. This dish celebrates the freshness and quality of each ingredient, allowing the natural flavors to shine through. When creating a sashimi platter, it is essential to use only sashimi-grade fish, ensuring the highest standards of taste and texture. In this particular arrangement, I have chosen to showcase the delicate flavors of lean tuna, chutoro (fatty) tuna, salmon, yellowtail, and squid.

1. Place the soy sauce and dashi in a bowl and stir to combine. Set the dipping sauce aside.

2. If you are starting with pieces of fish, use one of the following methods to prepare the sashimi:

3. Hirazukuri: This straight-cut method is suitable for cutting thicker and softer fish, such as tuna, bonito, yellowtail, and salmon. To use the hirazukuri method, place ⅔-inch blocks of fish on a cutting board so that the fibers are oriented diagonally from bottom left to top right. If the thickness of the fish is not uniform, position it so that the thinner side is closer to you and the thicker side is furthest away.

4. Position the blade of the knife at a 90-degree angle to the fish, about ⅜ inch away from the edge of your dominant hand. Curl the fingers of your off hand to form it into a claw and gently hold the fish in place. Make a single cut starting from the base of the blade, pulling the knife down and toward you until it reaches the chopping board. Use the knife to push the piece of sashimi to the side and repeat.

5. Sogi-giri: This method results in a slanted cut, and is best for cutting whitefish with firm flesh, such as sea bream and flatfish. To use the sogi-giri method, place the fish on the cutting board at a 30- to 45-degree angle. If you are right-handed, the right side should be tilted toward the top right corner of the cutting board.

6. Cut off the top corner opposite of your dominant hand. Discard the piece resulting from this initial cut. Position the base of the blade against the fish at an angle and gently place your fingers on top of the area you want to cut. Carefully pull the knife down toward you, but don't cut all the way through. As the knife is about to reach the cutting board, turn the knife so that it is at a 90-degree angle (as shown in photo) and complete the cut. Use your other hand to push the piece of sashimi to the side and repeat. To con-

INGREDIENTS:

- ¼ CUP SOY SAUCE
- ¼ CUP AWASE DASHI STOCK, (SEE PAGE 38), CHILLED
- ⅔ LB. SASHIMI-GRADE SEAFOOD
- 1 TABLESPOON WASABI (SEE PAGE 500)

trol, the width and thickness of the sashimi produced via the sogi-giri method, simply change the angle of the blade.

7. Kaku-zukuri (dice cut): This straightforward method produces diced seafood, and is often used to process tuna, bonito, and other fish. Place blocks of fish on a cutting board and cut them into ⅔-inch cubes.

8. Arrange the sashimi on a serving platter and serve alongside the dipping sauce and Wasabi.

Sashimi Platter, see page 502

SEA BREAM KOMBU-JIME

YIELD: 4 SERVINGS / **ACTIVE TIME:** 10 MINUTES / **TOTAL TIME:** 25 HOURS

Kombu-jime is a traditional Japanese technique that involves layering kombu with fish or other ingredients to draw out excess moisture, enhancing the natural flavors of both the kombu and the sashimi. This method maximizes the umami element and creates a uniquely delicious texture. Here, we use sea bream, as it is one of the best choices for this approach.

1. Season the sea bream with the salt. Moisten the kombu with the sake. Let the sea bream and kombu sit for 1 hour.

2. Pat the sea bream and kombu dry with paper towels. Sandwich the sea bream between the kombu and cover the mixture tightly with plastic wrap. Place it in the refrigerator and let the sea bream cure for 1 day.

3. Place the soy sauce and dashi in a bowl and stir to combine. Set the dipping sauce aside.

4. Carefully unwrap the sea bream and remove the kombu. Discard the kombu. Cut the sea bream into thin slices and serve it alongside the dipping sauce and Wasabi.

INGREDIENTS:

1   (7 OZ.) PIECE OF SASHIMI-GRADE SEA BREAM

½   TEASPOON KOSHER SALT

2   SHEETS OF DRIED KOMBU (EACH ABOUT 4 X 6 INCHES)

1   TABLESPOON SAKE

3   TABLESPOONS SOY SAUCE

3   TABLESPOONS AWASE DASHI STOCK (SEE PAGE 38)

1   TEASPOON WASABI (SEE PAGE 500)

MARINATED TUNA SASHIMI

YIELD: 4 SERVINGS / **ACTIVE TIME:** 5 MINUTES / **TOTAL TIME:** 45 MINUTES

This marinated tuna can be used in a variety of sushi dishes. However, do not limit yourself to tuna here, as other sashimi-grade seafood can also be marinated with this sauce.

1. Place the mirin and sake in a small saucepan and bring to a boil over medium-high heat. Boil for 1 minute, turn off the heat, add the soy sauce, and swirl the pan to incorporate it.

2. Transfer the marinade to a wide container and let it cool for 10 minutes.

3. Add kombu and let the mixture steep until it is cool to the touch.

4. Dip the tuna into the marinade, ensuring that each piece gets coated on both sides. Arrange the tuna in a single layer in the container, place plastic wrap directly on the surface of the tuna, and let it marinate in the refrigerator for 30 minutes before using.

INGREDIENTS:

3	TABLESPOONS MIRIN
3	TABLESPOONS SAKE
3	TABLESPOONS SOY SAUCE
1	SMALL PIECE OF DRIED KOMBU
½	LB. SASHIMI-GRADE TUNA, SLICED

Sea Bream Kombu-Jime, see page 506

IKURA

YIELD: 6 SERVINGS / ACTIVE TIME: 30 MINUTES / TOTAL TIME: 25 HOURS AND 30 MINUTES

Ikura refers to the individual roe of salmon or trout, carefully separated from the membrane. This delicacy is particularly associated with Hokkaido, Japan's northernmost prefecture, and is a popular topping for sashimi and sushi. In Japanese cuisine, ikura is typically marinated in a soy sauce–based mixture, enhancing its natural flavor and adding a savory depth.

1. Open the sujiko by hand and gently massage it to loosen the eggs from the membrane. Remove as many eggs as possible from the membrane and place them in a heatproof bowl. Don't worry if some won't come loose at this point. Place the water and 1 teaspoon of salt in a pot and warm it to 160°F. The water is ready when you see small bubbles forming.

2. Place the sujiko in a heatproof bowl and pour the salted water over it. Use chopsticks to gently stir the sujiko to loosen any stubborn eggs. Remove the membrane as you go, continuing until most of the membrane is gone and the roe has separated into individual eggs. For any especially stubborn grains of roe, gently pinch them between your thumb and forefinger to push them out.

3. Once all of the membrane has been removed, pour out the salted water, add cold water, and gently stir the roe by hand to remove any remaining debris or thin skin. Pour out the water and repeat this rinsing process until the eggs are completely clean.

4. Transfer the cleaned eggs to a colander. Place the colander over a bowl and sprinkle the remaining salt over the eggs, shaking the colander to distribute it evenly. Cover the colander with plastic wrap and refrigerate the roe for 1 hour. Don't worry if the eggs appear white at this point; they will turn a beautiful red after this process is complete.

5. Place the sake and mirin in a small saucepan and bring to a boil over medium heat. Boil for 30 seconds, transfer the mixture to a sealable container, and add the soy sauce, dashi, and kombu. Let the marinade cool completely.

6. Remove the roe from the refrigerator and add it to the container with the cooled marinade, making sure that the roe is completely submerged. Seal the container and let it marinate in the refrigerator for 1 day before using.

INGREDIENTS:

1	SACK OF SUJIKO (SALMON ROE)
4	CUPS WATER
1½	TEASPOONS KOSHER SALT
¼	CUP SAKE
2	TABLESPOONS MIRIN
2	TABLESPOONS LIGHT SOY SAUCE
3	TABLESPOONS AWASE DASHI STOCK (SEE PAGE 38)
	2-INCH SQUARE OF DRIED KOMBU

NEGITORO

YIELD: 4 SERVINGS / **ACTIVE TIME:** 5 MINUTES / **TOTAL TIME:** 35 MINUTES

Negitoro is a beloved sushi filling known for its soft, melt-in-your-mouth texture. The key to creating authentic negitoro is incorporating oil. I used rice bran oil for this recipe, but it can also be made with olive oil or the oil from a canned oily fish.

1. Season the tuna with the salt and place it in a container. Prop up the container on one side to let any excess liquid drain off and let the tuna sit for 30 minutes.

2. Pat the tuna dry with paper towels. Use a spoon to scrape the surface of the tuna, removing and discarding any stringy parts as you go. Once all of the tuna has been scraped, use a knife to mash it further.

3. Transfer the mashed tuna to a mixing bowl. Add the rice bran oil and mayonnaise, stir until well combined, and use as desired.

INGREDIENTS:

½   LB. SASHIMI-GRADE TUNA

1   TEASPOON KOSHER SALT

1   TABLESPOON RICE BRAN OIL

2   TEASPOONS JAPANESE MAYONNAISE (SEE PAGE 46)

BUTTERFLIED SHRIMP

YIELD: 4 SERVINGSS/ **ACTIVE TIME:** 20 MINUTES / **TOTAL TIME:** 30 MINUTES

This is a recipe for boiling large shrimp that can be used for all types of sushi rolls. Black tiger shrimp are recommended here, but any large shrimp will do.

1. Straighten the shrimp while keeping the shells attached. Insert bamboo skewers between the shells and the meat along the backs of the shrimp to keep them straight.

2. Prepare a bowl of cold water. Bring water to a boil in a pot. Stir in the vinegar and salt and then add the skewered shrimp. Cook for 2 minutes and then immediately transfer the shrimp to the bowl of cold water. Let them cool completely.

3. Carefully remove the bamboo skewers, peel the shrimp, and use a knife to cut off the pointy protrusion in the middle of each tail. Also, trim any parts of the shrimp's other end that are not neatly shaped.

4. Gently insert a knife into the stomach of each shrimp and carefully open them by applying pressure, taking care not to cut all the way through.

5. Rinse the shrimp under cold water and use as desired.

INGREDIENTS:

10   BLACK TIGER SHRIMP, HEADS REMOVED

1   TEASPOON RICE VINEGAR

1   TEASPOON KOSHER SALT

Butterflied Shrimp, see page 513

SAKURA DENBU

YIELD: 4 SERVINGS / **ACTIVE TIME:** 15 MINUTES / **TOTAL TIME:** 15 MINUTES

Sakura denbu is a sweet and fluffy Japanese condiment made from boiled white fish. It gets its name from the Japanese word for cherry blossoms due to its beautiful pink color, and is typically used to decorate sushi, rice balls, and bento boxes. Make sure to remove every last pinbone from the fillet.

INGREDIENTS:

- 7 OZ. SKINLESS COD FILLET
- 4 TEASPOONS SUGAR
- PINCH OF KOSHER SALT
- 1 TABLESPOON SAKE
- 1 DROP OF RED FOOD DYE OR BEET JUICE

1. Bring a pot of water to a gentle boil. Slip the cod into the boiling water and cook until it is cooked through, 3 to 5 minutes. Be sure not to let the water boil too rapidly, as the cod is delicate and prone to breaking.

2. While the cod is boiling, place a fine-mesh sieve over a large mixing bowl and fill the bowl with cold water. Use a mesh strainer to transfer the cod to the bowl of cold water. Rub the surface of the fish gently to wash it. Drain and repeat, washing the cod once more.

3. Pat the cod dry with paper towels and then break it into fine flakes by rubbing it between your fingers, sprinkling the resulting flakes into a cold nonstick skillet.

4. Place the sugar, salt, sake, and dye in a small bowl and stir until the sugar has dissolved. Pour the mixture into the pan and stir until the cod is pink.

5. Place the pan over low heat and cook, stirring continually to make sure the cod does not brown, until the liquid has completely evaporated and the flakes are mostly dry. Use as desired.

DASHIMAKI TAMAGO

YIELD: 6 SERVINGS / **ACTIVE TIME:** 15 MINUTES / **TOTAL TIME:** 15 MINUTES

This is a traditional Japanese omelet that stands out from tamagoyaki through the incorporation of dashi stock. In the sushi world, it is a common ingredient in futomaki and nigiri.

1. Crack the eggs into a bowl and lightly beat them with chopsticks, using a back-and-forth motion. Avoid whisking in a circular motion to prevent too many bubbles from forming.

2. Place the dashi, mirin, sugar, salt, and soy sauce in a separate bowl and whisk until the sugar and salt have dissolved.

3. Place a fine-mesh sieve over the bowl containing the dashi mixture. Pour the beaten eggs into the sieve to strain them into the dashi mixture. Gently mix the eggs and dashi mixture to combine, again taking care not to create too many air bubbles.

4. Heat a tamagoyaki (rectangular) pan over medium heat. Add the canola oil and use a paper towel to spread the canola oil evenly and wipe away any excess. Keep the oiled paper towel nearby for later use.

5. Once the pan has heated up, pour a thin, even layer of the egg mixture into the pan, just enough to coat the bottom. The layer should be thin enough to cook quickly but not so thin that it breaks. If you notice any air bubbles, pierce them with a chopstick. If parts of the egg are cooking too quickly or the pan feels too hot, temporarily lift the pan off the heat and readjust as necessary.

6. When the egg is half-cooked, use chopsticks or a spatula to start rolling it from the far edge of the pan toward you. Start the roll by making a small fold at the furthest edge, then continue to roll toward you while holding the pan's handle with your other hand. As you roll up the egg, quickly tilt the pan up as if you were going to flip a pancake, as this motion will help keep the egg from breaking. Continue rolling the egg until it reaches the edge closest to you. Use the oiled paper towel to coat the empty space in the pan. Push the rolled-up tamagoyaki back to the far end of the pan and lightly coat the remaining area with the oiled paper towel.

7. Pour another layer of the egg mixture into the pan, gently lifting the rolled piece and tilting the pan so that some of the mixture goes underneath it. Tilt the pan again to ensure the uncooked egg mixture is flat and even. Cook as instructed in Steps 5 and 6.

8. Repeat the process until all of the egg mixture has been used and the dashimaki tamago is formed.

9. Transfer it to a bamboo sushi mat lined with plastic wrap, press on the edges to form it into a block, and use as desired.

INGREDIENTS:

4	EGGS
3	TABLESPOONS AWASE DASHI STOCK (SEE PAGE 38)
1½	TABLESPOONS MIRIN
1	TEASPOON SUGAR
¼	TEASPOON KOSHER SALT
½	TEASPOON LIGHT SOY SAUCE
1	TEASPOON CANOLA OIL

Sakura Denbu, see page 516

KANPYO & SHIITAKE MUSHROOMS

YIELD: 4 SERVINGS / ACTIVE TIME: 10 MINUTES / TOTAL TIME: 30 MINUTES

Simmered kampyo and shiitake mushrooms are popular ingredients in sushi rolls like futomaki and hosomaki, and are the perfect way to add sweetness and richness to your sushi rolls.

1. Place the kanpyo and salt in a bowl and rub them together. Rinse the kanpyo under cold water, place it in a bowl, and cover it with water. Place the mushrooms in a separate bowl and cover them with water. Place a drop lid, aluminum foil, or parchment paper on the surface to keep the mushrooms submerged. Let them soak until they are rehydrated, about 30 minutes.

2. Drain the mushrooms and reserve ½ cup of the soaking liquid. Place this liquid in a small saucepan with the soy sauce, sugar, and sake and bring to a boil over medium heat. Reduce the heat to low and add the mushrooms. Drain the kanpyo and add it to the pan. Simmer until the liquid has reduced by three-quarters.

3. Stir in the mirin and simmer until almost all of the liquid has evaporated. Turn off the heat and let the mixture cool.

4. Cut the kanpyo into the desired lengths, slice the mushrooms, and use as desired.

INGREDIENTS:

¾	OZ. KANPYO (DRIED GOURD STRIPS)
1	TEASPOON KOSHER SALT
4	DRIED SHIITAKE MUSHROOMS
1½	TABLESPOONS SOY SAUCE
1½	TABLESPOONS SUGAR
1½	TABLESPOONS SAKE
1½	TABLESPOONS MIRIN

KINSHI TAMAGO

YIELD: 2 SERVINGS / **ACTIVE TIME:** 10 MINUTES / **TOTAL TIME:** 10 MINUTES

Kinshi tamago is a simple yet elegant garnish made by slicing a thin egg crepe into delicate strings. This versatile topping is commonly used to adorn dishes like chirashizushi and hiyashi chuka, adding a visual appeal and a subtle flavor.

1. Crack the egg into a bowl, add the salt, and whisk until well combined.

2. Place a fine-mesh sieve over another bowl. Pour the egg through the sieve and use a spoon to gently work it into the bowl.

3. Warm a small nonstick skillet over medium-low heat. Add the canola oil and spread it evenly over the entire pan with a paper towel. Remove any excess canola oil with another paper towel.

4. Pour the strained egg mixture into the pan and swirl to distribute the egg evenly. You want it to be in a thin, even layer. If you're using a very small pan, you will need to cook the egg mixture in batches to ensure the crepe has the proper thinness.

5. Cook until the egg it is about 80 percent cooked; the surface should still be slightly soft and not fully set. This should take about 2 to 3 minutes, depending on the heat of your stove. Take care not to let the bottom of the crepe brown.

6. Remove the pan from heat, carefully peel the egg crepe out of the pan, and transfer it to a cutting board. Gently roll the egg crepe into a tight cylinder. Using a sharp knife, slice the crepe into rounds that are about 1/16 inch thick and use as desired.

INGREDIENTS:

1   EGG

      PINCH OF KOSHER SALT

1   TEASPOON CANOLA OIL

Kanpyo & Shiitake Mushrooms,
see page 520

YOSHOKU

─────────────────────────────────

*Y*oshoku refers to Western-inspired dishes that have been integrated into Japanese cuisine. Originating in the late nineteenth century, these dishes have evolved significantly from their Western roots, often bearing little resemblance to their original forms. Yoshoku represents a fascinating culinary fusion, showcasing how Japanese interpreted and reimagined Western flavors and techniques to suit local tastes.

KOROKKE

YIELD: 4 SERVINGS / **ACTIVE TIME:** 30 MINUTES / **TOTAL TIME:** 1 HOUR AND 20 MINUTES

This is a popular Japanese style croquette made with creamy potatoes, ground meat, and onions, all of which gets coated in a crispy layer of panko.

1. Chop the potatoes, making sure the pieces are similarly sized, place them in a pot of cold water, and add the salt. Bring to a rolling boil, reduce the heat so that the potatoes gently boil, and cook until they are fork-tender, 15 to 20 minutes.

2. While the potatoes are boiling, place the butter in a large skillet and melt it over medium heat. Add the onion and cook, stirring occasionally, until it is translucent, about 3 minutes. Add the beef, season with salt, the pepper, and nutmeg and cook until it is cooked through, about 6 minutes, breaking up the beef with a wooden spoon. Stir in the soy sauce, sugar, and mirin and cook until the beef has absorbed all of the liquid. Remove the pan from heat and let the mixture cool.

3. Drain the potatoes, transfer them to a heatproof bowl, and add the milk. Mash until the potatoes are smooth and stir in the onion and beef. Transfer the mixture to a wide container and let it cool.

4. Cover the container and chill the mixture in the refrigerator for 30 minutes.

5. Add rice bran oil to a Dutch oven until it is about 2 inches deep and warm it to 355°F. Place the water, egg, and flour in a bowl and stir until the mixture comes together as a smooth batter. Place flour in a shallow bowl and the panko in another shallow bowl.

6. Remove the potato mixture from the fridge and divide it into 4 to 6 pieces. Roll these into balls, flatten them, and shape them into ovals. Roll them in the flour until coated, dip them into the batter, and then dredge them in the panko until they are coated by a generous layer of bread crumbs.

7. Working in batches if necessary to avoid overcrowding the pot, gently slip the korokke into the hot oil and fry until they are crispy and golden brown, 3 to 5 minutes. Transfer the fried korokke to a wire rack to drain before serving them with Worcestershire sauce.

INGREDIENTS:

⅔ LB. STARCHY POTATOES, WASHED AND PEELED

1½ TEASPOONS KOSHER SALT, PLUS MORE TO TASTE

1 TABLESPOON UNSALTED BUTTER

1 SMALL ONION, FINELY DICED

3 OZ. GROUND BEEF

PINCH OF BLACK PEPPER

PINCH OF FRESHLY GRATED NUTMEG

1½ TABLESPOONS SOY SAUCE

1 TEASPOON SUGAR

2 TEASPOONS MIRIN

1 TABLESPOON WHOLE MILK

RICE BRAN OIL, AS NEEDED

3½ TABLESPOONS COLD WATER

1 EGG

5 TABLESPOONS ALL-PURPOSE FLOUR, PLUS MORE AS NEEDED

1¼ CUPS NAMA PANKO (SEE PAGE 66)

WORCESTERSHIRE SAUCE, FOR SERVING

JAPANESE-STYLE POTATO SALAD

YIELD: 6 SERVINGS / **ACTIVE TIME:** 10 MINUTES / **TOTAL TIME:** 30 MINUTES

Potato salad is a global favorite, and Japan is not an exception to that claim. A common sight in home kitchens, bento boxes, and alongside various dishes, this potato salad recipe offers a comforting, creamy taste that embodies the essence of simplicity.

1. Peel the potatoes and cut them in half. Place them in a large pot, cover with cold water, and bring to a boil. Cook until the potatoes are fork-tender, 15 to 20 minutes.

2. While the potatoes are boiling, place the onion and cucumber in a bowl, season with the salt, and rub it into the vegetables. Set the vegetables aside, allowing them to release their liquid.

3. Drain the potatoes and mash until the consistency is to your liking.

4. Return to the bowl of salted onion and cucumber. By now, they should have released a fair amount of water. Squeeze the vegetables firmly to remove any excess moisture, drain, and add them to the mashed potatoes.

5. Add the remaining ingredients and work the mixture until well combined.

6. Let the potato salad cool slightly until it is cool enough to touch. Serve slightly warm or chilled.

INGREDIENTS:

3	MEDIUM POTATOES
¼	ONION, SLICED THIN
⅓	CUP THINLY SLICED AND HALVED CUCUMBER
¼	TEASPOON KOSHER SALT
1	TEASPOONS HONEY
3	TABLESPOONS JAPANESE MAYONNAISE (SEE PAGE 46)
½	CUP DICED HAM (SMALL DICE)
1	TEASPOON SMOOTH DIJION MUSTARD
1	TABLESPOON HEAVY CREAM
½	TEASPOON LIGHT SOY SAUCE
	PINCH OF BLACK PEPPER

HAMBAGU

Hambagu is a beloved yoshoku dish, tracing its roots back to Hamburg, Germany. This meal found its way into the heart of Japanese home cooking during the 1950s and '60s. Since then, it has remained a cherished favorite among both children and adults, gracing the tables of homes and restaurants alike. Hambagu is traditionally served with a side of fluffy white rice, creamy potato salad, and tender boiled vegetables, creating a well-rounded, satisfying meal.

1. Place the butter in a large skillet and melt it over medium heat. Add the onion and cook, stirring occasionally, until it is translucent, about 3 minutes. Remove the pan from heat and let the onion cool completely.

2. Place the milk and panko in a bowl and let the mixture soak. Place the beef, salt, pepper, nutmeg, and cooled onion in a separate bowl and work the mixture by hand until just combined. Add the panko mixture and work the mixture until it is just incorporated.

3. Divide the meat into four portions and shape them into patties, tossing them between your hands to remove any air pockets. Press a dent into one side of the patties, place them on a plate, and chill them in the refrigerator for 20 to 30 minutes.

4. Place the canola oil in a large skillet and warm it over medium-high heat. Place the patties in the pan, dent side up, and cook until they are browned, about 3 minutes. Flip them over and cook for another 3 minutes. For a well-done center, reduce the heat, cover the pan with a lid, and cook until the hambagu are cooked to your liking. Remove the hambagu from the pan and wrap them in aluminum foil.

5. Add the Worcestershire sauce, ketchup, mustard, and honey to the pan, stir to combine, and simmer on low heat until the sauce starts to thicken, 2 to 3 minutes.

6. Top the hambagu with a generous amount of the sauce and serve.

INGREDIENTS:

2	TABLESPOONS UNSALTED BUTTER
1	ONION, FINELY DICED
6	TABLESPOONS WHOLE MILK
½	CUP NAMA PANKO (SEE PAGE 66)
1¼	LBS. GROUND BEEF
½	TEASPOON KOSHER SALT
¼	TEASPOON BLACK PEPPER
⅛	TEASPOON FRESHLY GRATED NUTMEG
1	TABLESPOON CANOLA OIL
3	TABLESPOONS WORCESTERSHIRE SAUCE
6	TABLESPOONS KETCHUP
1½	TEASPOONS SMOOTH DIJON MUSTARD
1	TABLESPOON HONEY

JAPANESE-STYLE MACARONI SALAD

YIELD: 6 SERVINGS / **ACTIVE TIME:** 10 MINUTES / **TOTAL TIME:** 20 MINUTES

Macaroni salad, a beloved dish enjoyed in many countries around the world, has found a special place in Japanese cuisine as well. This version has become a staple in homes across Japan, where it is seen as a simple yet satisfying addition to meals.

1. Fill a large pot with water and bring to a boil over high heat. While you are waiting for the water to come to a boil, wash the eggs.

2. Add the macaroni, eggs, and salt to the pot and cook until the macaroni is al dente.

3. While the macaroni and eggs are boiling, place the cucumber and carrot in a bowl, season with salt, and gently toss to coat. Set the vegetables aside, allowing them to release their liquid.

4. Fill a bowl with cold water. Drain the macaroni and eggs and rinse them under cold water. Transfer the eggs to the bowl of cold water.

5. Squeeze the cucumber and carrot to remove any excess water. Peel the eggs and place them in a large bowl. Using a spatula or fork, mash the eggs. Add the mayonnaise, ponzu, dashi granules, garlic paste, mustard, Parmesan, macaroni, cucumber, and carrot and gently work the mixture until well combined.

6. Garnish the macaroni salad with black pepper and serve.

INGREDIENTS:

1	CUP DRIED MACARONI
2	EGGS
¼	TEASPOON KOSHER SALT, PLUS MORE TO TASTE
½	JAPANESE OR PERSIAN CUCUMBER, SLICED THIN
¼	CARROT, PEELED AND JULIENNED
3	TABLESPOONS JAPANESE MAYONNAISE (SEE PAGE 46)
1½	TEASPOONS PONZU SAUCE (SEE PAGE 45)
½	TEASPOON DASHI GRANULES
½	TEASPOON GARLIC PASTE
½	TEASPOON JAPANESE MUSTARD
1½	TEASPOONS GRATED PARMESAN CHEESE
	BLACK PEPPER, FOR GARNISH

Japanese-Style Macaroni Salad, see page 533

TAMAGO SANDO

YIELD: 4 SERVINGS / **ACTIVE TIME:** 15 MINUTES / **TOTAL TIME:** 25 MINUTES

Tamago sando is Japan's take on the humble egg salad sandwich. In my recipe, a hint of honey and touch of fiery mustard create a slightly sweet and punchy filling that takes things to the next level.

1. Bring a pot of water to a rolling boil. Prepare an ice bath. Add the eggs to the boiling water and cook for 10 minutes.

2. Remove the eggs from the boiling water and plunge them into the ice bath. Peel the eggs in the water, pat them dry, and transfer them to a large mixing bowl.

3. Add the salt and pepper and mash the eggs with a wooden spoon. Add the mayonnaise and honey and stir until well combined.

4. Spread the butter on half of the slices of bread. Spread the mustard on the other slices of the bread. Spread the egg mixture over the buttered pieces of bread and assemble the sandwiches with the other slices of bread. Chill the sandwiches in the refrigerator for 20 to 30 minutes.

5. Cut the sandwiches into halves or thirds and serve.

INGREDIENTS:

8	EGGS
½	TEASPOON KOSHER SALT
¼	TEASPOON GROUND BLACK PEPPER
½	CUP JAPANESE MAYONNAISE (SEE PAGE 46)
1½	TEASPOONS HONEY
1	TABLESPOON UNSALTED BUTTER, SOFTENED
8	SLICES OF WHITE BREAD, CRUSTS REMOVED
2	TEASPOONS JAPANESE MUSTARD

JAPANESE-STYLE CABBAGE ROLLS

YIELD: 4 SERVINGS / **ACTIVE TIME:** 15 MINUTES / **TOTAL TIME:** 25 MINUTES

Cabbage rolls are a beloved preparation around the world, including in Japan. These can be served as a side dish or used in hot pots.

1. Fill a large pot with water and bring to a boil. Add the cabbage and cook for 1 minute. Using tongs, remove the cabbage leaves from the pot and place them in a colander. Let the cabbage leaves cool.

2. While you are waiting for the cabbage leaves to cool, place the dashi, sake, soy sauce, mirin, brown sugar, salt, ginger, and garlic in a medium saucepan and cook over medium heat. When the broth is about to come to a boil, turn off the heat and let the broth sit, allowing the flavors to continue melding.

3. When the cabbage leaves are cool enough to handle, lay them out on a flat surface. Place two slices of pork belly on each cabbage leaf and season with pepper. Fold the two long sides of the cabbage leaves over the pork, then tightly roll the leaves up from the bottom to top to create a neat package. Arrange the cabbage rolls in a single layer, seam side down, in a large pot.

4. Pour the broth over the cabbage rolls, ensuring they are evenly covered. Place a drop lid, aluminum foil, or parchment paper on the surface and bring to a boil over medium heat. Reduce the heat to low and let the cabbage rolls simmer for 15 minutes.

5. Use tongs to carefully transfer the cooked cabbage rolls to a serving plate, reserving the remaining broth in the pot.

6. In a small bowl, combine the potato starch and water. Slowly pour the slurry into the broth, stirring continually to prevent lumps from forming. Place the pot over medium heat and cook, stirring gently, until the sauce thickens and becomes glossy.

7. Pour the thickened sauce over the cabbage rolls, garnish with parsley, and serve.

INGREDIENTS:

12	GREEN CABBAGE LEAVES
2	CUPS AWASE DASHI STOCK (SEE PAGE 38)
2	TABLESPOONS SAKE
1½	TABLESPOONS LIGHT SOY SAUCE
1	TABLESPOON MIRIN
1½	TEASPOONS LIGHT BROWN SUGAR
1	TEASPOON KOSHER SALT
1	TEASPOON GRATED FRESH GINGER
1	TEASPOON GRATED GARLIC
24	THIN SLICES OF PORK BELLY
	BLACK PEPPER, TO TASTE
1	TABLESPOON POTATO STARCH
1	TABLESPOON WATER
	DRIED PARSLEY, FOR GARNISH

OMURICE

YIELD: 6 SERVINGS / **ACTIVE TIME:** 40 MINUTES / **TOTAL TIME:** 40 MINUTES

Here's is a popular Yoshoku dish made with chicken fried rice encased in a fluffy omelet.

1. Place 1 tablespoon of olive oil and the butter in a large skillet and warm the mixture over medium heat. Once the butter has melted, add the onion and cook, stirring occasionally, until it has softened. Add the chicken and mushrooms and cook until the chicken is browned all over. Add the wine and cook, stirring occasionally, until the chicken is cooked through.

2. Add the rice and season with the salt and pepper. Add the ketchup and Worcestershire sauce and stir until they are evenly distributed through the rice. Add the peas and parsley and stir until evenly distributed. Remove the pan from heat and cover it to keep the rice mixture warm. I recommend dividing it into six equal portions for efficiency when making the omelet.

3. For best results, each omelet should be made separately. Warm an 8-inch skillet over medium heat and lightly coat it with some of the canola oil, wiping away any excess with a paper towel.

4. Crack the eggs into a large bowl and add the milk and remaining olive oil. Whisk until well combined and then pour the mixture into a clean bowl through a fine-mesh sieve to make it smooth.

5. Pour about ½ cup of the egg mixture into the heated pan and tilt it to spread the mixture evenly, including up the sides a little. Whisk with chopsticks until the edges start to set, then stop whisking. Once the omelet is half-cooked, place one portion of the rice in the center and form it into the shape of an American football. Carefully lift the edges of the omelet from the pan using a silicone spatula and then fold two opposite sides of the omelet over the rice. It's okay if the sides don't overlap. Use the spatula to make sure that the bottom of the omelet isn't stuck to the pan. Carefully flip it onto a plate, cover the omelet with plastic wrap or a paper towel, and gently press on it to shape it. Repeat this process for each omelet.

6. When all of the omelets have been cooked, garnish with additional ketchup and dried parsley and serve.

INGREDIENTS:

1	TABLESPOON PLUS 2 TEASPOONS EXTRA-VIRGIN OLIVE OIL
2	TEASPOONS UNSALTED BUTTER
1	ONION, FINELY DICED
⅔	LB. BONELESS, SKINLESS CHICKEN BREASTS, DICED
12	CHESTNUT MUSHROOMS, SLICED THIN
2	TABLESPOONS WHITE WINE
2½	CUPS PERFECT JAPANESE RICE (SEE PAGE 80), COOLED AND SLIGHTLY DRIED OUT
2	PINCHES OF KOSHER SALT
2	PINCHES OF BLACK PEPPER
⅓	CUP KETCHUP, PLUS MORE FOR GARNISH
2	TEASPOONS WORCESTERSHIRE SAUCE
2	TABLESPOONS GREEN PEAS
2	PINCHES OF DRIED PARSLEY, PLUS MORE FOR GARNISH
1	TABLESPOON CANOLA OIL
12	EGGS
¼	CUP MILK

JAPANESE-STYLE CURRY RICE

YIELD: 4 SERVINGS / **ACTIVE TIME:** 30 MINUTES / **TOTAL TIME:** 1 HOUR AND 15 MINUTES

From India to England, and then from England to Japan, curry evolved in its own unique way. Often called European curry in Japan to distinguish it from Indian varieties, this dish blends Indian spices, Western seasonings, and Japanese flavors. While many Japanese home cooks rely on store-bought cubes to prepare the roux, this from-scratch recipe offers a more flavorful alternative. Some ingredients may seem bizarre, but they're crucial for achieving the best flavor.

1. Place the onion and 1 tablespoon of olive oil in a large skillet, season with salt, and stir to combine. Cook over medium-low heat, stirring occasionally, for 10 minutes. Reduce the heat to low and cook until the onion is dark and caramelized, 15 to 20 minutes, stirring occasionally. If the onion starts to stick to the pan, add small amounts of water as needed. Remove the pan from heat and set the caramelized onion aside.

2. Place the remaining olive oil in a pot and warm it over medium heat. Add the beef, season with salt and pepper, and cook over medium heat until it is browned all over, turning it as necessary. Transfer the beef to a plate and set it aside.

3. Reduce the heat to medium-low, add the butter, ginger, and garlic to the pan and cook, stirring occasionally, until it is fragrant. Add the caramelized onion, curry powder, and flour and stir until the mixture becomes a golden brown paste.

4. Add a small amount of the stock and whisk to loosen the mixture. Add the rest of the stock along with the potatoes, carrot, bay leaf, and blueberry jam and stir to dissolve any clumps. Bring to a simmer and cook for 15 minutes, stirring occasionally.

5. Add all of the remaining ingredients, except for the rice and fukujinzuke, and stir until well incorporated. Simmer the curry for another 10 minutes.

6. Divide the rice among the serving plates and ladle the curry over it. Garnish with fukujinzuke and serve.

INGREDIENTS:

1	LARGE ONION, SLICED THIN
1½	TABLESPOONS EXTRA-VIRGIN OLIVE OIL
	SALT AND PEPPER, TO TASTE
14	OZ. BEEF SHANK OR CHUCK, CHOPPED
2	TABLESPOONS UNSALTED BUTTER
	1-INCH PIECE OF FRESH GINGER, PEELED AND MINCED
3	GARLIC CLOVES, MINCED
2½	TABLESPOONS JAPANESE CURRY POWDER (SEE PAGE 65)
3	TABLESPOONS CAKE FLOUR
3¼	CUPS BEEF STOCK
3	POTATOES, CHOPPED
1	CARROT, PEELED AND CHOPPED
1	BAY LEAF
1	TABLESPOON BLUEBERRY JAM
2	TABLESPOONS RED WINE
1	TABLESPOON SOY SAUCE
1	TABLESPOON MIRIN
1½	TEASPOONS HONEY
1½	TEASPOONS APPLE JAM OR APPLE BUTTER
1½	TEASPOONS KETCHUP
1½	TEASPOONS WORCESTERSHIRE SAUCE
½	TEASPOON GARAM MASALA
½	TEASPOON INSTANT COFFEE POWDER
¼	TEASPOON FRESHLY GRATED NUTMEG
4	CUPS PERFECT JAPANESE RICE (SEE PAGE 80)
	FUKUJINZUKE (PICKLED RADISH), FOR GARNISH

TACO RICE

YIELD: 4 SERVINGS / **ACTIVE TIME:** 10 MINUTES / **TOTAL TIME:** 15 MINUTES

Here's is a standout dish in Okinawan cuisine, born from a creative blend of Tex-Mex and Japanese cuisine. It emerged in the 1980s, crafted by a local restaurant owner catering to US soldiers stationed in Okinawa. This recipe transforms the classic comfort food into a chic, café-style dish.

1. Place the olive oil in a large skillet and warm it over medium heat. Add the onion and garlic and cook, stirring occasionally, until the onion has softened, about 5 minutes. Add the beef and cook until it is browned all over and cooked through, about 8 minutes, breaking it up with a wooden spoon.

2. Stir in the soy sauce, mirin, Worcestershire sauce, ketchup, curry powder, and coffee and cook until the sauce has reduced by half.

3. Divide the rice among the serving plates or bowls. Top the rice with the lettuce and then the beef mixture. Top the beef with a fried egg, sprinkle the cheese and tortilla chips over each portion, and then top with the avocado and tomato. Drizzle hot sauce over the top and serve.

INGREDIENTS:

1½ TEASPOONS EXTRA-VIRGIN OLIVE OIL

1 ONION, FINELY DICED

2 GARLIC CLOVES, FINELY DICED

10 OZ. GROUND BEEF

1 TEASPOON SOY SAUCE

1 TABLESPOON MIRIN

3 TABLESPOONS WORCESTERSHIRE SAUCE

3 TABLESPOONS KETCHUP

½ TABLESPOON JAPANESE CURRY POWDER (SEE PAGE 65)

½ TEASPOON INSTANT COFFEE POWDER

4 CUPS PERFECT JAPANESE RICE (SEE PAGE 80)

8 LEAVES OF BUTTER LETTUCE, CUT INTO STRIPS

4 FRIED EGGS

¼ CUP GRATED CHEDDAR OR GOUDA CHEESE

1 CUP CRUSHED TORTILLA CHIPS

FLESH OF 1 AVOCADO, SLICED

1 TOMATO, DICED

HOT SAUCE, TO TASTE

HAYASHI RICE

YIELD: 4 SERVINGS / ACTIVE TIME: 20 MINUTES / TOTAL TIME: 25 MINUTES

Hayashi rice combines tender beef, onions, bell peppers, and mushrooms in a rich demi-glace-like sauce. Eschewing the premade roux that is popular, this recipe focuses on layering flavors for a more authentic and comforting experience.

1. Sprinkle the salt, pepper, and two-thirds of the flour over the beef, making sure it is evenly coated. Place 2 tablespoons of butter in a large skillet and melt it over medium heat. Add half of the garlic and cook until it is fragrant, about 1 minute. Add the beef and cook until it is browned all over, turning as necessary.

2. Add the onion and cook, stirring occasionally, until it has softened, about 5 minutes. Add the bell peppers and mushrooms, reduce the heat to low, and cook, gently stirring occasionally.

3. Sprinkle the remaining flour over the mixture and stir to incorporate. Add the ketchup, red wine, and Worcestershire sauce, stirring to incorporate each one before adding the next. Add the stock, raise the heat to medium-high, and cook, stirring occasionally, until the sauce thickens. Reduce the heat to the lowest possible setting.

4. Place the remaining butter in a separate pan and melt it over medium heat. Add the remaining garlic and cook until it is fragrant, about 1 minute. Add the rice and cook until it is lightly browned, 3 to 5 minutes, stirring occasionally. Stir in the parsley and remove the pan from heat.

5. To serve, portion the rice on one side of the serving plates and the hayashi beef on the other and garnish with additional parsley.

INGREDIENTS:

2	PINCHES OF KOSHER SALT
2	PINCHES OF BLACK PEPPER
2	TABLESPOONS ALL-PURPOSE FLOUR
1	LB. BEEF ROUND OR BONELESS BEEF SHORT RIBS, SLICED THIN
2	TABLESPOONS PLUS 2 TEASPOONS UNSALTED BUTTER
4	GARLIC CLOVES, MINCED
1	ONION, SLICED
2	BELL PEPPERS, STEMMED, SEEDED, AND DICED
6	BROWN BUTTON MUSHROOMS, SLICED
¼	CUP KETCHUP
½	CUP RED WINE
¼	CUP WORCESTERSHIRE SAUCE
2½	CUPS BEEF STOCK
4	CUPS PERFECT JAPANESE RICE (SEE PAGE 80)
2	TEASPOONS FINELY CHOPPED FRESH PARSLEY, PLUS MORE FOR GARNISH

Hayashi Rice, see page 543

MEAT DORIA

YIELD: 6 SERVINGS / **ACTIVE TIME:** 40 MINUTES / **TOTAL TIME:** 1 HOUR

Today's Japan offers myriad variations of this rice gratin, including seafood and curry dorias, but this particular recipe supplies layers of garlic-infused rice, creamy béchamel, and a rich meat sauce. This Western-influenced dish is a fantastic choice for family gatherings, certain to be a hit at any party or family meal.

1. Preheat the oven to 430°F. To prepare the rice, place the butter in a large skillet and melt it over medium heat. Add the garlic and cook until it is fragrant, about 1 minute. Add the rice, salt, pepper, and soy sauce and stir-fry for 2 to 3 minutes. Add the parsley and stir until it is evenly distributed. Spread the rice in a large baking dish or divide it among ramekins, cover it, and set it aside.

2. To begin preparations for the meat sauce, place the olive oil in a large skillet and warm it over medium heat. Add the onion and garlic and cook for 2 minutes, stirring frequently. Add the beef and cook until it is browned all over, about 5 minutes, breaking it up with wooden spoon. Add the salt, pepper, and flour and stir until the flour is completely incorporated. Stir in the tomatoes and their juices and bring to a boil.

3. Reduce the heat to low, stir in the soy sauce, sugar, and curry powder and cover the pan. Simmer on low for 10 minutes.

4. To prepare the béchamel, place the butter in a medium saucepan and melt it over low heat. Add the flour and stir continually until the mixture is smooth. Add one-third of the milk in a slow stream and whisk the mixture vigorously to prevent lumps from forming. As the sauce thickens, slowly add the remaining milk in two increments, continuing to whisk continually. If you notice the sauce thickening too quickly, briefly remove the pan from heat. Keep whisking until the sauce is smooth and thickens to a point where it can coat the back of a wooden spoon. Remove the pan from heat and stir in the salt and nutmeg.

5. Pour the béchamel over the rice and use the back of a spoon to spread it evenly. Carefully top the béchamel with the meat sauce and spread it into an even layer. Sprinkle the cheeses over the top, place the baking dish or ramekins on the middle rack in the oven, and bake for 10 minutes.

6. Move the baking dish or ramekins to the upper rack and bake for another 10 minutes.

7. Remove the doria from the oven and serve.

INGREDIENTS:

FOR THE RICE

1	TABLESPOON UNSALTED BUTTER
3	GARLIC CLOVES, MINCED
3½	CUPS PERFECT JAPANESE RICE (SEE PAGE 80)
¼	TEASPOON KOSHER SALT
⅛	TEASPOON BLACK PEPPER
1	TEASPOON LIGHT SOY SAUCE
1	TEASPOON DRIED PARSLEY

FOR THE MEAT SAUCE

1½	TEASPOONS EXTRA-VIRGIN OLIVE OIL
1	ONION, FINELY DICED
2	GARLIC CLOVES, MINCED
½	LB. GROUND BEEF
⅛	TEASPOON SALT
⅛	TEASPOON BLACK PEPPER
1½	TEASPOONS ALL-PURPOSE FLOUR
1	(14 OZ.) CAN OF DICED TOMATOES, WITH THEIR JUICE
2	TEASPOONS SOY SAUCE
1	TABLESPOON SUGAR
¼	TEASPOON JAPANESE CURRY POWDER (SEE PAGE 65)

FOR THE BÉCHAMEL

¼	CUP UNSALTED BUTTER
¼	CUP ALL-PURPOSE FLOUR
1¾	CUPS WHOLE MILK
½	TEASPOON KOSHER SALT
⅛	TEASPOON FRESHLY GRATED NUTMEG
1½	CUP GRATED GOUDA CHEESE
⅓	CUP GRATED PECORINO CHEESE

CREAM STEW

YIELD: 6 SERVINGS / ACTIVE TIME: 20 MINUTES / TOTAL TIME: 30 MINUTES

This hearty white stew is a beloved dish in Japan, especially during the colder months. While opinions are divided on whether rice or bread is the best accompaniment, serving it with a toasted baguette is my personal go-to.

1. Season the chicken with the salt and pepper and coat it with half of the flour. Place the olive oil in a Dutch oven and warm it over medium-high heat. Add the chicken, skin side down, and stir-fry until the chicken is browned all over. Remove the chicken from the pan and set it aside.

2. Add the onion, potatoes, carrots, and bell peppers and stir-fry until the onion has softened, about 5 minutes. Return the chicken to the pot and deglaze the pot with the white wine, scraping up any browned bits from the bottom. Sprinkle the remaining flour over the mixture and stir until well combined.

3. Reduce the heat to low and add the milk. Add the chicken bouillon and stir until it has completely dissolved. Add the cheese and butter, stir until they have melted, and then stir in the cream.

4. Let the stew simmer until the carrots and potatoes are tender, about 10 minutes, stirring occasionally.

5. While the stew is simmering, place the broccoli and a small amount of water in a microwave-safe bowl, cover it with plastic wrap, and microwave on high for 3 minutes.

6. Divide the stew and broccoli among the serving bowls, garnish with parsley, and serve with slices of toasted baguette.

INGREDIENTS:

1⅓	LBS. BONELESS, SKIN-ON CHICKEN THIGHS, CHOPPED
¼	TEASPOON KOSHER SALT
¼	TEASPOON BLACK PEPPER
¼	CUP ALL-PURPOSE FLOUR
3	TABLESPOONS EXTRA-VIRGIN OLIVE OIL
1	LARGE ONION, SLICED THIN
2	WAXY POTATOES, PEELED AND DICED
2	CARROTS, PEELED AND DICED
2	RED BELL PEPPERS, STEMMED, SEEDED, AND DICED
¼	CUP WHITE WINE
3½	CUPS WHOLE MILK
4	TEASPOONS CHICKEN BOUILLON
2	TABLESPOONS GRATED PARMESAN OR PECORINO CHEESE
2	TABLESPOONS UNSALTED BUTTER
¼	CUP HEAVY CREAM
1	HEAD OF BROCCOLI, CUT INTO FLORETS
	FRESH PARSLEY, FINELY CHOPPED, FOR GARNISH
	BAGUETTE, SLICED AND TOASTED, FOR SERVING

BUTTER & SOY SAUCE WAFU PASTA

YIELD: 4 SERVINGS / ACTIVE TIME: 10 MINUTES / TOTAL TIME: 15 MINUTES

Wafu pasta refers to a unique fusion of pasta dishes that incorporate distinctly Japanese ingredients and flavors. In this recipe, I highlight a classic and beloved combination: butter, soy sauce, and shiitake mushrooms.

1. Bring a large pot of water to a boil. Add the salt, let the water return to a boil, and add the pasta. Cook the pasta until it is al dente.

2. While the pasta is cooking, place the canola oil in a large skillet and warm it over medium heat. Add the garlic and cook until it is fragrant, about 1 minute. Add the bacon and cook, stirring occasionally, until it starts to get crispy, 4 to 6 minutes. Stir in the spinach and mushrooms, season with salt, the pepper, and dashi granules, and cook, stirring occasionally, until the spinach has wilted, 2 to 3 minutes.

3. Add 2 tablespoons of the pasta water to the pan and reduce the heat to low. Cook, stirring occasionally, to let the flavors develop.

4. Drain the pasta, add it to the pan, and top it with the butter and soy sauce. Toss to combine.

5. Divide the pasta among the serving plates, garnish with green onions and sesame oil, and serve.

INGREDIENTS:

1 TABLESPOON KOSHER SALT, PLUS MORE TO TASTE

14 OZ. DRIED SPAGHETTI

1 TABLESPOON CANOLA OIL

4 GARLIC CLOVES, SLICED

1 CUP CHOPPED BACON

4 CUPS SPINACH

4 SHIITAKE MUSHROOMS, STEMMED AND SLICED

PINCH OF BLACK PEPPER

1 TEASPOON DASHI GRANULES

1 TABLESPOON UNSALTED BUTTER

2 TABLESPOONS SOY SAUCE

GREEN ONIONS, CHOPPED, FOR GARNISH

SESAME OIL, FOR GARNISH

SALMON & MISO CREAM PASTA

YIELD: 4 SERVINGS / ACTIVE TIME: 10 MINUTES / TOTAL TIME: 20 MINUTES

Japanese-style pasta is known for its innovative fusion of flavors, a daring that has created a variety of unique dishes. One of the recent popular choices is a creamy pasta dish featuring white miso, using its umami-laden flavor to great effect.

1. Bring a large pot of water to a boil. Add the salt, let the water return to a boil, and add the pasta. Cook the pasta until it is al dente.

2. While the pasta is cooking, season the salmon with salt and set it aside. Place the olive oil in a large skillet and warm it over medium heat. Add the garlic and onion and cook, stirring frequently, until they are fragrant, about 2 minutes.

3. Add the salmon, mushrooms, and sake to the pan and cook until the sake has almost completely evaporated.

4. Stir in the heavy cream and white miso and simmer the mixture, stirring occasionally, until the sauce begins to thicken. Add about 3 tablespoons of the pasta water to the sauce and stir in the spinach.

5. Drain the pasta, add it to the pan, and toss to combine.

6. Divide the pasta among the serving plates, garnish with Parmesan, yuzu zest, and pepper, and serve.

INGREDIENTS:

- 1 TABLESPOON KOSHER SALT, PLUS MORE TO TASTE
- 14 OZ. DRIED SPAGHETTI
- 2 SALMON FILLETS, CHOPPED
- 1 TABLESPOON EXTRA-VIRGIN OLIVE OIL
- 2 GARLIC CLOVES, MINCED
- ½ ONION, FINELY DICED
- 5 BROWN BUTTON MUSHROOMS, QUARTERED
- 2 TABLESPOONS SAKE
- ½ CUP HEAVY CREAM
- 1½ TABLESPOONS WHITE MISO PASTE
- 1 CUP SPINACH, CHOPPED
- PARMESAN CHEESE, GRATED, FOR GARNISH
- YUZU ZEST, FOR GARNISH
- BLACK PEPPER, FOR GARNISH

Butter & Soy Sauce Wafu Pasta, see page 550

MENTAIKO PASTA

YIELD: 4 SERVINGS / **ACTIVE TIME:** 10 MINUTES / **TOTAL TIME:** 15 MINUTES

This pasta dish leverages the unique flavor of mentaiko, a seasoned delicacy made from pollock roe that is cured with chile pepper, supplying a spicy kick that complements the creamy texture of the pasta beautifully.

1. Bring a large pot of water to a boil. Add the salt, let the water return to a boil, and add the pasta. Cook the pasta until it is al dente.

2. While the pasta is cooking, combine the mentaiko, butter, olive oil, soy sauce, sugar, dashi granules, pepper, and milk in a large bowl.

3. Add 2 tablespoons of pasta water to the bowl and stir until the mixture is smooth.

4. Drain the pasta, add it to the mentaiko sauce, and toss to coat.

5. Divide the pasta among the serving plates, garnish with shiso leaves and kizami nori, and serve with lemon slices.

INGREDIENTS:

1   TABLESPOON KOSHER SALT, PLUS MORE TO TASTE

14   OZ. DRIED SPAGHETTI

1   CUP MENTAIKO, SKIN REMOVED

2   TABLESPOONS UNSALTED BUTTER, SOFTENED

2   TABLESPOONS EXTRA-VIRGIN OLIVE OIL

2   TEASPOONS LIGHT SOY SAUCE

½   TEASPOON SUGAR

½   TEASPOON DASHI GRANULES

⅛   TEASPOON GROUND BLACK PEPPER

2   TABLESPOONS WHOLE MILK

SHISO LEAVES, SLICED THIN, FOR GARNISH

KIZAMI (SHREDDED) NORI, FOR GARNISH

LEMON SLICES, FOR SERVING

CARBO UDON

YIELD: 2 SERVINGS / ACTIVE TIME: 15 MINUTES / TOTAL TIME: 15 MINUTES

This modern fusion dish marries the creamy richness of the Italian carbonara with chewy Japanese udon. It recently has stirred up quite a buzz, especially on social media, making its way into both convenience stores and restaurant menus in Japan.

1. Place the eggs and Parmesan in a small bowl and whisk to combine. Set the mixture aside.

2. Place the olive oil in a large skillet and warm it over medium-low heat. Add the garlic, pepper, bay leaf, and bacon and cook, stirring occasionally, until the bacon is crispy. Remove half of the bacon from the pan and set it aside.

3. Add the dashi and soy sauce to the pan, reduce the heat to low, and simmer the mixture.

4. Cook the udon noodles for 1 minute less than specified in the directions on the package or in the recipe.

5. Remove the bay leaf and garlic from the pan and discard them. Drain the noodles, add them to the pan, and toss to combine.

6. Turn the heat to the lowest possible setting and let the pan cool slightly. Add the egg mixture and stir until well combined.

7. Transfer the noodles to a large serving bowl and top with the reserved bacon. Garnish with the parsley and additional Parmesan cheese and pepper and serve.

INGREDIENTS:

2	PASTEURIZED EGGS
¼	CUP GRATED PARMESAN OR PECORINO CHEESE, PLUS MORE FOR GARNISH
1	TABLESPOON EXTRA-VIRGIN OLIVE OIL
1	GARLIC CLOVE, LIGHTLY CRUSHED
¼	TEASPOON COARSELY GROUND BLACK PEPPER, PLUS MORE FOR GARNISH
1	BAY LEAF
¼	LB. BACON, SHREDDED
½	CUP AWASE DASHI STOCK (SEE PAGE 38)
1½	TEASPOONS SOY SAUCE
2	SERVINGS OF UDON NOODLES (SEE PAGE 414 FOR HOMEMADE)
	PINCH OF DRIED PARSLEY, FOR GARNISH

CHUKA

Chuka refers to Chinese-inspired dishes that have been adapted to Japanese tastes and cooking styles. This cuisine is strongly influenced by Sichuan cuisine, and often differs from Chinese food found in Western countries, creating a distinct subset of Japanese cuisine. Interestingly, ramen, though originally a Chinese dish, has been modified so significantly that it's often no longer categorized as chuka, but grouped into its own distinct category.

MABO NASU

YIELD: 4 SERVINGS / **ACTIVE TIME:** 20 MINUTES / **TOTAL TIME:** 30 MINUTES

Mabo nasu is a chuka dish inspired by the Sichuan dish yu xiang eggplant. It has been tweaked to cater to Japanese tastes by reducing the spiciness and altering the flavor with various seasonings.

1. Rinse the eggplants under cold water, cut off the stems, slice them lengthwise down the middle, and then chop them into rough chunks. Place the eggplants in a bowl of cold water, add a pinch of salt, and let them soak for 5 minutes to remove any bitterness.

2. Drain the eggplants and pat them dry with paper towels.

3. Place the canola oil in a large skillet or wok and warm it over medium heat. Add the garlic, ginger, and onion and cook, stirring frequently, until they are fragrant, about 2 minutes.

4. Stir in the chili bean sauce, sugar, and black pepper and then add the pork. Cook until it is browned all over, about 5 minutes, breaking it up with a wooden spoon.

5. Pour in the sake and soy sauce and cook, stirring frequently, for 3 to 4 minutes.

6. Add the eggplants and drizzle the sesame oil over the dish. Stir-fry until the eggplants have softened slightly, about 5 minutes.

7. Add the stock and bring the mixture to a boil.

8. Combine the water and cornstarch in a small bowl. Gradually pour the slurry into the pan, stirring continually. Cook until the sauce thickens to your liking, about 5 minutes.

9. Garnish with the green onions and serve.

INGREDIENTS:

1	LB. JAPANESE OR CHINESE EGGPLANTS
	SALT, TO TASTE
1	TABLESPOON CANOLA OIL
4	GARLIC CLOVES, MINCED
2	TABLESPOONS MINCED FRESH GINGER
¼	MEDIUM ONION, FINELY DICED
2	TABLESPOONS CHILI BEAN SAUCE
1	TEASPOON SUGAR
⅛	TEASPOON BLACK PEPPER
½	LB. GROUND PORK
2	TABLESPOONS SAKE
2	TABLESPOONS SOY SAUCE
2	TABLESPOONS SESAME OIL
2½	CUPS CHICKEN STOCK
¼	CUP WATER
2	TABLESPOONS CORNSTARCH
	GREEN ONIONS, FINELY CHOPPED, FOR GARNISH

CHINJAO ROSU

YIELD: 4 SERVINGS / **ACTIVE TIME:** 10 MINUTES / **TOTAL TIME:** 20 MINUTES

This dish has become a staple in Japanese households and is similar to the pepper steak dish that is popular in the US. The primary difference between the Japanese and Chinese versions of this preparation is the taste, due to the prominent use of beef in the Japanese iteration.

1. Place the oyster sauce, soy sauce, sugar, chicken bouillon, water, and 1 teaspoon of cornstarch in a bowl and whisk until the sugar has completely dissolved. Place the sauce next to the stove.

2. Crack the eggs into a bowl and beat until scrambled. Add the beef, sake, salt, black pepper, and soy sauce and stir until well combined. Sprinkle the remaining cornstarch into the bowl and stir until it is incorporated. Stir in the sesame oil and set the mixture aside.

3. Place half of the canola oil in a large skillet or wok and warm it over medium-high heat. Add the beef mixture and stir-fry until the beef is seared all over. Transfer the beef to a plate and set it aside.

4. Add the remaining canola oil to the pan and warm it. Add the bamboo shoots and stir-fry for 1 minute. Add the bell peppers, ginger, and garlic and stir-fry until the vegetables have softened slightly, 2 to 3 minutes.

5. Return the beef to the pan stir to combine. Stir the sauce, pour it over the beef and vegetables, and turn off the heat. Stir to coat everything with the sauce. The residual heat from the pan will warm the sauce, allowing it to thicken slightly. Serve immediately.

INGREDIENTS:

¼	CUP OYSTER SAUCE
2	TABLESPOONS SOY SAUCE
1	TABLESPOON SUGAR
1	TABLESPOON CHINESE CHICKEN BOUILLON
2	TABLESPOONS WATER
¼	CUP PLUS 1 TEASPOON CORNSTARCH
2	EGGS
1	LB. BEEF CHUCK, CUT INTO STRIPS
4	TEASPOONS SAKE
¼	TEASPOON KOSHER SALT
⅛	TEASPOON BLACK PEPPER
2	TEASPOONS SOY SAUCE
2	TEASPOONS SESAME OIL
2	TABLESPOONS CANOLA OIL
¾	LB. BOILED BAMBOO SHOOTS, JULIENNED
4	BELL PEPPERS, STEMMED, SEEDED, AND JULIENNED
2	TABLESPOONS JULIENNED FRESH GINGER
4	GARLIC CLOVES, SLICED THIN

Mabo Nasu, see page 562

SUBUTA

YIELD: 6 SERVINGS / **ACTIVE TIME:** 30 MINUTES / **TOTAL TIME:** 30 MINUTES

Subuta is a popular dish inspired by Chinese sweet-and-sour dishes. Made with crispy deep-fried pork belly and vibrant vegetables, this is a satisfying recipe guaranteed to taste better than any takeout.

1. Add rice bran oil to a Dutch oven until it is about 2 inches deep and warm it to 355°F.

2. Place the pork belly in a bowl, season with salt and pepper, and sprinkle the flour over it. Stir until coated, add the egg yolks, and stir until they coat the pork belly.

3. Sprinkle ¼ cup of cornstarch onto a plate, roll the pork belly in the cornstarch until completely coated, and gently slip it into the hot oil. Fry until it is crispy and golden brown, 3 to 4 minutes. Transfer the fried pork belly to a wire rack to drain.

4. Gently slip the carrots into the hot oil, set a timer for 2 minutes, and fry them for this amount of time. Transfer the fried carrots to the wire rack to drain. Add the onion and bell peppers, set a timer for 1 minute, and fry the vegetables for this amount of time. Transfer the fried onion and bell peppers to the wire rack to drain.

5. Place the ketchup, rice vinegar, sake, sugar, water, soy sauce, chicken bouillon, and remaining cornstarch in a large skillet and cook, stirring continually, over medium heat until the sauce starts to thicken.

6. Add the fried pork belly and vegetables and toss to combine.

7. Sprinkle the sesame seeds over the dish and serve.

INGREDIENTS:

	RICE BRAN OIL, AS NEEDED
1	LB. PORK BELLY, CUBED
	SALT AND PEPPER, TO TASTE
2	TABLESPOONS ALL-PURPOSE FLOUR
2	EGG YOLKS
¼	CUP PLUS 1 TEASPOON CORNSTARCH
2	CARROTS, PEELED AND CHOPPED
1	ONION, SLICED
2	BELL PEPPERS, STEMMED, SEEDED, AND CUBED
¼	CUP KETCHUP
¼	CUP RICE VINEGAR
1	TABLESPOON SAKE
¼	CUP SUGAR
6	TABLESPOONS WATER
2	TEASPOONS SOY SAUCE
1	TEASPOON CHINESE CHICKEN BOUILLON
1	TEASPOON WHITE SESAME SEEDS

EBI CHILI

YIELD: 4 SERVINGS / **ACTIVE TIME:** 10 MINUTES / **TOTAL TIME:** 20 MINUTES

The chili bean paste keys this flavorful and mildly spicy dish, which pairs perfectly with white rice.

1. To prepare the sauce, place all of the ingredients in a small bowl and whisk to combine. Set the sauce aside.

2. To begin preparations for the shrimp, sprinkle the sake, salt, pepper, and potato starch over the shrimp, and toss until they are evenly coated.

3. Place half of the canola oil in a large skillet and warm it over medium heat. Add the shrimp and cook until they are a light golden brown on each side, 1 to 2 minutes, turning them over once. Remove the shrimp from the pan and set them aside.

4. Add the remaining canola oil to the pan and warm it. Add the leek, garlic, ginger, chile, and chili bean paste and cook, stirring occasionally, until the mixture is fragrant, about 2 minutes. Return the shrimp to the pan, pour the prepared sauce over them, and stir-fry until the sauce thickens.

5. Transfer the dish to a serving bowl, garnish with green onions and sesame seeds, and serve.

INGREDIENTS:

FOR THE SAUCE

2	TABLESPOONS WATER
2	TABLESPOONS KETCHUP
2	TABLESPOONS SAKE
1½	TEASPOONS SESAME OIL
1	TEASPOON SUGAR
1	TEASPOON CHINESE CHICKEN BOUILLON
1	TEASPOON LIGHT SOY SAUCE
1	TEASPOON YELLOW MISO PASTE

FOR THE SHRIMP

1	TABLESPOON SAKE
1	LB. SHRIMP, SHELLS REMOVED, DEVEINED
	PINCH OF KOSHER SALT
	PINCH OF BLACK PEPPER
1	TABLESPOON POTATO STARCH
1	TABLESPOON CANOLA OIL
1	JAPANESE LEEK, WHITE PART ONLY, FINELY DICED
1	GARLIC CLOVE, MINCED
1	TEASPOON MINCED FRESH GINGER
1	DRIED RED CHILE PEPPER, SLICED THIN
1½	TEASPOONS CHILI BEAN PASTE
	GREEN ONIONS, FINELY CHOPPED, FOR GARNISH
	SESAME SEEDS, FOR GARNISH

Subuta, see page 566

YURINCHI

YIELD: 4 SERVINGS / ACTIVE TIME: 15 MINUTES / TOTAL TIME: 45 MINUTES

Yurinchi is one of the most enjoyed chuka dishes in Japan, and can be found at almost any Chinese restaurant in the country. It differs from the original Chinese version in a few respects. First, the Chinese version is batterless. Second, boneless meat is used in the Japanese version. Last, the sauce in the Japanese version is very sweet and sour in comparison with its forerunner.

1. To begin preparations for the chicken, cut the chicken into four equally sized rectangular pieces or bite-size pieces. Place the chicken in a bowl, add the ginger, garlic, soy sauce, sake, and pepper, and stir until these ingredients coat the chicken. Let the chicken marinate in the refrigerator for 30 minutes.

2. While the chicken is marinating, prepare the sauce. Place all of the ingredients, except for the leek, in a small saucepan and bring to a simmer over medium-low heat. Simmer for 1 to 2 minutes, stir in the leek, and remove the pan from heat. Set the sauce aside.

3. Add the tapioca starch to the bowl containing the chicken and stir until the chicken is evenly coated.

4. Add rice bran oil to a Dutch oven until it is 2 inches deep and warm it to 320°F. Working in batches to avoid overcrowding the pot, gently slip the chicken into the hot oil and fry until it is golden brown all over, about 4 minutes, turning it over halfway through. Transfer the fried chicken to a wire rack to drain.

5. Once all of the chicken has been fried, warm the oil to 360°F. Return the chicken to the hot oil in batches and fry until it is cooked through, about 1 minute, turning it over halfway through.

6. Transfer the fried chicken to a cutting board and, if you did not cut it into bite-size pieces initially, slice it into large pieces. Pour the sauce over the top and serve.

INGREDIENTS:

FOR THE CHICKEN

1⅓ LBS. BONELESS, SKIN-ON CHICKEN THIGHS

1½ TEASPOONS GINGER PASTE

1½ TEASPOONS GARLIC PASTE

1½ TABLESPOONS SOY SAUCE

3 TABLESPOONS.SAKE

¼ TEASPOON WHITE PEPPER

½ CUP TAPIOCA STARCH

RICE BRAN OIL, AS NEEDED

FOR THE SAUCE

1 TABLESPOON MINCED FRESH GINGER

1 TEASPOON MINCED GARLIC

2 TABLESPOONS SOY SAUCE

1 TEASPOON WORCESTERSHIRE SAUCE

1 TABLESPOON APPLE CIDER VINEGAR

1 TEASPOON FRESH LEMON JUICE

½ TABLESPOON MIRIN

1½ TEASPOONS SUGAR

1½ TEASPOONS SESAME OIL

½ TEASPOON MINCED DRIED CHILE PEPPER

½ JAPANESE LEEK, FINELY DICED

EBI MAYO

YIELD: 4 SERVINGS / ACTIVE TIME: 20 MINUTES / TOTAL TIME: 30 MINUTES

This dish is a delectable appetizer made with succulent prawns and a sweet, mildly tangy mayonnaise-based sauce that can be used to coat the prawns or served on the side.

1. To begin preparations for the batter, combine the cake flour, rice flour, baking powder, salt, and pepper in a bowl and place the bowl in the freezer.

2. To prepare the sauce, place all of the ingredients in a bowl, stir to combine, and set the sauce aside.

3. To begin preparations for the prawns, place the prawns in a bowl, sprinkle the salt and 2 teaspoons of cornstarch over them, and rub these ingredients into the prawns. Rinse the prawns under cold water and pat them dry with paper towels.

4. Add rice bran oil to a Dutch oven until it is 2 inches deep and warm it to 375°F. Add the garlic cloves to the oil, remove them when they turn brown, and discard them.

5. Sprinkle the remaining cornstarch over the prawns and stir until they are evenly coated.

6. Remove the bowl of dried batter ingredients from the freezer, add the lager, and stir until the mixture comes together as a smooth batter.

7. Working in batches to avoid overcrowding the pot, dip the prawns into the batter until completely coated and gently slip them into the hot oil. Fry until they are cooked through and golden brown, 2 to 3 minutes. Transfer the fried prawns to a wire rack to drain.

8. Either add the fried prawns to the sauce and stir until coated or serve the sauce on the side. Garnish with parsley and serve.

INGREDIENTS:

FOR THE BATTER

1¼	CUPS CAKE FLOUR
2	TABLESPOONS RICE FLOUR
1	TEASPOON BAKING POWDER
2	PINCHES OF KOSHER SALT
2	PINCHES OF BLACK PEPPER
6½	OZ. LAGER, CHILLED

FOR THE SAUCE

½	CUP JAPANESE MAYONNAISE (SEE PAGE 46)
2	TABLESPOONS CONDENSED MILK
2	TEASPOONS KETCHUP
2	TEASPOONS RICE VINEGAR
1	TEASPOON SOY SAUCE
1	TEASPOON FRESH LEMON JUICE
1	TEASPOON PAPRIKA

FOR THE PRAWNS

1	LB. KING PRAWNS, SHELLS REMOVED, DEVEINED
¼	TEASPOON KOSHER SALT
6	TABLESPOONS PLUS 2 TEASPOONS CORNSTARCH
	RICE BRAN OIL, AS NEEDED
4	GARLIC CLOVES
	DRIED PARSLEY, FOR GARNISH

Yurinchi, see page 570

TENSHINHAN

YIELD: 2 SERVINGS / **ACTIVE TIME:** 10 MINUTES / **TOTAL TIME:** 40 MINUTES

Made with fluffy white rice encased in a tender crab omelet and topped with a rich, creamy sauce, tenshinhan is a tasty side dish. The flavor of the sauce varies according to region—this recipe is based on the Tokyo version, which favors a sweet, vinegar-based sauce.

1. To begin preparations for the sauce, place the butter in a medium saucepan and melt it over low heat. Add the soy sauce, stock, brown sugar, and salt, stir to combine, raise the heat to medium, and bring to a boil.

2. Combine the cornstarch and water in a small bowl. Boil the sauce for 1 minute and then add the slurry and rice vinegar, stirring continually. Cook until the sauce has thickened slightly and is glossy. Turn off the heat, cover the pan, and leave it on the burner.

3. To begin preparations for the omelet, crack the eggs into a bowl and whisk until combined. Add the leek and canned crab, whisk to combine, and add the ginger, salt, and pepper. Whisk to combine.

4. Warm a large nonstick skillet over medium-high heat. Add the canola oil and swirl the pan to evenly coat it. Pour the egg mixture into the pan and whisk vigorously for about 30 seconds. Reduce the heat to medium and cook without mixing the omelet. Pack the cooked rice into a bowl and flip the shaped mound onto a plate. When the omelet is cooked to your liking, loosen the edges with a spatula and carefully slide it over the rice.

5. Pour the sauce over the omelet and drizzle the sesame oil over the top. Garnish with green onions and serve.

INGREDIENTS:

FOR THE SAUCE

1	TABLESPOON UNSALTED BUTTER
1½	TEASPOONS LIGHT SOY SAUCE
¾	CUP CHICKEN STOCK
1½	TEASPOONS LIGHT BROWN SUGAR
	PINCH OF KOSHER SALT
1	TEASPOON CORNSTARCH
1	TABLESPOON COLD WATER
1½	TEASPOONS RICE VINEGAR

FOR THE OMELET

4	EGGS
1	TABLESPOON FINELY DICED JAPANESE LEEK, WHITE PART ONLY
4¼	OZ. CANNED CRABMEAT, DRAINED
1	TEASPOON GRATED FRESH GINGER
	PINCH OF KOSHER SALT
	PINCH OF BLACK PEPPER
1	TABLESPOON CANOLA OIL
1⅓	CUPS COOKED JAPANESE SHORT-GRAIN RICE
1	TEASPOON SESAME OIL
	GREEN ONIONS, CHOPPED, FOR GARNISH

CHAHAN

YIELD: 2 SERVINGS / **ACTIVE TIME**: 10 MINUTES / **TOTAL TIME**: 10 MINUTES

Chahan is a Japanese term used to refer to fried rice, which is a versatile and popular dish that often appears on the menus in ramen restaurants.

1. Before you start cooking, cut and measure all of the ingredients. Cooking will proceed quickly over high heat, so having everything ready to go is crucial.

2. Place the lard in a wok and melt it over high heat. The high heat is essential for achieving the characteristic smoky flavor of properly made chahan. Crack the eggs directly into the pan and quickly break them up with a spatula. Fry until they achieve a slightly runny, scrambled consistency. Add the rice, break up any clumps, and stir until thoroughly combined with the eggs.

3. Add the pork belly, kamaboko, and leek and stir-fry until they are evenly distributed. Add the soy sauce, sake, mirin, ginger, garlic, sugar, salt, pepper, and chicken bouillon and stir-fry for 1 to 2 minutes, tossing occasionally to slightly dry out and crisp the rice.

4. To serve, pack the fried rice into a ladle or a small bowl and flip it onto a plate so that it sits in a neat mound. Garnish with Benishoga.

INGREDIENTS:

1½ TEASPOONS LARD

2 EGGS

1⅓ CUPS PERFECT JAPANESE RICE (SEE PAGE 80), COOLED AND SLIGHTLY DRIED OUT

½ CUP COOKED PORK BELLY OR PORK CHASHU (SEE PAGE 376 OR 382), CUBED

3 SLICES OF KAMABOKO FISH CAKE, CUBED

2 TABLESPOONS FINELY DICED JAPANESE LEEK, WHITE PART ONLY

1 TABLESPOON SOY SAUCE

1 TEASPOON SAKE

1 TEASPOON MIRIN

½ TEASPOON GRATED FRESH GINGER

½ TEASPOON GRATED GARLIC

¼ TEASPOON SUGAR

¼ TEASPOON KOSHER SALT

¼ TEASPOON WHITE PEPPER

½ TEASPOON CHINESE CHICKEN BOUILLON

BENISHOGA (SEE PAGE 315), FOR GARNISH

PORK YAKI GYOZA

YIELD: 25 TO 30 GYOZA / **ACTIVE TIME:** 30 MINUTES / **TOTAL TIME:** 40 MINUTES

Gyoza is a type of dumpling that originated from Chinese cuisine but has been widely adopted and adapted by the Japanese. It has become a popular dish in a wide range of dining and retail establishments, from izakayas and ramen shops to supermarkets.

1. To prepare the sauce, place all of the ingredients in a bowl and stir to combine. Set the sauce aside.

2. To begin preparations for the filling, place all of the ingredients in a large mixing bowl and work the mixture with your hands until the ingredients are evenly distributed, taking care not to overwork the mixture.

3. Lay a wrapper flat in the palm of your hand. Place approximately 1 tablespoon of filling in the center of the wrapper, leaving a generous border around the edge. Avoid overfilling, as this will prevent the gyoza from being sealed properly.

4. Moisten the edge along the top half of the wrapper with water. Fold the gyoza in half, not letting the edges touch immediately. Start pinching at one corner of the half-moon, then create small pleats with your thumbs. Press each pleat firmly to seal the gyoza completely. Gently tap the base of the sealed gyoza on the counter or your palm to create a flat bottom, which will allow them to sit upright while they cook. Repeat with the remaining wrappers and filling.

5. Place the rice bran oil in a large skillet and warm it over medium heat. Place the gyoza in the pan, flat side down, and fry until the bottoms are golden brown, 3 to 5 minutes. Carefully pour the boiling water into the pan around the gyoza. Cover the pan with a lid and cook until the water has nearly evaporated.

6. Uncover the pan and cook until all of the liquid has evaporated and the gyoza are cooked through.

7. Drizzle the sesame oil over the gyoza, remove them from the pan, and flip them onto a serving plate so that the browned bases are facing up. Serve alongside the sauce.

INGREDIENTS:

FOR THE SAUCE

1	TABLESPOON RICE VINEGAR
2	TEASPOONS SOY SAUCE
½	TEASPOON CHILI OIL
¼	TEASPOON WHITE PEPPER

FOR THE FILLING

5½	OZ. GROUND PORK
1	CUP FINELY DICED GREEN CABBAGE
½	CUP FINELY DICED GARLIC CHIVES
1	TABLESPOON MINCED FRESH GINGER
1	GARLIC CLOVE, MINCED
⅛	TEASPOON KOSHER SALT
⅛	TEASPOON WHITE PEPPER
1	TEASPOON SOY SAUCE
1	TEASPOON OYSTER SAUCE
1	TEASPOON CHINESE CHICKEN BOUILLON
1	TEASPOON SESAME OIL
½	TEASPOON SUGAR
1½	TEASPOONS SAKE
25–30	GYOZA WRAPPERS (SEE PAGE 74)
1	TABLESPOON RICE BRAN OIL
½	CUP BOILING WATER
1½	TEASPOONS SESAME OIL

VEGETABLE GYOZA

YIELD: 20 LARGE GYOZA OR 30 REGULAR GYOZA / **ACTIVE TIME:** 30 MINUTES / **TOTAL TIME:** 40 MINUTES

This recipe blends imitation soy-based meat with vegetables and umami-rich seasonings. The result is a harmonious, flavorful filling that's both satisfying and vegan.

1. To prepare the sauce, place all of the ingredients in a bowl and stir to combine. Set the sauce aside.

2. To begin preparations for the filling, place the cabbage and salt in a bowl and rub the salt into the cabbage. Let the cabbage sit for 10 minutes.

3. Place all of the remaining ingredients in a bowl and stir until well combined, making sure the miso paste is well distributed.

4. After 10 minutes, the cabbage will have released some of its liquid. Squeeze it to remove any excess water, drain it, and then transfer it to the bowl containing the other filling ingredients. Stir until well combined.

5. Lay a wrapper flat in the palm of your hand. Place approximately 1½ teaspoons to 1 tablespoon of filling in the center of the wrapper, leaving a generous border around the edge. Avoid overfilling, as this will prevent the gyoza from being sealed properly.

6. Moisten the edge along the top half of the wrapper with water. Fold the gyoza in half, not letting the edges touch immediately. Start pinching at one corner of the half-moon, then create small pleats with your thumbs. Press each pleat firmly to seal the gyoza completely. Gently tap the base of the sealed gyoza on the counter or your palm to create a flat bottom, which will allow them to sit upright while they cook.

7. Place the rice bran oil in a large skillet and arrange the gyoza in the pan, flat side down. Cook over medium heat until the bottoms of the gyoza are golden brown, 3 to 5 minutes.

8. Combine the warm water and flour in a small bowl. Carefully pour the slurry into the pan around the gyoza. Cover the pan with a lid and cook until the water has nearly evaporated, about 3 minutes.

9. Uncover the pan and cook until all of the liquid has evaporated and the gyoza are cooked through.

10. Remove the gyoza from the pan and flip them onto a serving plate so that the browned bases are facing up. Serve alongside the sauce.

INGREDIENTS:

FOR THE SAUCE

1	TABLESPOON RICE VINEGAR
2	TEASPOONS SOY SAUCE
½	TEASPOON CHILI OIL
¼	TEASPOON GROUND BLACK PEPPER

FOR THE FILLING

⅛	NAPA CABBAGE, DICED
½	TEASPOON KOSHER SALT
3½	OZ. MINCED SOY-BASED IMITATION MEAT
2	SHIITAKE MUSHROOMS, STEMMED AND DICED
⅓	CUP BOILED BAMBOO SHOOTS, FINELY DICED
⅓	CUP GARLIC CHIVES, FINELY DICED
1½	TEASPOONS GARLIC PASTE
1	TEASPOON GINGER PASTE
¼	TEASPOON GROUND BLACK PEPPER
1	TEASPOON SAKE
1	TEASPOON MIRIN
1	TABLESPOON CORNSTARCH
1	TABLESPOON SESAME OIL
1½	TEASPOONS SOY SAUCE
1	TABLESPOON YELLOW MISO PASTE
20	LARGE OR 30 REGULAR GYOZA WRAPPERS (SEE PAGE 74)
1½	TEASPOONS RICE BRAN OIL
¼	CUP WARM WATER
½	TEASPOON ALL-PURPOSE FLOUR

SHUMAI

YIELD: 6 SERVINGS / ACTIVE TIME: 25 MINUTES / TOTAL TIME: 35 MINUTES

Shumai is the Japanese adaptation of the Chinese dim sum offering shomai or siu mai, a steamed dumpling filled with a blend of ground pork, seasonings, and vegetables, which is encased in a delicate flour dough. The Japanese version is typically topped with green peas and served with soy sauce and Japanese mustard.

1. Finely dice the pork belly. Scoop it into a large bowl and add the ground pork, soy sauce, oyster sauce, sake, sesame oil, sugar, salt, and pepper. Work the mixture with your hands until all of the ingredients are evenly distributed.

2. Place the leek, bamboo shoots, and potato starch in a separate bowl and toss until the vegetables are evenly coated. Add this mixture to the pork mixture. Add the onion and ginger and knead until everything is evenly distributed.

3. Fill a pot halfway with water and bring it to a boil. Line a steaming basket with a sheet of parchment paper.

4. Place a wonton wrapper in the palm of your hand and place 1 tablespoon of filling in the center, leaving a border around the edges. Make the OK gesture with your thumb and index finger and balance the wonton wrapper on top of the circle, with the filling over the hole. Use a knife to push the wonton down through the hole, pushing the edges of the wrapper up. Pat the base of the shumai with the knife until it is flat and place it in a steaming basket. Repeat until all of the wonton wrappers and filling have been used up.

5. Push a pea into the center of each shumai. Cover the steaming basket and place it over the boiling water. Steam until the shumai are cooked through, about 8 minutes.

6. Serve with soy sauce and Japanese mustard.

INGREDIENTS:

⅔	LB. PORK BELLY
⅔	LB. GROUND PORK
1	TEASPOON SOY SAUCE
1	TEASPOON OYSTER SAUCE
2	TEASPOONS SAKE
2	TEASPOONS SESAME OIL
1	TABLESPOON SUGAR
1	TEASPOON KOSHER SALT
2	PINCHES OF BLACK PEPPER
1	JAPANESE LEEK, WHITE PART ONLY, FINELY DICED
5	OZ. BOILED BAMBOO SHOOTS, FINELY DICED
¼	CUP POTATO STARCH
½	ONION, GRATED
	1-INCH PIECE OF FRESH GINGER, PEELED AND GRATED
60	SQUARE WONTON WRAPPERS
60	GREEN PEAS
	SOY SAUCE, FOR SERVING
	JAPANESE MUSTARD, FOR SERVING

Shumai, see page 579

HARUMAKI

YIELD: 4 SERVINGS / **ACTIVE TIME:** 30 MINUTES / **TOTAL TIME:** 1 HOUR

Harumaki, directly translated as "spring roll" in Japanese, is one of Japan's most beloved fried dishes, and is widely available in supermarkets and convenience stores. What sets Japanese harumaki apart from the Chinese version is its generous helping of vegetables, which creates a distinctive texture.

1. Mince the pork, place it in a bowl with the salt, black pepper, and sesame oil, and stir to combine.

2. Warm a large skillet over medium-low heat, add the pork, and stir-fry until it starts to brown, about 5 minutes. Add the ginger, garlic, and leek and stir-fry until they are fragrant, 1 to 2 minutes. Add the mushrooms, carrot, bell pepper, and bamboo shoots and stir-fry until they are tender, about 5 minutes.

3. Stir in the sake, soy sauce, oyster sauce, and sugar, add the stock, and bring to a simmer. Combine the water and potato starch in a bowl and pour the slurry into the pan, stirring continually. Cook until the mixture thickens and becomes glossy. Remove the pan from heat and transfer the filling to a container. Let the filling cool for about 30 minutes.

4. Combine water and flour in a 2:1 ratio in a small bowl. Place a wrapper in front of you and position it at a 45-degree angle, so that it looks like a diamond. Place some of the filling horizontally just beneath the center of the wrapper, keeping it away from the edges. Fold the bottom point of the wrapper tightly over the filling. Fold in the left and right sides and press down to secure them. Roll the wrapper up until only the top point remains. Dab the flour mixture on the top edges and seal the roll. Repeat with the remaining wrappers and filling.

5. Add rice bran oil to a Dutch oven until it is 1 inch deep and warm it to 320°F. Place the spring rolls in the hot oil, seams facing down, and fry until they are golden brown and crispy, turning them over once. Transfer the fried spring rolls to a wire rack to drain.

6. Serve with soy sauce and Japanese mustard.

INGREDIENTS:

5½ OZ. PORK SHOULDER OR PORK BELLY, SLICED THIN

PINCH OF KOSHER SALT

PINCH OF BLACK PEPPER

1 TEASPOON SESAME OIL

1½ TEASPOONS MINCED FRESH GINGER

1 GARLIC CLOVE, MINCED

½ JAPANESE LEEK, FINELY DICED

2 SHIITAKE MUSHROOMS, STEMMED AND SLICED

½ CARROT, PEELED AND JULIENNED

1 GREEN BELL PEPPER, STEMMED, SEEDED, AND JULIENNED

2 OZ. BOILED BAMBOO SHOOTS, JULIENNED

2 TABLESPOONS SAKE

1½ TEASPOONS SOY SAUCE, PLUS MORE FOR SERVING

1½ TEASPOONS OYSTER SAUCE

1 TEASPOON SUGAR

½ CUP CHICKEN STOCK

1 TABLESPOON COLD WATER, PLUS MORE AS NEEDED

1 TEASPOON POTATO STARCH

ALL-PURPOSE FLOUR, AS NEEDED

8 SQUARE SPRING ROLL WRAPPERS

RICE BRAN OIL, AS NEEDED

JAPANESE MUSTARD, FOR SERVING

BAN BAN ZII

YIELD: 4 SERVINGS / **ACTIVE TIME:** 15 MINUTES / **TOTAL TIME:** 30 MINUTES

Ban ban zii has transformed itself into a beloved Chinese-style salad in Japan. Originally a cold dish featuring steamed chicken and a spicy sauce, it evolved to cater to Japanese palates unaccustomed to chile peppers. The spicy sauce in the original was replaced with a creamy and nutty sesame sauce that beautifully complements the tender chicken and crisp vegetables.

1. Pat the chicken dry with paper towels. Using a fork, poke holes all over the chicken and sprinkle the salt and cornstarch over it.

2. Add the sake and chicken to a microwave-safe bowl. Loosely cover the bowl with plastic wrap, place it in the microwave, and microwave on high for 2 minutes.

3. Carefully remove the bowl from the microwave, being cautious of the hot steam. Turn the chicken over, cover the bowl loosely with the plastic wrap again, and return the bowl to the microwave. Microwave on high for 2 minutes.

4. Leave the bowl in the microwave and let the chicken steam for 10 minutes. The residual heat will continue to gently cook the chicken.

5. Place the sesame paste, rice vinegar, soy sauce, sugar, leek, chili oil, and sesame oil in a bowl and whisk to combine. Set the sauce aside.

6. Remove the chicken from the microwave and let it cool. When it is cool enough to handle, use your hands to shred the chicken. If you prefer a chilled salad, you can refrigerate the chicken at this point.

7. Arrange the cucumbers in a bed on a serving plate. Place the shredded chicken on top of the cucumbers and surround it with the tomatoes. Drizzle the sauce over the dish and serve.

INGREDIENTS:

⅔	LB. BONELESS, SKINLESS CHICKEN BREASTS
2	PINCHES OF KOSHER SALT
1	TEASPOON CORNSTARCH
1	TABLESPOON SAKE
2	TABLESPOONS SESAME PASTE
2	TABLESPOONS RICE VINEGAR
1½	TABLESPOONS SOY SAUCE
1	TABLESPOON SUGAR
1	TABLESPOON FINELY DICED JAPANESE LEEK, WHITE PART ONLY
1	TEASPOON CHILI OIL
1	TEASPOON TOASTED SESAME OIL
2	JAPANESE OR PERSIAN CUCUMBERS, JULIENNED
12	CHERRY OR GRAPE TOMATOES, HALVED

REBANIRA ITAME

YIELD: 4 SERVINGS / **ACTIVE TIME:** 20 MINUTES / **TOTAL TIME:** 20 MINUTES

This stir-fry has captured the hearts of diners, due in part to its affordability. Traditionally, it was prepared using pork or beef liver, which imparted a rich and distinctive taste, but in recent years there has been a shift toward using chicken liver, especially when it is prepared at home. This recipe is meant to be generously seasoned in order to perfectly complement white rice, so be sure to serve it with some.

1. To begin preparations for the chicken livers, place the chicken livers in a bowl and rinse them with cold water. Drain and pat the chicken livers dry with paper towels. Place the salt, pepper, sake, garlic paste, ginger paste, and potato starch in a bowl and stir to combine. Add the chicken livers, stir to coat, and let the chicken livers marinate.

2. To prepare the sauce, place all of the ingredients in a bowl and stir to combine. Set the sauce aside.

3. Place the sesame oil in a wok or large skillet and warm it over medium-high heat. Add the minced ginger, minced garlic, and leek and stir-fry until fragrant, about 30 seconds. Add the marinated chicken livers and stir-fry until they are browned all over.

4. Add the bean sprouts and stir-fry until they have softened. Pour the sauce into the pan and stir to combine. Cook until the sauce thickens and becomes sticky.

5. Add the garlic chives and stir-fry until they start to wilt, about 30 seconds. Season the dish with pepper and serve, garnishing each portion with chili oil.

INGREDIENTS:

FOR THE CHICKEN LIVERS

½   LB. CHICKEN LIVERS, CHOPPED

½   TEASPOON KOSHER SALT

    PINCH OF GROUND BLACK PEPPER, PLUS MORE TO TASTE

1   TABLESPOON SAKE

1   TEASPOON GARLIC PASTE

1   TEASPOON GINGER PASTE

1   TABLESPOON POTATO STARCH

1   TABLESPOON TOASTED SESAME OIL

1   TABLESPOON MINCED FRESH GINGER

1   TABLESPOON MINCED GARLIC

1   TABLESPOON FINELY DICED JAPANESE LEEK, WHITE PART ONLY

½   LB. BEAN SPROUTS, RINSED WELL

¼   LB. GARLIC CHIVES, CHOPPED

    CHILI OIL, FOR GARNISH

FOR THE SAUCE

1   TABLESPOON SOY SAUCE

1   TABLESPOON OYSTER SAUCE

1   TABLESPOON SUGAR

1   TABLESPOON SAKE

1   TABLESPOON MIRIN

1   TEASPOON POTATO STARCH

1   TEASPOON CHINESE CHICKEN BOUILLON

YASAI ITAME

YIELD: 4 SERVINGS / **ACTIVE TIME:** 10 MINUTES / **TOTAL TIME:** 15 MINUTES

This is a popular stir-fried dish that is prominently featured in Japanese teishokuya (a type of restaurant that is similar to an American diner) and Chinese eateries throughout Japan. The direct translation for the dish is "vegetable stir-fry," however, yasai itame typically includes a small amount of pork.

1. Place the sugar, chicken bouillon, garlic paste, soy sauce, oyster sauce, and sake in a small bowl and whisk to combine. Set the sauce aside.

2. Season the pork belly with the salt and pepper and then lightly coat it with the flour.

3. Place the canola oil in a large skillet or wok and warm it over medium-high heat. Add the pork and cook until it is browned all over, turning it as necessary. Remove the pork from the pan and set it aside.

4. Add the sliced garlic, cabbage, carrot, and onion and stir-fry until the cabbage and carrot have softened, about 5 minutes.

5. Pour the sauce into the pan and stir to combine. Return the pork to the pan and stir-fry until the sauce has thickened and the pork is cooked through.

6. Add the bean sprouts and garlic chives and stir-fry until the bean sprouts are heated through and the garlic chives have wilted, about 1 minute. Serve immediately.

INGREDIENTS:

½ TEASPOON SUGAR

1 TEASPOON CHINESE CHICKEN BOUILLON

1 TEASPOON GARLIC PASTE

1 TEASPOON SOY SAUCE

1 TABLESPOON OYSTER SAUCE

1 TABLESPOON SAKE

5 OZ. PORK BELLY, SLICED THIN

PINCH OF KOSHER SALT

PINCH OF BLACK PEPPER

1 TABLESPOON ALL-PURPOSE FLOUR

1 TEASPOON CANOLA OIL

2 GARLIC CLOVES, SLICED

¼ GREEN CABBAGE, CHOPPED

½ CARROT, PEELED AND JULIENNED

½ ONION, SLICED THIN

3½ OZ. BEAN SPROUTS

½ CUP CHOPPED GARLIC CHIVES (2-INCH-LONG PIECES)

NIKUMAN

YIELD: 8 SERVINGS / **ACTIVE TIME:** 50 MINUTES / **TOTAL TIME:** 1 HOUR AND 50 MINUTES

Nikuman is a soft and fluffy steamed bun filled with seasoned pork and chopped vegetables. It's a popular snack inspired by Chinese baozi and, while it can be found in convenience stores across Japan year-round, nothing beats biting into a nikuman on a cold winter day.

1. To begin preparations for the buns, place the water, sugar, and yeast in a bowl, gently stir, and let the mixture sit until it starts to foam, about 10 minutes.

2. Sift the flours into a large mixing bowl, add the salt and baking powder, and whisk to combine. Add the milk and yeast mixture and mix until the resulting mixture comes together as a rough dough.

3. Transfer the dough to a flour-dusted work surface and knead until it is smooth, 5 to 10 minutes. Place the dough in a bowl, cover it with the plastic wrap, and let the dough rest in a naturally warm place until it has doubled in size, 40 minutes to 1½ hours.

4. To begin preparations for the filling, place the soy sauce, oyster sauce, yellow miso, vinegar, sake, sugar, honey, salt, pepper, and chicken bouillon in a bowl and stir to combine. Place the bowl beside the stove.

5. Place the sesame oil in a large skillet and warm it over medium heat. Add the onion, bamboo shoots, mushrooms, ginger, and garlic and stir-fry for 2 minutes. Add the soy sauce mixture and stir-fry until the vegetables have absorbed most of the liquid.

6. Combine the water and potato starch in a bowl. Turn off the heat and stir the slurry into the pan, whisking until the mixture is glossy. Transfer the mixture to a wide container and let it cool.

7. When the mixture is cool enough to handle, stir the pork and lard into it. Cover the container and chill the mixture in the refrigerator until the dough for the buns has doubled in size.

8. Punch the dough to deflate it, place it on a flour-dusted work surface, and roll it into a cylinder. Cut the dough into eight equal pieces, form each piece into a ball, and flatten the balls into disks. Cover the buns with plastic wrap and let them rest for 15 minutes.

9. Line a steaming basket with parchment paper. Divide the filling into eight portions. Roll out the buns until they are a little less than ¼ inch thick. Pinch the edges of the buns to make the dough thinner, preventing there from being too much dough at the seams.

INGREDIENTS:

FOR THE BUNS

3.4	OZ. WARM WATER (105°F)
5	TEASPOONS SUGAR
½	TEASPOON ACTIVE DRY YEAST
7	OZ. CAKE FLOUR
3½	OZ. BREAD FLOUR, PLUS MORE AS NEEDED
½	TEASPOON KOSHER SALT
1	TEASPOON BAKING POWDER
1.7	OZ. WHOLE MILK

FOR THE FILLING

1	TABLESPOON SOY SAUCE
2	TEASPOONS OYSTER SAUCE
2	TEASPOONS YELLOW MISO PASTE
2	TEASPOONS BLACK VINEGAR
1	TABLESPOON SAKE
2	TEASPOONS SUGAR
2	TEASPOONS HONEY
2	PINCHES OF KOSHER SALT
2	PINCHES OF BLACK PEPPER
2	TEASPOONS CHINESE CHICKEN BOUILLON
1	TABLESPOON SESAME OIL
½	ONION, FINELY DICED
2½	OZ. BOILED BAMBOO SHOOTS, FINELY DICED
¾	CUP FINELY DICED SHIITAKE MUSHROOMS
	1-INCH PIECE OF FRESH GINGER, PEELED AND GRATED

Place the one portion of the filling in the center of the each bun, fold the buns into half-moons, and pinch the seams to seal them. Place the buns in the steaming basket, cover the basket, and let the buns rest for 15 minutes.

10. Place the steaming basket over a pot filled halfway with cold water and bring the water to a boil over high heat. Gradually bringing up the temperature prevents the buns from becoming misshapen or developing holes as they cook. When the water starts to boil, set a timer for 13 minutes and cook the nikuman for that amount of time. Remove the nikuman from the steaming basket and serve.

2	GARLIC CLOVES, GRATED
1	TABLESPOON COLD WATER
1	TEASPOON POTATO STARCH
7	OZ. GROUND PORK
2	TEASPOONS LARD

IZAKAYA

An izakaya restaurant is a Japanese-style pub, offering a unique dining experience focused on sharing small, tapas-style dishes with friends or colleagues while enjoying drinks. This Japanese version of small plates features a wide variety of dishes, all designed to complement beer and other alcoholic beverages. The diversity of izakaya cuisine is vast, with the common thread being its compatibility with drinks. Why not bring this convivial atmosphere home by creating your own izakaya experience at home?

YAKITORI IN A FRYING PAN

YIELD: 4 SERVINGS / **ACTIVE TIME:** 15 MINUTES / **TOTAL TIME:** 35 MINUTES

Yakitori is a beloved staple at izakaya restaurants and features bite-sized chicken pieces skewered and grilled over an open flame. While yakitori specialty restaurants utilize every part of the chicken, the most popular choice in the izakaya is the juicy and flavorful chicken thigh. In this recipe, I simplify the preparation by using a frying pan instead of a traditional charcoal grill.

1. To prepare the sauce, place all of the ingredients in a saucepan and bring to a simmer over medium heat. Reduce the heat to the lowest possible setting and let the sauce gently simmer for 10 minutes, stirring occasionally. After 10 minutes, turn off the heat and set the sauce aside.

2. To begin preparations for the skewers, thread the chicken and leeks onto bamboo skewers in the following order: chicken, leek, chicken, leek, and chicken. Repeat this pattern for each skewer until all of the chicken and leeks have been used. If you are left with only chicken at some point, you can just make skewers that are solely chicken. Place the prepared skewers in a container or dish and sprinkle the sake over them.

3. Lightly coat a large skillet with the canola oil and warm it over medium-high heat. Place the skewers in the pan and cook until they are browned on both sides, about 4 minutes, turning them over halfway through.

4. Reduce the heat to low and cover the pan with a lid. Let the skewers steam until the chicken is cooked through, about 5 minutes.

5. Remove the lid and raise the heat to medium-low. Using a brush, apply a thin layer of the sauce to the skewers. Cook for 30 seconds, turn the skewers over, and brush the other side with some sauce. Cook for another 30 seconds. Repeat once more, giving the skewers a nice glaze.

6. Remove the skewers from the pan and serve immediately.

INGREDIENTS:

FOR THE SAUCE

3   TABLESPOONS SOY SAUCE

3   TABLESPOONS MIRIN

1½ TABLESPOONS SAKE

1   TABLESPOON TURBINADO SUGAR

½   TEASPOON GARLIC PASTE

½   TEASPOON DUCK FAT

FOR THE SKEWERS

1½ LBS. BONELESS, SKIN-ON CHICKEN THIGHS, CHOPPED

2   JAPANESE LEEKS, WHITE PARTS ONLY, CHOPPED INTO ¾-INCH-LONG PIECES

2   TABLESPOONS SAKE

1   TEASPOON CANOLA OIL

YAKITON

YIELD: 4 SERVINGS / ACTIVE TIME: 15 MINUTES / TOTAL TIME: 20 MINUTES

Yakiton is essentially the pork equivalent of the popular chicken yakitori, and has been gaining significant popularity across Japan, with specialty restaurants featuring this dish increasingly dotting the streets of Tokyo and beyond. If you don't feel like firing up the grill, you can also prepare this using the broiler on your oven.

1. To prepare the sauce, place all of the ingredients in a saucepan and bring to a boil over medium heat. Reduce the heat to low and let the sauce gently simmer for 5 minutes, stirring continually, until the sauce is smooth and thick. After 10 minutes, turn off the heat and set the sauce aside.

2. To begin preparations for the skewers, cut the leeks into 1-inch-long pieces. Slice the pork into pieces that match the leeks in terms of length and thickness. Thread the pork and leek onto bamboo skewers in the following order: pork, leek, pork, leek, and pork. Repeat this pattern for each skewer until all of the pork and leeks have been used. If you are left with only pork at some point, you can just make skewers that are solely pork.

3. Prepare a grill for high heat (about 500°F). Place the skewers on the grill and season them with the pepper. Cook until they are lightly charred and the pork is almost cooked through, 6 to 8 minutes, turning them over halfway through. Keep a close eye on the skewers, as you do not want the pork to burn.

4. Using a brush, apply a thin layer of the sauce to the skewers. Cook for 1 to 2 minutes, turn the skewers over, and brush the other side with some sauce. Cook for another 1 to 2 minutes, until the skewers have a nice glaze.

5. Remove the skewers from the grill and serve immediately.

INGREDIENTS:

FOR THE SAUCE

⅓ CUP SAKE

2 TABLESPOONS RED MISO PASTE

2 TABLESPOONS SUGAR

1 TABLESPOON GARLIC PASTE

1½ TEASPOONS SESAME OIL

1 TEASPOON DASHI GRANULES

1 TEASPOON CHILI POWDER

FOR THE SKEWERS

2 JAPANESE LEEKS, WHITE PARTS ONLY

¾ LB. PORK SHOULDER

⅛ TEASPOON BLACK PEPPER

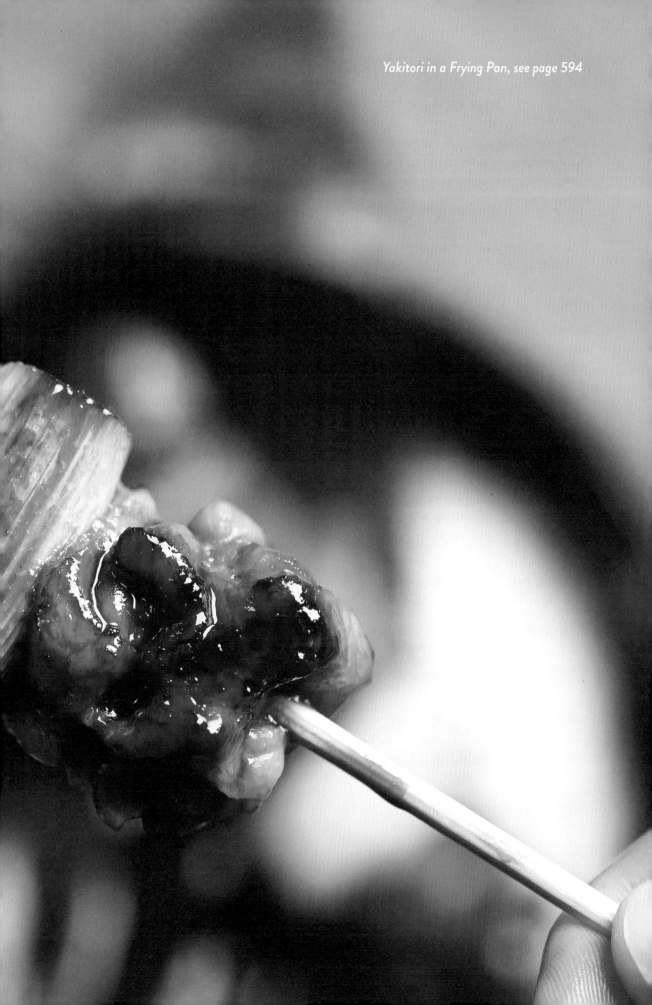

Yakitori in a Frying Pan, see page 594

NAGOYA'S TEBASAKI

YIELD: 4 SERVINGS / ACTIVE TIME: 10 MINUTES / TOTAL TIME: 20 MINUTES

One of Nagoya's specialties is deep-fried chicken wings coated with a rich sweet and savory sauce. As someone from that area, I've created what I feel is an authentic recipe, perfect for enhancing any gathering, from casual drinks with friends to lively game nights and festive parties.

1. To begin preparations for the wings, use a fork to poke holes all over the chicken wings. Combine the tapioca starch and flour in a shallow bowl and dredge the wings in the mixture until they are lightly coated.

2. Add rice bran oil to a Dutch oven until it is 2 inches deep and warm it 320°F. Use an instant-read thermometer to get the exact right temperature for this initial frying stage.

3. To prepare the sauce, place all of the ingredients in a small saucepan and bring the mixture to a simmer. Simmer for 2 minutes, remove the pan from heat, and set the sauce aside.

4. Working in batches to avoid overcrowding the pot, gently slip the chicken wings into the hot oil and fry them for 3 minutes, turning them over halfway through. Transfer the fried wings to a wire rack to drain. The wings will continue to cook as they rest.

5. Once all of the wings have been fried and allowed to rest for at least 3 minutes, warm the oil to 370°F. Gently slip the wings back into the hot oil and fry until they are cooked through and slightly browned and crispy, about 1 minute.

6. Transfer the fried wings to a container, brush them with the sauce, and season with white pepper. Garnish with sesame seeds and serve.

INGREDIENTS:

FOR THE WINGS

15	CHICKEN WINGS
2	TABLESPOONS TAPIOCA STARCH
1	TABLESPOON ALL-PURPOSE FLOUR
	RICE BRAN OIL, AS NEEDED
	WHITE PEPPER, TO TASTE
	WHITE SESAME SEEDS, FOR GARNISH

FOR THE SAUCE

¼	CUP SOY SAUCE
1	TABLESPOON SAKE
3	TABLESPOONS MIRIN
1	TABLESPOON SUGAR
1	TEASPOON GARLIC PASTE

CHICKEN HAM WITH UME SAUCE

YIELD: 4 SERVINGS / **ACTIVE TIME:** 10 MINUTES / **TOTAL TIME:** 2 HOURS AND 10 MINUTES

Chicken ham is an innovative Japanese dish that mimics the texture of ham, yet is crafted entirely from chicken. In this recipe, the chicken ham is paired with a tangy Ume Sauce, adding a lovely contrast to the chicken's savory flavor.

1. Use kitchen shears to cut through the thicker parts of the chicken, aiming to get it as flat as possible. Using a fork, poke holes all over the chicken. Rub the salt and sugar into the chicken and then tightly roll it up, with the side where the skin was on the inside of the roll. Cover the chicken in two or three pieces of plastic wrap, making sure it's completely sealed.

2. Place the water in a pot and bring to a boil. Carefully place the wrapped chicken in the water. Boil for 1 minute and then turn off the heat. Cover the pot with a lid and let the chicken sit in the hot water until it cools down to a point where it can be handled comfortably. This gentle cooking is the key to producing the ham-like texture.

3. When the chicken is cool enough to handle, remove the plastic wrap and cut the chicken into thin slices. Arrange the slices on a plate, drizzle the Ume Sauce over them, and serve.

INGREDIENTS:

⅔ LB. BONELESS, SKINLESS CHICKEN BREASTS

½ TEASPOON KOSHER SALT

½ TEASPOON SUGAR

12 CUPS WATER

UME SAUCE (SEE PAGE 678)

TORIKAWA PONZU

YIELD: 4 SERVINGS / ACTIVE TIME: 20 MINUTES / TOTAL TIME: 30 MINUTES

If you have leftover chicken skin and want to put it to good use, try making this popular and refreshing tapa, which is simple to prepare and offers a delightful mix of textures and flavors.

1. Prepare an ice bath. Place the water and sake in a medium saucepan and bring to a boil. Add the chicken skin and boil for 3 minutes.

2. Transfer the chicken skin to the ice bath and rub and wash it thoroughly. Pat the chicken skin dry with paper towels and cut it into thin strips.

3. Arrange the cucumber on a serving plate and place the strips of chicken skin strips on top. If you prefer to serve the dish colder, cover the plate with plastic wrap and chill it in the refrigerator.

4. Top the dish with the radish and drizzle the ponzu, lemon juice, and sesame oil over the top. Garnish with shichimi togarashi and serve.

INGREDIENTS:

3   CUPS WATER

1   TABLESPOON SAKE

2   OZ. CHICKEN SKIN

1   CUCUMBER, JULIENNED

2   TABLESPOONS GRATED DAIKON RADISH

3   TABLESPOONS PONZU SAUCE (SEE PAGE 45)

1½   TEASPOONS FRESH LEMON JUICE

1½   TEASPOONS SESAME OIL

     SHICHIMI TOGARASHI, FOR GARNISH

BEEF YAWATA MAKI

YIELD: 4 SERVINGS / **ACTIVE TIME**: 15 MINUTES / **TOTAL TIME**: 20 MINUTES

Yawata maki is a traditional dish that wraps vegetables with meat or eel. Initially, this dish featured burdock roots encased in eel or loach. Over time, it has evolved to include a variety of vegetable-and-protein pairings, maintaining its reputation as a visually appealing and flavorful dish.

1. Bring water to a boil in a pot. Prepare an ice bath. Cut the carrot into eight batons that are the same width and length as the green beans.

2. Add the carrots and green beans to the boiling water and cook until they have softened, about 3 minutes. Transfer them to the ice bath and let them cool.

3. Lay the slices of beef on a cutting board, gently stretch them out, and sprinkle some of the flour over them. Place a piece of carrot and a green bean beside each other at each end of the slices of beef and roll the beef up tightly. Sprinkle the remaining flour over the rolls.

4. Place the canola oil in a large skillet and warm it over medium heat. Place the beef rolls in the pan, seam side down, and fry until they are browned all over, turning them as necessary.

5. Place all of the remaining ingredients in a bowl and stir to combine. Pour the sauce into the pan and cook, turning the rolls to coat them with the sauce.

6. Remove the pan from heat. Trim the ends of the beef rolls and cut them into halves or thirds, revealing the colorful vegetable filling inside. Serve immediately.

INGREDIENTS:

1	CARROT, PEELED
8	GREEN BEANS, TRIMMED
4	LARGE SLICES OF THINLY SLICED BEEF
1	TABLESPOON ALL-PURPOSE FLOUR
1	TABLESPOON CANOLA OIL
2	TABLESPOONS SAKE
2	TABLESPOONS MIRIN
2	TABLESPOONS SOY SAUCE
1	TEASPOON SUGAR

Torikawa Ponzu, see page 600

TAKO WASA

YIELD: 4 SERVINGS / **ACTIVE TIME:** 5 MINUTES / **TOTAL TIME:** 8 HOURS AND 5 MINUTES

This refreshing appetizer is a popular dish on izakaya menus. Due to the extensive preparation and resting process involved, it is usually purchased ready-made in pouches. However, this recipe provides a simplified version of the dish that can easily be prepared at home.

1. Cut the octopus into bite-size pieces. Place the kombu, mirin, and sake in a small saucepan and warm the mixture for about 30 seconds, until the smell of alcohol dissipates. Remove the saucepan from heat.

2. Pour the mixture into a resealable plastic bag. Add the octopus, soy sauce, wasabi, and chile to the bag, seal it, and rub the ingredients together. Place the bag in the refrigerator and let the octopus marinate overnight.

3. Remove the octopus from the bag and serve as an appetizer, side dish, or snack.

INGREDIENTS:

3½   OZ. SASHIMI-GRADE OR
      BOILED OCTOPUS

      2-INCH SQUARE OF DRIED
      KOMBU

1   TABLESPOON MIRIN

1   TABLESPOON SAKE

1   TABLESPOON LIGHT SOY
      SAUCE

1½   TEASPOONS WASABI (SEE
      PAGE 500 FOR HOMEMADE)

1   DRIED RED CHILE PEPPER,
      SLICED THIN

UME & BUTTER SQUID STIR-FRY

YIELD: 4 SERVINGS / **ACTIVE TIME:** 10 MINUTES / **TOTAL TIME:** 10 MINUTES

This unique stir-fry breaks the mold by incorporating a distinctly Japanese element—pickled plums. Once you understand the balance of flavors in this sauce, it will open up endless possibilities.

1. Place the butter in a large skillet and melt it over medium heat. Add the squid and mushrooms, season with the salt, and cook, stirring occasionally, until the squid and mushrooms are nicely browned.

2. Add the cabbage and cook, stirring occasionally, until the cabbage has softened slightly.

3. While the vegetables are cooking, combine the Umeboshi, soy sauce, sake, and sugar in a small bowl.

4. Pour the sauce into the pan and stir-fry the mixture until the sauce has thickened.

5. Transfer the mixture to a serving dish. Season with pepper, garnish with the shiso leaves, and serve.

INGREDIENTS:

2 TABLESPOONS UNSALTED BUTTER

⅔ LB. CLEANED SQUID, CHOPPED

2 KING OYSTER MUSHROOMS, CHOPPED

⅛ TEASPOON KOSHER SALT

1 CUP CHOPPED GREEN CABBAGE

6 UMEBOSHI (SEE PAGE 329), SEEDED AND MASHED

2 TABLESPOONS SOY SAUCE

2 TABLESPOONS SAKE

1 TABLESPOON SUGAR

BLACK PEPPER, TO TASTE

6 SHISO LEAVES, SLICED THIN, FOR GARNISH

Tako Wasa, see page 604

ASARI NO SAKAMUSHI

YIELD: 4 SERVINGS / **ACTIVE TIME:** 10 MINUTES / **TOTAL TIME:** 1 HOUR AND 10 MINUTES

In Japan, the most popular way to prepare clams is by steaming them in sake. If you are fortunate enough to have access to fresh clams, give it a try!

1. Place the water and salt in a large bowl and stir to combine. Rinse the clams under cold water and add them to the bowl of salt water. Let the clams soak for 1 hour.

2. Drain the clams and rinse them under cold water. Transfer the clams to a large pot and add the sake. Bring to a simmer over medium heat. Once the sake begins to bubble slightly, reduce the heat to maintain a gentle simmer. Cover the pot and steam the clams until the majority of them have opened, about 5 minutes. Discard any clams that did not open.

3. Add the butter and soy sauce to the pot and gently shake the pot to incorporate them.

4. Divide the clams among the serving plates, garnish with green onions, and serve.

INGREDIENTS:

2 CUPS WATER

2 TEASPOONS KOSHER SALT

1 LB. CLAMS

3 TABLESPOONS SAKE

1½ TEASPOONS UNSALTED BUTTER

1 TEASPOON LIGHT SOY SAUCE

GREEN ONIONS, CHOPPED, FOR GARNISH

TANUKI HIYAYAKKO

Hiyayakko transforms chilled tofu into a refreshing and simple dish, elegantly served with soy sauce and a variety of toppings like green onions, ginger, and dried bonito flakes. While traditionally presented in a square shape, this adaptation slices the tofu for convenience. Hiyayakko allows for numerous toppings, and this recipe highlights my favorite one, a delightful combination of textures and flavors that enhance the delicate taste of the tofu.

1. Wrap the tofu in a paper towel and let it rest for 10 minutes.

2. Cut the tofu into slices or cubes and arrange them on a serving plate. Generously top each slice with some of the bonito flakes, Tenkasu, and green onion.

3. Pour the soy sauce and then the sesame oil over the tofu, sprinkle the sesame seeds over the top, garnish with the kizami nori, and serve.

INGREDIENTS:

¾   LB. SILKEN TOFU, DRAINED

2   TABLESPOONS BONITO FLAKES

2   TABLESPOONS TENKASU (SEE PAGE 68)

1   TABLESPOON FINELY CHOPPED GREEN ONION

1½   TEASPOONS SOY SAUCE

1½   TEASPOONS SESAME OIL

1   TEASPOON SESAME SEEDS

1   TEASPOON KIZAMI (SHREDDED) NORI, FOR GARNISH

TOFU STEAK

YIELD: 2 SERVINGS / **ACTIVE TIME:** 10 MINUTES / **TOTAL TIME:** 20 MINUTES

Tofu steak transforms the typically understated tofu into the star of the dish. In this recipe, the tofu is prepared teriyaki style, featuring a rich and savory sauce that enhances its flavor and produces a perfect appetizer or side dish.

1. Wrap the tofu in a paper towel, place it in the microwave, and microwave on high for 2 minutes.

2. While the tofu is in the microwave, place the soy sauce, mirin, sake, sugar, garlic, ginger, and chili bean sauce in a small bowl and whisk to combine. Set the sauce aside.

3. Remove the tofu from the microwave, remove the paper towel, and let the tofu cool. When the tofu is cool enough to handle, cut the tofu into thick slices.

4. Place the canola oil in a large skillet and warm it over medium heat. Place the tapioca starch in a shallow bowl and dredge the tofu in it. Place the tofu in the pan and fry until it is crispy all over, turning it as necessary.

5. Pour the sauce into the pan and toss until the tofu is evenly coated.

6. Transfer the tofu to a serving plate, garnish with green onions, bonito flakes, and shichimi togarashi, and serve.

INGREDIENTS:

14	OZ. FIRM TOFU, DRAINED
1½	TABLESPOONS SOY SAUCE
1½	TABLESPOONS MIRIN
1½	TABLESPOONS SAKE
1½	TEASPOONS SUGAR
1	TEASPOON GARLIC PASTE
½	TEASPOON GINGER PASTE
½	TEASPOON CHILI BEAN SAUCE
2	TABLESPOONS CANOLA OIL
2	TABLESPOONS TAPIOCA STARCH
	GREEN ONIONS, CHOPPED, FOR GARNISH
	BONITO FLAKES, FOR GARNISH
	SHICHIMI TOGARASHI, FOR GARNISH

TAMAGOYAKI

YIELD: 2 SERVINGS / ACTIVE TIME: 15 MINUTES / TOTAL TIME: 15 MINUTES

In Japan, tamagoyaki is usually prepared in a square frying pan tailored for the preparation. However, such specialized pans may not be readily available outside Japan, prompting a need for alternative methods. This recipe is designed for those with access only to a standard round skillet, ensuring that even without the specialized equipment, you can achieve a beautiful and delicious result.

1. Crack the eggs into a bowl and beat until scrambled. Add the sugar, soy sauce, salt, and water and whisk until the mixture is well combined and smooth.

2. Warm a skillet over high heat, add the canola oil, and spread it evenly across the pan with a paper towel.

3. Once the pan is hot, reduce the heat to medium-low.

4. Pour one-third of the egg mixture into the center of the pan and tilt it until the mixture covers the pan. As the egg begins to set, fold two opposing sides in toward the center to create parallel edges. Carefully roll the omelet up from the back to the front.

5. Push the omelet to the back edge of the pan and pour in another one-third of the egg mixture while carefully lifting up the omelet; this will help bind it to the raw egg mixture. As it starts to set, repeat the process in Step 4.

6. Repeat the process with the remaining egg mixture.

7. Remove the tamagoyaki from the pan and immediately cover it with plastic wrap to help it achieve the proper shape. For a more defined shape, you can also use a sushi mat to gently roll the tamagoyaki into the proper form.

8. Let the tamagoyaki cool slightly so that its shape becomes set. Unwrap it, slice it, and serve.

INGREDIENTS:

2	EGGS
1	TEASPOON SUGAR
½	TEASPOON LIGHT SOY SAUCE
⅛	TEASPOON KOSHER SALT
1	TABLESPOON WATER
1	TEASPOON CANOLA OIL

STIR-FRIED EDAMAME

YIELD: 6 SERVINGS / **ACTIVE TIME:** 5 MINUTES / **TOTAL TIME:** 5 MINUTES

Edamame is a popular snack in Japan, usually enjoyed alongside beer. However, in this recipe, I take a step further from the traditional method of boiling the edamame with salt. Instead, I season the edamame to improve its flavor, making it the perfect companion for a beer or cocktail. If you're using frozen edamame that already contains salt, make sure to decrease the amount of added salt accordingly to avoid overseasoning.

1. Place a large skillet over low heat and add the frozen edamame. Cook, stirring occasionally, until all of the water the edamame releases has evaporated.

2. Raise the heat to high, add the sesame oil, salt, pepper, and dashi granules, and stir-fry until the edamame is evenly coated and the ingredients are well combined.

3. Transfer the edamame to a serving bowl, garnish with shichimi togarashi, and serve.

INGREDIENTS:

¾ LB. FROZEN EDAMAME IN PODS

1 TABLESPOON SESAME OIL

½ TEASPOON KOSHER SALT

¼ TEASPOON GROUND BLACK PEPPER

¼ TEASPOON DASHI GRANULES

SHICHIMI TOGARASHI, FOR GARNISH

WAFU ADDICTIVE CABBAGE

YIELD: 4 SERVINGS / **ACTIVE TIME:** 5 MINUTES / **TOTAL TIME:** 5 MINUTES

Yamitsuki kyabetsu, or Addictive Cabbage, is a straightforward-yet-irresistible cabbage dish commonly found in izakaya and yakiniku restaurants in Japan. This version builds upon one of my blog's most beloved recipes, infusing it with a distinctly Japanese flair to produce a novel taste experience.

1. Cut the green cabbage into large bite-size pieces.

2. Place the sesame oil, ground sesame seeds, dashi granules, salt, Japanese mustard, and shichimi togarashi in a large mixing bowl and stir to combine. Add the cabbage and toss until the cabbage is evenly coated.

3. Using your hands, massage and gently crush the cabbage, making it more tender and helping it absorb the dressing. Serve once the flavor and texture are to your liking.

INGREDIENTS:

¼ LB. GREEN CABBAGE

1½ TABLESPOONS SESAME OIL

1 TABLESPOON GROUND SESAME SEEDS

½ TEASPOON DASHI GRANULES

¼ TEASPOON KOSHER SALT

¼ TEASPOON JAPANESE MUSTARD

¼ TEASPOON SHICHIMI TOGARASHI

Stir-Fried Edamame, see page 614

NASU DENGAKU

YIELD: 4 SERVINGS / **ACTIVE TIME:** 15 MINUTES / **TOTAL TIME:** 30 MINUTES

Dengaku is a traditional dish of grilled eggplant, tofu, or the root vegetable konnyaku coated with a sweet miso-based sauce. It has been enjoyed in Japan since the 1500s and is a speciality dish of Aichi Prefecture, where it commonly features the local red miso.

1. Prepare a grill for medium heat (about 400°F). Wash the eggplants and pat them dry with paper towels. Cut the eggplants in half lengthwise and make shallow diagonal incisions in a crosshatch pattern on the flesh of the eggplants, taking care not to cut through the skin.

2. Place the eggplants on the grill, skin side up. Grill until the flesh has grill marks on it, about 3 minutes. Turn the eggplants over and grill until the skin is lightly charred and the flesh is tender, about 5 minutes.

3. While the eggplants are grilling, place the yellow miso, sake, sesame oil, brown sugar, and mirin in a saucepan and bring to a boil over medium-high heat, stirring continually. Reduce the heat to low and let the sauce simmer for a few minutes, stirring occasionally. Remove the pan from heat and set the sauce aside.

4. Remove the eggplants from the grill and generously brush the sauce onto the flesh of the eggplants.

5. Return the eggplants to the grill with the flesh facing up. Cook until the sauce begins to develop a slightly dark appearance. Remove the eggplants from the grill and transfer them to a serving plate.

6. Garnish with sesame seeds and shiso leaves and serve.

INGREDIENTS:

2   JAPANESE OR CHINESE EGGPLANTS

2   TABLESPOONS YELLOW MISO PASTE

2   TABLESPOONS SAKE

1½   TEASPOONS TOASTED SESAME OIL

1½   TEASPOONS LIGHT BROWN SUGAR

1   TEASPOON MIRIN

    SESAME SEEDS, FOR GARNISH

    SHISO LEAVES, SLICED THIN, FOR GARNISH

ERYNGII STEAK

YIELD: 2 SERVINGS / **ACTIVE TIME:** 5 MINUTES / **TOTAL TIME:** 10 MINUTES

Eryngii mushrooms, or king oyster mushrooms, reign supreme in the culinary world thanks to their uniquely meaty texture. This recipe celebrates their regal qualities by transforming them into steaks.

1. Cut the mushrooms into segments that are just shy of 1 inch long. On the cut surface of each piece, carefully make three to four cuts in a crosshatch pattern on both sides. The depth and pattern of these cuts will help to create a wonderful texture when the mushrooms are cooked.

2. Warm a large skillet over medium-high heat. Add the butter and wait until it's melted and slightly bubbling. Place the mushrooms in the pan, season with the salt and pepper, and cook until they are nicely browned on both sides, turning occasionally.

3. Pour the soy sauce over the mushrooms. The heat of the pan will cause the soy sauce to sizzle and reduce slightly, creating a rich glaze. Turn off the heat and gently stir to evenly coat the mushrooms with the glaze.

4. Transfer the mushrooms to a serving bowl. While they're still hot, top them with the radish. Garnish with shichimi togarashi and green onions and serve.

INGREDIENTS:

4 KING OYSTER MUSHROOMS

2 TABLESPOONS UNSALTED BUTTER

PINCH OF KOSHER SALT

PINCH OF BLACK PEPPER

2 TABLESPOONS SOY SAUCE

2 TABLESPOONS GRATED DAIKON RADISH

SHICHIMI TOGARASHI, FOR GARNISH

GREEN ONIONS, FINELY CHOPPED, FOR GARNISH

Eryngii Steak, see page 619

MUGEN CABBAGE

The term mugen, which translates to "infinite" in Japanese, has sparked a culinary trend in which straightforward yet exceptionally tasty dishes are labeled "mugen XX," suggesting that they're so good one could enjoy them endlessly. Often focusing on vegetable-based creations, this naming trend emphasizes both simplicity and irresistible flavor.

1. In a large microwave-safe bowl, combine the cabbage, tuna, garlic, sesame oil, chicken bouillon, and salt. Cover the bowl with plastic wrap and microwave on high for 3 minutes.

2. Remove the bowl from the microwave, carefully remove the plastic wrap, and stir the mixture. Transfer it to a serving plate, season with pepper, garnish with bonito flakes and sesame seeds, and serve.

INGREDIENTS:

¼ GREEN CABBAGE, SHREDDED

5 OZ. CANNED TUNA IN WATER, DRAINED

½ TEASPOON GARLIC PASTE

2 TABLESPOONS SESAME OIL

1 TEASPOON CHINESE CHICKEN BOUILLON

¼ TEASPOON KOSHER SALT

BLACK PEPPER, TO TASTE

BONITO FLAKES, FOR GARNISH

SESAME SEEDS, FOR GARNISH

YATAIMESHI
(STREET FOOD)

*Y*ataimeshi, Japanese street food, has long been a beloved part of festival culture in Japan. Unlike in other Asian countries where street food is deeply integrated into daily life, in Japan, it's primarily associated with festivals or simple evening snacks. While historically limited to specific events or evening hours, recent years have seen a rise in mobile street food vendors who use vans to bring their delicious bites to a wider audience. Yataimeshi represents a unique aspect of Japanese culture, blending convenience with traditional flavors.

TAKOYAKI

YIELD: 4 SERVINGS / **ACTIVE TIME:** 30 MINUTES / **TOTAL TIME:** 40 MINUTES

Takoyaki, a beloved local delicacy from Osaka, is made by encasing pieces of octopus and various condiments in a flour-based batter and cooking them into spherical treats. Celebrated as Osaka's most popular street food, takoyaki is renowned for its crispy exterior and gooey interior. For those who may not be fond of octopus, alternative fillings such as shrimp, squid, or king oyster mushrooms are good options.

1. To prepare the sauce, place all of the ingredients in a small bowl and whisk to combine. Set the sauce aside.

2. To begin preparations for the takoyaki, place the dashi, soy sauce, and egg in a mixing bowl and whisk to combine. Sift the flour into a separate bowl, make a well in the center, and gradually pour the dashi mixture into the well, whisking until the resulting mixture comes together as a smooth batter.

3. Warm a takoyaki pan over medium heat and generously coat the wells with sesame oil. Pour the batter into the wells, filling them halfway. Place a piece of octopus in the center of the batter and then cover it with more batter, filling the wells completely. Sprinkle the Benishoga, green onion, and Tenkasu over the top.

4. Let the takoyaki cook for 1 to 2 minutes. Using a long bamboo skewer, draw lines between the wells, dividing the batter around each takoyaki. Roll the takoyaki over approximately halfway by scraping the skewer around the edge of the wells, working your wrist in a circular motion. It's OK if they still look messy at this point. Cook the takoyaki for a few more minutes and then roll them over again, tucking any misshapen parts into the bottom to firm up their round shape.

5. Brush the takoyaki with sesame oil and roll them occasionally to ensure even cooking. Swap the paler takoyaki into the wells containing the more golden brown ones to ensure that they all are cooked evenly, crispy, and golden brown. The centers of the takoyaki may still be a bit runny, which is normal.

6. Remove the cooked takoyaki from the pan and place them on a plate. Brush them with the sauce, top with mayonnaise, aonori powder, and bonito flakes, and serve.

INGREDIENTS:

FOR THE SAUCE

- 1½ TABLESPOONS WORCESTERSHIRE SAUCE
- 1½ TEASPOONS SOY SAUCE
- 1½ TEASPOONS KETCHUP
- 1 TABLESPOON HONEY
- ⅛ TEASPOON DASHI GRANULES

FOR THE TAKOYAKI

- 2½ CUPS AWASE DASHI STOCK, COOLED (SEE PAGE 38)
- 1½ TEASPOONS LIGHT SOY SAUCE
- 1 LARGE EGG
- 1 CUP CAKE FLOUR
- SESAME OIL, AS NEEDED
- 4 OZ. BOILED OCTOPUS, CUT INTO SMALL PIECES
- ¼ CUP BENISHOGA (SEE PAGE 315), FINELY DICED
- ¼ CUP FINELY DICED GREEN ONION
- ¼ CUP TENKASU (SEE PAGE 68)
- JAPANESE MAYONNAISE (SEE PAGE 46), FOR GARNISH
- AONORI POWDER, FOR GARNISH
- BONITO FLAKES, FOR GARNISH

OSAKA-STYLE OKONOMIYAKI

YIELD: 2 SERVINGS / **ACTIVE TIME:** 30 MINUTES / **TOTAL TIME:** 1 HOUR

Okonomiyaki, often translated as Japanese savory pancakes, stands as a celebrated emblem of Osaka's teppanyaki (hibachi in the US) street food culture. While premade okonomiyaki kits are commonly used in Japan for convenience, crafting this dish from scratch with regular flour is surprisingly straightforward.

1. To begin preparations for the okonomiyaki, sift the flour into a large bowl, add the water, dashi granules, milk, and 1 egg, and gently stir until the mixture just comes together as a smooth batter, taking care not to overmix. Cover the bowl with plastic wrap and chill the batter in the refrigerator for 30 minutes.

2. To prepare the sauce, place all of the ingredients in a small bowl and whisk to combine. Set the sauce aside.

3. Divide the batter between two bowls. Warm a large skillet over medium to medium-high heat. Divide the cabbage, Tenkasu, green onion, and remaining eggs between the bowls of batter and stir until well combined. Chill one portion of the batter in the refrigerator.

4. Add the canola oil to the pan and swirl to coat. Pour one portion of the batter into the pan and shape it with a spatula. Lay half of the pork belly on top and cook until the bottom of the okonomiyaki is brown and crispy. Carefully flip it over, cover the pan with a lid, reduce the heat to medium-low, and cook until the pork belly and okonomiyaki are cooked all the way through. To test the okonomiyaki for doneness, a toothpick inserted into its center should come out clean.

5. Remove the okonomiyaki from the pan and brush half of the prepared sauce over it. Garnish with half of the mayonnaise, bonito flakes, and aonori powder and serve.

6. Repeat Steps 4 and 5 with the remaining okonomiyaki batter, sauce, and garnishes.

INGREDIENTS:

FOR THE OKONOMIYAKI

¾	CUP CAKE FLOUR
5	TABLESPOONS WATER
2	TEASPOONS DASHI GRANULES
1	TEASPOON WHOLE MILK
3	EGGS
2½	CUPS CHOPPED GREEN CABBAGE
2	TABLESPOONS TENKASU (SEE PAGE 68)
2	TABLESPOONS FINELY CHOPPED GREEN ONION
2	TABLESPOONS CANOLA OIL
4–6	THIN SLICES OF COOKED PORK BELLY
1	TABLESPOON JAPANESE MAYONNAISE (SEE PAGE 46), FOR GARNISH
1	TABLESPOON BONITO FLAKES, FOR GARNISH
1	TEASPOON AONORI POWDER, FOR GARNISH

FOR THE SAUCE

1	TABLESPOON WORCESTERSHIRE SAUCE
1	TABLESPOON OYSTER SAUCE
2	TABLESPOONS KETCHUP
1	TABLESPOON HONEY
1	TEASPOON SOY SAUCE

HIROSHIMA-STYLE OKONOMIYAKI

YIELD: 2 SERVINGS (1 PANCAKE) / **ACTIVE TIME:** 20 MINUTES / **TOTAL TIME:** 30 MINUTES

In Hiroshima, okonomiyaki is completely different than it is in Osaka. It is layered, features a thin, crepe-like batter, and contains yakisoba noodles.

---

1. To prepare the sauce, place all of the ingredients in a small bowl and whisk to combine. Set the sauce aside.

2. To begin preparations for the okonomiyaki, place half of the canola oil in a large skillet and warm it over medium-high heat. Add the ramen noodles and fry until they are slightly crispy. Pour half of the sauce over the noodles, stirring until they are evenly coated. Remove the pan from heat and set the fried noodles aside.

3. Place the remaining canola oil in a clean large skillet and warm it over medium-low heat. Use a paper towel to spread the canola oil over the pan and wipe away any excess.

4. Place the flour, water, dashi granules, and sugar in a measuring cup and whisk until the mixture comes together as a smooth batter. Pour three-quarters of the batter into the center of the pan, spreading it out with the back of a spoon. Layer the cabbage, ikaten, and bean sprouts on top of the batter and drizzle the remaining batter over the top of these ingredients so that it covers them and will hold them. Top the crepe with the pork belly and cover the pan with a lid. Cook for 5 minutes.

5. Uncover the pan, carefully turn the crepe over, cover the pan, and cook until the pork belly and crepe are cooked through, about 5 minutes. Transfer the crepe to a plate and set it aside.

6. Crack the egg into a bowl, add the salt, and whisk to combine. Wipe out the pan with a paper towel and lightly coat it with canola oil. Pour the egg mixture into the pan, swirling the pan so that the egg coats the bottom. Cook until it's about 80 percent done. Top with the fried noodles and then carefully place the crepe on top of the noodles, with the bottom of the crepe facing up. Loosen the edges of the egg with a spatula and flip the entire okonomiyaki onto a plate, with the egg on top.

7. Brush the okonomiyaki with the remaining sauce, garnish with the green onion and Benishoga, and serve.

INGREDIENTS:

FOR THE SAUCE

- 1 TABLESPOON WORCESTERSHIRE SAUCE
- 1 TABLESPOON OYSTER SAUCE
- 2 TABLESPOONS KETCHUP
- 1 TABLESPOON HONEY
- 1 TEASPOON SOY SAUCE

FOR THE OKONIMIYAKI

- 1 TABLESPOON CANOLA OIL, PLUS MORE AS NEEDED
- 1 SERVING OF COOKED RAMEN NOODLES (SEE PAGE 372 FOR HOMEMADE)
- 3 TABLESPOONS CAKE FLOUR
- ¼ CUP WATER
- ⅛ TEASPOON DASHI GRANULES
- ⅛ TEASPOON SUGAR
- 2 CUPS SHREDDED GREEN CABBAGE
- ¼ CUP IKATEN (SQUID TEMPURA) OR TENKASU (SEE PAGE 68)
- 1 CUP BEAN SPROUTS
- 3½ OZ. PORK BELLY, SLICED THIN
- 1 EGG

  PINCH OF KOSHER SALT
- 1 TABLESPOON FINELY DICED GREEN ONION, FOR GARNISH
- 1 TABLESPOON BENISHOGA (SEE PAGE 315), FOR GARNISH

Osaka-Style Okonomiyaki, see page 630

TONPEIYAKI

YIELD: 2 SERVINGS / **ACTIVE TIME:** 15 MINUTES / **TOTAL TIME:** 15 MINUTES

Known as "easy okonomiyaki" in English, tonpeiyaki is a dish that can be described as a cross between an omelet and okonomiyaki. It is a classic Kansai dish and is popular at many teppanyaki restaurants and izakayas in western Japan.

1. To prepare the sauce, place all of the ingredients in a small bowl and whisk to combine. Set the sauce aside.

2. To begin preparations for the tonpeiyaki, crack the eggs into a large mixing bowl, add the milk, and whisk until well combined. Set the mixture aside.

3. Place the canola oil in a large skillet and warm it over medium heat. Add the cabbage and green onion, season with the salt and pepper, and stir-fry until the cabbage has softened slightly, 5 to 7 minutes. Transfer the mixture to a plate.

4. Add the pork belly and cook over medium heat until both sides are seared and it is crispy and cooked through, 4 to 6 minutes. Transfer the pork belly to the plate with the cabbage mixture.

5. Reduce the heat to medium-low and remove any excess fat from the pan, leaving just enough to cook the egg mixture. Pour the egg mixture into the pan. Once the eggs are half-cooked and still slightly runny on top, arrange the cabbage mixture in a line down the center of the eggs. Place the pork belly on top of the cabbage and carefully fold the sides of the eggs over the filling, forming them into an omelet shape. While cooking the eggs, reduce the heat if necessary to prevent the bottom from browning too much.

6. Carefully turn the tonpeiyaki out onto a plate and drizzle the sauce over it. Garnish with the mayonnaise, bonito flakes, and aonori powder and serve.

INGREDIENTS:

FOR THE SAUCE

1	TABLESPOON WORCESTERSHIRE SAUCE
1	TABLESPOON OYSTER SAUCE
2	TABLESPOONS KETCHUP
2	TEASPOONS HONEY
1	TEASPOON SOY SAUCE

FOR THE TONPEIYAKI

2	EGGS
2	TABLESPOONS WHOLE MILK
1	TEASPOON CANOLA OIL
1	CUP SHREDDED GREEN CABBAGE
1	TABLESPOON FINELY CHOPPED GREEN ONION
	PINCH OF KOSHER SALT
	PINCH OF BLACK PEPPER
4	THIN SLICES OF PORK BELLY
1	TEASPOON JAPANESE MAYONNAISE (SEE PAGE 46), FOR GARNISH
1	TEASPOON BONITO FLAKES, FOR GARNISH
½	TEASPOON AONORI POWDER, FOR GARNISH

YAKISOBA

YIELD: 3 SERVINGS / **ACTIVE TIME:** 10 MINUTES / **TOTAL TIME:** 15 MINUTES

Yakisoba, with its roots in Chinese chow mein, has evolved into a distinct and popular dish in Japan, frequently served at festivals and for a quick lunch. While many households in Japan opt for convenient store-bought yakisoba kits, this recipe guides you through the process. The secret? A dash of curry powder.

1. To prepare the sauce, place all of the ingredients in a small bowl and whisk to combine. Set the sauce aside.

2. To begin preparations for the yakisoba, place the water in a large pot and bring to a boil. Add the salt and half of the canola oil and let the water return to a boil. Place the cabbage in a colander and submerge it in the boiling water. Let it cook for 1 minute, drain the cabbage, and set it aside.

3. Add the noodles to the boiling water and cook them according to the directions on the package or in the recipe. Drain the noodles and set them aside.

4. While the noodles are cooking, place the remaining canola oil in a large skillet or wok and warm it over medium-high heat. Add the onion, carrot, and pork belly and stir-fry until the pork is crispy, 4 to 6 minutes.

5. Add the cooked noodles and cabbage to the pan. Pour the prepared sauce over the dish and sprinkle the bonito flakes over it. Stir-fry until the noodles are well coated with the sauce and the ingredients are evenly distributed.

6. Cook until most of the liquid has evaporated or been absorbed and the noodles are glossy.

7. Transfer the yakisoba to a serving dish, garnish with aonori powder and Benishoga, and serve.

INGREDIENTS:

FOR THE SAUCE

1	TABLESPOON SAKE
1	TABLESPOON OYSTER SAUCE
1	TABLESPOON SOY SAUCE
1	TABLESPOON WORCESTERSHIRE SAUCE
1	TEASPOON YELLOW MISO PASTE
1	TEASPOON SUGAR
½	TEASPOON CHINESE CHICKEN BOUILLON
1	TEASPOON GRATED GARLIC
1	TEASPOON GRATED FRESH GINGER
¼	TEASPOON JAPANESE CURRY POWDER (SEE PAGE 65)
1	TABLESPOON BONITO FLAKES, CRUSHED

FOR THE YAKISOBA

8	CUPS WATER
¼	TEASPOON KOSHER SALT
2	TEASPOONS CANOLA OIL
2	CUPS CHOPPED GREEN CABBAGE
2	SERVINGS OF RAMEN NOODLES (SEE PAGE 372 FOR HOMEMADE)
½	ONION, SLICED THIN
½	CARROT, PEELED AND JULIENNED
5	OZ. PORK BELLY, SLICED THIN AND CHOPPED
1	TABLESPOON BONITO FLAKES
	AONORI POWDER, FOR GARNISH
	BENISHOGA (SEE PAGE 315), FOR GARNISH

SHIO & LEMON YAKISOBA

YIELD: 4 SERVINGS / **ACTIVE TIME:** 15 MINUTES / **TOTAL TIME:** 15 MINUTES

In Japan, the most popular version of yakisoba is the Worcestershire sauce–based version, but shio yakisoba, which features a lighter, salt-based seasoning, comes in a close second. This recipe introduces a twist on the beloved dish, infusing it a refreshing burst of lemon.

1. To prepare the sauce, place all of the ingredients in a bowl and whisk to combine. Set the sauce aside.

2. To begin preparations for the yakisoba, place half of the canola oil in a large skillet and warm it over medium-high heat. Add the noodles to the pan and cook until they are crispy and golden brown, stirring to prevent them from sticking. Transfer the noodles to a plate and set them aside.

3. Add the remaining canola oil and warm it. Add the seafood mixture, carrots, and cabbage, season with the salt and pepper, and stir-fry until the vegetables have softened slightly.

4. Add the garlic chives and noodles to the pan and drizzle the sauce over the dish. Stir-fry until the sauce has been fully absorbed by the noodles.

5. Transfer the yakisoba to a serving dish, garnish with the shiso leaves and kizami nori, and serve with the lemon slices or wedges.

INGREDIENTS:

FOR THE SAUCE

ZEST AND JUICE OF 1 LEMON

1 TEASPOON KOSHER SALT

¼ TEASPOON BLACK PEPPER

½ TEASPOONS SUGAR

1 TEASPOON LIGHT SOY SAUCE

2 TABLESPOONS SAKE

1 TEASPOON GRATED GARLIC

1½ TEASPOONS SESAME OIL

2 TEASPOONS DASHI GRANULES

1½ TEASPOONS WHITE SESAME SEEDS

2 TABLESPOONS FINELY CHOPPED GREEN ONIONS

FOR THE YAKISOBA

2 TABLESPOONS CANOLA OIL

4 SERVINGS OF COOKED RAMEN NOODLES (SEE PAGE 372 FOR HOMEMADE)

1 LB. SEAFOOD MIXTURE

2 CARROTS, PEELED AND JULIENNED

4 CUPS CHOPPED GREEN CABBAGE

PINCH OF KOSHER SALT

PINCH OF BLACK PEPPER

1 CUP CHOPPED GARLIC CHIVES (1-INCH-LONG PIECES)

10 SHISO LEAVES, SLICED THIN, FOR GARNISH

¼ CUP KIZAMI (SHREDDED) NORI, FOR GARNISH

1 LEMON, SLICED OR CUT INTO WEDGES, FOR SERVING

YAKIUDON

YIELD: 2 SERVINGS / **ACTIVE TIME:** 10 MINUTES / **TOTAL TIME:** 15 MINUTES

Yakiudon is a stir-fry made with udon noodles, meat, vegetables, and a medley of seasonings. The key distinction lies in the flavoring: while yakisoba typically features a tangy sauce, yakiudon embraces a distinctly Japanese profile with a soy sauce and dashi–based sauce.

1. Bring water to a boil in a large saucepan. While you wait, measure out the sake, soy sauce, bonito flakes, dashi granules, sugar, and ginger and set them aside. Place the cabbage in a colander and submerge it in the boiling water. Cook for 1 minute, drain the cabbage, and set it aside.

2. Add the noodles to the boiling water and cook them for 2 minutes less than directed on the package or in the recipe. Drain the noodles, rinse them under cold water, and drain again. Add the sesame oil, toss to combine, and set the noodles aside.

3. Warm a large skillet over medium-high heat. Add the pork belly, season it with the salt and black pepper, and fry until the pork belly is slightly crispy, 4 to 6 minutes.

4. Add the carrot and bell pepper to the pan and stir-fry until the carrot is just tender, 5 to 7 minutes.

5. Add the bean sprouts and stir-fry for 1 minute. Add the noodles and all of the measured-out ingredients and stir-fry until most of the liquid has evaporated, 3 to 5 minutes.

6. Transfer the yakiudon to a serving dish, garnish with the sesame seeds, green onions, Onsen Tamago, and Benishoga, and serve.

INGREDIENTS:

2	TABLESPOONS SAKE
1	TABLESPOON SOY SAUCE
2	TABLESPOONS BONITO FLAKES, CRUSHED
1	TEASPOON DASHI GRANULES
¼	TEASPOON SUGAR
1	TEASPOON GRATED FRESH GINGER
2	CUPS CHOPPED GREEN CABBAGE
2	SERVINGS OF UDON NOODLES (SEE PAGE 414 FOR KHOMEMADE)
1	TABLESPOON SESAME OIL
5	OZ. PORK BELLY, SLICED THIN AND CHOPPED
	PINCH OF KOSHER SALT
	PINCH OF BLACK PEPPER
½	CARROT, PEELED AND JULIENNED
½	CUP JULIENNED GREEN BELL PEPPER
1	CUP BEAN SPROUTS
	WHITE SESAME SEEDS, FOR GARNISH
	GREEN ONIONS, FINELY CHOPPED, FOR GARNISH
	ONSEN TAMAGO (SEE PAGE 57), FOR GARNISH
	BENISHOGA (SEE PAGE 315), FOR GARNISH

NIKUMAKI ONIGIRI

YIELD: 3 SERVINGS / **ACTIVE TIME:** 10 MINUTES / **TOTAL TIME:** 20 MINUTES

Nikumaki onigiri offers a unique and satisfying twist on the traditional rice ball, featuring a core of rice enveloped in thinly sliced pork belly. While pork belly is recommended for its flavor, the recipe is adaptable to other cuts of pork, so long as they are sliced thin.

1. Divide the rice into six equal portions. Carefully form each portion into a compact ball, making sure they will hold their shapes.

2. Take a slice of pork and wrap it around a rice ball. Take another slice of pork and wrap in the opposite direction of the first to completely cover up the rice. You want a nice, tight wrap that conceals the rice entirely. If you have any excess pork, trim it with scissors to prevent overlapping and use it for the other rice balls. Repeat with the remaining rice balls and pork.

3. Place the cornstarch on a plate and roll the rice balls in it until they are lightly coated.

4. Place the canola oil in a large skillet and warm it over medium heat. Carefully place the rice balls in the pan and cook, turning occasionally, until they are golden brown and crispy all over and the pork is cooked through, 6 to 8 minutes.

5. Place the sake, soy sauce, mirin, sugar, ginger, and garlic in a bowl and whisk to combine.

6. Drain any excess oil from the pan, raise the heat to high, and pour the sake mixture over the rice balls. Cook, turning the balls to coat them evenly, until the mixture has reduced to a thick, syrupy glaze.

7. Sprinkle sesame seeds over the rice balls. Serve with the shiso leaves, using them to wrap the rice balls—adding a touch of freshness and keeping everyone's hands clean.

INGREDIENTS:

2	CUPS PERFECT JAPANESE RICE (SEE PAGE 80)
9	THIN SLICES OF PORK (EACH ABOUT 1 FOOT LONG)
1	TABLESPOON CORNSTARCH
1½	TEASPOONS CANOLA OIL
3	TABLESPOONS SAKE
3	TABLESPOONS SOY SAUCE
2	TABLESPOONS MIRIN
1	TABLESPOON SUGAR
1	TEASPOON GRATED FRESH GINGER
1	TEASPOON GRATED GARLIC
	SESAME SEEDS, FOR GARNISH
6	SHISO LEAVES, FOR SERVING

SWEET KUSHI DANGO

YIELD: 6 SERVINGS / **ACTIVE TIME:** 20 MINUTES / **TOTAL TIME:** 40 MINUTES

Dango is a traditional Japanese snack made with rice dumplings, and is most commonly served on skewers (kushi). Dango can be sweet or savory—we opt for the former here.

1. Soak six wooden skewers in a glass of water. Place the flour, tapioca starch, and sugar in a microwave-safe bowl and whisk to combine, breaking up any lumps of sugar. Add the water and whisk until the mixture is smooth.

2. Cover the bowl with plastic wrap, place it in the microwave, and microwave on high for 1½ minutes. Remove the bowl from the microwave, remove the plastic wrap, and knead the mixture with a rice paddle. Cover the bowl with the plastic wrap, return it to the microwave, and microwave on high for 1 minute. Remove the bowl from the microwave, remove the plastic wrap, and knead the mixture again with a rice paddle. Cover the bowl with the plastic wrap, return it to the microwave, and microwave on high for 30 seconds.

3. Remove the dough from the microwave and knead it with the rice paddle. Scoop it onto a large piece of plastic wrap. Cover the dough with another piece of plastic wrap (I usually use the one from the bowl) and roll it out until it is about ½ inch thick. Let the dough cool for 5 to 10 minutes.

4. Remove the plastic wrap and fold the dough in half twice. Cover it with the plastic wrap and roll out again. Repeat this process until the dough is smooth, about 5 minutes.

5. Cut the dough in half and roll each piece into a long cylinder. Cut each cylinder into nine equal pieces, each about 1 inch in diameter.

6. Fill a bowl with cold water and lightly moisten your hands with it. Roll the pieces into balls, moistening your hands any time the dough becomes too sticky to handle.

7. Thread the balls of dough onto the skewers, gently twisting them to help ease them onto the skewers without misshaping them.

8. Warm a nonstick skillet over medium heat and place the skewered dango in it. Cook until browned on both sides, 4 to 8 minutes, turning them over halfway through. Serve with the Anko or Mitarashi Sauce, drizzling the latter over the dango.

INGREDIENTS:

- 2.7 OZ. RICE FLOUR
- 2 TABLESPOONS TAPIOCA STARCH
- ¼ CUP SUGAR
- ¾ CUP HOT WATER (160°F)
- 6 TABLESPOONS ANKO (SEE PAGE 646), FOR TOPPING (OPTIONAL)

  MITARASHI SAUCE (SEE PAGE 678), FOR TOPPING (OPTIONAL)

DESSERTS

Japanese sweets fall into two completely different categories: yōcgashi and wagashi. Yōcgashi are Western-inspired desserts adapted to Japanese tastes, while wagashi are traditional Japanese confections. Wagashi, in particular, is known for its simple flavors and intricate aesthetics, often considered an art form. These meticulously crafted confections require professional skill and are best appreciated as edible art when visiting Japan. The contrast between yōcgashi and wagashi show-cases the diversity in Japanese confectionery, from Western-influenced creations to traditional sweets that embody centuries of cultural refinement.

ANKO

YIELD: 6 SERVINGS / ACTIVE TIME: 20 MINUTES / TOTAL TIME: 1 HOUR AND 45 MINUTES

Anko is a sweet paste made from boiled adzuki beans and sugar, and it is one of the most common ingredients in Japanese desserts, frequently appearing in mochi, sweet dumplings, bread, and doughnuts, and even as a spread on toast. The two main types of anko are chunky tsubuan which contains crushed whole beans, and the smoother koshian, which is made by removing the skins and grinding the beans into a smooth and refined paste. Directions on preparing both of these are included below.

1. Wash the beans and remove any that seem damaged. Pour them into a pot, cover them with water by 1 to 2 inches, and bring to a boil over medium heat. Cook for 10 to 15 minutes and drain the beans, which will help remove the astringency from them.

2. Rinse out the pot, add the beans, and once again cover them with water by 1 to 2 inches. Place a drop lid or parchment paper on the surface, bring to a boil, and reduce the heat so that the beans simmer. Cook for 40 minutes to 1 hour, checking the pot occasionally to ensure the beans are always submerged and adding more water as necessary. Skim off any foam that forms around the edge of the lid.

3. Test the beans by running a few under cold water and mashing them between your fingers. The beans are completely cooked when their insides feel smooth. If they feel grainy or their cores are still hard, continue cooking the beans and repeat this test every 5 to 10 minutes. When the beans are fully cooked, remove the pot from heat.

4. To produce tsubuan anko, drain the beans through a fine-mesh sieve and transfer them to a clean pot. Add ½ cup of water and bring to a simmer over medium-low heat, stirring continually while gently mashing the beans. Add the sugar and brown sugar in three increments, making sure that each addition has completely dissolved before adding the next increment. Cook until the mixture has thickened and you can draw a line through it and see the bottom of the pot. Stir in the salt and remove the pot from heat.

5. To produce koshian anko, place a fine-mesh sieve over a large heatproof bowl and drain the beans, reserving the cooking liquid in the bowl. Use a pestle or wooden spoon to crush and grind the beans, working them through the sieve until only their skins remain. Lift the sieve and pour fresh water through it to catch any leftover pulp. Wait a few minutes for the bean paste to settle to the bottom of the bowl. Drain the top of the water, top it up with

INGREDIENTS:

1	CUP ADZUKI BEANS
⅔	CUP SUGAR
⅓	CUP LIGHT BROWN SUGAR
¼	TEASPOON KOSHER SALT

more water, and let the beans settle for a few minutes again. Repeat this process three times.

6. Pour the mixture through a piece of cheesecloth and squeeze until you are left with a pale, crumbly paste.

7. Place ½ cup water, the sugar, and brown sugar in a clean pot and warm over medium-low heat, stirring continually. When the sugars have dissolved, add the bean paste to the pot and stir continually until the mixture has thickened and you can draw a line through it and see the bottom of the pot. Remove the pot from heat and stir in the salt. The paste will firm up more as it cools.

8. Transfer the anko to a container and let it cool to room temperature. Cover and chill in the refrigerator until ready to use. You can also divide the anko into individual portions and freeze it for long-term storage.

ICHIGO DAIFUKU

YIELD: 6 SERVINGS / **ACTIVE TIME:** 30 MINUTES / **TOTAL TIME:** 45 MINUTES

This is a classic Japanese sweet that encases fresh, tart strawberries and sweet red bean paste in a soft and stretchy rice dough called gyuhi.

1. Fill a pot halfway with water and bring it to a boil over medium-high heat. Place the flour and sugar in a mixing bowl and whisk to combine. Add the water and work the mixture until it comes together as a smooth batter.

2. Line a heatproof container small enough to fit in your steaming basket, but large enough to hold the mixture, with a large piece of scrunched-up parchment paper. Make sure the parchment paper goes up the sides of the container, as this will prevent the mochi batter from leaking out. Pour the batter into the parchment paper and wrap the steaming basket's lid with a kitchen towel to prevent water droplets from forming. Place the lid on the steaming basket, place it over the boiling water, and steam the batter, stirring it twice in the first 5 minutes. Reduce the heat to medium and steam the mochi until it is set and translucent, 10 to 12 minutes.

3. While the mochi is steaming, sprinkle 3 tablespoons of corn-starch over a baking sheet. Dust a rubber spatula with cornstarch. When the mochi is done, turn off the heat and remove the con-tainer from the steaming basket. Carefully lift the parchment paper out of the container and scrape the mochi onto the cornstarch, spreading it evenly. Sprinkle the remaining cornstarch over the top of the mochi and let it cool for 5 to 10 minutes.

4. While the mochi is cooling, divide the Anko into six portions and roll them into balls. Wash the strawberries, pat them dry with paper towels, and cut off the stems.

5. Generously dust your hands with cornstarch and keep a small bowl of cornstarch nearby. Use your hands to spread and flatten the mochi on the tray until it is about ⅛ inch thick. Dust your hands with cornstarch if the mochi becomes too sticky.

6. Cut the dough into six pieces and wrap the balls of Anko with them, pinching the edges together to seal the Anko within. Flip the dough over so that the seams are hidden underneath. Dip your fin-gers in the cornstarch any time the dough starts to stick. Place the filled ichigo daifuku back on the cornstarch-dusted baking sheet while you work on the others. Transfer the ichigo daifuku to a plate and brush them to remove any excess cornstarch. Using kitchen scissors, cut a slit across their centers, open up the slits, and place a strawberry inside each one. Serve immediately.

INGREDIENTS:

- ¾ CUP GLUTINOUS RICE FLOUR (MOCHIKO OR SHIRATAMAKO)
- 3 TABLESPOONS SUGAR
- ⅔ CUP WATER
- ¼ CUP CORNSTARCH, PLUS MORE AS NEEDED
- 5.2 OZ. KOSHIAN ANKO (SEE PAGE 646)
- 6 STRAWBERRIES

CHOMEIJI SAKURA MOCHI, KANTO STYLE

YIELD: 10 SERVINGS / **ACTIVE TIME**: 30 MINUTES / **TOTAL TIME**: 1 HOUR AND 30 MINUTES

Sakura mochi is a traditional Japanese sweet typically enjoyed during cherry blossom season. This seasonal delicacy comes in two regional variations: the Kansai version, known for the sticky texture derived from domyojiko, a dried glutinous rice, and the Kanto version, characterized by its crepe-like wrapping. This preparation employs the latter style.

1. Place the salted cherry blossom leaves in a bowl of cold water and let them soak for 1 hour.

2. Drain the leaves and pat them dry with paper towels. Divide the Anko into 10 portions and form them into cylinders.

3. Warm a large nonstick skillet over low heat. Place the flours and sugar in a mixing bowl and stir to combine. Add the water and food coloring and whisk until the mochi batter is smooth and light pink.

4. Place a small amount of the canola oil in the pan and spread it around with a paper towel. Wipe away any excess to prevent hot spots.

5. Place 1 tablespoon of the batter in the pan and spread it out lengthwise, making a long oval that is about 2 x 4½ inches. Repeat until you can't fit any more mochi in the pan, making sure to leave plenty of space between each oval. Cook until air bubbles start to appear on the surface, flip the mochi over, and cook the other side for 30 seconds to 1 minute.

6. Transfer the cooked mochi to a plate to cool and repeat with the remaining batter.

7. When the mochi are cool enough to handle, wrap them around the cylinders of red bean paste. Wrap the cherry blossom leaves around the mochi and serve. The cherry blossom leaves are edible, so you can enjoy the mochi with or without the leaves, according to your preference.

INGREDIENTS:

10	SALTED CHERRY BLOSSOM LEAVES
8.8	OZ. KOSHIAN ANKO (SEE PAGE 646)
¼	CUP GLUTINOUS RICE FLOUR
⅓	CUP ALL-PURPOSE FLOUR
1	TABLESPOON SUGAR
½	CUP WATER
1	SMALL DROP OF RED FOOD COLORING
½	TEASPOON CANOLA OIL

Ichigo Daifuku, see page 648

WARABI MOCHI

YIELD: 4 SERVINGS / **ACTIVE TIME:** 20 MINUTES / **TOTAL TIME:** 1 HOUR AND 15 MINUTES

Warabi mochi is a traditional dessert from Kyoto made with starch derived from the bracken fern's rhizome, known in Japanese as warabiko. Although not technically mochi, it has a wonderful stretchy texture and is one of the most-loved wagashi in Japan.

1. To begin preparations for the mochi, sift the matcha powder (if using) into a bowl, add the sugar and bracken starch, and whisk to combine. Add the water and work the mixture until the sugar, starch, and matcha have dissolved.

2. Place a strainer over a medium saucepan and pour the mixture into the pan through the strainer. Place the pan on the stove and warm the mixture over medium heat, stirring continually with a silicone spatula. Scrape the bottom of the pan regularly to prevent the mixture from burning. When the mixture starts to thicken, reduce the heat to low and continue to cook until the mixture becomes thick and translucent with a viscous texture. Remove the pan from heat.

3. Transfer the mixture to a container and spread it out until it is about 1 inch thick. Let the mixture cool to room temperature. Cover the container and chill the mochi in the refrigerator for 1 hour.

4. While the mochi is chilling, prepare the syrup. Place all of the ingredients in a small saucepan and bring to a boil over medium heat. Reduce the heat to low and simmer until the syrup has thickened slightly, 2 to 3 minutes. Remove the pan from heat and let the syrup cool. Pour it into a measuring cup or mason jar.

5. Remove the mochi from the refrigerator and cut it into bite-size pieces.

6. To prepare the kinako powder, place all of the ingredients in a bowl and whisk to combine. Roll the warabi mochi in the powder, drizzle the syrup over them, and serve immediately.

INGREDIENTS:

FOR THE MOCHI

1½ TEASPOONS MATCHA POWDER (OPTIONAL)

3 TABLESPOONS SUGAR

3 TABLESPOONS BRACKEN STARCH OR TAPIOCA STARCH

1 CUP WATER

FOR THE SYRUP

2 TABLESPOONS DARK BROWN SUGAR

2 TABLESPOONS SUGAR

3 TABLESPOONS WATER

FOR THE KINAKO POWDER

1 TABLESPOON ROASTED SOYBEAN POWDER

½ TEASPOON MATCHA POWDER (OPTIONAL)

1 TABLESPOON SUGAR

PINCH OF KOSHER SALT

OHAGI

YIELD: 8 SERVINGS / ACTIVE TIME: 30 MINUTES / TOTAL TIME: 2 HOURS

Ohagi, also known as botamochi, is a traditional Japanese sweet made by lightly crushing cooked glutinous rice (mochigome) and shaping it into a ball. There are two main variations of ohagi, one is wrapped with sweet bean paste, while the other is filled with the paste and then coated in roasted soybean powder. They are often enjoyed during the spring and autumn equinoxes and supposedly ward off bad luck.

1. Place the glutinous rice into a bowl and cover it with cold water. Gently swish the rice and drain it. Repeat this process three times.

2. After the final rinse, cover the rice with cold water and let it soak for 30 minutes.

3. Drain the rice and let it dry for 5 minutes. Place it in a heavy-bottomed pot and add the water. Cover the pot with a lid and bring the rice to a boil over a medium heat. Let it boil for 30 seconds, reduce the heat to low, and simmer the rice for 7 minutes.

4. Turn the heat to high and cook for 10 seconds. Turn off the heat and let the rice steam on the warm stove for 15 minutes. Resist the urge to remove the lid while the rice is steaming.

5. Form the Anko into four balls for wrapping (approximately 2½ tablespoons each) and four balls for filling (approximately 1½ tablespoons each). Place them on a plate, cover them with plastic wrap, and chill the balls of Anko in the refrigerator.

6. Place the roasted soybean powder in a container, add sugar and salt to taste, whisk to combine, and set the mixture aside.

7. Uncover the pot and stir the sugar and salt into the cooked rice, mixing thoroughly while mashing the grains of rice. Once half of the rice has been mashed, transfer the rice to a wide container, cover it with plastic wrap, and let it cool.

8. When the rice is cool enough to handle, wet your hands and form the rice into eight balls—four large balls, and four small balls. Take one of the large rice balls, place it on a piece of plastic wrap, and flatten it. Place one of the small balls of Anko in the center of the rice and form the rice around it until the Anko is no longer visible. Roll the ball in the roasted soybean powder mixture until it is completely coated. Repeat with the remaining large rice balls and small balls of Anko. Place a large ball of Anko on a piece of plastic wrap and flatten it. Place a small rice ball in the center and form the Anko around it until the rice ball is no longer visible. Repeat with the remaining large balls of Anko and small balls of rice. Serve immediately.

INGREDIENTS:

¾ CUP MOCHIGOME (SWEET GLUTINOUS RICE)

¾ CUP WATER

1 CUP ANKO (SEE PAGE 646)

1 TABLESPOON ROASTED SOYBEAN POWDER

2 TEASPOONS SUGAR, PLUS MORE TO TASTE

PINCH OF KOSHER SALT, PLUS MORE TO TASTE

Warabi Mochi, see page 652

KURI YOKAN

YIELD: 10 SERVINGS / **ACTIVE TIME:** 15 MINUTES / **TOTAL TIME:** 1 HOUR AND 45 MINUTES

Yokan is a traditional wagashi made with anko and kanten powder, a plant-based gelling agent made from red algae. This jelly-like dessert has a pleasantly firm texture, and the addition of candied chestnuts adds a luxurious touch.

1. Drain the candied chestnuts and reserve 2 tablespoons of the syrup. Cut the chestnuts into halves or quarters. Sprinkle water over a 6 x 3–inch loaf pan and arrange half of the chestnuts in the bottom of the pan. Set the other half of the chestnuts aside.

2. Place the kanten powder and brown sugar in a saucepan and stir to combine. Add the water gradually, whisking continually to prevent lumps from forming. Place the pan on the stove and bring the mixture to a boil over medium heat, stirring continually. Boil the mixture for 2 minutes.

3. Turn off the heat and add the Anko in three increments, whisking until each addition has been incorporated and the mixture is smooth before adding the next. Set the heat to low and cook the mixture, stirring continually, until small bubbles appear around the edge of the pan. Turn off the heat and stir in the reserved syrup and salt.

4. Fill a large pot with cold water and place the pan with the yokan in the water. Stir the yokan for 5 minutes to help it cool. It will thicken slightly as it cools.

5. Pour the yokan into the loaf pan, sprinkle the remaining chestnuts evenly over the top, and gently push down on them with a spoon to submerge them in the yokan. Smooth the top of the yokan and pop any air bubbles with a toothpick.

6. Let the yokan cool at room temperature for 20 to 30 minutes. Place it in the refrigerator and chill for 1 hour.

7. Remove the yokan from the pan, cut it into thick slices, and serve.

INGREDIENTS:

10   CANDIED CHESTNUTS IN SYRUP

1½   TEASPOONS KANTEN POWDER

1   TABLESPOON LIGHT BROWN SUGAR

1   CUP WATER

10½   OZ. KOSHIAN ANKO (SEE PAGE 646)

PINCH OF KOSHER SALT

ANMITSU

YIELD: 6 SERVINGS / **ACTIVE TIME:** 40 MINUTES / **TOTAL TIME:** 1 HOUR AND 30 MINUTES

Anmitsu is a traditional dessert made with cubes of kanten jelly topped with red bean paste, fruits, and soft mochi (gyuhi or shiratama dango). Anmitsu dates back to the Meiji Era and is often served with whipped cream or ice cream and drizzled with kuromitsu, a bittersweet syrup made with dark brown sugar.

1. To begin preparations for the kanten jelly, place the kanten powder and sugar in a saucepan and whisk to combine. Gradually add 1 cup of water, whisking to incorporate it. Bring the mixture to a boil over medium heat, stirring occasionally. Set a timer for 2 minutes. After 2 minutes, add the remaining water and stir until thoroughly combined. Remove the pan from heat and pour the mixture into a square 7-inch cake pan. Let the mixture cool for about 20 minutes. Place it in the refrigerator and chill until it is set.

2. While the kanten jelly is setting, prepare the syrup. Place all of the ingredients in a medium saucepan and bring to a boil over medium heat, stirring continually to dissolve the sugars. Stop stirring once it starts to boil and tilt the pan occasionally to prevent the syrup from burning. Boil the syrup until it has thickened slightly, about 5 minutes. Remove the pan from heat and pour the syrup into a measuring cup or mason jar.

3. Bring a pot of water to a rolling boil. To begin preparations for the dango, place the shiratamako in a bowl and gradually incorporate the water. Use your hands to knead the mixture until it comes together as a smooth, not-tacky dough. If the dough is too crumbly, incorporate water 1 teaspoon at a time until it has the proper texture.

4. Divide the dough into 12 pieces and roll them into 1-inch balls. Gently drop the balls into the boiling water. When all of the balls are floating, set a timer for 2 minutes and prepare an ice bath. After 2 minutes, use a strainer to scoop out the dango. Place them in the ice bath and let them cool.

5. Remove the kanten jelly from the refrigerator, cut it into 1-inch cubes, and divide it among serving bowls. Drain the dango and top each portion with these, the fruits, Anko, and whipped cream or ice cream. Drizzle the kuromitsu syrup over the top and serve.

INGREDIENTS:

FOR THE KANTEN JELLY

1½	TEASPOONS KANTEN POWDER
3	TABLESPOONS SUGAR
2	CUPS WATER

FOR THE SYRUP

¼	CUP DARK BROWN SUGAR
¼	CUP SUGAR
½	CUP WATER

FOR THE DANGO

½	CUP SHIRATAMAKO (GLUTINOUS RICE FLOUR)
¼	CUP WATER, PLUS MORE AS NEEDED
1	KIWI, PEELED, HALVED LENGTHWISE AND CUT INTO 12 HALF-MOONS, FOR TOPPING
12	SEGMENTS OF MANDARIN ORANGE (CANNED OR FRESH), FOR TOPPING
6	PEACH SLICES (CANNED OR FRESH), FOR TOPPING
6	MARASCHINO CHERRIES, FOR TOPPING
10½	OZ. ANKO (SEE PAGE 646), FOR TOPPING
	WHIPPED CREAM OR ICE CREAM, FOR TOPPING

SILKY CUSTARD PURIN

YIELD: 4 TO 6 SERVINGS / **ACTIVE TIME:** 20 MINUTES / **TOTAL TIME:** 4 HOURS AND 30 MINUTES

A much-loved dessert consisting of a simple caramel topped with silky custard.

1. To begin preparations for the custard, place the milk and sugar in a microwave-safe bowl and whisk until the sugar has dissolved. Sprinkle the gelatin over the mixture, gently stir, and let the gelatin bloom for 5 to 10 minutes.

2. To begin preparations for the caramel, place the sugar in a saucepan and add 2 tablespoons of water. Stir until the sugar has dissolved, place the pan on the stove, and warm the mixture over low heat. When the mixture starts to bubble, resist the urge to mix it. If the pan has hot spots, swirl it occasionally to ensure that the mixture cooks evenly.

3. When the caramel starts to turn golden, add 1 tablespoon of water. Make sure to stand back from the stove and wear protective gloves in case the caramel spatters. Cook until the caramel turns amber, remove it from heat, and carefully add the remaining water. Swirl the pan to incorporate the water and cool the caramel. Divide the caramel between 4 to 6 ramekins and let it cool for a few minutes. Transfer the ramekins to the refrigerator and let the caramel set.

4. When the gelatin has bloomed, place the milk mixture in the microwave and microwave on high for 2 minutes. Remove the mixture from the microwave, stir it well, and return it to the microwave. Microwave on high in 20- to 30-second increments, stirring after each one, until the gelatin has completely dissolved.

5. Place the eggs, heavy cream, and vanilla in a bowl and whisk to combine. Add a small amount of the hot milk mixture and whisk to temper the egg mixture. While gently whisking continually, gradually add all of the remaining milk mixture.

6. Strain the custard through a fine-mesh sieve to ensure that it is smooth.

7. Remove the ramekins from the refrigerator and pour the custard over the caramel, leaving a little room at the top of the ramekins to prevent spills.

8. Cover the ramekins with plastic wrap and chill the purin in the refrigerator for at least 3 to 4 hours before serving. If time allows, chill the purin overnight.

INGREDIENTS:

FOR THE CUSTARD

1¼ CUPS WHOLE MILK

¼ CUP SUGAR

¼ OZ. UNFLAVORED GELATIN

3 PASTEURIZED EGGS

½ CUP HEAVY CREAM

½ TEASPOON PURE VANILLA EXTRACT

FOR THE CARAMEL

¼ CUP SUGAR

¼ CUP HOT WATER

Silky Custard Purin, see page 659

COFFEE JELLY

YIELD: 4 SERVINGS / **ACTIVE TIME:** 10 MINUTES / **TOTAL TIME:** 4 HOURS AND 10 MINUTES

This is a popular summertime treat crafted from robust black coffee and a touch of sweetener, and it often comes topped with a dollop of fresh whipped cream.

1. Place 1 cup of water in a bowl and sprinkle the gelatin over it. Gently stir and let the gelatin bloom for 5 minutes.

2. Place the remaining water in a saucepan and bring to a boil. Remove the pan from heat, let the water cool for a few minutes, and then add the espresso powder and 2 to 3 tablespoons of sugar. Stir until they have completely dissolved.

3. Pour the sweetened coffee mixture into the gelatin mixture and stir until the gelatin has dissolved.

4. Divide the coffee jelly among four ramekins and let it cool to room temperature. Chill it in the refrigerator until it has set, about 4 hours.

5. Place the heavy cream in a chilled mixing bowl, add the vanilla and remaining sugar, and whip until the mixture is thick. Top each portion of coffee jelly with the whipped cream and serve immediately.

INGREDIENTS:

2 CUPS WATER

½ OZ. UNFLAVORED GELATIN

2 TABLESPOONS INSTANT ESPRESSO POWDER

2–3 TABLESPOONS SUGAR, PLUS 1 TABLESPOON FOR THE WHIPPED CREAM

½ CUP HEAVY CREAM

2 DROPS OF PURE VANILLA EXTRACT

DORAYAKI

YIELD: 8 SERVINGS / **ACTIVE TIME**: 30 MINUTES / **TOTAL TIME**: 50 MINUTES

Dorayaki is a delicious sweet snack made by sandwiching red bean paste between two castella-inspired pancakes, though it can also be made with other fillings such as whipped cream, custard, and chestnuts.

1. Crack the eggs into a bowl, add the sugar, honey, and mirin, and whisk until the mixture is pale and well combined. Place the baking soda and water in a separate bowl and stir to combine. Add this mixture to the egg mixture and whisk to combine. Sift the flour over the mixture and whisk until the resulting mixture is smooth. Add the milk and whisk until the mixture comes together as a smooth batter. Cover the bowl with plastic wrap and chill the batter in the refrigerator for 30 minutes.

2. Warm a large nonstick skillet over low heat for 5 to 10 minutes. Place a small amount of the canola oil in the pan and spread into a thin, even layer with a paper towel.

3. Remove the batter from the refrigerator and pour 1½ teaspoons of the mixture into the pan for each pancake. Fry the pancakes in batches of two or three, depending on the size of your pan. Cover the pan with a lid and cook until bubbles appear on top of the pancakes. Turn the pancakes over and fry on the other side for 30 seconds. Transfer the cooked pancakes to a plate and loosely tent them with aluminum foil.

4. Spoon about 2 tablespoons of red bean paste over half of the pancakes, spreading it thick in the middle and thinner on the edges. Place the other half of the pancakes on top and gently press the edges of the dorayaki to seal. Serve immediately or cover with plastic wrap and store them in the refrigerator if serving later.

INGREDIENTS:

2	EGGS
6	TABLESPOONS SUGAR
1	TABLESPOON HONEY
1	TEASPOON MIRIN
½	TEASPOON BAKING SODA
½	TEASPOON WATER
4	OZ. CAKE FLOUR
¼	CUP WHOLE MILK
1	TEASPOON CANOLA OIL
10½	OZ. ANKO (SEE PAGE 646)

Coffee Jelly, see page 662

CASTELLA

YIELD: 16 SERVINGS / **ACTIVE TIME:** 30 MINUTES / **TOTAL TIME:** 25 HOURS

Castella is a sweet honey-flavored cake known for its iconic rectangular shape. The cake was introduced to Japan by Portuguese merchants in the sixteenth century and has since become a specialty of Nagasaki, and a staple confection across Japan.

1. Measure out all of the ingredients. Place the egg whites and egg yolks in separate bowls and cover them. Let all of the ingredients come to room temperature, sitting for about 20 minutes.

2. Line a square 7-inch cake pan with parchment paper and sprinkle the turbinado sugar over it. Sift the flours twice, combine them, and set the mixture aside.

3. Preheat the oven to 350°F. Whip the egg whites with a handheld mixer on medium until they are foamy. Add the caster sugar in three increments, whipping until each addition is fully incorporated before adding the next increment. Continue to whip the mixture until it holds stiff peaks. Add the egg yolks to the meringue one at a time, whipping for 5 to 10 seconds to incorporate each one. Drizzle the honey into the meringue and whip for 10 seconds before switching to a rubber spatula to work the mixture.

4. Sift the flours into the meringue in three increments, gently folding to incorporate each increment and making sure not remove too much air from the mixture.

5. Place the milk and canola oil in a small bowl and whisk to combine. Add 2 to 3 tablespoons of the batter to the bowl and whisk to combine. Pour the milk mixture into the remaining batter and fold to incorporate it.

6. Pour the batter into the cake pan and tap it on the counter to remove any large air bubbles. Use a skewer or chopstick to draw lines on the surface of the batter, moving back and forth three times for each line.

7. Place the pan on the top rack in the oven and bake for 10 minutes. Move the cake to the middle rack, reduce the oven's temperature to 320°F, and bake until a toothpick inserted into the center of the cake comes out clean, 30 to 40 minutes. Check the cake frequently around the 30-minute mark.

8. Remove the cake from the oven and tap it on the counter to prevent it from sinking. Let the cake cool in the pan for a few minutes. Remove it from the pan and cover it with plastic wrap. Place the warm cake in a container with a lid, cover it, and let it rest for 24 hours. Trim the edges of the cake and cut it in half. Cut the cake into thick slices and serve.

INGREDIENTS:

3	EGG WHITES
4	EGG YOLKS
1	TABLESPOON TURBINADO SUGAR
3½	OZ. BREAD FLOUR
2½	TABLESPOONS CAKE FLOUR
⅔	CUP CASTER (SUPERFINE) SUGAR
2	TABLESPOONS HONEY
2	TABLESPOONS WHOLE MILK
2	TABLESPOONS CANOLA OIL

MATCHA & ADZUKI POUND CAKE

YIELD: 8 TO 10 SERVINGS / **ACTIVE TIME:** 20 MINUTES / **TOTAL TIME:** 1 HOUR

Matcha is a high-quality green tea powder traditionally served as part of Japanese tea ceremonies. These days, Western-style cakes and confections often feature this profoundly Japanese flavor, which is earthy yet refreshing.

1. Preheat the oven to 350°F. Line a 7 x 3–inch loaf pan with parchment paper.

2. Crack the eggs into a measuring cup, add the milk and vanilla, and gently whisk to combine. Set the mixture aside.

3. Sift the flour and matcha into a mixing bowl and whisk to combine. Remove 1 tablespoon of the mixture and set it aside. Add the baking powder and salt to the mixing bowl and whisk to combine.

4. Place the butter in the work bowl of a stand mixer fitted with the paddle attachment and beat until it is smooth. Add the sugar and beat to incorporate. With the mixer running, gradually pour the egg mixture into the work bowl a little at a time. Add the dry mixture in three increments and beat until the resulting mixture comes together as a smooth batter.

5. Sprinkle the reserved matcha mixture over the adzuki beans and toss to coat. Add them to the batter and fold until they are evenly distributed.

6. Pour the batter into the loaf pan and place it on the middle rack in the oven. Bake until a toothpick inserted into the center of the cake comes out clean, 40 to 50 minutes.

7. Remove the cake from the oven and let it cool in the pan for a few minutes. Remove the cake from the pan, transfer it to a wire rack, and let it cool completely before slicing and serving.

INGREDIENTS:

2	EGGS, AT ROOM TEMPERATURE
1½	TABLESPOONS WHOLE MILK, AT ROOM TEMPERATURE
2–3	DROPS OF PURE VANILLA EXTRACT
3½	OZ. CAKE FLOUR, SIFTED
1	TABLESPOON MATCHA POWDER
½	TEASPOON BAKING POWDER
	PINCH OF KOSHER SALT
3½	OZ. BUTTER, SOFTENED
½	CUP SUGAR
½	CUP COOKED ADZUKI BEANS, PATTED DRY

STRAWBERRY SHORTCAKE

YIELD: 4 TO 6 SERVINGS / **ACTIVE TIME:** 30 MINUTES / **TOTAL TIME:** 1 HOUR AND 30 MINUTES

This shortcake is Japan's favorite cake to celebrate with, and suitable for any festive occasion.

1. To begin preparations for the shortcake, coat a round 6-inch cake pan with butter and line it with parchment paper. Preheat the oven to 350°F. Separate the eggs, placing egg whites in a clean glass bowl, and the egg yolks in a separate bowl. Set the egg yolks aside. Add the lemon juice to the egg whites and whisk until the mixture is foamy. Add the caster sugar in three increments and whip the mixture with a handheld mixer on medium until the mixture is glossy and holds stiff peaks.

2. Add the egg yolks to the mixture one at a time, whipping for 10 seconds to incorporate each one. Sift the flour into a separate mixing bowl. Add the whipped egg white mixture to it in three increments, folding to incorporate.

3. Place the butter and milk in a small microwave-safe bowl, place it in the microwave, and microwave on high until the butter has melted, 20 to 30 seconds. Add 1 to 2 tablespoons of the cake batter and stir until well combined. Pour the milk mixture into the rest of the batter and carefully fold to incorporate it, taking care not to overmix the batter.

4. Pour the batter into the cake pan and tap it on the counter to remove any large air bubbles. Place it in the oven and bake until it is golden brown, 22 to 26 minutes, checking on it frequently around the 20-minute mark. Remove the cake from the oven and tap it on the counter.

5. Remove the cake from the pan immediately and let it cool on a wire rack for 1 hour. While the cake is cooling, chill a mixing bowl in the freezer.

6. To prepare the syrup, place all of the ingredients in a small microwave-safe bowl, place it in the microwave, and microwave for 1 minute. Remove the syrup from the microwave, stir to combine, and let it cool.

7. Place the heavy cream, confectioners' sugar, and vanilla in the chilled bowl and whip until the mixture holds stiff peaks.

8. Cut the cake in half at the equator and brush the top of each piece with the syrup. Spread some of the whipped cream over one piece and top it with the sliced strawberries. Place the other piece of cake on top, cover the entire cake with the remaining whipped cream, top it with the whole strawberries, and garnish with mint. Refrigerate the cake and enjoy it within 2 days.

INGREDIENTS:

FOR THE SHORTCAKE

- 1½ TABLESPOONS UNSALTED BUTTER, MELTED, PLUS MORE AS NEEDED
- 2 EGGS, AT ROOM TEMPERATURE
- ½ TEASPOON FRESH LEMON JUICE
- 6 TABLESPOONS CASTER (SUPERFINE) SUGAR
- 1¾ OZ. CAKE FLOUR, SIFTED
- 1 TABLESPOON WHOLE MILK
- 1¼ CUPS HEAVY WHIPPING CREAM, CHILLED
- 3 TABLESPOONS CONFECTIONERS' SUGAR, PLUS MORE FOR TOPPING
- ¼ TEASPOON PURE VANILLA EXTRACT
- 16 STRAWBERRIES, HALF SLICED THIN, HALF LEFT WHOLE

  FRESH MINT, FOR GARNISH

FOR THE SYRUP

- 2 TABLESPOONS CASTER (SUPERFINE) SUGAR
- 2½ TABLESPOONS WATER
- 1 TABLESPOON LIQUEUR (OPTIONAL)

MATCHA RARE CHEESECAKE

YIELD: 6 TO 8 SERVINGS / **ACTIVE TIME:** 30 MINUTES / **TOTAL TIME:** 8 HOURS AND 30 MINUTES

This is Japan's take on no-bake cheesecake. It is typically made with yogurt to give it a lighter taste and a slightly tangy flavor, and is often stabilized with gelatin. This variation of the recipe highlights the earthy flavor of matcha, which perfectly pairs with the other ingredients. If using an 8- or 9-inch springform pan, double the recipe.

1. Line a 6-inch springform pan with parchment paper and coat the edge with butter. Place the graham crackers in a resealable plastic bag, add the melted butter, and massage the butter into the graham crackers until no dry crumbs remain, shaking the bag occasionally. Pour the mixture into the pan and press it flat with the back of a wooden spoon or a heavy glass. Chill the crust in the refrigerator while you make the filling.

2. Place the cream cheese in a large microwave-safe bowl and whisk until it is smooth. If the cream cheese is too stiff, microwave it on high for 20 to 30 seconds. Add the yogurt, vanilla, and confectioners' sugar and whisk until well combined. Set the mixture aside for now.

3. Place the water in a small microwave-safe bowl, sprinkle the gelatin over the top, and stir to combine. Let the gelatin bloom for 5 to 10 minutes.

4. Place several ice cubes in a large mixing bowl and place a smaller bowl on top of them. Add ¼ cup of the heavy cream and gradually sift in the matcha while whipping the mixture with a handheld mixer on medium. When the matcha is fully incorporated and there are no lumps, add the remaining heavy cream and whip until the mixture holds firm peaks.

5. Combine the matcha cream and cream cheese mixture. Place the gelatin mixture in the microwave and microwave on high in 20- to 30-second increments, stirring between each one, until the gelatin has dissolved. Pour the gelatin mixture into the filling mixture and stir until it has been evenly distributed.

6. Remove the crust from the refrigerator and pour the filling over the top. Smooth the top with a rubber spatula, cover the pan with plastic wrap, and chill the cheesecake in the refrigerator overnight.

7. Use a warm knife to loosen the edge of the cheesecake and remove it from the pan. Transfer it to a serving plate, top with berries and additional matcha, and serve.

INGREDIENTS:

3	TABLESPOONS UNSALTED BUTTER, MELTED, PLUS MORE AS NEEDED
¾	CUP CRUSHED GRAHAM CRACKERS
1	CUP CREAM CHEESE
5.3	OZ. PLAIN YOGURT
1–2	DROPS OF PURE VANILLA EXTRACT
½	CUP CONFECTIONERS' SUGAR
1	TABLESPOON WATER
1	TEASPOON UNFLAVORED GELATIN
¾	CUP HEAVY WHIPPING CREAM
1½	TABLESPOONS MATCHA POWDER, PLUS MORE FOR TOPPING
	FRESH BERRIES, FOR TOPPING

SUITO POTETO

YIELD: 10 SERVINGS / **ACTIVE TIME:** 30 MINUTES / **TOTAL TIME:** 1 HOUR

Suito poteto is a creamy, cake-like dessert shaped to resemble the sweet potatoes which provide its unique flavor. This is a seasonal snack, most commonly enjoyed in the fall.

INGREDIENTS:

1	LB. JAPANESE SWEET POTATOES
2	TABLESPOONS UNSALTED BUTTER
2	TABLESPOONS SUGAR
2	TABLESPOONS HEAVY CREAM OR WHOLE MILK
2	TEASPOONS HONEY
¼	TEASPOON PURE VANILLA EXTRACT
1–2	EGG YOLKS
	BLACK SESAME SEEDS, FOR TOPPING

1. Fill a pot with cold water. Peel the sweet potatoes and cut them into similar-sized pieces, placing them in the pot as you go to prevent discoloration. Place the pot on the stove, bring to a gentle boil over medium heat, and cook until the sweet potatoes are fork-tender, 15 to 20 minutes.

2. Drain the sweet potatoes and mash until they are completely smooth. Add the butter and stir to combine. Add the remaining ingredients, except for the egg yolks and sesame seeds, and stir until well combined.

3. Transfer the mixture to a saucepan and warm it over the lowest possible heat, stirring continually until the moisture has evaporated and the mixture is thick enough to cling to a wooden spoon.

4. Scoop the mixture into a wide container, spread it thin, and let it cool.

5. Preheat the oven to 360°F. When the mixture is cool enough to handle, divide it into 10 equal portions and form each one into a football-shape. Wrap the base of each suito poteto with aluminum foil and place them on a baking sheet.

6. Place the egg yolks in a small bowl and whisk to combine. Generously brush the tops and sides of the suito poteto with the egg wash. Sprinkle black sesame seeds in the center of the suito poteto, place them on the top rack in the oven, and bake until they are golden brown, 10 to 15 minutes.

7. Remove the suito poteto from the oven and let them cool to room temperature. Chill them in the refrigerator before serving.

DAIGAKU IMO

YIELD: 4 SERVINGS / ACTIVE TIME: 20 MINUTES / TOTAL TIME: 35 MINUTES

Daigaku imo is an addictive snack featuring Japanese sweet potatoes coated in a sweet glaze. It is believed to get its unusual name, which translates to "university potato," from the fact that it is much loved by college students.

1. Wash the sweet potatoes, gently rubbing them to remove any dirt or debris. Fill a bowl with cold water and add the salt. Cut the ends off the sweet potatoes and cut them into ½-inch-thick slices. Cut each round vertically into thirds, place them in the bowl of salted water, and let them soak for 5 minutes.

2. Drain the sweet potatoes and pat them dry with paper towels. Place them in a pot and cover them with rice bran oil. Place the pot on the stove and warm over medium heat. Check the heat occasionally and don't let it exceed 360°F. Cook until the sweet potatoes are crispy and golden brown. Remove one piece from the hot oil and check to see that the inside is soft. When they are soft inside, transfer the sweet potatoes to a wire rack to drain.

3. Place a glass of cold water beside the stove. Line a nonstick baking sheet with a Silpat mat and place it beside the stove. Place the caster sugar, mirin, water, and vinegar in a heavy-bottom bottom, stir to combine, and warm over low heat, stirring until the sugar has dissolved. Stop mixing as soon as the caramel starts to bubble. Cook the caramel until it turns golden. Dip a chopstick into it and plunge the caramel it into the glass of cold water. If it hardens, it's ready. Test the caramel every 20 to 30 seconds until it is ready.

4. Carefully add the soy sauce and black sesame seeds to the caramel and quickly stir to combine.

5. Add the sweet potatoes and turn off the heat. The caramel will cool quickly and start to become sticky, so you will need to work fast. Quickly turn the sweet potatoes in the caramel to coat them and then transfer them to the Silpat mat. If the caramel cools too much and becomes overly sticky, heat it on low until it has softened and then turn off the heat. Repeat as many times as necessary until all of the sweet potatoes have been coated in the caramel.

6. Let the sweet potatoes cool for 5 minutes before serving.

INGREDIENTS:

1	LB. JAPANESE SWEET POTATOES
	PINCH OF KOSHER SALT
	RICE BRAN OIL, AS NEEDED
⅓	CUP CASTER (SUPERFINE) SUGAR
1½	TABLESPOONS MIRIN
1	TABLESPOON WATER
½	TEASPOON RICE VINEGAR
½	TEASPOON SOY SAUCE
½	TEASPOON BLACK SESAME SEEDS

APPENDIX

MITARASHI SAUCE

YIELD: ¾ CUP / ACTIVE TIME: 10 MINUTES / TOTAL TIME: 10 MINUTES

1. Place all of the ingredients in a saucepan and bring to a simmer over low heat, stirring to dissolve the sugar.

2. Cook until the sauce has thickened slightly and serve immediately.

INGREDIENTS:

2	TABLESPOONS SOY SAUCE
¼	CUP SUGAR
2	TABLESPOONS MIRIN
2	TEASPOONS TAPIOCA STARCH
¼	CUP COLD WATER

UME SAUCE

YIELD: ½ CUP / ACTIVE TIME: 10 MINUTES / TOTAL TIME: 10 MINUTES

1. Place the dashi, soy sauce, rice vinegar, and Umeboshi in a small saucepan and bring to a boil.

2. Combine the tapioca starch and water in a bowl and add the slurry to the pan, stirring continually.

3. Cook until the sauce has thickened. Remove the pan from heat and let the sauce cool completely. Chill the sauce in the refrigerator before serving.

INGREDIENTS:

6	TABLESPOONS AWASE DASHI STOCK (SEE PAGE 38)
1½	TEASPOONS LIGHT SOY SAUCE
1½	TEASPOONS RICE VINEGAR
2	TABLESPOONS UMEBOSHI (SEE PAGE 329), MASHED
½	TEASPOON TAPIOCA STARCH
½	TEASPOON WATER

WARISHITA SAUCE

YIELD: 1¼ CUPS / ACTIVE TIME: 10 MINUTES / TOTAL TIME: 45 MINUTES

1. Place the mirin and sake in a medium saucepan and bring to a boil over medium heat. Reduce the heat to medium-low and let the mixture simmer for 1 to 2 minutes. Stir in the soy sauce, brown sugar, and water and cook, stirring to dissolve the brown sugar. Add the dried kombu, remove the pan from heat, and let the sauce steep for 30 minutes.

2. Remove the kombu from the sauce, discard it, and serve the sauce.

INGREDIENTS:

¼	CUP MIRIN
¼	CUP SAKE
⅓	CUP SOY SAUCE
¼	CUP LIGHT BROWN SUGAR
½	CUP WATER
	4 X 6–INCH SHEET OF DRIED KOMBU

YAKINIKU SAUCE

YIELD: ¾ CUP / ACTIVE TIME: 10 MINUTES / TOTAL TIME: 10 MINUTES

1. Place all of the ingredients in a saucepan and bring to a gentle simmer over medium-low heat, stirring occasionally.

2. Let the sauce simmer for 3 minutes and serve immediately.

INGREDIENTS:

3	TABLESPOONS LIGHT SOY SAUCE
3	TABLESPOONS MIRIN
3	TABLESPOONS DARK SOY SAUCE
1½	TABLESPOONS KETCHUP
1½	TEASPOONS HONEY
1	GARLIC CLOVE, GRATED
¼	ONION, GRATED
¼	TEASPOON FRESH LEMON JUICE
1	TABLESPOON GRATED APPLE
½	TEASPOON CAYENNE PEPPER
1½	TEASPOONS SESAME OIL
1½	TEASPOONS SESAME SEEDS
½	TEASPOON GRATED FRESH GINGER

TANGY TARTAR SAUCE

YIELD: ½ CUP / **ACTIVE TIME:** 5 MINUTES / **TOTAL TIME:** 5 MINUTES

1. Place all of the ingredients in a bowl, stir until well combined, and use as desired.

INGREDIENTS:

2	HARD-BOILED EGGS, DICED
¼	ONION, FINELY DICED
2	SMALL GHERKINS, FINELY DICED
¼	CUP JAPANESE MAYONNAISE (SEE PAGE 46)
1	TEASPOON KETCHUP
1	TABLESPOON FRESH LEMON JUICE
2	TEASPOONS SUGAR
⅛	TEASPOON KOSHER SALT
⅛	TEASPOON BLACK PEPPER

TARTAR SAUCE

YIELD: ½ CUP / **ACTIVE TIME:** 5 MINUTES / **TOTAL TIME:** 20 MINUTES

1. Place the cucumber and onion in a bowl, season with the salt, and let the mixture rest for 15 minutes.

2. Squeeze the cucumber and onion to remove any excess water and drain them.

3. Place the hard-boiled egg in a bowl and mash it. Add the cucumber, onion, and the remaining ingredients, stir until well combined, and use as desired.

INGREDIENTS:

½	JAPANESE CUCUMBER, FINELY DICED
¼	ONION, FINELY DICED
½	TEASPOON KOSHER SALT
1	HARD-BOILED EGG
3	TABLESPOONS JAPANESE MAYONNAISE (SEE PAGE 46)
	PINCH OF BLACK PEPPER
1	TEASPOON HONEY
1	TEASPOON FRESH LEMON JUICE
½	TEASPOON KETCHUP
½	TEASPOON JAPANESE MUSTARD (OPTIONAL)

HOMEMADE CROUTONS

YIELD: 4 SERVINGS / ACTIVE TIME: 10 MINUTES / TOTAL TIME: 20 MINUTES

1. Preheat the oven to 355°F. Place the olive oil, butter, dried herbs, and salt in a bowl and stir to combine. Add the baguette pieces and toss to coat evenly.

2. Place the baguette pieces on a baking sheet in a single layer, making sure they don't overlap. Place the pan in the oven and bake until the croutons are golden brown and crispy, about 10 minutes.

3. Remove the croutons from the oven and use as desired.

INGREDIENTS:

1	TEASPOON EXTRA-VIRGIN OLIVE OIL
1	TEASPOON UNSALTED BUTTER, MELTED
1	TEASPOON MIXED DRIED HERBS
⅛	TEASPOON KOSHER SALT
5	OZ. DAY-OLD BAGUETTE, CUBED

SPICY SESAME SAUCE

YIELD: ½ CUP / ACTIVE TIME: 5 MINUTES / TOTAL TIME: 5 MINUTES

1. Place all of the ingredients in a bowl, whisk to combine, and use as desired.

INGREDIENTS:

3	TABLESPOONS SESAME PASTE
2	TABLESPOON SOY SAUCE
¼	CUP WATER
1	TEASPOON CHILI OIL
1	TEASPOON RICE VINEGAR
½	TEASPOON SUGAR

CONVERSION TABLE

WEIGHTS

1 oz. = 28 grams

2 oz. = 57 grams

4 oz. (¼ lb.) = 113 grams

8 oz. (½ lb.) = 227 grams

16 oz. (1 lb.) = 454 grams

VOLUME MEASURES

⅛ teaspoon = 0.6 ml

¼ teaspoon = 1.23 ml

½ teaspoon = 2.5 ml

1 teaspoon = 5 ml

1 tablespoon (3 teaspoons) = ½ fluid oz. = 15 ml

2 tablespoons = 1 fluid oz. = 29.5 ml

¼ cup (4 tablespoons) = 2 fluid oz. = 59 ml

⅓ cup (5⅓ tablespoons) = 2.7 fluid oz. = 80 ml

½ cup (8 tablespoons) = 4 fluid oz. = 120 ml

⅔ cup (10⅔ tablespoons) = 5.4 fluid oz. = 160 ml

¾ cup (12 tablespoons) = 6 fluid oz. = 180 ml

1 cup (16 tablespoons) = 8 fluid oz. = 240 ml

TEMPERATURE EQUIVALENTS

°F	°C	Gas Mark
225	110	¼
250	130	½
275	140	1
300	150	2
325	170	3
350	180	4
375	190	5
400	200	6
425	220	7
450	230	8
475	240	9
500	250	10

LENGTH MEASURES

1/16 inch = 1.6 mm

⅛ inch = 3 mm

¼ inch = 1.35 mm

½ inch = 1.25 cm

¾ inch = 2 cm

1 inch = 2.5 cm

ABOUT THE AUTHOR

Yuto Omura is the founder of Sudachi, a contemporary Japanese recipe blog that focuses on introducing how to make both homestyle and restaurant-quality Japanese dishes using both authentic and accessible ingredients.

Yuto's passion for cooking started from an early age, and he would often experiment without using cookbooks or online recipes, allowing him to express his creativity without limits.

After spending several years in the UK, he began to try to recreate the flavors of home using local ingredients. Although challenging at first, this experience helped him realize that Japanese food can be created anywhere in the world, and he became inspired to share this with others through sudachirecipes.com.

His mission is to demystify Japanese cuisine for home cooks and focus on the joy and simplicity of preparing unfamiliar dishes while emphasizing creativity over strict adherence to tradition. The ultimate goal is not to globalize Japanese cuisine, but to share the pleasure of cooking and enjoying it at home.

INDEX

Abura Soba, 404
Abura-age
  Chanko Nabe, 478
  Chirashizushi, 496
  Classic Miso Soup, 114
  Curry Udon, 437
  Inarizushi, 491
  Kenchin Jiru, 125
  Kiriboshi Daikon, 189
  Kitsune Udon/Soba, 425
  Kyoto-Style Udon, 431
  Maze Gohan with Bamboo Shoots,
    103
  Miso Nikomi Udon, 438
  Oden, 474
  recipe, 69
  Red Miso Soup, 122
  Salmon Miso Nabe, 475
  Salmon Takikomi Gohan, 109
  Tori Nanban Soba, 450
adzuki beans
  Anko, 646–647
  Matcha & Adzuki Pound Cake,
    667
  Sekihan, 86–87
Ae Soba with Canned Tuna, 456
Agedashi Tofu, 291
Ajitama
  Miso Ramen, 396
  recipe, 378
  Shoyu Ramen, 393
  Tonkotsu-Style Ramen Hack, 397
amazake
  Bettarazuke, 316
Anko
  Anmitsu, 658
  Dorayaki, 663
  Ohagi, 653
  recipe, 646–647
  Sweet Kushi Dango, 641
Anmitsu, 658
aonori powder
  Chikuwa no Isobeage, 300
  Osaka-Style Okonomiyaki, 630

Potato Iso Cheese-ae, 165
Takoyaki, 628
Tonpeiyaki, 635
Yakisoba, 636
apples
  Shogayaki, 241
  Yakiniku Sauce, 679
Asari Miso Soup, 118
Asari no Sakamushi, 608
asparagus
  Shojin-age, 279
  Shrimp & Asparagus Sumiso-ae,
    157
Atsuage Tofu
  Oden, 474
  recipe, 73
avocados
  Avocado & Cucumber Ume-
    Goma-ae, 162
  Chirashizushi, 496
  Futomaki, 488
  Natto Gohan, 89
  Taco Rice, 542
  Temakizushi, 490
Awase Dashi Stock
  Agedashi Tofu, 291
  Beef Niku Udon, 434
  Carbo Udon, 557
  Chawanmushi, 142
  Chicken Hambagu with Ume-an
    Sauce, 250
  Classic Miso Soup, 114
  Curry Udon, 437
  Dashimaki Tamago, 517
  Gyudon, 337
  Ikura, 510
  Inarizushi, 491
  Japanese-Style Cabbage Rolls, 538
  Jibuni, 209
  Kakitamajiru, 133
  Kamo Nanban Soba, 445
  Kitsune Udon/Soba, 425
  Kyoto-Style Udon, 431
  Miso Nikomi Udon, 438

Miso Stir-Fry, 265
Motsunabe, 471
Nagasaki Champon, 401
Nagoya's Taiwan Ramen, 400
Nanbanzuke, 324
Niku Bukkake Udon, 441
Oden, 474
Onsen Tamago, 57
Orandani, 193
Osuimono, 134
Ozoni, 135
Pork Niku Soba, 449
recipe, 38
Red Miso Soup, 122
Salmon Ochazuke, 99
Sashimi Platter, 502–503
Sawaniwan, 130
Sea Bream Kombu-Jime, 506
Shoyu Ramen, 393
Simmered Sweet Potatoes, 188
Soba Noodle Broth, 421
Soboro Daikon, 203
Somen with Homemade Dipping
  Sauce, 457
Takoyaki, 628
Tempura, 272
Tonjiru, 124
Tori Nanban Soba, 450
Torijiru, 129
Udon Noodle Broth, 417
Ume Sauce, 678
White Miso Soup, 121

bacon
  Butter & Soy Sauce Wafu Pasta,
    550
  Carbo Udon, 557
Baked Chicken Katsu, 255
Baked Cod Saikyo-yaki, 229
Baked Shiozake, 220
bamboo shoots
  Bamboo Shoot Okaka-ni, 183
  Chikuzenni, 201
  Chinjao Rosu, 563

Gomoku Mame, 194
Harumaki, 583
Jibuni, 209
Maze Gohan with Bamboo Shoots, 103
Menma-Style Bamboo Shoots, 383
Nikuman, 588–589
Shio Ramen, 394
Shojin-age, 279
Shumai, 579
Tonkotsu-Style Ramen Hack, 397
Tsukemen, 408
Vegetable Gyoza, 578
Ban Ban Zii, 584
bean sprouts
    Chanko Nabe, 478
    Hiroshima-Style Okonomiyaki, 631
    Miso Ramen, 396
    Rebanira Itame, 585
    Seasoned Bean Sprouts, 389
    Shio Lemon Nabe, 466
    Soy Milk Tantan Nabe, 470
    Yakiudon, 638
    Yasai Itame, 587
beans and legumes
    Anko, 646–647
    Beef Yawata Maki, 601
    Butadon, 343
    Chikuzenni, 201
    Chirashizushi, 496
    Cold Soba Salad, 454
    Eggplant Zunda-ae, 171
    Gomoku Mame, 194
    Green Bean Gomaae, 156
    Kakiage Udon/Soba, 426
    Mame Gohan, 84
    Matcha & Adzuki Pound Cake, 667
    Niku Dofu, 202
    Nikujaga, 208
    Omurice, 539
    Red Kidney Beans Amani, 197
    Sawaniwan, 130
    Sekihan, 86–87
    Shojin Dashi Stock, 41
    Shumai, 579
    Simmered Taro & Squid, 210
    Soboro Don, 344
    Stir-Fried Edamame, 614
    White Miso Soup, 121
beef
    Beef Niku Udon, 434
    Beef Shigureni, 211
    Beef Sukiyaki, 464
    Beef Yawata Maki, 601

Bifukatsu, 295
Chinjao Rosu, 563
Gyudon, 337
Hambagu, 532
Hayashi Rice, 543
Japanese-Style Curry Rice, 541
Korokke, 528
Meat Doria, 546
Menchi Katsu, 287
Miso-Marinated Beef Steaks, 246
Niku Bukkake Udon, 441
Niku Dofu, 202
Nikujaga, 208
Sukiyaki Donburi, 356
Taco Rice, 542
Teriyaki Beef Donburi, 355
Yakiniku Don, 347
beef intestines
    Motsunabe, 471
beef stock
    Hayashi Rice, 543
    Japanese-Style Curry Rice, 541
beef tallow
    Beef Sukiyaki, 464
    Gyudon, 337
beef tendon
    Oden, 474
beer
    Beer-Pickled Cucumbers, 328
    Buta no Kakuni, 206
    Ebi Mayo, 571
Benishoga
    Chahan, 575
    Gyudon, 337
    Hiroshima-Style Okonomiyaki, 631
    Hiyashi Chuka, 405
    recipe, 315
    Sukiyaki Donburi, 356
    Takoyaki, 628
    Tonkotsu-Style Ramen Hack, 397
    Yakisoba, 636
    Yakiudon, 638
Bettarazuke, 316
Bifukatsu, 295
bok choy
    Chuka Don, 361
    Ponzu Chicken Donburi, 351
    Sakana no Nitsuke, 230
    Tantanmen, 403
bonito flakes
    Avocado & Cucumber Ume-Goma-ae, 162
    Awase Dashi Stock, 38
    Bamboo Shoot Okaka-ni, 183
    Broccoli Karashi-ae, 159

Chicken & Cucumber Bainiku-ae, 164
Goya Champuru, 264
Hiyashi Mentaiko Udon, 444
Mentsuyu, 42
Mugen Cabbage, 622
Napa Cabbage Ohitashi, 155
Omusubi, 92
Orandani, 193
Oroshi Soba, 451
Osaka-Style Okonomiyaki, 630
Ponzu Sauce, 45
Takoyaki, 628
Tanuki Hiyayakko, 611
Tofu Steak, 612
Tonpeiyaki, 635
Ultimate Tamago Kake Gohan, 93
Ume Cucumber, 175
Wakame Salad, 148
Yakisoba, 636
Yakiudon, 638
broccoli
    Broccoli Karashi-ae, 159
    Cream Stew, 549
    Oyako Don, 336
    Salmon & Ikura Oyakodon, 366
buckwheat flour
    Homemade Soba Noodles, 420
burdock root
    Beef Shigureni, 211
    Motsunabe, 471
    Torijiru, 129
Buri Daikon, 215
Buta no Kakuni, 206
Butadon, 343
Butter & Soy Sauce Wafu Pasta, 550
Butterflied Shrimp
    Futomaki, 488
    recipe, 513
    Temarizushi, 495

cabbage
    Hiroshima-Style Okonomiyaki, 631
    Japanese-Style Cabbage Rolls, 538
    Motsunabe, 471
    Mugen Cabbage, 622
    Nagasaki Champon, 401
    Osaka-Style Okonomiyaki, 630
    Pork Yaki Gyoza, 576
    Salmon Chan Chan-yaki, 235
    Shio & Lemon Yakisoba, 637
    Soy Milk Tantan Nabe, 470
    Teriyaki Beef Donburi, 355
    Tonkatsu, 284
    Tonpeiyaki, 635

Tonteki, 245
Ume & Butter Squid Stir-Fry, 605
Wafu Addictive Cabbage, 615
Yakisoba, 636
Yakiudon, 638
Yasai Itame, 587
See also napa cabbage
Camambert cheese
Kushiage, 288
Carbo Udon, 557
carrots
Beef Sukiyaki, 464
Beef Yawata Maki, 601
Carrot Masago-ae, 170
Carrot Peanut-ae, 158
Chanko Nabe, 478
Chicken Zosui, 98
Chikuzenni, 201
Chirashizushi, 496
Chuka Don, 361
Cream Stew, 549
Gomoku Mame, 194
Harumaki, 583
Hiyashi Chuka, 405
Japanese-Style Curry Rice, 541
Japanese-Style Macaroni Salad, 533
Jibuni, 209
Kakiage Udon/Soba, 426
Kenchin Jiru, 125
Kiriboshi Daikon, 189
Kohaku Namasu, 325
Maze Gohan with Bamboo Shoots, 103
Nagasaki Champon, 401
Nanbanzuke, 324
Nikujaga, 208
Nukazuke-Style Pickles, 308
Oden, 474
Okra & Carrot Shira-ae, 169
Ozoni, 135
Pork & Garlic Nabe, 467
Salmon Chan Chan-yaki, 235
Salmon Takikomi Gohan, 109
Sawaniwan, 130
Shio & Lemon Yakisoba, 637
Shojin Dashi Stock, 41
Subuta, 566
Tonjiru, 124
Torijiru, 129
White Miso Soup, 121
Yakisoba, 636
Yakiudon, 638
Yasai Itame, 587
Castella, 666
Chahan, 575
Chanko Nabe, 478

Chashu
Chicken Breast Chashu, 377
Classic Pork Chashu, 376
Oven-Roasted Chashu, 382
Tsukemen, 408
Chawanmushi, 142
cheddar cheese
Kani Kurimu Korokke, 273
Taco Rice, 542
cheese. *See individual cheese types*
cherries, Maraschino
Anmitsu, 658
cherry blossom leaves
Chomeiji Sakura Mochi, Kanto Style, 649
chestnuts, candied
Kuri Yokan, 656
chia seeds
Jukkokumai, 83
chicken
Baked Chicken Katsu, 255
Ban Ban Zii, 584
Chanko Nabe, 478
Chicken & Cucumber Bainiku-ae, 164
Chicken Breast Chashu, 377
Chicken Drumstick Sappari-ni, 254
Chicken Ham with Ume Sauce, 599
Chicken Hambagu with Ume-an Sauce, 250
Chicken Miso Yuan-yaki, 258
Chicken Nanban, 247
Chicken Zosui, 98
Chikuzenni, 201
Citrusy Chicken Karaage, 283
Cream Stew, 549
Jibuni, 209
Kushiage, 288
Maze Gohan with Bamboo Shoots, 103
Miso Nikomi Udon, 438
Nagoya's Tebasaki, 598
Omurice, 539
Oyako Don, 336
Ozoni, 135
Ponzu Chicken Donburi, 351
Shio Lemon Nabe, 466
Shio Ramen, 394
Soboro Daikon, 203
Soy-Glazed Roasted Chicken Legs, 261
Teriyaki Chicken, 240
Tori Nanban Soba, 450
Tori no Karaage, 280

Torijiru, 129
Toriten, 276
Yakitori in a Frying Pan, 594
Yurinchi, 570
chicken livers
Rebanira Itame, 585
chicken skin
Torikawa Ponzu, 600
chicken stock
Harumaki, 583
Mabo Nasu, 562
Tenshiinhan, 574
chikuwa fish cakes
Chikuwa no Isobeage, 300
Oden, 474
Chikuwa no Isobeage, 300
Chikuzenni, 201
chili bean paste
Ebi Chili, 567
Mabo Dofu Don, 357
Miso Stir-fry, 265
Soy Milk Tantan Nabe, 470
Spicy Negi, 390
Tantanmen, 403
Tofu Steak, 612
chili bean sauce
Fragrant Pork Mince, 381
Mabo Nasu, 562
Miso Ramen, 396
Nagoya's Taiwan Ramen, 400
chili threads
Mabo Dofu Don, 357
Chinjao Rosu, 563
Chirashizushi, 496
Chomeiji Sakura Mochi, Kanto Style, 649
chrysanthemums
Beef Sukiyaki, 464
Sukiyaki Donburi, 356
Chuka Don, 361
citrus/citrus juice
Baked Shiozake, 220
Ponzu Sauce, 45
Saba no Shioyaki, 221
Sanma no Shioyaki, 224
Yellowtail Yuan-yaki, 232
See also individual fruits
Citrusy Chicken Karaage, 283
clams
Asari Miso Soup, 118
Asari no Sakamushi, 608
Classic Miso Soup, 114
Classic Pork Chashu, 376
cod fillets
Baked Cod Saikyo-yaki, 229

Kawari Age, 303
Sakura Denbu, 516
Coffee Jelly, 662
Cold Soba Salad, 454
condensed milk
Ebi Mayo, 571
conversion table, 682
corn
Corn Potage, 139
Miso Ramen, 396
Nagasaki Champon, 401
Salmon Miso Nabe, 475
crab, imitation
Futomaki, 488
Sunomono, 151
crabmeat
Kani Kurimu Korokke, 273
Tenshiinhan, 574
cream cheese
Matcha Rare Cheesecake, 670
Potato Iso Cheese-ae, 165
Cream Stew, 549
Crispy Garlic Chips
Ae Soba with Canned Tuna, 456
Motsunabe, 471
recipe, 386
Shoyu Ramen, 393
cucumbers
Ae Soba with Canned Tuna, 456
Avocado & Cucumber Ume-
goma-ae, 162
Ban Ban Zii, 584
Beer-Pickled Cucumbers, 328
Chicken & Cucumber Bainiku-ae,
164
Cucumber Misozuke, 321
Fukujinzuke, 310
Futomaki, 488
Hiyashi Chuka, 405
Hiyashi Tanuki Udon/Soba, 430
Hosomaki, 485
Japanese-Style Macaroni Salad, 533
Japanese-Style Potato Salad, 531
Nukazuke-Style Pickles, 308
Salmon & Ikura Oyakodon, 366
Shabu-Shabu Salad, 152
Shibazuke, 317
Sunomono, 151
Tartar Sauce, 680
Temakizushi, 490
Temarizushi, 495
Torikawa Ponzu, 600
Ume Cucumber, 175
Wakame Salad, 148
Curry Powder, Japanese, 65
Curry Udon, 437

Daigaku Imo, 674
daikon radishes
Agedashi Tofu, 291
Atsuage Tofu, 73
Bettarazuke, 316
Buri Daikon, 215
Chicken Miso Yuan-yaki, 258
Daikon Amazuzuke, 322
Eryngii Steak, 619
Fukujinzuke, 310
Kenchin Jiru, 125
Kohaku Namasu, 325
Niku Bukkake Udon, 441
Nukazuke-Style Pickles, 308
Oden, 474
Oroshi Soba, 451
Ozoni, 135
Saba no Shioyaki, 221
Salmon Nanban-yaki, 234
Sanma no Shioyaki, 224
Sawaniwan, 130
Shojin Dashi Stock, 41
Soboro Daikon, 203
Takuan, 318
Torijiru, 129
Torikawa Ponzu, 600
Zaru Udon/Soba, 429
dashi granules
Abura Soba, 404
Broccoli Karashi-ae, 159
Butter & Soy Sauce Wafu Pasta,
550
Chicken Breast Chashu, 377
Chicken Nanban, 247
Chicken Zosui, 98
Cucumber Misozuke, 321
Eggplant Zunda-ae, 171
Fukujinzuke, 310
Goya Champuru, 264
Hiroshima-Style Okonomiyaki,
631
Hiyashi Mentaiko Udon, 444
Japanese-Style Macaroni Salad, 533
Kabocha no Nimono, 182
Kushiage, 288
Maze Gohan with Bamboo Shoots,
103
Mentaiko Pasta, 554
Napa Cabbage Ohitashi, 155
Niku Dofu, 202
Nikujaga, 208
Okayu, 97
Okra & Carrot Shira-ae, 169
Osaka-Style Okonomiyaki, 630
Oyako Don, 336
Pork Katsudon, 340

Salmon Takikomi Gohan, 109
Satsumaimo Gohan, 90
Shio & Lemon Yakisoba, 637
Shio Ramen, 394
Soboro Don, 344
Stir-Fried Edamame, 614
Sukiyaki Donburi, 356
Takoyaki, 628
Tendon, 350
Tonkotsu-Style Ramen Hack, 397
Tsukemen, 408
Wafu Addictive Cabbage, 615
Wakame Salad, 148
Yaki Onigiri Dashi Chazuke, 102
Yakiton, 595
Yakiudon, 638
Dashimaki Tamago
Chirashizushi, 496
Futomaki, 488
recipe, 517
Temakizushi, 490
Dorayaki, 663
dressings
Goma Dressing, 51
Ponzu Dressing, 54
Shiso Dressing, 56
Wafu Dressing, 50
duck
Jibuni, 209
Kamo Nanban Soba, 445

Ebi Chili, 567
Ebi Furai, 292
Ebi Mayo, 571
edamame
Butadon, 343
Eggplant Zunda-ae, 171
Stir-Fried Edamame, 614
eels
Unaju/Unadon, 367
eggplants
Cold Soba Salad, 454
Eggplant Zunda-ae, 171
Fukujinzuke, 310
Kushiage, 288
Mabo Nasu, 562
Miso Stir-Fry, 265
Nasu Dengaku, 618
Orandani, 193
Saba no Misoni, 228
Shibazuke, 317
Tempura, 272
Tendon, 350
eggs
Abura Soba, 404
Ajitama, 378

Beef Sukiyaki, 464
Bifukatsu, 295
Buta no Kakuni, 206
Carbo Udon, 557
Castella, 666
Chahan, 575
Chanko Nabe, 478
Chicken Drumstick Sappari-ni, 254
Chicken Nanban, 247
Chicken Zosui, 98
Chinjao Rosu, 563
Citrusy Chicken Karaage, 283
Dashimaki Tamago, 517
Dorayaki, 663
Ebi Furai, 292
Goya Champuru, 264
Hiroshima-Style Okonomiyaki, 631
Japanese Mayonnaise, 46
Japanese-Style Macaroni Salad, 533
Kakitamajiru, 133
Kani Kurimu Korokke, 273
Kinshi Tamago, 521
Korokke, 528
Kushiage, 288
Matcha & Adzuki Pound Cake, 667
Menchi Katsu, 287
Miso Nikomi Udon, 438
Nabeshigi, 174
Niku Bukkake Udon, 441
Niratama Soup, 138
Oden, 474
Omurice, 539
Onsen Tamago, 57
Osaka-Style Okonomiyaki, 630
Oyako Don, 336
Pork Katsudon, 340
Salmon Fry, 294
Shio Ramen, 394
Silky Custard Purin, 659
Soboro Don, 344
Stamina Don, 346
Strawberry Shortcake, 669
Subuta, 566
Suito Poteto, 673
Sukiyaki Donburi, 356
Taco Rice, 542
Takoyaki, 628
Tamago Sando, 536
Tamagoyaki, 613
Tangy Tartar Sauce, 680
Tartar Sauce, 680
Tempura, 272
Tenshiinhan, 574

Tonkatsu, 284
Tonpeiyaki, 635
Toriten, 276
Tororo Tsukimi Udon, 442
Tsukemen, 408
Ultimate Tamago Kake Gohan, 93
eggs, quail
    Chuka Don, 361
    Kushiage, 288
Eryngii Steak, 619
espresso powder, instant
    Coffee Jelly, 662

fish
    Ae Soba with Canned Tuna, 456
    Baked Cod Saikyo-yaki, 229
    Baked Shiozake, 220
    Buri Daikon, 215
    Carrot Masago-ae, 170
    Chahan, 575
    Chawanmushi, 142
    Chikuwa no Isobeage, 300
    Curry Udon, 437
    Fish Teriyaki, 225
    Futomaki, 488
    Hosomaki, 485
    Kawari Age, 303
    Kitsune Udon/Soba, 425
    Mackerel Ume-ni, 233
    Marinated Kaisen-Don, 364
    Marinated Tuna Sashimi, 507
    Miso Nikomi Udon, 438
    Mugen Cabbage, 622
    Nagasaki Champon, 401
    Nanbanzuke, 324
    Negitoro, 512
    Oden, 474
    Omusubi, 92
    Osuimono, 134
    Saba no Misoni, 228
    Saba no Shioyaki, 221
    Sakana no Nitsuke, 230
    Salmon & Ikura Oyakodon, 366
    Salmon & Miso Cream Pasta, 551
    Salmon Chan Chan-yaki, 235
    Salmon Flakes, 61
    Salmon Fry, 294
    Salmon Miso Nabe, 475
    Salmon Nanban-yaki, 234
    Salmon Ochazuke, 99
    Salmon Takikomi Gohan, 109
    Sanma no Shioyaki, 224
    Sea Bream Kombu-Jime, 506
    Taimeshi, 106
    Temakizushi, 490
    Temarizushi, 495

Tsukemen, 408
Yellowtail Yuan-yaki, 232
See also seafood
fish cakes, chikuwa
    Chikuwa no Isobeage, 300
    Oden, 474
fish cakes, kamaboko
    Chahan, 575
    Chawanmushi, 142
    Curry Udon, 437
    Kitsune Udon/Soba, 425
    Miso Nikomi Udon, 438
    Nagasaki Champon, 401
    Oden, 474
    Osuimono, 134
fish cakes, narutomaki
    Tsukemen, 408
Fragrant Pork Mince, 381
Fukujinzuke
    Japanese-Style Curry Rice, 541
    recipe, 310
Futomaki, 488

gardenia fruit
    Takuan, 318
Gari
    Futomaki, 488
    recipe, 499
garlic
    Ae Soba with Canned Tuna, 456
    Butter & Soy Sauce Wafu Pasta, 550
    Chahan, 575
    Chinjao Rosu, 563
    Chuka Don, 361
    Citrusy Chicken Karaage, 283
    Classic Pork Chashu, 376
    Crispy Garlic Chips, 386
    Ebi Mayo, 571
    Fragrant Pork Mince, 381
    Gyudon, 337
    Hayashi Rice, 543
    Japanese-Style Curry Rice, 541
    Mabo Dofu Don, 357
    Mabo Nasu, 562
    Meat Doria, 546
    Miso Ramen, 396
    Miso Stir-Fry, 265
    Motsunabe, 471
    Nagoya's Taiwan Ramen, 400
    Nikuman, 588–589
    Oven-Roasted Chashu, 382
    Pork & Garlic Nabe, 467
    Pork Niku Soba, 449
    Shio & Lemon Yakisoba, 637
    Shio Ramen, 394

Soy Milk Tantan Nabe, 470
Squid Karaage, 299
Stamina Don, 346
Tantanmen, 403
Teriyaki Tofu Donburi, 360
Tonteki, 245
Tori no Karaage, 280
Toriten, 276
Yakisoba, 636
Yasai Itame, 587
Yurinchi, 570
garlic chives
   Motsunabe, 471
   Nagoya's Taiwan Ramen, 400
   Niratama Soup, 138
   Pork Yaki Gyoza, 576
   Rebanira Itame, 585
   Shio & Lemon Yakisoba, 637
   Soy Milk Tantan Nabe, 470
   Stamina Don, 346
   Vegetable Gyoza, 578
   Yasai Itame, 587
garlic paste
   Abura Soba, 404
   Ajitama, 378
   Chanko Nabe, 478
   Cucumber Misozuke, 321
   Japanese-Style Macaroni Salad, 533
   Mugen Cabbage, 622
   Nabeshigi, 174
   Nagasaki Champon, 401
   Nagoya's Tebasaki, 598
   Niratama Soup, 138
   Rebanira Itame, 585
   Shoyu Ramen, 393
   Tofu Steak, 612
   Tonkotsu-Style Ramen Hack, 397
   Tonteki, 245
   Tsukemen, 408
   Vegetable Gyoza, 578
   Yaki Onigiri Dashi Chazuke, 102
   Yakiton, 595
   Yakitori in a Frying Pan, 594
   Yasai Itame, 587
   Yurinchi, 570
ginger, fresh
   Beef Niku Udon, 434
   Beef Shigureni, 211
   Benishoga, 315
   Buri Daikon, 215
   Buta no Kakuni, 206
   Chahan, 575
   Chicken Breast Chashu, 377
   Chicken Drumstick Sappari-ni, 254
   Chinjao Rosu, 563

Chuka Don, 361
Citrusy Chicken Karaage, 283
Classic Pork Chashu, 376
Ebi Chili, 567
Fragrant Pork Mince, 381
Fukujinzuke, 310
Gari, 499
Gyudon, 337
Harumaki, 583
Japanese-Style Cabbage Rolls, 538
Japanese-Style Curry Rice, 541
Joya Nabe, 479
Kamaage Udon, 418
Kyoto-Style Udon, 431
Mabo Nasu, 562
Mackerel Ume-ni, 233
Miso Ramen, 396
Miso Stir-Fry, 265
Miso-Marinated Beef Steaks, 246
Motsunabe, 471
Niku Bukkake Udon, 441
Nikuman, 588–589, 640
Oden, 474
Oven-Roasted Chashu, 382
Plant-Based Miso Soup, 115
Pork Yaki Gyoza, 576
Rayu, 49
Rebanira Itame, 585
Saba no Misoni, 228
Sakana no Nitsuke, 230
Salmon Takikomi Gohan, 109
Shibazuke, 317
Shogayaki, 241
Shumai, 579
Simmered Sweet Potatoes, 188
Soboro Daikon, 203
Soy Milk Tantan Nabe, 470
Squid Karaage, 299
Taimeshi, 106
Tenshiinhan, 574
Tori no Karaage, 280
Torijiru, 129
Toriten, 276
Yakiniku Sauce, 679
Yakisoba, 636
Yakiudon, 638
Yurinchi, 570
ginger paste
   Chanko Nabe, 478
   Kamo Nanban Soba, 445
   Nagasaki Champon, 401
   Rebanira Itame, 585
   Soboro Don, 344
   Tofu Steak, 612
   Tsukemen, 408

Wakame Salad, 148
Yurinchi, 570
Goma Dressing, 51
Gomoku Mame, 194
gouda cheese
   Meat Doria, 546
   Taco Rice, 542
Goya Champuru, 264
graham crackers
   Matcha Rare Cheesecake, 670
green beans
   Beef Yawata Maki, 601
   Cold Soba Salad, 454
   Green Bean Gomaae, 156
   Kakiage Udon/Soba, 426
green onions
   Butadon, 343
   Curry Udon, 437
   Hiroshima-Style Okonomiyaki, 631
   Kitsune Udon/Soba, 425
   Mabo Dofu Don, 357
   Miso Ramen, 396
   Oroshi Soba, 451
   Osaka-Style Okonomiyaki, 630
   Salmon Chan Chan-yaki, 235
   Shio & Lemon Yakisoba, 637
   Somen with Homemade Dipping Sauce, 457
   Stamina Don, 346
   Takoyaki, 628
   Tantanmen, 403
   Tanuki Hiyayakko, 611
   Tonpeiyaki, 635
   Tsukemen, 408
green tea
   Salmon Ochazuke, 99
greens
   Shabu-Shabu Salad, 152
Gyoza Wrappers
   Pork Yaki Gyoza, 576
   recipe, 74
   Vegetable Gyoza, 578
Gyudon, 337

Hakusai no Asazuke, 311
ham
   Hiyashi Chuka, 405
   Japanese-Style Potato Salad, 531
Hambagu, 532
haricots verts
   Cold Soba Salad, 454
   See also green beans
Harumaki, 583
Hayashi Rice, 543
Hiroshima-Style Okonomiyaki, 631

Hiyashi Chuka, 405
Hiyashi Mentaiko Udon, 444
Hiyashi Tanuki Udon/Soba, 430
Homemade Croutons
    Corn Potage, 139
    recipe, 681
Homemade Ramen Noodles
    Abura Soba, 404
    Hiroshima-Style Okonomiyaki,
        631
    Miso Ramen, 396
    Motsunabe, 471
    Nagasaki Champon, 401
    Nagoya's Taiwan Ramen, 400
    Pork & Garlic Nabe, 467
    recipe, 372–373
    Salmon Miso Nabe, 475
    Shio & Lemon Yakisoba, 637
    Shio Lemon Nabe, 466
    Shio Ramen, 394
    Shoyu Ramen, 393
    Soy Milk Tantan Nabe, 470
    Tantanmen, 403
    Tonkotsu-Style Ramen Hack, 397
    Tsukemen, 408
    Yakisoba, 636
Homemade Soba Noodles
    Ae Soba with Canned Tuna, 456
    Cold Soba Salad, 454
    Hiyashi Tanuki Udon/Soba, 430
    Kakiage Udon/Soba, 426
    Kamo Nanban Soba, 445
    Kitsune Udon/Soba, 425
    Oroshi Soba, 451
    Pork Niku Soba, 449
    recipe, 420
    Tori Nanban Soba, 450
    Zaru Udon/Soba, 429
Homemade Udon Noodles
    Beef Niku Udon, 434
    Beef Sukiyaki, 464
    Carbo Udon, 557
    Curry Udon, 437
    Hiyashi Mentaiko Udon, 444
    Hiyashi Tanuki Udon/Soba,
        430
    Joya Nabe, 479
    Kakiage Udon/Soba, 426
    Kamaage Udon, 418
    Kitsune Udon/Soba, 425
    Kyoto-Style Udon, 431
    Miso Nikomi Udon, 438
    Niku Bukkake Udon, 441
    Pork & Garlic Nabe, 467
    recipe, 414
    Shio Lemon Nabe, 466

Yakiudon, 638
Zaru Udon/Soba, 429
horse mackerel fillets
    Nanbanzuke, 324
Hosomaki, 485

Ichigo Daifuku, 648
ikaten
    Hiroshima-Style Okonomiyaki,
        631
Ikura
    Futomaki, 488
    recipe, 510
    Salmon & Ikura Oyakodon, 366
    Temarizushi, 495
Inarizushi, 491

Japanese Curry Powder
    Curry Udon, 437
    Japanese-Style Curry Rice, 541
    Kawari Age, 303
    Meat Doria, 546
    recipe, 65
    Taco Rice, 542
    Yakisoba, 636
Japanese Mayonnaise
    Baked Chicken Katsu, 255
    Chicken Hambagu with Ume-an
        Sauce, 250
    Ebi Mayo, 571
    Goma Dressing, 51
    Hiyashi Chuka, 405
    Hiyashi Mentaiko Udon, 444
    Japanese-Style Macaroni Salad, 533
    Japanese-Style Potato Salad, 531
    Kawari Age, 303
    Negitoro, 512
    Osaka-Style Okonomiyaki, 630
    recipe, 46
    Takoyaki, 628
    Tamago Sando, 536
    Tangy Tartar Sauce, 680
    Tartar Sauce, 680
    Tonpeiyaki, 635
Japanese-Style Cabbage Rolls, 538
Japanese-Style Curry Rice, 541
Japanese-Style Macaroni Salad, 533
Japanese-Style Potato Salad, 531
Jibuni, 209
Joya Nabe, 479
Jukkokumai, 83

Kabocha no Nimono, 182
kabosu juice
    Toriten, 276
Kakiage Udon/Soba, 426

Kakitamajiru, 133
Kamaage Udon, 418
kamaboko fish cake
    Chahan, 575
    Chawanmushi, 142
    Curry Udon, 437
    Kitsune Udon/Soba, 425
    Miso Nikomi Udon, 438
    Oden, 474
    Osuimono, 134
kamaboko fish cakes
    Nagasaki Champon, 401
Kamo Nanban Soba, 445
Kani Kurimu Korokke, 273
Kanpyo
    Futomaki, 488
    Hosomaki, 485
    Kanpyo & Shiitake Mushrooms,
        520
kanten powder
    Anmitsu, 658
    Kuri Yokan, 656
karashi
    Beer-Pickled Cucumbers, 328
katsuobushi
    Abura Soba, 404
    Kawari Age, 303
Kenchin Jiru, 125
ketchup
    Bifukatsu, 295
    Hayashi Rice, 543
    Omurice, 539
    Subuta, 566
Kidney Beans Amani, Red, 197
Kinpira Renkon, 186
Kinshi Tamago
    Hiyashi Chuka, 405
    recipe, 521
    Temarizushi, 495
Kiriboshi Daikon, 189
kirimochi
    Ozoni, 135
Kitsune Udon/Soba, 425
kiwi
    Anmitsu, 658
kizami nori
    Abura Soba, 404
    Ae Soba with Canned Tuna, 456
    Hiyashi Mentaiko Udon, 444
    Mentaiko Pasta, 554
    Salmon & Ikura Oyakodon, 366
    Shio & Lemon Yakisoba, 637
    Stamina Don, 346
    Tanuki Hiyayakko, 611
    Tororo Tsukimi Udon, 442
    Tsukemen, 408

Kohaku Namasu, 325
kombu
  Ajitama, 378
  Asari Miso Soup, 118
  Awase Dashi Stock, 38
  Bettarazuke, 316
  Buri Daikon, 215
  Chanko Nabe, 478
  Daikon Amazuzuke, 322
  Fukujinzuke, 310
  Gari, 499
  Gomoku Mame, 194
  Hakusai no Asazuke, 311
  Ikura, 510
  Joya Nabe, 479
  Kohaku Namasu, 325
  Kombu No Tsukudani, 60
  Mackerel Ume-ni, 233
  Mame Gohan, 84
  Marinated Kaisen-Don, 364
  Marinated Tuna Sashimi, 507
  Mentsuyu, 42
  Omusubi, 92
  Plant-Based Miso Soup, 115
  Ponzu Sauce, 45
  Pork & Garlic Nabe, 467
  Salmon Miso Nabe, 475
  Sea Bream Kombu-Jime, 506
  Shio Lemon Nabe, 466
  Shojin Dashi Stock, 41
  Soy Milk Tantan Nabe, 470
  Sumeshi, 484
  Taimeshi, 106
  Tako Wasa, 604
  Takuan, 318
  Warishita Sauce, 679
  Yudofu with Spicy Sesame Sauce, 198
konnyaku
  Chikuzenni, 201
Korokke, 528
Koshian Anko
  Chomeiji Sakura Mochi, Kanto Style, 649
  Ichigo Daifuku, 648
  Kuri Yokan, 656
Kuri Yokan, 656
Kushiage, 288
Kyoto-Style Udon, 431

lager
  Buta no Kakuni, 206
  Ebi Mayo, 571
leeks, Japanese
  Ae Soba with Canned Tuna, 456
  Ban Ban Zii, 584

Beef Sukiyaki, 464
Buta no Kakuni, 206
Chahan, 575
Chanko Nabe, 478
Chicken Breast Chashu, 377
Chicken Zosui, 98
Classic Miso Soup, 114
Classic Pork Chashu, 376
Curry Udon, 437
Ebi Chili, 567
Fragrant Pork Mince, 381
Harumaki, 583
Jibuni, 209
Kakitamajiru, 133
Kamo Nanban Soba, 445
Kenchin Jiru, 125
Miso Nikomi Udon, 438
Miso Ramen, 396
Oden, 474
Oven-Roasted Chashu, 382
Pork & Garlic Nabe, 467
Pork Niku Soba, 449
Rayu, 49
Rebanira Itame, 585
Saba no Misoni, 228
Salmon Miso Nabe, 475
Shio Lemon Nabe, 466
Shio Ramen, 394
Shumai, 579
Spicy Negi, 390
Sukiyaki Donburi, 356
Tenshiinhan, 574
Teriyaki Tofu Donburi, 360
Tonjiru, 124
Tori Nanban Soba, 450
Torijiru, 129
Yakiton, 595
Yakitori in a Frying Pan, 594
Yurinchi, 570
lemon peel/zest
  Kohaku Namasu, 325
  Shio & Lemon Yakisoba, 637
lemons/lemon juice
  Citrusy Chicken Karaage, 283
  Kohaku Namasu, 325
  Lemon Teriyaki Pork, 253
  Shio & Lemon Yakisoba, 637
  Shio Lemon Nabe, 466
  Temarizushi, 495
  Toriten, 276
  Wafu Dressing, 50
lettuce
  Taco Rice, 542
lotus roots
  Chikuzenni, 201
  Fukujinzuke, 310

Kinpira Renkon, 186
Kushiage, 288
Shojin-age, 279

Mabo Dofu Don, 357
Mabo Nasu, 562
mackerel
  Mackerel Ume-ni, 233
  Nanbanzuke, 324
  Saba no Misoni, 228
  Saba no Shioyaki, 221
Mame Gohan, 84
Marinated Kaisen-Don, 364
Marinated Tuna Sashimi
  Chirashizushi, 496
  recipe, 507
matcha powder
  Matcha & Adzuki Pound Cake, 667
  Matcha Rare Cheesecake, 670
  Shojin-age, 279
  Warabi Mochi, 652
Maze Gohan with Bamboo Shoots, 103
meat, imitation
  Vegetable Gyoza, 578
Meat Doria, 546
melons
  Goya Champuru, 264
Menchi Katsu, 287
Menma-Style Bamboo Shoots
  recipe, 383
  Shio Ramen, 394
  Shoyu Ramen, 393
  Tonkotsu-Style Ramen Hack, 397
  Tsukemen, 408
mentaiko
  Hiyashi Mentaiko Udon, 444
  Mentaiko Pasta, 554
Mentsuyu
  Ae Soba with Canned Tuna, 456
  Hiyashi Tanuki Udon/Soba, 430
  Kamaage Udon, 418
  Oroshi Soba, 451
  recipe, 42
  Tororo Tsukimi Udon, 442
  Zaru Udon/Soba, 429
mirin
  Agedashi Tofu, 291
  Ajitama, 378
  Baked Cod Saikyo-yaki, 229
  Bamboo Shoot Okaka-ni, 183
  Beef Niku Udon, 434
  Beef Shigureni, 211
  Beef Yawata Maki, 601
  Buri Daikon, 215

Butadon, 343
Chahan, 575
Chanko Nabe, 478
Chawanmushi, 142
Chicken & Cucumber Bainiku-ae,
   164
Chicken Breast Chashu, 377
Chicken Hambagu with Ume-an
   Sauce, 250
Chicken Miso Yuan-yaki, 258
Chicken Nanban, 247
Chicken Zosui, 98
Chikuzenni, 201
Chirashizushi, 496
Classic Pork Chashu, 376
Cold Soba Salad, 454
Curry Udon, 437
Daigaku Imo, 674
Dashimaki Tamago, 517
Dorayaki, 663
Fish Teriyaki, 225
Fragrant Pork Mince, 381
Gomoku Mame, 194
Gyudon, 337
Ikura, 510
Inarizushi, 491
Japanese-Style Cabbage Rolls, 538
Japanese-Style Curry Rice, 541
Jibuni, 209
Kabocha no Nimono, 182
Kamo Nanban Soba, 445
Kanpyo & Shiitake Mushrooms,
   520
Kenchin Jiru, 125
Kinpira Renkon, 186
Kiriboshi Daikon, 189
Kitsune Udon/Soba, 425
Kombu No Tsukudani, 60
Korokke, 528
Kushiage, 288
Kyoto-Style Udon, 431
Lemon Teriyaki Pork, 253
Mackerel Ume-ni, 233
Marinated Kaisen-Don, 364
Marinated Tuna Sashimi, 507
Maze Gohan with Bamboo Shoots,
   103
Menma-Style Bamboo Shoots, 383
Mentsuyu, 42
Miso Nikomi Udon, 438
Miso Ramen, 396
Miso-Marinated Beef Steaks, 246
Mitarashi Sauce, 678
Motsunabe, 471
Nabeshigi, 174
Nagoya's Tebasaki, 598

Nanbanzuke, 324
Nasu Dengaku, 618
Niku Bukkake Udon, 441
Nikujaga, 208
Nikuman, 640
Oden, 474
Onsen Tamago, 57
Orandani, 193
Oven-Roasted Chashu, 382
Oyako Don, 336
Ponzu Chicken Donburi, 351
Ponzu Dressing, 54
Ponzu Sauce, 45
Pork & Garlic Nabe, 467
Pork Katsudon, 340
Pork Niku Soba, 449
Pork Rikyu-yaki, 260
Rebanira Itame, 585
Saba no Misoni, 228
Sakana no Nitsuke, 230
Salmon Chan Chan-yaki, 235
Salmon Flakes, 61
Salmon Miso Nabe, 475
Salmon Nanban-yaki, 234
Salmon Takikomi Gohan, 109
Satsumaimo Gohan, 90
Sawaniwan, 130
Shio Lemon Nabe, 466
Shogayaki, 241
Simmered Sweet Potatoes, 188
Simmered Taro & Squid, 210
Soba Noodle Broth, 421
Soboro Daikon, 203
Soboro Don, 344
Soy-Glazed Roasted Chicken Legs,
   261
Stamina Don, 346
Sukiyaki Donburi, 356
Sunomono, 151
Taco Rice, 542
Taimeshi, 106
Tako Wasa, 604
Tempura, 272
Tendon, 350
Teriyaki Beef Donburi, 355
Teriyaki Chicken, 240
Teriyaki Tofu Donburi, 360
Tofu Steak, 612
Tonteki, 245
Tori Nanban Soba, 450
Udon Noodle Broth, 417
Unaju/Unadon, 367
Vegetable Gyoza, 578
Warishita Sauce, 679
Yaki Onigiri Dashi Chazuke, 102
Yakiniku Sauce, 679

Yakitori in a Frying Pan, 594
Yellowtail Yuan-yaki, 232
Yurinchi, 570
miso paste, awase
   Miso Ramen, 396
   Torijiru, 129
miso paste, red
   Red Miso Soup, 122
   Yakiton, 595
miso paste, red hatcho
   Miso Nikomi Udon, 438
miso paste, white
   Baked Cod Saikyo-yaki, 229
   Okra & Carrot Shira-ae, 169
   Salmon & Miso Cream Pasta, 551
   White Miso Soup, 121
miso paste, yellow
   Asari Miso Soup, 118
   Chanko Nabe, 478
   Chicken Hambagu with Ume-an
      Sauce, 250
   Classic Miso Soup, 114
   Cold Soba Salad, 454
   Cucumber Misozuke, 321
   Ebi Chili, 567
   Goya Champuru, 264
   Mabo Dofu Don, 357
   Miso Stir-Fry, 265
   Miso-Marinated Beef Steaks, 246
   Nabeshigi, 174
   Nasu Dengaku, 618
   Nikuman, 588–589
   Nukazuke-Style Pickles, 308
   Okayu, 97
   Oven-Roasted Chashu, 382
   Plant-Based Miso Soup, 115
   Saba no Misoni, 228
   Salmon Chan Chan-yaki, 235
   Salmon Miso Nabe, 475
   Shrimp & Asparagus Sumiso-ae,
      157
   Soboro Daikon, 203
   Soy Milk Tantan Nabe, 470
   Stamina Don, 346
   Tonjiru, 124
   Tsukemen, 408
   Vegetable Gyoza, 578
   Yaki Onigiri Dashi Chazuke, 102
   Yakisoba, 636
Miso Ramen, 396
Miso-Marinated Beef Steaks, 246
Mitarashi Sauce
   recipe, 678
   Sweet Kushi Dango, 641
mitsuba
   Chawanmushi, 142

Osuimono, 134
Ozoni, 135
Pork Katsudon, 340
mochigome
   Ohagi, 653
Motsunabe, 471
Mugen Cabbage, 622
mushrooms
   Beef Sukiyaki, 464
   Butter & Soy Sauce Wafu Pasta,
      550
   Chanko Nabe, 478
   Chawanmushi, 142
   Chicken Hambagu with Ume-an
      Sauce, 250
   Chicken Zosui, 98
   Chikuzenni, 201
   Chirashizushi, 496
   Chuka Don, 361
   Classic Miso Soup, 114
   Curry Udon, 437
   Eryngii Steak, 619
   Gomoku Mame, 194
   Harumaki, 583
   Hayashi Rice, 543
   Jibuni, 209
   Kanpyo & Shiitake Mushrooms,
      520
   Kenchin Jiru, 125
   Kiriboshi Daikon, 189
   Kushiage, 288
   Lemon Teriyaki Pork, 253
   Maze Gohan with Bamboo Shoots,
      103
   Miso Nikomi Udon, 438
   Miso-Marinated Beef Steaks, 246
   Nagasaki Champon, 401
   Niku Dofu, 202
   Nikuman, 588–589
   Omurice, 539
   Osuimono, 134
   Ozoni, 135
   Plant-Based Miso Soup, 115
   Ponzu Chicken Donburi, 351
   Saba no Misoni, 228
   Salmon & Miso Cream Pasta, 551
   Salmon Chan Chan-yaki, 235
   Salmon Miso Nabe, 475
   Salmon Takikomi Gohan, 109
   Sawaniwan, 130
   Shojin Dashi Stock, 41
   Shojin-age, 279
   Sukiyaki Donburi, 356
   Tendon, 350
   Tonjiru, 124
   Tonkotsu-Style Ramen Hack, 397

Torijiru, 129
Ume & Butter Squid Stir-Fry, 605
Vegetable Gyoza, 578
myoga
   Shibazuke, 317

Nabeshigi, 174
Nagasaki Champon, 401
Nagoya's Taiwan Ramen, 400
Nagoya's Tebasaki, 598
Nama Panko
   Baked Chicken Katsu, 255
   Bifukatsu, 295
   Ebi Furai, 292
   Hambagu, 532
   Kani Kurimu Korokke, 273
   Korokke, 528
   Kushiage, 288
   Menchi Katsu, 287
   recipe, 66
   Salmon Fry, 294
   Tonkatsu, 284
Nanbanzuke, 324
napa cabbage
   Beef Sukiyaki, 464
   Chanko Nabe, 478
   Chuka Don, 361
   Hakusai no Asazuke, 311
   Napa Cabbage Ohitashi, 155
   Pork & Garlic Nabe, 467
   Salmon Miso Nabe, 475
   Shio Lemon Nabe, 466
   Tonjiru, 124
   Vegetable Gyoza, 578
narutomaki fish cakes
   Tsukemen, 408
Nasu Dengaku, 618
Natto Gohan, 89
Negitoro
   recipe, 512
   Temakizushi, 490
Niku Bukkake Udon, 441
Niku Dofu, 202
Nikujaga, 208
Nikumaki Onigiri, 640
Nikuman, 588–589
Niratama Soup, 138
noodles and pasta
   Abura Soba, 404
   Ae Soba with Canned Tuna, 456
   Beef Niku Udon, 434
   Beef Sukiyaki, 464
   Butter & Soy Sauce Wafu Pasta,
      550
   Carbo Udon, 557
   Cold Soba Salad, 454

Curry Udon, 437
Futomaki, 488
Hiroshima-Style Okonomiyaki,
   631
Hiyashi Chuka, 405
Hiyashi Mentaiko Udon, 444
Hiyashi Tanuki Udon/Soba, 430
Homemade Ramen Noodles,
   372–373
Homemade Soba Noodles, 420
Homemade Udon Noodles, 414
Japanese-Style Macaroni Salad, 533
Joya Nabe, 479
Kakiage Udon/Soba, 426
Kamaage Udon, 418
Kamo Nanban Soba, 445
Kitsune Udon/Soba, 425
Kyoto-Style Udon, 431
Mentaiko Pasta, 554
Miso Nikomi Udon, 438
Miso Ramen, 396
Motsunabe, 471
Nagoya's Taiwan Ramen, 400
Niku Bukkake Udon, 441
Oroshi Soba, 451
Pork & Garlic Nabe, 467
Pork Niku Soba, 449
Salmon & Miso Cream Pasta, 551
Salmon Miso Nabe, 475
Shio & Lemon Yakisoba, 637
Shio Lemon Nabe, 466
Shio Ramen, 394
Shoyu Ramen, 393
Somen with Homemade Dipping
   Sauce, 457
Soy Milk Tantan Nabe, 470
Spaghetti Ramen Hack, 375
Tonkotsu-Style Ramen Hack, 397
Tori Nanban Soba, 450
Tororo Tsukimi Udon, 442
Tsukemen, 408
Udon Noodle Broth, 417
Yakisoba, 636
Yakiudon, 638
Zaru Udon/Soba, 429
nori
   Abura Soba, 404
   Ae Soba with Canned Tuna, 456
   Chicken & Cucumber Bainiku-ae,
      164
   Hiyashi Mentaiko Udon, 444
   Hosomaki, 485
   Mentaiko Pasta, 554
   Miso Ramen, 396
   Omusubi, 92
   Potato Iso Cheese-ae, 165

Salmon & Ikura Oyakodon, 366
Salmon Ochazuke, 99
Shio & Lemon Yakisoba, 637
Shoyu Ramen, 393
Stamina Don, 346
Tanuki Hiyayakko, 611
Temakizushi, 490
Tempura, 272
Tendon, 350
Tonkotsu-Style Ramen Hack, 397
Tororo Tsukimi Udon, 442
Tsukemen, 408
Yaki Onigiri Dashi Chazuke, 102
Nukazuke-Style Pickles, 308

octopus
    Tako Wasa, 604
    Takoyaki, 628
Oden, 474
Ohagi, 653
Okayu, 97
okra
    Cold Soba Salad, 454
    Okra & Carrot Shira-ae, 169
Omurice, 539
Omusubi, 92
onions
    Beef Niku Udon, 434
    Chanko Nabe, 478
    Chicken Hambagu with Ume-an
        Sauce, 250
    Classic Pork Chashu, 376
    Corn Potage, 139
    Cream Stew, 549
    Hambagu, 532
    Hayashi Rice, 543
    Japanese-Style Curry Rice, 541
    Japanese-Style Potato Salad, 531
    Kakiage Udon/Soba, 426
    Kani Kurimu Korokke, 273
    Korokke, 528
    Mabo Dofu Don, 357
    Mabo Nasu, 562
    Meat Doria, 546
    Menchi Katsu, 287
    Miso Stir-Fry, 265
    Nagasaki Champon, 401
    Nanbanzuke, 324
    Niku Dofu, 202
    Nikujaga, 208
    Nikuman, 588–589
    Omurice, 539
    Oyako Don, 336
    Pork Katsudon, 340
    Salmon & Miso Cream Pasta, 551
    Salmon Chan Chan-yaki, 235

Shogayaki, 241
Shumai, 579
Stamina Don, 346
Subuta, 566
Taco Rice, 542
Tangy Tartar Sauce, 680
Tantanmen, 403
Tartar Sauce, 680
Torijiru, 129
White Miso Soup, 121
Yakiniku Sauce, 679
Yakisoba, 636
Yasai Itame, 587
Onsen Tamago
    Niku Bukkake Udon, 441
    recipe, 57
    Stamina Don, 346
    Yakiniku Don, 347
    Yakiudon, 638
Orandani, 193
orange peel
    Kohaku Namasu, 325
oranges
    Anmitsu, 658
    Wafu Dressing, 50
Oroshi Soba, 451
Osaka-Style Okonomiyaki, 630
Osuimono, 134
Oven-Roasted Chashu, 382
Oyako Don, 336
oyster sauce
    Abura Soba, 404
    Beef Niku Udon, 434
    Chinjao Rosu, 563
    Chuka Don, 361
    Fragrant Pork Mince, 381
    Goya Champuru, 264
    Harumaki, 583
    Hiroshima-Style Okonomiyaki,
        631
    Mabo Dofu Don, 357
    Menchi Katsu, 287
    Menma-Style Bamboo Shoots, 383
    Miso Ramen, 396
    Motsunabe, 471
    Nagasaki Champon, 401
    Nagoya's Taiwan Ramen, 400
    Nikuman, 588–589
    Niratama Soup, 138
    Oden, 474
    Osaka-Style Okonomiyaki, 630
    Oven-Roasted Chashu, 382
    Pork & Garlic Nabe, 467
    Pork Yaki Gyoza, 576
    Rebanira Itame, 585
    Shoyu Ramen, 393

Shumai, 579
Stamina Don, 346
Tonkotsu-Style Ramen Hack, 397
Tonpeiyaki, 635
Tori no Karaage, 280
Tsukemen, 408
Yakisoba, 636
Yasai Itame, 587
Ozoni, 135

Pacific saury
    Sanma no Shioyaki, 224
panko
    Baked Chicken Katsu, 255
    Bifukatsu, 295
    Ebi Furai, 292
    Hambagu, 532
    Kani Kurimu Korokke, 273
    Korokke, 528
    Kushiage, 288
    Menchi Katsu, 287
    Nama Panko, 66
    Salmon Fry, 294
    Tonkatsu, 284
Parmesan cheese
    Carbo Udon, 557
    Cream Stew, 549
    Japanese-Style Macaroni Salad,
        533
    Potato Iso Cheese-ae, 165
    Salmon & Miso Cream Pasta, 551
pasta. See noodles and pasta
peaches
    Anmitsu, 658
peanut butter
    Carrot Peanut-ae, 158
    Miso Ramen, 396
    Tantanmen, 403
peanuts
    Carrot Peanut-ae, 158
peas
    Mame Gohan, 84
    Omurice, 539
    Shumai, 579
peas, snow
    Chikuzenni, 201
    Chirashizushi, 496
    Niku Dofu, 202
    Nikujaga, 208
    Sawaniwan, 130
    Simmered Taro & Squid, 210
    Soboro Don, 344
    White Miso Soup, 121
Pecorino cheese
    Carbo Udon, 557
    Cream Stew, 549

Meat Doria, 546
Potato Iso Cheese-ae, 165
peppers, bell
  Chinjao Rosu, 563
  Cream Stew, 549
  Harumaki, 583
  Hayashi Rice, 543
  Miso Stir-Fry, 265
  Nabeshigi, 174
  Nanbanzuke, 324
  Orandani, 193
  Subuta, 566
  Teriyaki Tofu Donburi, 360
  Yakiudon, 638
peppers, chile
  Bettarazuke, 316
  Buri Daikon, 215
  Chicken Miso Yuan-yaki, 258
  Cucumber Misozuke, 321
  Ebi Chili, 567
  Japanese Curry Powder, 65
  Kinpira Renkon, 186
  Menma-Style Bamboo Shoots, 383
  Motsunabe, 471
  Nabeshigi, 174
  Nagoya's Taiwan Ramen, 400
  Orandani, 193
  Pork Rikyu-yaki, 260
  Rayu, 49
  Soy Milk Tantan Nabe, 470
  Tako Wasa, 604
  Tempura, 272
  Tendon, 350
  Unaju/Unadon, 367
Perfect Japanese Rice
  Butadon, 343
  Chicken Zosui, 98
  Chuka Don, 361
  Gyudon, 337
  Hayashi Rice, 543
  Japanese-Style Curry Rice, 541
  Mabo Dofu Don, 357
  Marinated Kaisen-Don, 364
  Maze Gohan with Bamboo Shoots, 103
  Meat Doria, 546
  Natto Gohan, 89
  Nikuman, 640
  Okayu, 97
  Omurice, 539
  Omusubi, 92
  Oyako Don, 336
  Ponzu Chicken Donburi, 351
  Pork Katsudon, 340
  recipe, 80
  Salmon & Ikura Oyakodon, 366

Salmon Ochazuke, 99
Soboro Don, 344
Stamina Don, 346
Sukiyaki Donburi, 356
Taco Rice, 542
Tendon, 350
Teriyaki Beef Donburi, 355
Teriyaki Tofu Donburi, 360
Ultimate Tamago Kake Gohan, 93
Unaju/Unadon, 367
Yaki Onigiri Dashi Chazuke, 102
Yakiniku Don, 347
perilla leaves
  Shiso Dressing, 56
pickles
  Tangy Tartar Sauce, 680
Plant-Based Miso Soup, 115
plums
  Umeboshi, 329–331
pollock roe, salted
  Carrot Masago-ae, 170
Ponzu Chicken Donburi, 351
Ponzu Dressing
  recipe, 54
  Shabu-Shabu Salad, 152
Ponzu Sauce
  Japanese-Style Macaroni Salad, 533
  Joya Nabe, 479
  Ponzu Chicken Donburi, 351
  Ponzu Dressing, 54
  recipe, 45
  Torikawa Ponzu, 600
pork
  Butadon, 343
  Chahan, 575
  Cold Soba Salad, 454
  Fragrant Pork Mince, 381
  Harumaki, 583
  Kushiage, 288
  Lemon Teriyaki Pork, 253
  Mabo Dofu Don, 357
  Mabo Nasu, 562
  Menchi Katsu, 287
  Miso Ramen, 396
  Miso Stir-Fry, 265
  Nagoya's Taiwan Ramen, 400
  Nikuman, 588–589, 640
  Pork Katsudon, 340
  Pork Rikyu-yaki, 260
  Pork Yaki Gyoza, 576
  Shabu-Shabu Salad, 152
  Shogayaki, 241
  Shoyu Ramen, 393
  Shumai, 579
  Soboro Don, 344
  Soy Milk Tantan Nabe, 470

Tantanmen, 403
Tonkatsu, 284
Tonkotsu-Style Ramen Hack, 397
Tonteki, 245
Yakiniku Don, 347
Yakiton, 595
pork belly
  Buta no Kakuni, 206
  Butadon, 343
  Chahan, 575
  Chuka Don, 361
  Classic Pork Chashu, 376
  Curry Udon, 437
  Goya Champuru, 264
  Harumaki, 583
  Hiroshima-Style Okonomiyaki, 631
  Japanese-Style Cabbage Rolls, 538
  Joya Nabe, 479
  Miso Stir-Fry, 265
  Nagasaki Champon, 401
  Osaka-Style Okonomiyaki, 630
  Oven-Roasted Chashu, 382
  Pork & Garlic Nabe, 467
  Pork Niku Soba, 449
  Sawaniwan, 130
  Shumai, 579
  Stamina Don, 346
  Subuta, 566
  Tonjiru, 124
  Tonpeiyaki, 635
  Yakisoba, 636
  Yakiudon, 638
  Yasai Itame, 587
potatoes
  Cream Stew, 549
  Japanese-Style Curry Rice, 541
  Japanese-Style Potato Salad, 531
  Korokke, 528
  Nikujaga, 208
  Oden, 474
  Potato Iso Cheese-ae, 165
  White Miso Soup, 121
prawns
  Ebi Furai, 292
  Ebi Mayo, 571
  Tempura, 272
  See also shrimp
pumpkin
  Tempura, 272

quail eggs
  Chuka Don, 361
  Kushiage, 288

Rayu
  recipe, 49
  Soy Milk Tantan Nabe, 470
Rebanira Itame, 585
Red Kidney Beans Amani, 197
Red Miso Soup, 122
rice
  Butadon, 343
  Chahan, 575
  Chicken Zosui, 98
  Chuka Don, 361
  Gyudon, 337
  Hayashi Rice, 543
  Japanese-Style Curry Rice, 541
  Jukkokumai, 83
  Mabo Dofu Don, 357
  Mame Gohan, 84
  Marinated Kaisen-Don, 364
  Maze Gohan with Bamboo Shoots,
    103
  Meat Doria, 546
  Natto Gohan, 89
  Nikuman, 640
  Ohagi, 653
  Okayu, 97
  Omurice, 539
  Omusubi, 92
  Oyako Don, 336
  Perfect Japanese Rice, 80
  Ponzu Chicken Donburi, 351
  Pork Katsudon, 340
  Salmon & Ikura Oyakodon, 366
  Salmon Ochazuke, 99
  Salmon Takikomi Gohan, 109
  Satsumaimo Gohan, 90
  Sekihan, 86–87
  Soboro Don, 344
  Stamina Don, 346
  Sukiyaki Donburi, 356
  Sumeshi, 484
  Taco Rice, 542
  Taimeshi, 106
  Tendon, 350
  Tenshiinhan, 574
  Teriyaki Beef Donburi, 355
  Teriyaki Tofu Donburi, 360
  Ultimate Tamago Kake Gohan, 93
  Unaju/Unadon, 367
  Yaki Onigiri Dashi Chazuke, 102
  Yakiniku Don, 347
rice cakes, kirimochi
  Oden, 474
rice flour
  Anmitsu, 658
  Chomeiji Sakura Mochi, Kanto
    Style, 649

Ichigo Daifuku, 648
Sweet Kushi Dango, 641

Saba no Misoni, 228
Saba no Shioyaki, 221
Sakana no Nitsuke, 230
sake
  Agedashi Tofu, 291
  Ajitama, 378
  Asari Miso Soup, 118
  Asari no Sakamushi, 608
  Baked Cod Saikyo-yaki, 229
  Baked Shiozake, 220
  Bamboo Shoot Okaka-ni, 183
  Ban Ban Zii, 584
  Beef Yawata Maki, 601
  Buri Daikon, 215
  Butadon, 343
  Chahan, 575
  Chanko Nabe, 478
  Chicken & Cucumber Bainiku-ae,
    164
  Chicken Breast Chashu, 377
  Chicken Drumstick Sappari-ni,
    254
  Chicken Miso Yuan-yaki, 258
  Chicken Zosui, 98
  Chikuzenni, 201
  Chinjao Rosu, 563
  Chirashizushi, 496
  Chuka Don, 361
  Citrusy Chicken Karaage, 283
  Classic Pork Chashu, 376
  Ebi Chili, 567
  Fish Teriyaki, 225
  Gomoku Mame, 194
  Goya Champuru, 264
  Gyudon, 337
  Harumaki, 583
  Ikura, 510
  Japanese-Style Cabbage Rolls, 538
  Jibuni, 209
  Joya Nabe, 479
  Kabocha no Nimono, 182
  Kamo Nanban Soba, 445
  Kanpyo & Shiitake Mushrooms,
    520
  Kawari Age, 303
  Kenchin Jiru, 125
  Kinpira Renkon, 186
  Kiriboshi Daikon, 189
  Kitsune Udon/Soba, 425
  Kombu No Tsukudani, 60
  Lemon Teriyaki Pork, 253
  Mabo Dofu Don, 357
  Mabo Nasu, 562

Mackerel Ume-ni, 233
Mame Gohan, 84
Marinated Kaisen-Don, 364
Marinated Tuna Sashimi, 507
Maze Gohan with Bamboo Shoots,
  103
Menma-Style Bamboo Shoots, 383
Miso Stir-Fry, 265
Miso-Marinated Beef Steaks, 246
Motsunabe, 471
Nabeshigi, 174
Nagoya's Tebasaki, 598
Nasu Dengaku, 618
Niku Bukkake Udon, 441
Niku Dofu, 202
Nikujaga, 208
Nikuman, 588–589, 640
Oden, 474
Oven-Roasted Chashu, 382
Ozoni, 135
Ponzu Chicken Donburi, 351
Pork & Garlic Nabe, 467
Pork Katsudon, 340
Pork Niku Soba, 449
Pork Rikyu-yaki, 260
Pork Yaki Gyoza, 576
Rebanira Itame, 585
Saba no Misoni, 228
Saba no Shioyaki, 221
Sakana no Nitsuke, 230
Sakura Denbu, 516
Salmon & Miso Cream Pasta, 551
Salmon Chan Chan-yaki, 235
Salmon Flakes, 61
Salmon Fry, 294
Salmon Ochazuke, 99
Salmon Takikomi Gohan, 109
Sanma no Shioyaki, 224
Satsumaimo Gohan, 90
Sea Bream Kombu-Jime, 506
Sekihan, 86–87
Shabu-Shabu Salad, 152
Shio & Lemon Yakisoba, 637
Shio Lemon Nabe, 466
Shogayaki, 241
Shumai, 579
Simmered Taro & Squid, 210
Soboro Don, 344
Soy-Glazed Roasted Chicken Legs,
  261
Squid Karaage, 299
Stamina Don, 346
Subuta, 566
Sukiyaki Donburi, 356
Taimeshi, 106
Tako Wasa, 604

Tendon, 350
Teriyaki Beef Donburi, 355
Teriyaki Chicken, 240
Teriyaki Tofu Donburi, 360
Tofu Steak, 612
Tori Nanban Soba, 450
Tori no Karaage, 280
Torijiru, 129
Torikawa Ponzu, 600
Toriten, 276
Ume & Butter Squid Stir-Fry, 605
Unaju/Unadon, 367
Vegetable Gyoza, 578
Warishita Sauce, 679
Yakisoba, 636
Yakiton, 595
Yakitori in a Frying Pan, 594
Yakiudon, 638
Yasai Itame, 587
Yellowtail Yuan-yaki, 232
Yurinchi, 570
Sakura Denbu
    Futomaki, 488
    recipe, 516
salads
    Cold Soba Salad, 454
    Japanese-Style Macaroni Salad, 533
    Japanese-Style Potato Salad, 531
    Shabu-Shabu Salad, 152
    Wakame Salad, 148
salmon
    Baked Shiozake, 220
    Futomaki, 488
    Salmon & Ikura Oyakodon, 366
    Salmon & Miso Cream Pasta, 551
    Salmon Chan Chan-yaki, 235
    Salmon Flakes, 61
    Salmon Fry, 294
    Salmon Miso Nabe, 475
    Salmon Nanban-yaki, 234
    Salmon Ochazuke, 99
    Salmon Takikomi Gohan, 109
    Temakizushi, 490
Salmon Flakes
    Omusubi, 92
    recipe, 61
    Salmon & Ikura Oyakodon, 366
salmon roe
    Ikura, 510
Sanma no Shioyaki, 224
Sashimi Platter, 502–503
satoimo
    Kenchin Jiru, 125
Satsumaimo Gohan, 90
sausages, smoked
    Oden, 474

Sawaniwan, 130
scallops
    Chirashizushi, 496
    Salmon Miso Nabe, 475
    Temarizushi, 495
sea bream
    Sea Bream Kombu-Jime, 506
    Taimeshi, 106
seafood
    Asari Miso Soup, 118
    Asari no Sakamushi, 608
    Butterflied Shrimp, 513
    Chawanmushi, 142
    Chirashizushi, 496
    Chuka Don, 361
    Ebi Chili, 567
    Ebi Furai, 292
    Ebi Mayo, 571
    Eggplant Zunda-ae, 171
    Futomaki, 488
    Hiroshima-Style Okonomiyaki,
        631
    Kakiage Udon/Soba, 426
    Kani Kurimu Korokke, 273
    Kawari Age, 303
    Kushiage, 288
    Marinated Kaisen-Don, 364
    Motsunabe, 471
    Nagasaki Champon, 401
    Oden, 474
    Salmon Miso Nabe, 475
    Sashimi Platter, 502–503
    Shio & Lemon Yakisoba, 637
    Shrimp & Asparagus Sumiso-ae,
        157
    Simmered Taro & Squid, 210
    Squid Karaage, 299
    Sunomono, 151
    Tako Wasa, 604
    Takoyaki, 628
    Temakizushi, 490
    Temarizushi, 495
    Tempura, 272
    Tendon, 350
    Tenshiinhan, 574
    Ume & Butter Squid Stir-Fry, 605
    See also fish
Seasoned Bean Sprouts, 389
Sekihan, 86–87
sesame paste
    Ban Ban Zii, 584
    Pork Rikyu-yaki, 260
    Spicy Sesame Sauce, 681
sesame seeds
    Abura Soba, 404
    Ae Soba with Canned Tuna, 456

Baked Chicken Katsu, 255
Goma Dressing, 51
Green Bean Gomaae, 156
Hiyashi Chuka, 405
Pork & Garlic Nabe, 467
Pork Rikyu-yaki, 260
Salmon Ochazuke, 99
Soy Milk Tantan Nabe, 470
Stamina Don, 346
Tantanmen, 403
Tonkotsu-Style Ramen Hack, 397
Ume Cucumber, 175
Wafu Addictive Cabbage, 615
Shabu-Shabu Salad, 152
Shibazuke, 317
shichimi togarashi
    Agedashi Tofu, 291
    Beef Niku Udon, 434
    Chicken Nanban, 247
    Curry Udon, 437
    Eryngii Steak, 619
    Joya Nabe, 479
    Kakitamajiru, 133
    Kamo Nanban Soba, 445
    Kyoto-Style Udon, 431
    Seasoned Bean Sprouts, 389
    Shio Ramen, 394
    Soboro Daikon, 203
    Spicy Negi, 390
    Stir-Fried Edamame, 614
    Tofu Steak, 612
    Tori Nanban Soba, 450
    Torikawa Ponzu, 600
    Wafu Addictive Cabbage, 615
    Zaru Udon/Soba, 429
Shio & Lemon Yakisoba, 637
Shio Lemon Nabe, 466
Shio Ramen, 394
Shiraganegi
    Chicken Drumstick Sappari-ni,
        254
    Saba no Misoni, 228
shiratamako
    Anmitsu, 658
Shiso Dressing, 56
shiso leaves
    Ae Soba with Canned Tuna, 456
    Chicken & Cucumber Bainiku-ae,
        164
    Chicken Hambagu with Ume-an
        Sauce, 250
    Futomaki, 488
    Hiyashi Mentaiko Udon, 444
    Mackerel Ume-ni, 233
    Mentaiko Pasta, 554
    Nabeshigi, 174

Nasu Dengaku, 618
Nikuman, 640
Salmon & Ikura Oyakodon, 366
Shibazuke, 317
Shio & Lemon Yakisoba, 637
Temakizushi, 490
Temarizushi, 495
Tempura, 272
Ume & Butter Squid Stir-Fry, 605
Umeboshi, 329–331
shochu
  Umeboshi, 329–331
Shogayaki, 241
Shojin Dashi Stock
  Kenchin Jiru, 125
  recipe, 41
Shojin-age
  recipe, 279
  Tenkasu, 68
Shoyu Ramen, 393
shrimp
  Butterflied Shrimp, 513
  Chawanmushi, 142
  Ebi Chili, 567
  Eggplant Zunda-ae, 171
  Futomaki, 488
  Kakiage Udon/Soba, 426
  Kawari Age, 303
  Kushiage, 288
  Shrimp & Asparagus Sumiso-ae,
    157
  Temakizushi, 490
  Temarizushi, 495
  Tendon, 350
  See also prawns
Shumai, 579
shungiku
  Beef Sukiyaki, 464
Silky Custard Purin, 659
Simmered Sweet Potatoes, 188
Simmered Taro & Squid, 210
snow peas
  Chikuzenni, 201
  Chirashizushi, 496
  Niku Dofu, 202
  Nikujaga, 208
  Sawaniwan, 130
  Simmered Taro & Squid, 210
  Soboro Don, 344
  White Miso Soup, 121
Soba Noodle Broth
  Kakiage Udon/Soba, 426
  Kitsune Udon/Soba, 425
  recipe, 421
Soboro Daikon, 203
Soboro Don, 344

Somen with Homemade Dipping
  Sauce, 457
soups and broths
  Asari Miso Soup, 118
  Awase Dashi Stock, 38
  Chawanmushi, 142
  Classic Miso Soup, 114
  Corn Potage, 139
  Cream Stew, 549
  Kakitamajiru, 133
  Kenchin Jiru, 125
  Niratama Soup, 138
  Osuimono, 134
  Ozoni, 135
  Plant-Based Miso Soup, 115
  Red Miso Soup, 122
  Sawaniwan, 130
  Shojin Dashi Stock, 41
  Soba Noodle Broth, 421
  Tonjiru, 124
  Torijiru, 129
  Udon Noodle Broth, 417
  White Miso Soup, 121
  See also noodles and pasta
soy milk
  Soy Milk Tantan Nabe, 470
  Tonkotsu-Style Ramen Hack, 397
  Tsukemen, 408
soy sauce
  Abura Soba, 404
  Ajitama, 378
  Beef Niku Udon, 434
  Beef Shigureni, 211
  Buta no Kakuni, 206
  Butadon, 343
  Carrot Peanut-ae, 158
  Chicken Breast Chashu, 377
  Chicken Drumstick Sappari-ni,
    254
  Chicken Miso Yuan-yaki, 258
  Chicken Nanban, 247
  Chikuzenni, 201
  Classic Pork Chashu, 376
  Cold Soba Salad, 454
  Curry Udon, 437
  Fish Teriyaki, 225
  Fukujinzuke, 310
  Gyudon, 337
  Jibuni, 209
  Kamo Nanban Soba, 445
  Kenchin Jiru, 125
  Kiriboshi Daikon, 189
  Kitsune Udon/Soba, 425
  Kyoto-Style Udon, 431
  Marinated Kaisen-Don, 364
  Marinated Tuna Sashimi, 507

Meat Doria, 546
Mentsuyu, 42
Motsunabe, 471
Nagoya's Tebasaki, 598
Niku Bukkake Udon, 441
Niku Dofu, 202
Nikuman, 640
Oden, 474
Oven-Roasted Chashu, 382
Ponzu Sauce, 45
Sakana no Nitsuke, 230
Salmon Nanban-yaki, 234
Sashimi Platter, 502–503
Sawaniwan, 130
Sea Bream Kombu-Jime, 506
Shio Ramen, 394
Shiso Dressing, 56
Shogayaki, 241
Shoyu Ramen, 393
Soba Noodle Broth, 421
Somen with Homemade Dipping
  Sauce, 457
Soy-Glazed Roasted Chicken Legs,
  261
Sukiyaki Donburi, 356
Tantanmen, 403
Tendon, 350
Teriyaki Beef Donburi, 355
Teriyaki Chicken, 240
Teriyaki Tofu Donburi, 360
Tonteki, 245
Tori Nanban Soba, 450
Toriten, 276
Udon Noodle Broth, 417
Unaju/Unadon, 367
Wafu Dressing, 50
Yakiniku Sauce, 679
Yakitori in a Frying Pan, 594
Yurinchi, 570
soybean powder, roasted
  Ohagi, 653
  Warabi Mochi, 652
soybeans
  Gomoku Mame, 194
soybeans, dried
  Shojin Dashi Stock, 41
Spaghetti Ramen Hack, 375
Spicy Negi, 390
Spicy Sesame Sauce
  recipe, 681
  Yudofu with Spicy Sesame Sauce,
    198
spinach
  Butter & Soy Sauce Wafu Pasta,
    550
  Joya Nabe, 479

Miso Ramen, 396
Salmon & Miso Cream Pasta, 551
spring roll wrappers
Harumaki, 583
Kawari Age, 303
squash
Kabocha no Nimono, 182
squid
Futomaki, 488
Hiroshima-Style Okonomiyaki, 631
Oden, 474
Simmered Taro & Squid, 210
Squid Karaage, 299
Ume & Butter Squid Stir-Fry, 605
Stamina Don, 346
Stir-Fried Edamame, 614
strawberries
Ichigo Daifuku, 648
Strawberry Shortcake, 669
Subuta, 566
sudachi
Baked Shiozake, 220
Saba no Shioyaki, 221
Sanma no Shioyaki, 224
Suito Poteto, 673
sujiko
Ikura, 510
Sukiyaki Donburi, 356
Sumeshi
Chirashizushi, 496
Futomaki, 488
Hosomaki, 485
Inarizushi, 491
recipe, 484
Temakizushi, 490
Temarizushi, 495
Sunomono, 151
surimi sticks. See crab, imitation
Sweet Kushi Dango, 641
sweet potatoes
Daigaku Imo, 674
Satsumaimo Gohan, 90
Shojin-age, 279
Simmered Sweet Potatoes, 188
Suito Poteto, 673
Tonjiru, 124

Taco Rice, 542
Taimeshi, 106
Tako Wasa, 604
Takoyaki, 628
Takuan
Futomaki, 488
recipe, 318
Tamago Sando, 536

Tamagoyaki, 613
Tangy Tartar Sauce
Ebi Furai, 292
recipe, 680
Salmon Fry, 294
Tantanmen, 403
Tanuki Hiyayakko, 611
tarako
Carrot Masago-ae, 170
taro
Kenchin Jiru, 125
Simmered Taro & Squid, 210
Tartar Sauce
Chicken Nanban, 247
recipe, 680
Tangy Tartar Sauce, 680
Temakizushi, 490
temari fu
Osuimono, 134
Temarizushi, 495
Tempura
Kakiage Udon/Soba, 426
recipe, 272
Tendon, 350
Tenkasu, 68
Tendon, 350
Tenkasu
Hiroshima-Style Okonomiyaki, 631
Hiyashi Tanuki Udon/Soba, 430
Natto Gohan, 89
Niku Bukkake Udon, 441
Osaka-Style Okonomiyaki, 630
recipe, 68
Takoyaki, 628
Tanuki Hiyayakko, 611
Tendon, 350
Zaru Udon/Soba, 429
Tenshiinhan, 574
Teriyaki Beef Donburi, 355
Teriyaki Chicken, 240
Teriyaki Tofu Donburi, 360
tofu
Abura-age, 69
Agedashi Tofu, 291
Atsuage Tofu, 73
Beef Sukiyaki, 464
Classic Miso Soup, 114
Goya Champuru, 264
Joya Nabe, 479
Mabo Dofu Don, 357
Motsunabe, 471
Niku Dofu, 202
Oden, 474
Okra & Carrot Shira-ae, 169

Plant-Based Miso Soup, 115
Pork & Garlic Nabe, 467
Red Miso Soup, 122
Soy Milk Tantan Nabe, 470
Tanuki Hiyayakko, 611
Teriyaki Tofu Donburi, 360
Tofu Steak, 612
Wakame Salad, 148
Yudofu with Spicy Sesame Sauce, 198
tomatoes
Ban Ban Zii, 584
Cold Soba Salad, 454
Hiyashi Chuka, 405
Meat Doria, 546
Shabu-Shabu Salad, 152
Taco Rice, 542
Wakame Salad, 148
Tonjiru, 124
Tonkatsu
Pork Katsudon, 340
recipe, 284
Tonkotsu-Style Ramen Hack, 397
Tonpeiyaki, 635
Tonteki, 245
Tori Nanban Soba, 450
Tori no Karaage, 280
Torijiru, 129
Torikawa Ponzu, 600
Toriten, 276
Tororo Tsukimi Udon, 442
tortilla chips
Taco Rice, 542
Tsukemen, 408
tuna
Ae Soba with Canned Tuna, 456
Chirashizushi, 496
Futomaki, 488
Hosomaki, 485
Marinated Tuna Sashimi, 507
Mugen Cabbage, 622
Negitoro, 512
Temakizushi, 490
turnips
Tonjiru, 124

Udon Noodle Broth
Kakiage Udon/Soba, 426
Kitsune Udon/Soba, 425
recipe, 417
Ultimate Tamago Kake Gohan, 93
Ume & Butter Squid Stir-Fry, 605
Ume Cucumber, 175
ume plum vinegar, red
Benishoga, 315

Ume Sauce
    Chicken Ham with Ume Sauce,
      599
    recipe, 678
Umeboshi
    Avocado & Cucumber Ume-
      Goma-ae, 162
    Chicken & Cucumber Bainiku-ae,
      164
    Chicken Hambagu with Ume-an
      Sauce, 250
    Mackerel Ume-ni, 233
    Okayu, 97
    recipe, 329–331
    Tororo Tsukimi Udon, 442
    Ume & Butter Squid Stir-Fry, 605
    Ume Cucumber, 175
    Ume Sauce, 678
Unaju/Unadon, 367

Vegetable Gyoza, 578

Wafu Addictive Cabbage, 615
Wafu Dressing, 50
wakame seaweed
    Classic Miso Soup, 114
    Hiyashi Tanuki Udon/Soba, 430
    Red Miso Soup, 122
    Sunomono, 151
    Wakame Salad, 148
Warabi Mochi, 652
Warishita Sauce
    Beef Sukiyaki, 464
    recipe, 679

Wasabi
    Ae Soba with Canned Tuna, 456
    Eggplant Zunda-ae, 171
    Futomaki, 488
    Hiyashi Tanuki Udon/Soba, 430
    Hosomaki, 485
    Marinated Kaisen-Don, 364
    Ponzu Dressing, 54
    recipe, 500
    Salmon & Ikura Oyakodon, 366
    Salmon Ochazuke, 99
    Sashimi Platter, 502–503
    Sea Bream Kombu-Jime, 506
    Tako Wasa, 604
    Temakizushi, 490
    Temarizushi, 495
    Teriyaki Beef Donburi, 355
    Zaru Udon/Soba, 429
White Miso Soup, 121
wine, red
    Bifukatsu, 295
    Fukujinzuke, 310
    Hayashi Rice, 543
    Japanese-Style Curry Rice, 541
    Kushiage, 288
wine, white
    Beef Shigureni, 211
    Cream Stew, 549
    Gyudon, 337
    Omurice, 539
wonton wrappers
    Shumai, 579

Yaki Onigiri Dashi Chazuke, 102
Yakiniku Don, 347

Yakiniku Sauce
    recipe, 679
    Yakiniku Don, 347
Yakisoba, 636
Yakiton, 595
Yakitori in a Frying Pan, 594
Yakiudon, 638
yams
    Tororo Tsukimi Udon, 442
Yasai Itame, 587
yellowtail fillets
    Buri Daikon, 215
    Futomaki, 488
    Yellowtail Yuan-yaki, 232
yogurt
    Matcha Rare Cheesecake, 670
    Nukazuke-Style Pickles, 308
Yudofu with Spicy Sesame Sauce, 198
Yurinchi, 570
yuzu
    Chicken Miso Yuan-yaki, 258
    Hakusai no Asazuke, 311
    Osuimono, 134
    Soy-Glazed Roasted Chicken Legs,
      261
    Wafu Dressing, 50
    Yellowtail Yuan-yaki, 232
yuzu juice
    Kohaku Namasu, 325
    Toriten, 276
yuzu peel/zest
    Kohaku Namasu, 325
    Salmon & Miso Cream Pasta, 551

Zaru Udon/Soba, 429

ABOUT CIDER MILL PRESS BOOK PUBLISHERS

Good ideas ripen with time. From seed to harvest, Cider Mill Press brings fine reading, information, and entertainment together between the covers of its creatively crafted books. Our Cider Mill bears fruit twice a year, publishing a new crop of titles each spring and fall.

"Where Good Books Are Ready for Press"

501 Nelson Place
Nashville, Tennessee 37214

cidermillpress.com